JAPANESE MODERN ART

JAPANESE MODERN ART
Painting from 1910 to 1970

Edited by
Irmtraud Schaarschmidt-Richter

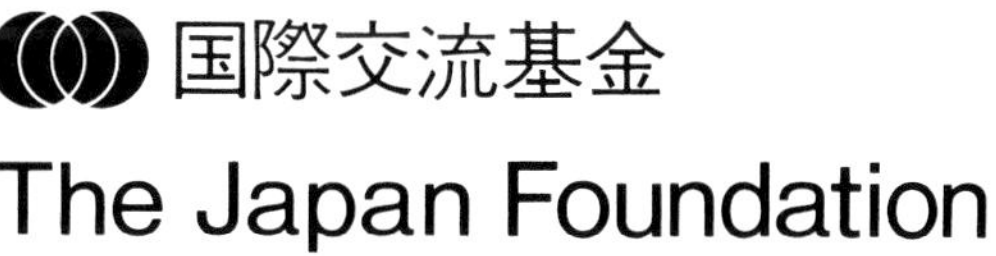

EDITION STEMMLE

Zurich New York

CONTENTS

LENDERS

National Museum of Modern Art, Tokyo
Kanagawa Prefecture Museum of Modern Art, Kamakura
Itabashiku Art Museum, Tokyo
Municipal Art Museum, Tokyo
Hyôgo Prefecture Museum of Modern Art, Kobe
Iwate Prefecture Museum, Morioka
National Museum of Modern Art, Kyoto
Aichi Prefecture Art Museum, Nagoya
Miyazaki Prefecture Art Museum, Miyazaki
Niigata Prefecture Art Museum, Nagaoka
Municipal Art Museum, Chiba
Municipal Art Museum, Kitakyûshu
Yokohama Art Museum, Yokohama
Municipal Art Museum, Kyoto
Nerimaku Art Museum, Tokyo
Meguroku Art Museum, Tokyo
Prefecture Museum of Modern Art, Toyama
Okamoto Tarô Art Museum, Kawasaki
Ono Tadashige Museum of Graphic Art, Tokyo
Nishimura Hatch Bunka Gakuin
Yorozu Tetsugorô Memorial Museum, Tôwa (Iwate)
Mainichi shimbun Newspapers
Kônan Gakuen, Ashiya
Taira Utaru
Nakajima Hiroshi, in conjunction with the Tokyo Gallery, Tokyo
Takamatsu Yasuko, in conjunction with the Chiba Assc., Tokyo
Hayashi Makiko, in conjunction with the Tokyo Gallery, Tokyo
Matsumoto Kan
Ham Gallery, Nagoya
Yonetsu Gallery
Ito Mitsumasa
Iida Yoshikuni

ACKNOWLEDGEMENTS

Ingrid Mössinger
Kunstsammlungen Chemnitz

Hellmut Seemann
Schirn Kunsthalle Frankfurt

The exhibition *Japanese Modern Art—Painting from 1910 to 1970* is one of the high points in a series of events entitled "Japan in Germany." The show plays a key role in the program, dedicated to promoting "new encounters between Japan and Germany in the twenty-first century." We are very pleased that the cities of Chemnitz and Frankfurt am Main have been chosen as venues for the exhibition.

Japanese Modern Art—Painting from 1910 to 1970 presents more than 100 works of art by 26 artists. It is the first such exhibition to explore the Japanese origins of twentieth-century Japanese painting, but it is also the most extensive exhibition devoted exclusively to modern Japanese painters ever shown in Germany. Previous large-scale exhibitions of Japanese art, such as the show presented in conjunction with the *Japan Art Festival,* have featured paintings as well as other forms of Japanese art. Focused on the medium of painting, the present exhibition offers a very special look at works from the period 1910 to 1970.

Because of the significance of these paintings, their large numbers and the great distance separating the exhibition sites from the lender locations, this exhibition could hardly have been financed by a single museum or exhibition center. We are therefore most grateful to The Japan Foundation of Tokyo and its president, Mr. Fujii Hiroaki, for their generous support of this project. Mr. Shimizu Yoichi, Mr. Ogo Hayato and Ms. Sato Atsuko as well as and the representatives of the Japanisches Kulturinstitut in Cologne, Mr. Ueda Takashi, Mr. Sakato Masaru and Ms. Kiyota Tokiko, also deserve our thanks for their commitment to the realization of the exhibition.

The exhibition *Japanese Modern Art—Painting from 1910 to 1970* was conceived by Ms. Irmtraud Schaarschmidt-Richter. She has pursued intensive research in the field of Japanese art for many years and is the wife of the late Siegfried Schaarschmidt, a well-known translator of Japanese literature who died in 1998. She established contact with the exhibiting institutions, persuaded the Japanese museums to provide works on loan, described the origins and development of modern Japanese painting in an extensive essay and, last but not least, served as editorial director for the catalogue. We are very grateful to Ms. Schaarschmidt-Richter for her extraordinary achievement.

For their insightful catalogue essays, we would like to express special thanks to Mr. Sakai Tadayasu, Director, and Mr. Mizusawa Tsutomu of the Kanagawa Prefecture Museum of Modern Art in Kamakura, Mr. Matsumoto Tôru, Chief Curator of the National Museum of Modern Art in Tokyo and Mr. Ozaki Shinzin, Chief Curator of the Itabashiku Art Museum in Tokyo.

We also wish to thank the translators of the texts and the Sprachzentrum für Japanisch e. V., Frankfurt am Main.

We are very grateful to the three museums mentioned above for their assistance in arranging for loans of numerous paintings. Without their dedicated support and generous cooperation, this exhibition project could not have been realized.

We would not have been able to compile and publish the extensive exhibition catalogue without the generous funding provided by the Kultur-Stiftung of the Deutsche Bank. We wish to express our sincere thanks to its director, Mr. Michael Münch.

We are also indebted to Japan Airlines for its contribution to the success of the exhibition.

All of these efforts and contributions—from concept development, research and scholarly assistance to financial support—would have been in vain if we had not been able to rely upon the willingness of numerous lenders to part from their works of art for such a long period of time and over such a great distance. We are therefore deeply grateful to all those who provided works on loan.

A WORD OF GREETING

Fujii Hiroaki
President of The Japan Foundation

As one of the organizers of the exhibition *Japanese Modern Art—Painting from 1910 to 1970,* which focuses on early high points in modern Japanese painting, I am particularly delighted that the exhibition will be shown at both the Museum der Kunstsammlungen Chemnitz and the Schirn Kunsthalle in Frankfurt.

Since its foundation in 1972, the main objective of The Japan Foundation has been to further mutual understanding at an international level, promote culture world-wide, and make a contribution to the well-being of mankind. In order to achieve this objective, the foundation has organized joint activities with more than 130 countries throughout the world and in many different fields, including the sciences, art, and sports.

Thus far, various projects in Germany have been realised or supported not only through exhibitions of the traditional arts of Japan, but also through presentations of contemporary art, which have now become our primary focus. In this way, we have tried to present works from the realm of the fine arts which, as it were, symbolically embody both the past and the present of Japanese culture.

The current exhibition presents a review of Japanese painting from 1910 to 1970. It contains many works by different artists, with special consideration devoted to those artists who, despite the constant influx of western influence into Japan, have maintained a keen awareness of their Japanese identity and produced original works in keeping with their own ideas. Irmtraud Schaarschmidt-Richter, guest curator of the exhibition, visited the exhibition *Japan and Europe: 1543 to 1929* organized in 1993 by our foundation together with the Society of the Berlin Festwochen and the Agency for Cultural Affairs, Japan. The idea for an exhibition centered on artists and works from the years after 1929 has now borne fruit, as it were, in this exhibition. It could thus be maintained that one of the foundation's previous enterprises has given rise to a new project, and this too, is a source of great satisfaction for me in my capacity as one of the organizers.

This year's activities are taking place under the motto "Japan in Germany," and large-scale cultural events such as theatre performances, concerts, and exhibitions are scheduled to take place throughout Germany. It is my sincere hope that, inspired by this particular exhibition, many Germans will spontaneously attend these various events highlighting Japanese culture, and that cultural exchange between Japan and Germany will thus continue to thrive.

Finally, I would like to express my heartfelt thanks to all those who placed valuable works at our disposal for inclusion in this exhibition. Thanks are also due to the Museum der Kunstsammlungen Chemnitz and the Schirn Kunsthalle Frankfurt, who, as co-organizers, enabled this exhibition to be realised, to the art critic Irmtraud Schaarschmidt-Richter, guest curator of the exhibition, and to the members of the Japanese executive committee, who co-operated in every way possible during the preliminary stages. I would also like to express my gratitude to Japan Airlines for their help in transporting the works of art, and to the many participants on both the Japanese and German sides who made their respective contributions toward the successful organization of the exhibition.

September 1999

THE GROWTH OF MODERN JAPANESE PAINTING

Irmtraud Schaarschmidt-Richter

The first encounters between Europe and East Asia, specifically Japan, date back several hundred years. At that time, in the seventeenth and eighteenth centuries, Chinese arts and crafts—which in many cases were actually Japanese arts and crafts—were in vogue in Europe. Europeans were less interested in Asian painting, which attracted little conscious attention, than in architecture and the applied arts. The first porcelain objects made in Europe were direct imitations of Japanese Arita porcelain, a style influenced by the Chinese. Pieces of furniture were sent to Japan to be decorated with painted lacquer panels. Among the works of the great German landscape architect Joseph Peter Lenné (1798–1866) are several that bear a striking resemblance to Japanese pond gardens. A similar development occurred in Japan during the sixteenth and seventeenth centuries, when Jesuit missionaries introduced Christian and secular western painting to that country. Japanese painters copied these works, often on paper and using mineral pigments, although the Jesuits taught the techniques of oil painting and etching. Japanese painters also adapted European motifs, depicting the arrival of Portuguese ships and scenes from the life of Jesuits and merchants in the Japanese genre style on wall screens. Large numbers of these wall screens were taken to Europe as souvenirs. From time to time Japanese artists experimented with European perspective painting, although perspective had already occasionally been used even before the advent of European influence.

Japanese and European artists did not begin to deal concretely with each other's traditions in painting until the late nineteenth and early twentieth century. From the European perspective, this interest was not limited merely to the use of Japanese motifs in western painting—images of ladies dressed in kimonos, of fans or *Nô* masks (of which there is evidence enough)—but rather represented the attempt to come to terms with very different pictorial approaches and modes of vision, with aesthetic concepts that were—and are—as fundamentally different from one another as the respective cultures themselves. At a time when European art found itself in danger of stagnation near the end of the last century, many artists ventured forth in search of new directions and possibilities. They found them, for example, in insights into the significance of plane, line and asymmetry gained from Japanese art. Thus Japanese painting had become quite familiar to late nineteenth-century Europeans through the world fairs and expositions that had come into fashion over a period of several decades. Along with woodcuts, Japanese painting exerted an appreciable influence upon Western art and artists, including such painters as Monet, van de Velde and others. Klimt, for example, almost literally adopted Kôrin's blue river and golden wave ornaments for his female figures (cf. Ill. 4), while van Gogh's tiger lilies would hardly have been conceivable apart from Kôrin's wall screen with tiger lilies (cf. Ill. 5).

Japan faced an entirely different situation. The latter half of the nineteenth century had witnessed the total transformation of existing state structures. The *shôgun* government had been dissolved, the emperor returned to his throne and a constitutional monarchy established. The capital was moved to Edo, which was renamed Tokyo or "Capital of the East." Foreign powers had played a part in all of this, deploying their threatening "black ships" off the coast of Japan and ultimately forcing the opening of the island empire that had remained relatively isolated from the outside world. Moreover, the sovereignty of Japan was severely restricted by unfair treaties. If Japan wished to maintain its independence and continue to exist as a sovereign state, it would have to open itself to the West and seek to achieve economic and political parity. This meant learning and applying much that could be useful and beneficial. The need for a radically new beginning was recognized in the arts and sciences as well. The Japanese were compelled to realize that it was just as important to become familiar with the Western mind as it was to learn new techniques—in order to discover the source of their adversary's great intellectual power. Efforts to this end were often thoroughly critical. But for the Japanese, this process also meant searching for new approaches in art in order to find their way back to themselves—even if it involved a detour, an exotic detour through the study of the entire range of Western styles. Thus the period in question—this much, at least, is clear—was a time of giving and taking on both sides, in the West and in Japan, and not a phase of influence from the West alone. Yet because they did study Western styles, Japanese artists were accused of having been mere imitators on the road to modern art and of having thrown overboard everything from their own past. Such assessments were often conditioned by Westerners' failure to look closely enough and most certainly by their Eurocentric, if not outright colonialistic way of thinking.

Gradually, however, many are beginning to realize that such was not the case and that modern Japanese art, especially painting, did not develop from Western influences alone, but had roots of its own that can be traced back to a very specific view of art, to uniquely Japanese modes of vision and aesthetic codes. Despite all attempts to understand and benefit from the lessons of Western art and the complex of underlying intellectual attitudes associated with it, Japanese artists retained a fundamental position of their own that played a significant role in later developments. This position is evident, and has been since the classical period, in an unmistakable tendency toward the abstract, toward the emphasis and dynamization of line and toward a unique kind of asymmetrical surface configuration. Nevertheless, Western observers of the history of early modern Japanese painting are often irritated by what they perceive as a wide range of European styles in a number of Japanese works of the period.

One should perhaps note at this juncture that style *per se* does not have the same restrictive meaning in East Asia that is attached to it in the West. The con-

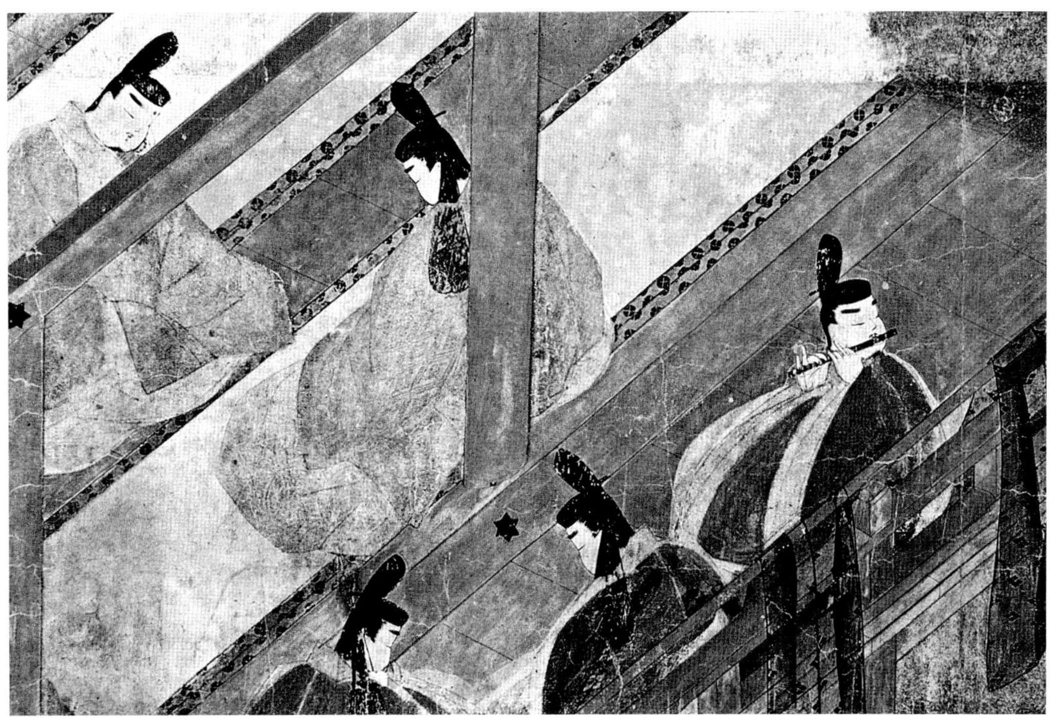

Ill. 1 *Flute Concert,* from the *Genji-monogatari-emaki,* Scroll, Mineral and Vegetable Pigment on Paper, 12th c., Goto Museum, Tokyo

cept of style in East Asia is not associated with a specific period; it does not refer to a style that, once fully exhausted, more or less gradually fades away. Instead, there is a constant diversity of prevailing styles, and this remained essentially true in the modern period as well. In Japanese modern art, style serves only as a vehicle for the artist's means of expression—in the expressive power of lines which, in many cases, still reveal the presence of the artist's hand, in the rhythm of forms, in their balance, in the individual approach to a general phenomenon. Since style therefore hardly defines a compulsory system, opportunities for invention remain, permitting a wide variety of stylistic and expressive forms to coexist at the same time. Obligations to specific styles are defined only by the object, its required iconography and the prevailing situation. Buddhist cult images provide an excellent example: Buddha is always depicted as a highly abstract figure in statuesque calm. His companions, the *Bodhisattva,* are more mobile and more elaborately decorated, while the divine generals and especially the priest and monk figures as well as the *Oni* devil are portrayed with a high degree of realism that often spills over into expressionism. In the seventeenth century, two important works of architecture were built almost simultaneously: the plain, very "modern"-looking Katsura villa, a summer residence for the Emperor, and the richly carved, vividly colored "baroque" Tôshôgu shrine, the mausoleum of the Tokugawa shôguns.

Even such masters of classical Japanese painting as Sesshû (fifteenth century), Sôtatsu (seventeenth century) and Kôrin (eighteenth century) drew simultaneously from a range of different styles and forms of expression. Moreover, it was also quite normal, even for a master, to study the works of his great predecessors and, having delved deeply into them, to work in their spirit—although not exclusively—from then on.

In the Japanese art of writing, *Sho,* there is even a word for this practice of study and emulation of feeling: *Rinsho.* The term does not denote imitation, however, but rather the attempt to grasp the underly-

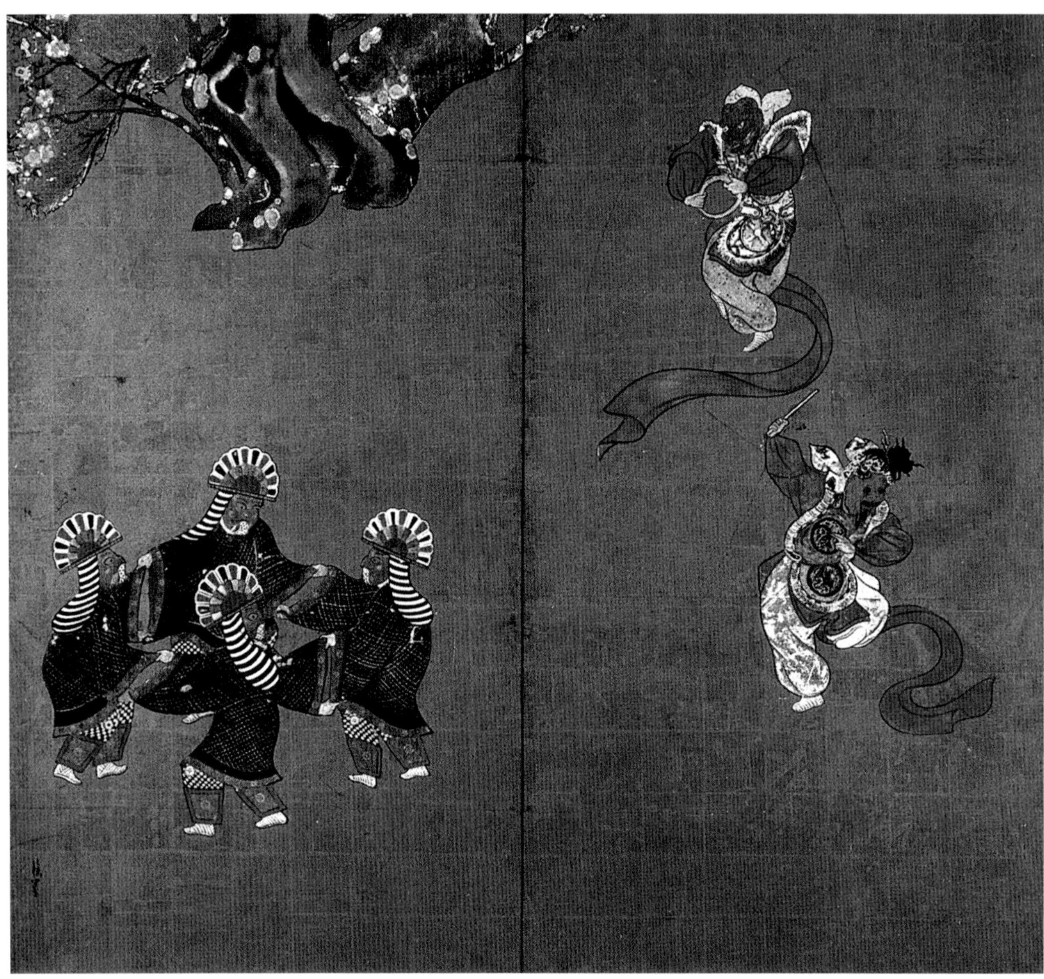

Ill. 2 Sôtatsu, *Bugaku Dance,* Wall Screen, Mineral and Vegetable Pigment on Gold Leaf, 17th c., Sambô' in Temple, Kyoto

ing experience of the master. Thus it is not regarded as a lack of creativity if an artist seeks to express himself in the style of another master. The result is not plagiarism and seldom a bad work of art, but more likely the opposite. The invention of something new was not the most important thing and was hardly considered essential (although it was certainly not meaningless); expression and intensity were everything. One could concentrate upon these qualities in the process of adapting the experience of a master. In a certain sense, the same interpretation applies to the study of European styles and forms of expression by Japanese artists. Their studies enabled them to comprehend the intellectual and spiritual positions of the other side. It was a way of coming to grips with the new, with Western art and culture. It is also worth noting that two hundred years of relative isolation had produced in the Japanese an irrepressible curiosity about everything on the outside, a general thirst for knowledge.

For the most part, this phase of study—which led to what is referred to as *Yôga,* or Western-style Japanese painting, works that often show unmistakably Western features—came to an end long ago and no longer plays an essential role. The term *Yôga* is often used only with respect to materials, which are now so international, diverse and highly individualized that they are of no significance for the development of style. Since then, a modern form of Japanese art has emerged, manifesting itself in different ways and in a variety of contemporary forms of expression, yet having developed from a Japanese perspective and through the process of dealing with a new situation and new encounters. It is an art that is clearly recognizable as new, an art that has grown forth from its own roots. These roots, as has been emphasized repeatedly, lie in a specific mode of vision combined with a highly sophisticated concept of form. The most important component of this formal concept, to summarize once again, is an emphatic flatness: the image is developed from the plane and is often asymmetrically organized through the intersection of shapes which ordinarily occupy the entire pictorial surface, without a horizon, as it were. This quality is also evident in the importance attached to line as contour, as a kind of "calligraphic" brushwork, and to the rhythmic distribution of colors. This inherent quality appears again and again—more often than one would imagine in the West—as a fundamental attitude that is always at work.

Evidence of this phenomenon extends far back into the past, to the medieval illuminated scrolls and, in fact, to the oldest of these: the twelfth-century scroll illustrating the *Genji-monogatari* or *History of Prince Genji,* an account written during the eleventh century by the courtesan Murasaki Shikibu. Although the parallel perspective creates a spatial continuum that is not entirely lacking in depth, the composition is developed entirely from the plane. The most striking example of this is the image of the *Flute Concert* (Ill. 1). The surface area is configured diagonally by the architecture, shown in parallel perspective. Three figures follow these lines, but one of them appears slightly out of kilter, creating a delicate sense of tension. Two other figures are seated at right angles to this group, forming an irregular pointed triangle with the fragment of a figure in the lower left-hand corner of the picture. This rhythm of forms is clearly underscored by the black courtly hats. It appears to be a precisely calculated, deliberately employed artistic device. The result is a strict yet transparent clarity and a cool tension which nonetheless seem unconstrained, almost accidental, and evokes a mood of great intensity. Even this illustration from such an early period in history points beyond its own narrative content to expression through form while at the same time creating a concentrated literary atmosphere. Thus we find even in this ancient work of art the roots of Japanese principles and concepts of design.

These fundamental elements are even more clearly recognizable in the works of the *Rimpa* school of the seventeenth to the nineteenth centuries. The *Rimpa* school is not a true school of art in the sense used by art historians, but rather a genealogy, as it were, of a certain painting technique that originated with two noteworthy master painters: Sôtatsu and Kôrin. The

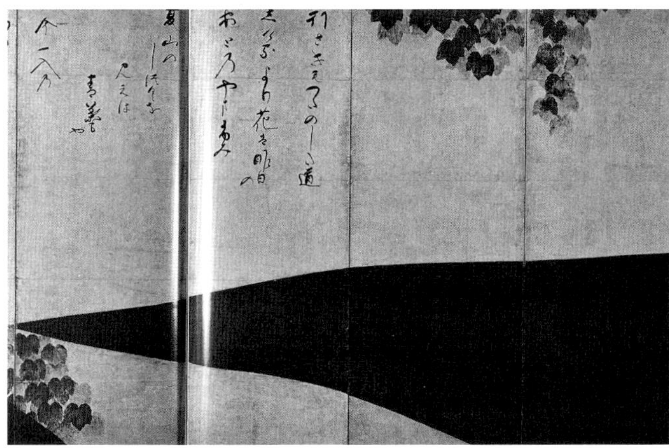

Ill. 3 Sôtatsu (attr.), *Ivy-Lined Path,* Wall Screen, Mineral and Vegetable Pigment on Gold Leaf, early 17th c., National Museum, Tokyo

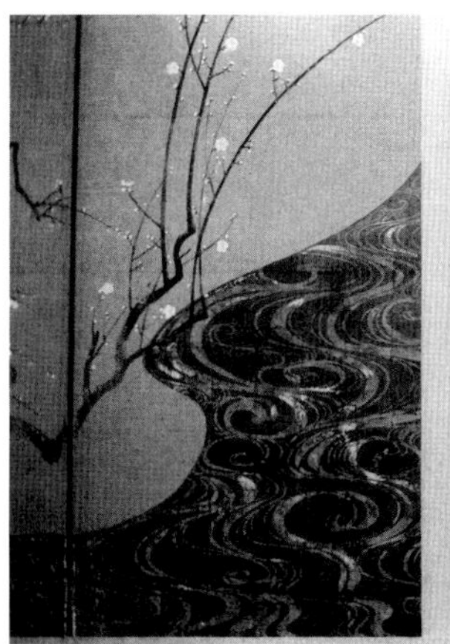

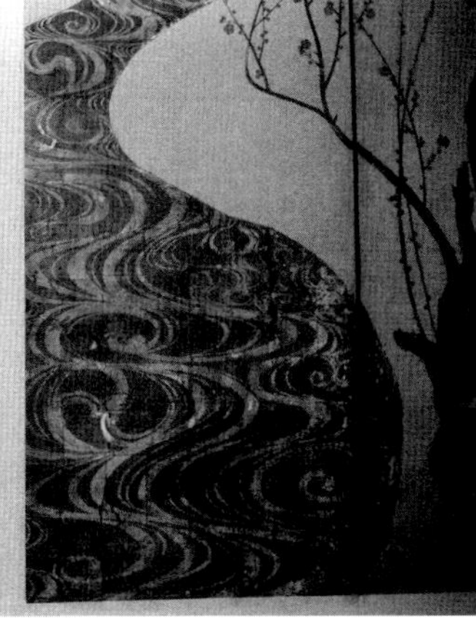

Ill. 4 Ogata Kôrin, *Red and White Plums (Plum Blossoms),* Wall Screen, Mineral and Vegetable Pigment on Gold Leaf, 18th c., Atami Museum MOA, Atami

works of these two masters, who are generally regarded as the direct forefathers of modern Japanese painting, offer particularly striking illustrations of these basic principles and concepts. Sôtatsu, active during the first half of the seventeenth century and probably the greatest genius among the painters of the *Rimpa* school, studied the classical paintings of the twelfth and thirteenth centuries in an effort to articulate them in a new way as a consciously extrapolated adaptation in forms. He achieved this by employing a unique form of abstraction in the pair of wall screens with *Bugaku* dancers (Ill. 2). Here, Sôtatsu distributed a few characteristic figures with rather ornamental features—figures found in virtually the same form in many images of *Bugaku* dancers from the period—in a diagonal arrangement, seemingly suspended above the gold ground as if the artist regarded them only as a point of departure from which to develop a rhythm of colors. The few supporting elements—the music tent with two barely visible drums and the two trees standing in opposite corners—are subordinated to the images of the *Bugaku* dancers to an unusual degree; they serve primarily a formal purpose and have virtually no substantive meaning. In order to prevent the diagonally arranged group of figures from escaping the boundaries of the picture, however, a group of vivid blue dancers is positioned opposite it. In spite of this abstract, entirely non-illustrative representation of the *Bugaku* dance, the viewer senses something of the rigid solemnity and restrained passion hidden behind the grotesque masks, something of the movement in non-movement that is characteristic of many forms of Japanese art: form and animation, animation through form.

Another work only tentatively attributed to Sôtatsu (Ill. 3) but undoubtedly a product of the same era and the general context of the *Rimpa* school is the wall-screen painting entitled *Ivy-Lined Path,* an illustration based upon *Ise-monogatari,* a literary work from the tenth century. Flat surface is the dominant

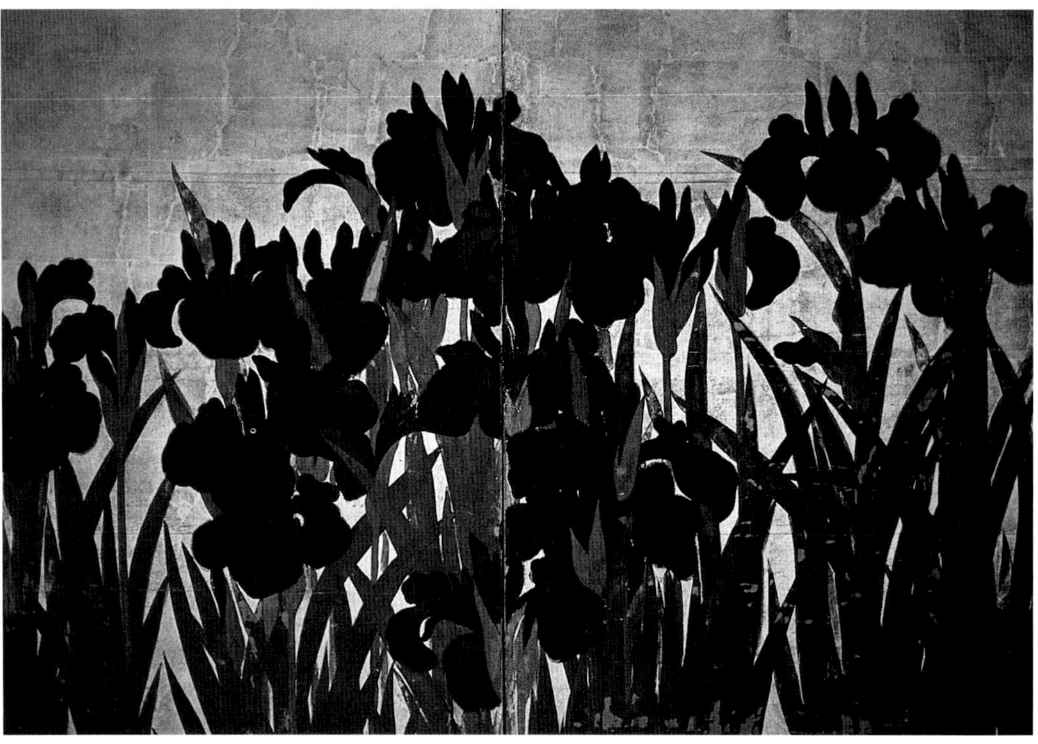

Ill. 5 Ogata Kôrin, *Tiger Lilies,* Wall Screen, Mineral and Vegetable Pigment on Gold Leaf, 18th c., Nezu Museum, Tokyo

Ill. 6 Sakai Hôitsu, *Fuji-san,* Mineral and Vegetable Pigment on Paper, early 19th c.

theme here. Were it not for the token suggestion of ivy vines, the image would be a pure two-dimensional abstraction. Opaque green triangles are applied to the gold ground, which itself is divided into diagonal segments by variations of the gold tone. These diagonally bordered areas are "lined" without any hint of realism by the ivy, which seems to have been applied with daubs of paint. Poems from the *Ise-monogatari* are written on several of the panels.

At first glance, one might be tempted to regard this as decorative painting, but it is more than that. It is the complete transposition of a motif from nature into form without any loss of vitality, of the scent in which the reality of the motif is concentrated. Japanese artists have the unique ability to comprehend things of all kinds, even the most banal, in formal terms, to see them as form. It is a gift with a long tradition whose influence is evident even in the most

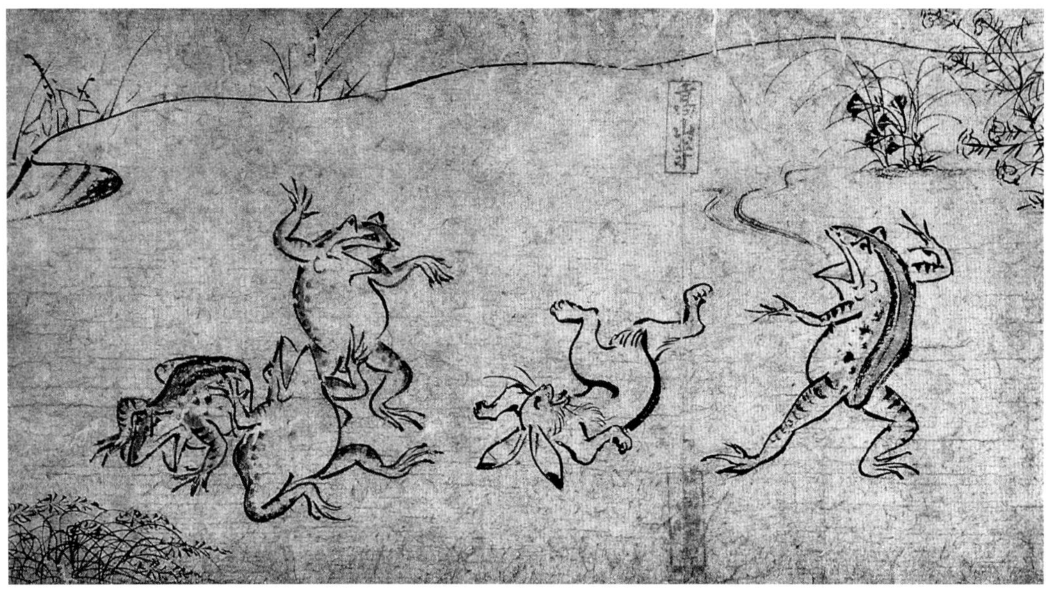

Ill. 7 *Chôjû giga,* Animal Caricatures, Scroll, Ink on Paper, 12th c., Kôzanji Temple, Kyoto

modern manifestations. And it also encompasses the possibility of shaping literary allusions, beyond the sphere of illustration, as autonomous artistic expressions.

The other great artist worthy of note in this context is Ogata Kôrin (1658–1716). His famous wall screen *Red and White Plums (Plum Blossoms)*—two gnarled plum trees separated by a blue and gold river (Ill. 4)—is a demonstration of complete planarity in combination with an almost impressionistic rendering of such botanical motifs as plum blossoms and "expressionistic" tree trunks. In reducing both trees and river, each in its own way, to their essential features—that is, by depicting them neither naturalistically nor even realistically—Kôrin pursues an approach encountered only rarely in Western art, at least not in such a definitive form or at such an early point in time. Kôrin's use of abstraction was deliberate, as numerous sketches clearly indicate. Step by step, he carefully approached the monumental, entirely flat river that appears almost upright on the pictorial surface. While models for the arabesques of the golden waves can surely be found in a number of stylized images of waves from various periods, no artist before him had depicted a river in such an ornamental form. The placement of the rudimentary, expressive forms of the plum trees on the left and right creates a unique tension between landscape elements that goes far beyond the limits of natural representation, yet still achieves the effect of a symbol of nature.

Much the same can be said of Kôrin's wall screens (Ill. 5), covered only with tiger lilies executed in blue and green on a gold ground and arranged twice in a rhythmic asymmetrical pattern over six panels. Although Kôrin did a series of precise sketches as studies for these flowers, they remain pure surface elements despite all appearances of layering, rendered in opaque colors and a somewhat impressionistic technique.

The aspect of flatness is taken a step further by Sakai Hôitsu (1761–1821), a later *Rimpa* painter. The picture is quite small: a flat, light-colored Mount Fuji set against a bright blue sky with an equally flat sun, painted around the beginning of the nineteenth century (Ill. 6). The motif, it appears, is merely an excuse to divide a plane. Apart from two-dimensionality, two other characteristics typical of Japanese painting are quite evident here: asymmetry and the emphasis on clear contour lines. These three painters are also singled out by Japanese scholars as forerunners—conceptual pioneers—of modern Japanese art.

In a culture in which written communication takes place through a system of complicated signs consisting of lines—vertical, horizontal and diagonal—line plays a very important role as a means of expression in art as well. Indeed, the practice of writing in signs developed into an advanced art in China very early on and somewhat later in Japan, retaining its relevance and significance to this day. The use of lines as contours in sketchlike drawings to create an extraordinary sense of tension and to intensify expression may well have its origins, at least to a certain extent, in the art of writing in signs. Examples of a highly energized, dynamic line can be found in the *Chôjû giga* (Ill. 7), animal-caricature scrolls from as early as the twelfth century. This tension of lines generated an unusually animated effect of motion marked by a heightened sense of realism in the visual image.

Yet the art of the line is not restricted to contour alone. In the course of a revival of Zen philosophy in the seventeenth century, the first Zen paintings—*Zen-ga* (Zen picture)—appeared. Like the *Kôan,* the paradoxical proverbs intended as aids to Zen pupils in their quest for enlightenment, Zen priests wrote such proverbs, often with a broad brush, in an artistic form or combined codelike signs with corresponding inscriptions, as in the case of Hakuin Ekaku (1685–1768) and his *Iron Club* (Ill. 8). This is a highly expressive kind of painting that penetrates into meditative depths with powerful brushstrokes often rounded to form the imperfect circle of perfection (Ill. 9), yet always remaining on the surface.

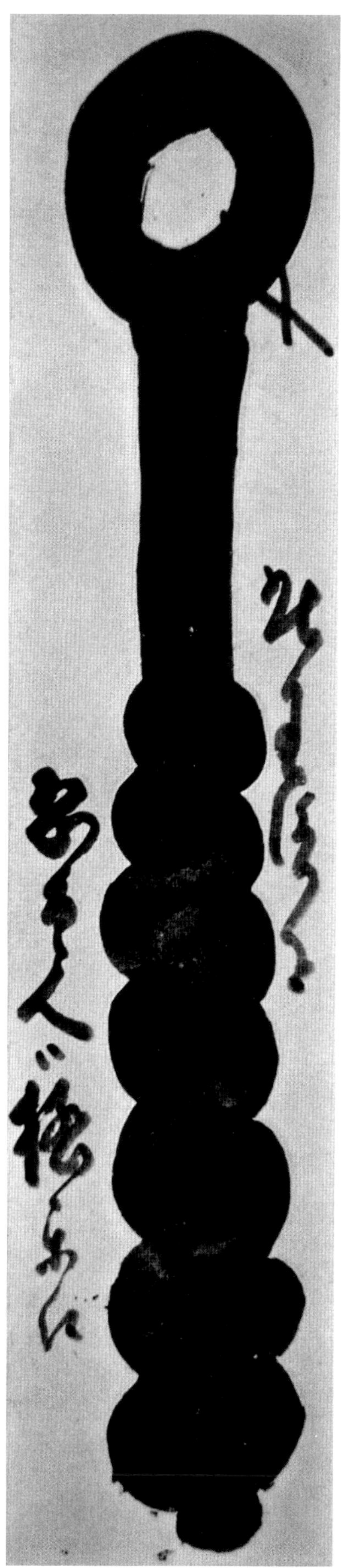

Ill. 8 Hakuin Ekaku, *Iron Club,* Hanging Scroll, Ink on Paper, 17th c., Hosokawa Collection, Tokyo

It was in this context that the first non-representational Japanese painting—perhaps the first non-representational painting anywhere—originated. It consists of lines that describe no object whatsoever and bears the short title *What is this?* (Ill. 10). It was painted by the Zen priest Tôrei Enji (1721–1792) in the eighteenth century. This is not to say that a general movement toward non-representational painting beyond the boundaries of *Zen-ga* emerged from this context. Yet it should be noted that "thinking in non-representational images," while not widespread, was at least recognized as a possible approach to visual art by the eighteenth century at the latest.

These fundamental criteria were not the only factors that influenced the development of modern painting. Japanese precursors in attitude and mode of expression already existed for certain stylistic forms that would later play a role in modern art. One of these was Surrealism. Not surprisingly, elements of the surreal appear in medieval Buddhist cult images—in the Amida Buddha figure known as *Raigô,* for example, who descends from the heavens on a cloud to receive one who is about to die, or in the esoteric configurations. Even if they are not perceived as "surrealistic," they represent at least a first step in that direction.

Yet the eighteenth century produced painting that is genuinely "surreal." The first artist who comes to mind in this context is Itô Jakuchû (1710?–1800). Although he is said to have been influenced by *Ming* painting, this contention relates primarily to his grotesque, unkempt plum trees. In his paintings of shells or cocks (Ill. 11), the arrangement of elements, the staggered configuration of the motifs and the often vivid color contrasts—red against gray—produce a constellation that evokes an uncanny, surreal atmosphere. Jakuchû also undertook intensive nature studies and is even said to have bred chickens. But he used his chickens and shells to create form, which he integrated into the flat surfaces of his paintings. A closer examination of Jakuchû's work

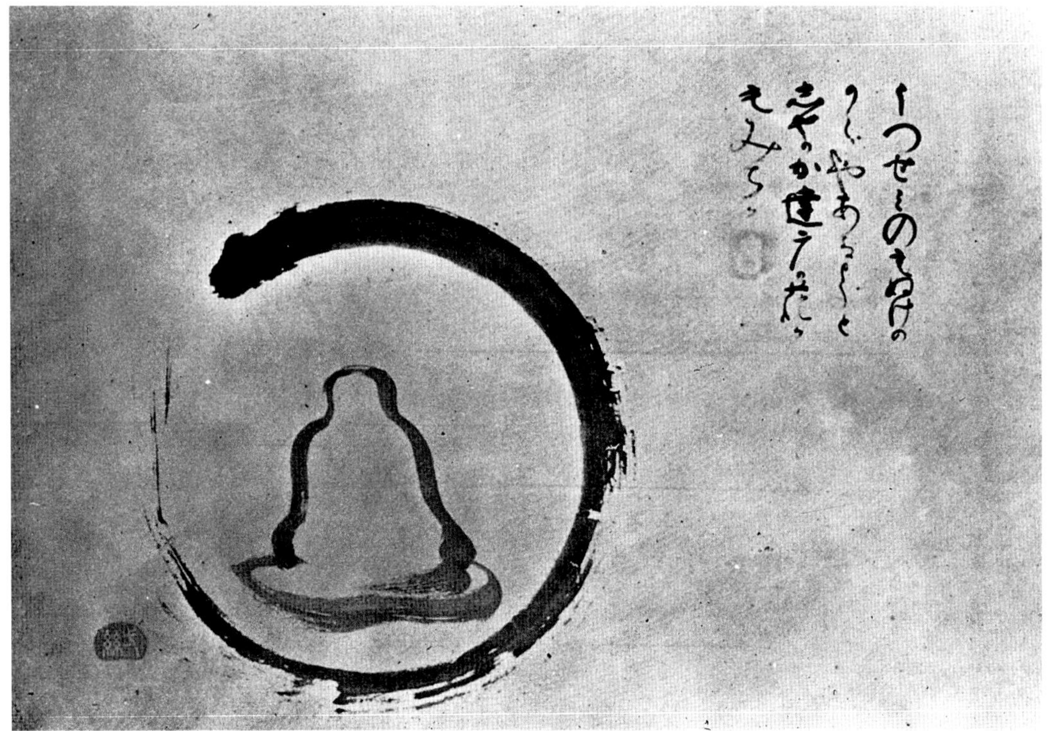

Ill. 9 *Bodhidaruma in a Circle,* Hanging Scroll, Ink on Paper, 18th c.

shows that the claim of some western scholars that his paintings are purely decorative, like tapestries, does not stand up to scrutiny. Quite apart from the fact that he wanted these pictures to be regarded as "self-portraits," the motifs are so consistently surreal that Japanese art scholars regard him as a forefather of the movement in its modern form.

One could easily pursue this investigation further and find "Cubist" or "Expressionist" elements in the paintings of the classical period, conceptual approaches to visual art which—whether consciously or unconsciously—relate to more recent times or, to be more precise, to the end of the nineteenth century. In any event, one has the distinct impression that the seeds of new developments from the outside fell on well-prepared, fertile ground.

It is even appropriate to speak of certain predispositions with respect to such "active" art forms as installations, performances and happenings of the kind that appeared during the 1920s and became increasingly popular after World War II. This comes to expression in the art of tea-drinking, known in Europe by the inappropriate designation "tea ceremony" and called *chanoyu*—"hot tea water"—in Japanese. A Japanese critic once referred to it as the "precursor of the happening," and he may not have been far from the truth. Essentially, the art of tea-drinking is nothing more than the practice of gathering together to drink tea. Yet the deliberate treatment of the tea-drinking utensils as works of art—from the sculptural teacups to the illustrated scroll in the decorative niche to the slim, carved teaspoon and the bamboo vase—clearly bears some resemblance to the happenings of later years. This artistic aspect is underscored by a strictly prescribed arrangement of the utensils, which nevertheless permits a flexible response to practical requirements, and especially by the manner in which they are shared and used by the host and the guests. A spatial work of art emerges from their concert of communicative movements, a work of art that incorporates and interprets space, transporting it into the realm of infinity, a work of art whose meaning is temporary but always reproducible. This context, it is safe to say, engendered a predisposition for art actions that would have been inconceivable as artistic expressions in Europe until much later.

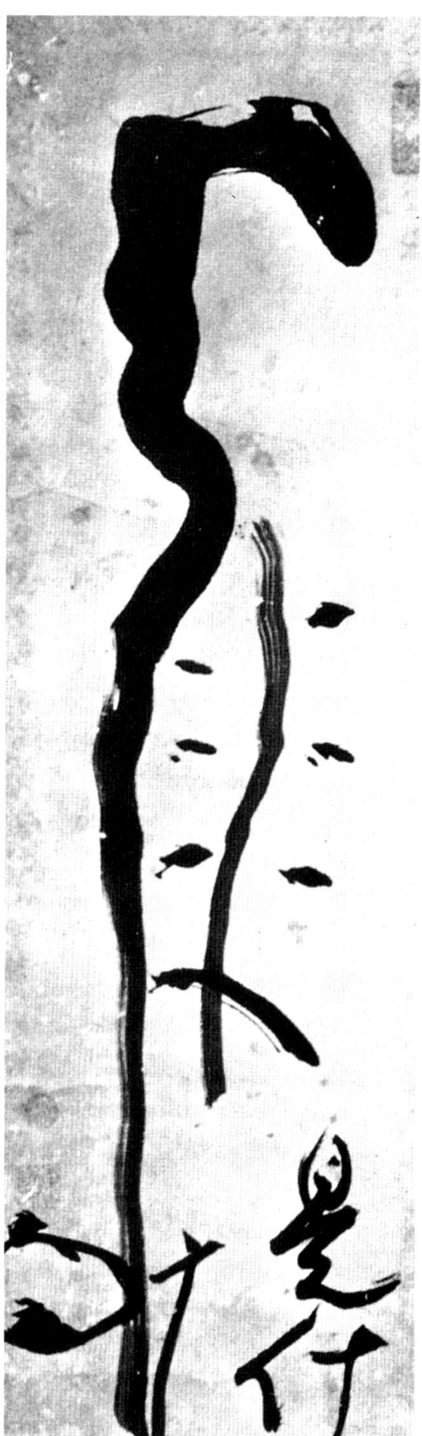

Ill. 10 Tôrei Enji, *What is This?,* Hanging Scroll, Ink on Paper, 18th c., Tanaka Collection, Numazu

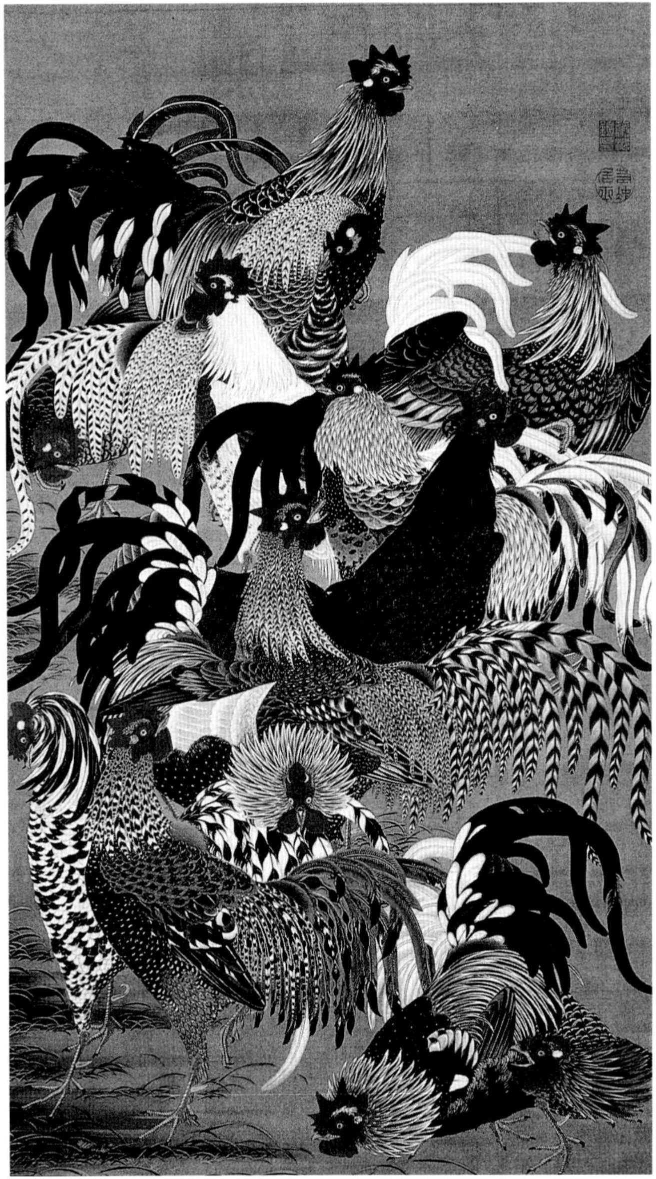

Ill. 11 Itô Jakuchû, *Cocks,* Hanging Scroll, Mineral and Vegetable Pigment on Silk, 18th c., Imperial Budget Office, Tokyo

Encouraged by the Dada movement, Japanese artists of the 1920s organized actions of their own. These were considerably more artistic, however, and much less oriented toward social criticism. Quite a different approach was taken by the *Gutai* group of 1954, whose actions—not referred to as "happenings," of course, but as "concrete" events—were based upon direct confrontation with material long before Kaprow organized his own form of happening.

A comparison of the aesthetic principles of classical Japanese art with what has emerged from them in our century shows that this development cannot be regarded as a simple linear progression of historical ideas in the traditional sense (although so-called Japanese *Nihonga* painting represented such a counter-movement). Rather, based upon the foundations of traditional views about art, new and independent phenomena took shape for which the classical foundation provided the nourishing soil, the ground in which its roots could take hold. Moreover, as we see from paintings such as the Ivy Wall Screen attributed to Sôtatsu and architectural structures such as the Katsura villa as well as the Japanese garden as *land art* and even the applied arts—lacquer art and lacquered utility objects whose functional austerity, simplicity and emphasis on material anticipated the Bauhaus—the very things we recognize as "modern" in Western art and architecture were already present at a number of different levels in Japan in the seventeenth century and earlier. The "leap" into modernism, therefore, was neither abrupt nor a venture into distant, unknown territories. These facts remain hidden from the outside observer by the Japanese practice of adopting Western painting materials, initially oils and canvas. This effect is intensified, as already demonstrated above, by the fact that the early artists of the modern period, like the classical masters before them, experimented with a number of different styles, including Western ones, before finding or rediscovering their own way, which did not exclude detours and reversals of direction. This is true of many of the artists presented here. Thus it is virtually impossible to assign the individual artists to single categories; nearly every one of them could easily be placed under a different heading as well. And that, too, is a fundamental attribute of Japanese art: diversity.

In light of these circumstances, it is remarkable that the first modern non-representational or abstract painting was created as early as 1912. Its painter was Yorozu Tetsugorô (1885–1927). Known as *Mu dai (Untitled),* it shows a bluish-reddish, almost tachistically painted flat surface with reddish contours. Its weight appears concentrated in the upper left-hand third of the canvas, where reflections of light appear here and there. Perhaps it is the impression of a landscape, but it is certainly not a likeness (Plate no. 1). The painting was done at nearly the same time as Kandinsky's abstract watercolor, i.e. 1910, or as some contend, 1913. But it was not until 1915 that Yorozu began to study Kandinsky's works, presumably shortly after *On the Spiritual in Art* was first translated into Japanese. Like all his fellow artists, Yorozu experimented with a number of different styles, doing several very interesting Cubist-style paintings, for example. His examination piece *The Naked Beauty* (Ill. 12), submitted upon completion of his academic studies, was painted under the influence of Matisse, as he himself stated. Yet even at that early point in his career, he transposed his predecessor's model into a visual concept of his own. It is not only the flatness and high horizon, but also the diagonal structure of the composition that negate the volumes of the body and reveal unmistakably Japanese elements of style.

Yorozu never simply imitated modern Western painting, but instead always approached it in his own individual way. The richly textured East Asian brushstrokes that inspired him in his landscapes and helped him to discover soft color tones was of great significance for him. It eventually encouraged him to abandon all of the categorizing styles and seek his own mode of expression, a quest that turned his attention to the study of East Asian, and specifically Japanese painting of the Literari, *Nanga,* of the eighteenth and nineteenth centuries. In his view, this meant investigating human rhythm and the rhythm of nature, a study which, one may safely conclude, helped him achieve his form of Japanese modernism. In this sense, Yorozu and his oeuvre exemplify the theme of this exhibition.

But there are many who sought their own direction in the same or similar ways. Onchi Kôshirô (1891–1955), for example, worked during the same period. Trained as a graphic artist, he was active in many different fields. He also painted in oil, which had become common practice in Japan around the turn of the century. His specialty was graphic art, however, and he even produced book illustrations at times. Kôshirô was very open to artistic developments of all kinds both in and outside of Japan. Some of his prints betray familiarity with the work of Franz Marc. He was also quite impressed with Kandinsky, although his knowledge of that artist's work was secondhand, and Kandinsky had exhibited only figural works at the "Sturm" (Berlin) show presented in

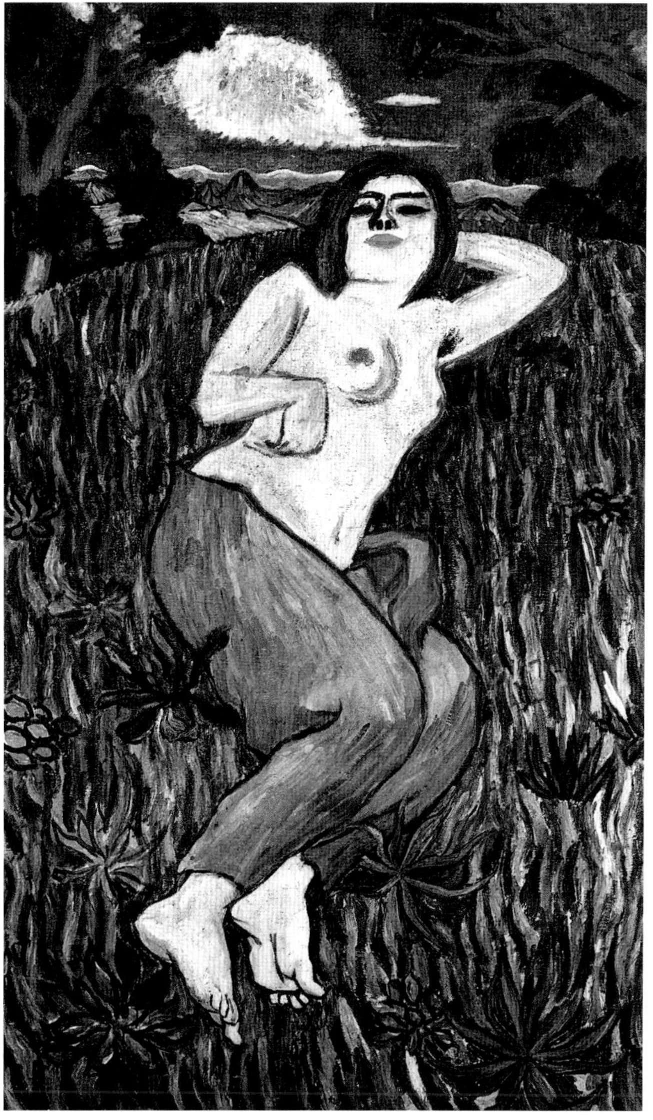

Ill. 12 Yorozu Tetsugorô, *The Naked Beauty,* Oil on Canvas, 1912, National Museum of Modern Art, Tokyo

Tokyo in 1914. Onchi also maintained close ties with the artists' group *Shirakaba (White Birch)* and the "life reformer" Mushanokôji Saneatsu. He incorporated many of these experiences into his prints, yet—and this is what makes him so interesting for the present exhibition—most of his works bear the dominant imprint of Japanese concepts of pictorial structure and composition. This is particularly evident in his print series *Tsukuhae—Reflections of the Moon,* comprised of woodcuts carved and printed by the artist himself (Plate no. 4 and 5), especially in the series *Lyric* (Ill. 13). Here we find all the elements that define the Japanese view of the pictorial image: sharp contours, total flatness, asymmetrical organization and abstract two-dimensional forms combined occasionally with small realistic references such as those familiar from the decorative Japanese paper collages of the twelfth century.

Receptive to everything new, Japanese artists were also willing to study the numerous "isms" emerging in Europe at the time and adopt them in their own work. Yet they did so in their own individual ways. In many cases, the names of schools and styles were taken literally—although they were usually not intended in that way—and imbued with an artist's own content and expression. The results often bore little resemblance to the models that had inspired them.

Kambara Tai (1898–1997), for example, an artist who was strongly attracted to Futurism and dedicated his first manifesto to Marinetti (see biographies), surely did not share the movement's desire to do away with the old values nor even its enthusiastic embrace of technology and science. Yet in his vividly colored paintings, we detect movements and gentle plays of light that seem to follow a musical rhythm influenced by emotional responses. Such titles as *Symphony* or *Pessimist,* which appear in several different variations, confirm this perception (Plate no. 9–12). Whereas Yorozu's color harmonies were often composed more or less in the style of landscapes, Kambara's works appear as "color spaces." They are almost always diagonally structured, a characteristic that may be interpreted as an unmistakable reference to the parallel perspective of the ancient illustrated scrolls. The impression of motion is evoked primarily through the use of relatively short but richly textured brushstrokes. From time to time, Kambara attempts almost paradoxically to freeze the movement in this dynamic plane by incorporating symbols of motion such as wheels or wheel-shaped flowers. It may be that in using these combinations, Kambara saw himself coming closer to Futurism, but it was a Futurism entirely in keeping with his own Japanese views and expressed in Japanese brush technique.

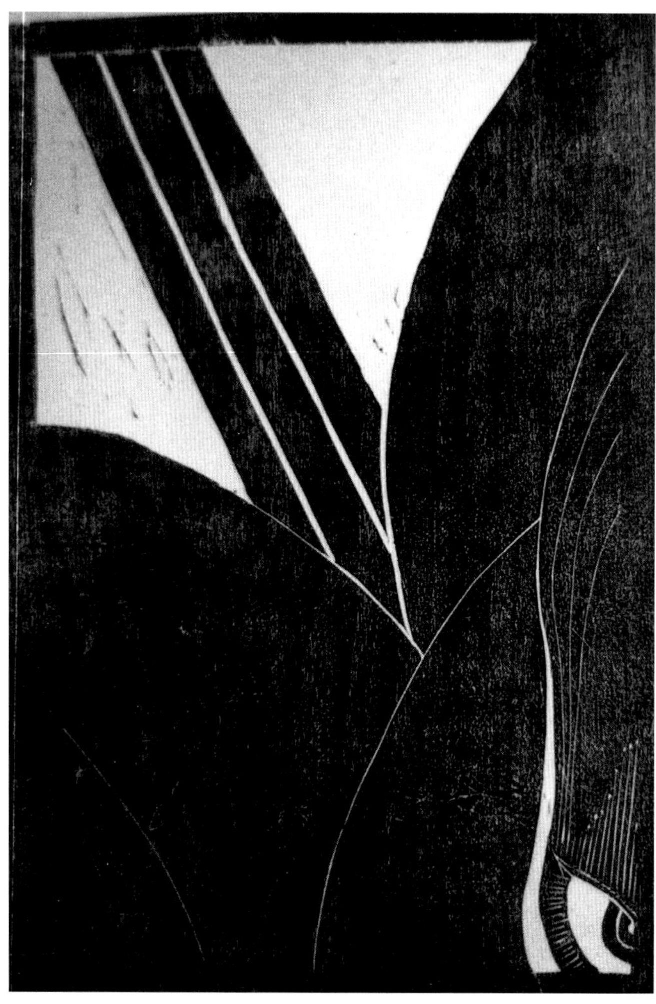

Ill. 13 Onchi Kôshirô, *Tsukuhae—Reflections of the Moon II–4, Lyric IX, 1914,* Wakayama Prefecture Museum, Wakayama

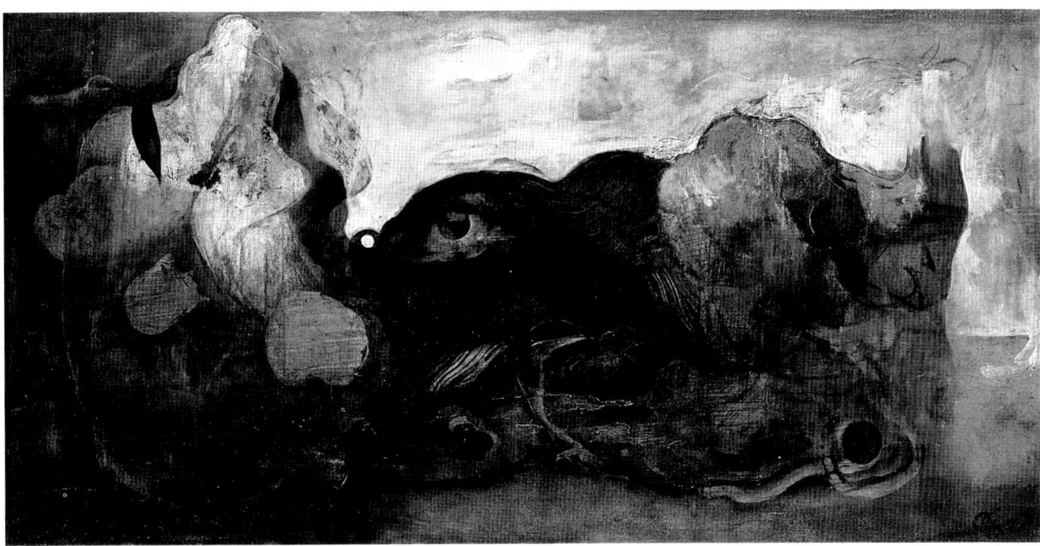

Ill. 14 Ai-Mitsu, *Landscape with Eye,* Oil on Canvas, 1938, National Museum of Modern Art, Tokyo

Some of the works of significant Japanese artists appear at first glance to be so directly inspired by Western art forms that one is tempted to deny them any autonomy whatsoever. Yet upon closer examination it becomes clear that this impression is false. Scholars have attempted, for example, to relate the work of Onosato Toshinobu (1912–1986) to that of Victor Vasarely. But Onosato did not seek to create optical illusions by distributing simple, visual-kinetic effects over the surface of the picture. His small geometric forms in vertical and horizontal rows are arranged in such a way that they point to a kind of infinity beyond the boundaries of the pictorial surface. With circular forms superimposed over them, they evoke a sense of cosmic unity, much in the manner of a mandala, the Buddhist diagram of the world. Thus it may require a philosophical interpretation to go beyond the superficial comparison with Vasarely, but Onosato's paintings provide more direct evidence.

The painting entitled *Black and White Round,* completed in 1940 (Plate no. 31), clearly points to Onosato's East Asian origin. The painting is dominated by a large, black circular form within which rectangles containing black dots are distributed. Two other rectangles, black with white dots, are positioned opposite the circular form. The presence of the black circular area shifts the center of gravity of the composition to the upper third of the painting, yet it is counterbalanced by the two black rectangles. The painting exhibits the balanced asymmetry characteristic of Japanese aesthetics, but also shows that white is more than simply a background for the black forms. Here, white is just as much an element of the composition as black, and is closely related to it. This "unformed" surface, which nonetheless possesses a strong formal quality, is typical of East Asian ink painting in general, particularly works containing landscape motifs, and plays a very important role in that genre. Much the same effect is achieved in Onosato's picture with the black circular form, where white exhibits the same formal power as black.

As we have seen, abstraction has been an important element of Japanese painting since the classical era. One explanation for this may be that artists have consistently sought to penetrate to the essential core of things, to cast off the superfluous. Yet again and again we find figures who rose above the great mass of abstractionists, pursued a path of their own and achieved works of singular excellence. One of these noteworthy painters, an artist of strongly introverted creative genius, was Yamaguchi Takeo (1902–1983), a member of the "Society of the Ninth Space," an association of abstract artists founded in 1938. Other members of the group were Yoshihara Jirô and Saitô Yoshishige. Yamaguchi began his career as a Late Impressionist during the 1920s. A decade later he had developed his own form of Cubism, although from here he immediately embarked upon his return to the two-dimensional surface. A little later he abandoned all traces of linear stability, retaining memories of objects but dissolving them in light and color, projecting them on the surface and negating depth entirely. A heavy framework, supported by vivid colors such as yellow and green, calls to mind written signs and gives rhythm to the flat space. Although several paintings from this period are reminiscent of Kandinsky, planar surface plays a much more definitive role in these works. Forms are not merely imposed upon the surface, but are generated from within it in a manner typical of much of Japanese painting.

Yamaguchi's later pursuit of progressive reduction was heralded as early as 1940 by the appearance of a few, seemingly suspended two-dimensional forms. Further development, however, was severely restricted by the ensuing war. In 1941 Yamaguchi was forbidden to exhibit his work, although he was allowed to continue painting. Abstract landscape forms began to appear in his paintings in 1942–43 and were condensed into almost realistic, red-outlined shapes after the war. This was his attempt to come to grips with the events of the wartime years. It was "the responsibility of artists" to deal with the problems of the war and the post-war period, or so it was said at the time. Many abstract artists sought to meet this obligation by devoting their efforts to the figural representation of pain and destruction. Yamaguchi, however, returned to his pre-war pursuit of reduction as early as 1948. His thin brush lines became broad, winding, intersecting bands combined with circular forms; his palette was reduced to red, ochre and

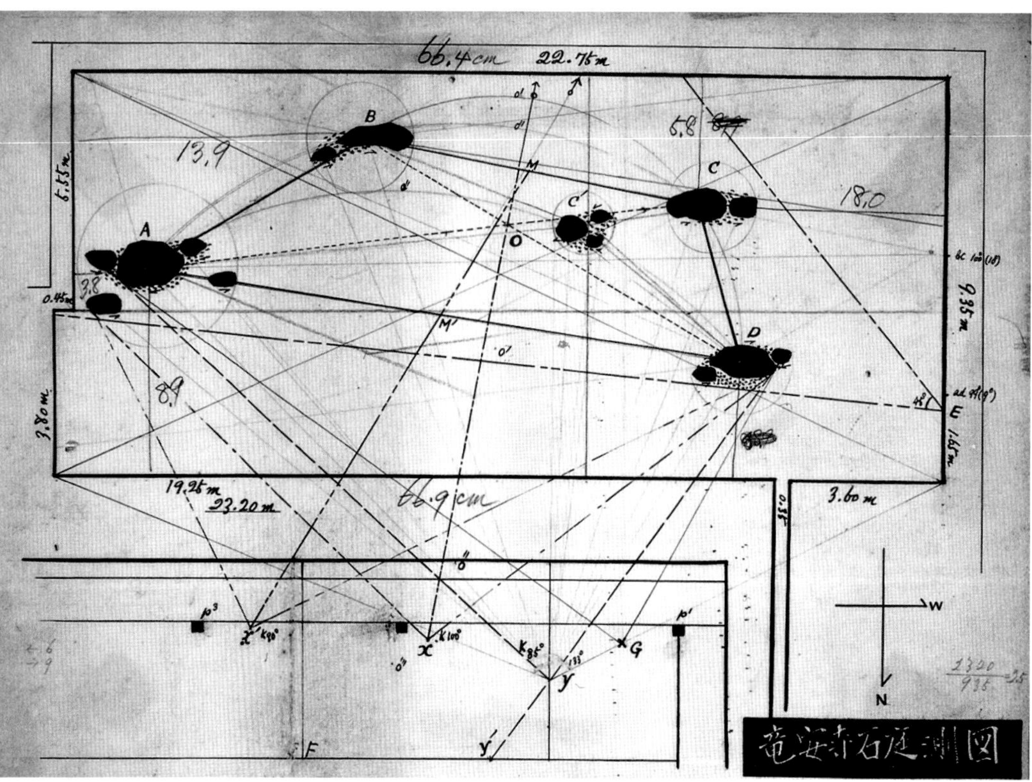

Ill. 15a Kitawaki Noboru, *Ryôanji Stone Garden* (Structural Plan), Ink on Paper, 1934, National Museum of Modern Art, Tokyo

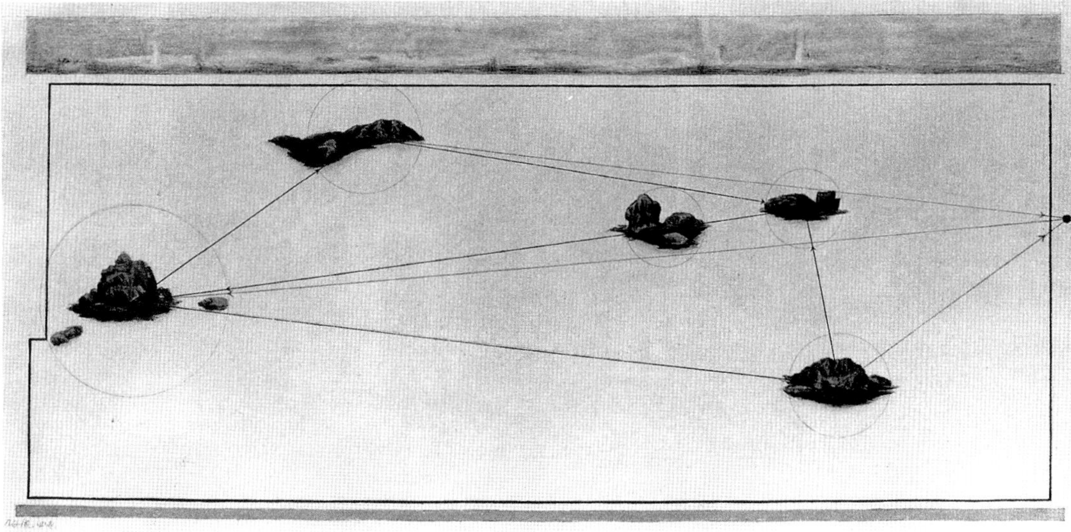

Ill. 15b Kitawaki Noboru, *Ryôanji Stone Garden* (Vectoral Structures), Oil on Canvas, 1941, National Museum of Modern Art, Tokyo

black. Associations with written signs reappeared. Toward the end of the 1950s these bands expanded to form surface areas, displacing more and more of the black background until only peripheral zones and slits remained. Ultimately, the black was almost completely eliminated, leaving behind only small traces. Yet it would be mistaken to equate these works with Color Field Painting. Yamaguchi's point of departure as a painter was the natural environment around him. The landscape and especially the fields of Japan remained as concrete images in his mind. He expressed them in a surface form that exposed their injuries and refused to hide their imperfections and, for that very reason, created the "imperfect image" of a landscape in which we recognize a typically East Asian attitude.

The works of Saitô Yoshishige (born in 1904) clearly demonstrate that even relief sculpture—if only bas relief—need not be resistant to Japanese surface aesthetics. Following several experiments in wooden carving, oil painting and literature during his youth, Saitô's attention shifted to his real calling and objective in 1930s. From this point on, he was concerned with the visual expression of the interrelationships of forms; thus it was not long before he produced the large-scale bas relief *Toro-wood* (a precise definition of the word has not been established) of 1938 (Plate no. 29). At the time, this work was one of his most famous. Such reliefs may contradict the Japanese aesthetics of surface—indeed, Saitô himself identified three-dimensional space as his point of departure—but can also be viewed in relation to two-dimensional space and time. Saitô categorically rejected the illusion of space: "The forms do not relate to one another as foreground and background but instead create a real space defined by flat surfaces."

Saitô's development, however, did not end with these reliefs. He went on to experiment in a number of different media. Following a figural phase during the post-war years—a shift he, like Yamaguchi, saw as an obligation—he arrived at a new kind of abstract painting, characterized now by a dynamic two-dimensional surface. He was fascinated first and foremost by the elasticity of East Asian brushwork. Thus it was only natural that signlike forms began to appear, only to dissolve again in the surface movement, like written signs chiseled into stone that are gradually worn away through weathering. Saitô amassed a fine collection of tracings taken with ink swabs from old inscribed stones. Although he did not make direct use of written signs in his elaborately structured pictures, they contributed significantly to the development of his formal vocabulary.

Saitô approached the theme of concrete space again and again in a number of different ways. He created asymmetrical lattice structures inspired by Japanese half-timbered houses. Taking up aspects of his *Toro-wood,* he began to employ simplified forms of everyday objects as motifs—the *Crane (Hook)* (Plate no. 72), for example, which he even attached as a

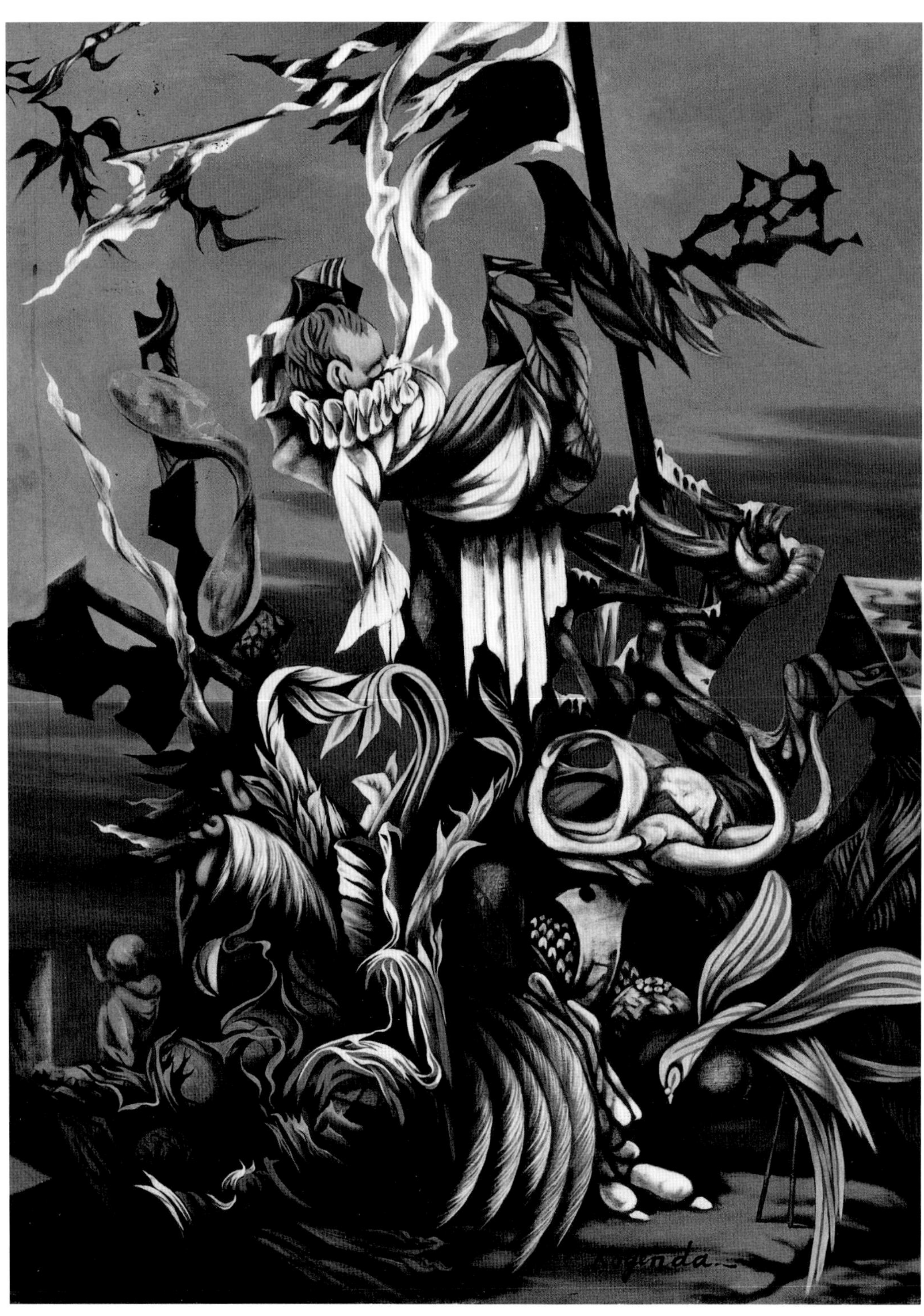

Ill. 16 Hamamatsu Kogenta, *Genealogy of the Century,* Oil on Canvas, 1938, Itabashiku Art Museum, Tokyo

moveable element. He did not abandon his basic objective of constructing spaces from flat elements even in his later installations, in which the space between the narrow, flat pieces of wood may serve the same function as the "empty" space in East Asian ink painting. Although some may still attempt to associate certain phases of Saitô's work with Western styles, there can be no doubt that a unique and specifically East Asian mode of thought and vision underlies everything he produced.

Although most of the important representatives of modern Japanese painting relied on traditional views and aesthetics, there were artists who drew upon their memories of old motifs and signlike forms, reformulating them and making them the basis for their quest for new directions. One such artist was Sugai Kumi (1918–1995). He is also typical of the many Japanese artists who traveled abroad, attempting to come to terms with what they found there and find a place within it and eventually returning to their own identity, their own creative selves. Having passed through the first phase after his arrival in Paris in 1952, Sugai shifted his focus to the old memories. In a style reminiscent of East Asian brushwork, yet in broad strokes, he "wrote out" the signs for *Moon* or for *Hill* (Plate no. 64 and 59), often rendering the Japanese ogre or devil *Oni* in shapes that closely resembled the written sign for *Oni*. He retained this signlike quality, although it later solidified into an individualized form of "hard edge"—that is, into starkly outlined curving bands in pure colors, their stringency apparently diminished by the addition of softer, almost shadowy accompanying forms. Elements of this kind began to appear in his work around 1961. These new paintings were a symbolic expression of his love of high speed and fast cars (Plate no. 69). In other words, on the basis of the original signlike quality of his works—itself a product of his brushwork—he developed a new quality which, despite its transformed appearance, was essentially the same. The artist himself saw this as an expression of two different selves. During his early phase he had regarded himself as an artist and a "doer"; in his late phase he achieved his true ego or self, which is expressed in the sign. Nothing shows more clearly that the roots of Sugai's art lie within himself and never wandered outside the sphere of Japanese culture.

For a certain period in his life, Takamatsu Jirô (1936–1998) could also be mentioned in the same context as Sugai. During this phase, i.e. primarily in the 1960s, he was concerned with a type of motif often used in painting and particularly in the woodcuts of the eighteenth and nineteenth centuries: the motif of shadow pictures. Jirô had begun his career with different kinds of installations and performances and later worked with changes in nature before taking up the theme of shadow imagery. The sliding doors used for entering and leaving the traditional Japanese house are covered with semi-translucent paper. The movement of people or animals in lighted rooms inside the house produces a fascinating, often uncanny play of shadows. This was presumably Takamatsu's inspiration, although he may well have been stimulated by the shadows of Hiroshima, the traces of the bodies of people left on walls after the bombing of that city.

Most of Takamatsu's shadow paintings are large-scale works featuring almost life-size figures in completely two-dimensional presentation. All spatial relationships appear to have been eliminated. Takamatsu returned to this theme again and again, for example in small paintings containing concrete objects such as nails and hooks. These elements added a new nuance and "movement" to the shadow pictures (Plate no. 75–77), as the real shadows could be set in motion by changing the location of the light source.

While non-representational, so-called abstract painting was developing in a variety of forms through a number of different approaches, Japanese Surrealism reached its zenith in the years just before, during

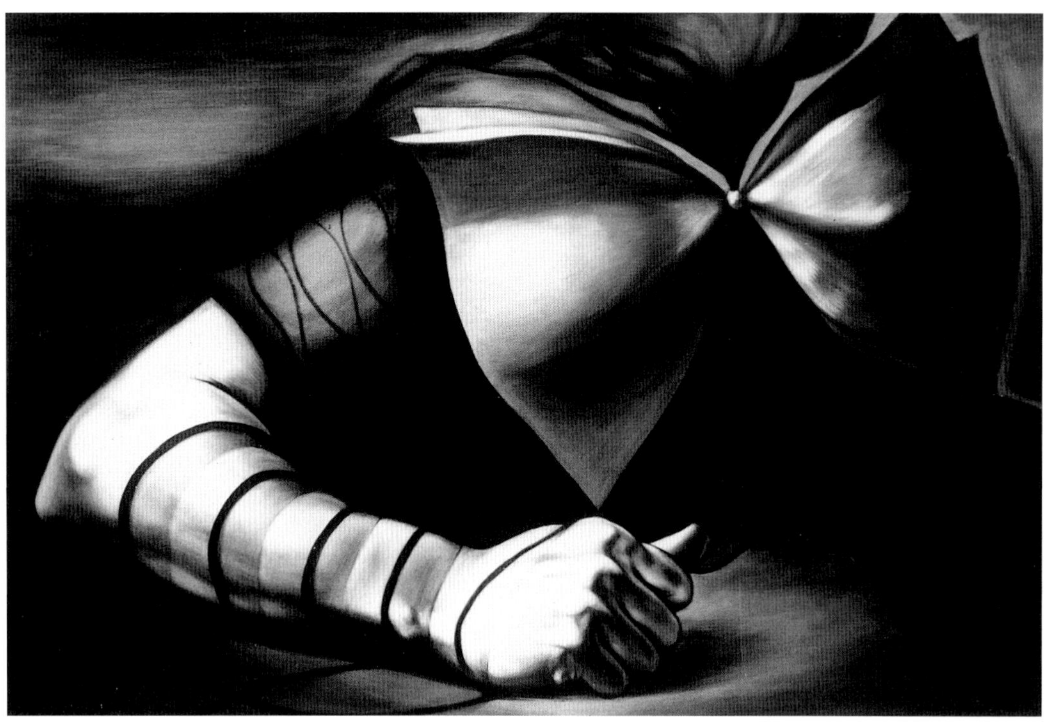

Ill. 17 Okamoto Tarô, *The Wounded Arm,* Oil on Canvas, 1936, Okamoto family, Tokyo

and after World War II. A cursory glance suggests that Japanese Surrealism resembles its international form and that it responded to certain external stimuli. But the two versions of Surrealism developed from quite different starting points. While Breton describes Surrealism as psychic automatism and demands the transformation of dream and reality into an absolute reality or super-reality, the essence of Japanese Surrealism consists in a juxtaposition of opposites: nature and the supernatural, reality and hyperreality. This opposition was postulated by Nishiwaki Junsaburô (1894–1984), one of the most important lyricists and art theorists of modern Japan, in his various essays on Surrealism, although he saw hyperreality as a kind of supranaturalism. The naturalism of which he speaks, however, differs from our definition of naturalism, and relates rather to an immediate view of nature. True nature was to be made visible through the juxtaposition of astonishing opposites. Yet Surrealism in Japan exhibits a range of different characteristics. There are certainly echoes of de Chirico or Dalí, but we find other, very different ideas as well. Ai-Mitsu painted *Landscape with Eye* (Ill. 14) in 1938. The landscape and the eye are not really opposing elements. Both are natural phenomena; they are merely different manifestations of existence, apparently separated from one another. Ai-Mitsu places them in a close relationship, without negating their difference—and the eye becomes an element of the landscape after all.

The work of Kitawaki Noboru (1901–1951), who is also referred to as a Surrealist, presents an entirely different face. He appears to have begun in the customary Surrealist manner, combining irreconcilable things in partially distorted perspectives. He found himself dealing increasingly with magical landscapes before finally turning to Constructivism in the late 1930s. His most significant works, which set him apart from all other movements, were completed between 1939 and 1941. In his cool constructions incorporating the magical signs of the *I Ching,* Kitawaki conjures up a world that lies *a priori* beyond the pale of palpable reality, yet is of essential importance to human existence—the latter represented in the form of a single human eye or the natural-looking image of a plant in the midst of all of these signs (Plate no. 36). Analysis appears to be both the point of departure and the primary objective of Kitawaki's later works. Somewhat earlier, he had studied the famous stone garden at the Ryôanji temple in Kyoto (Ill. 15 a/b). The motif in these works, the object of representation—which originated in the late fifteenth century—is itself a symbol of a "surreal" world that transcends all mundane reality. It points beyond the here and now toward cosmic relationships, passing over all boundaries in the process. Kitawaki sought to "comprehend" this, to fix it at the human level and to confront it with the aid of the intellect. Perhaps it is possible to draw the following conclusion from these works: Kitawaki appropriated concrete, existing "surreal" phenomena and attempted to make them accessible to his experience through lines of communication and construction.

In a general sense, it is true that most Japanese artists have concentrated upon themselves in an effort to discover their own identities and find expression for their perceptions and feelings. They have sought to explore the essence of things, of the world, in terms of its relevance to their own existence. Yet a number of artists, some of them perhaps only at certain times, have focused upon things outside themselves, upon social problems, questions of war and peace or the problems of the post-war era. We are reminded of those who believed, immediately after the end of the war, that it was "the responsibility of artists" to come to terms with the problems of the

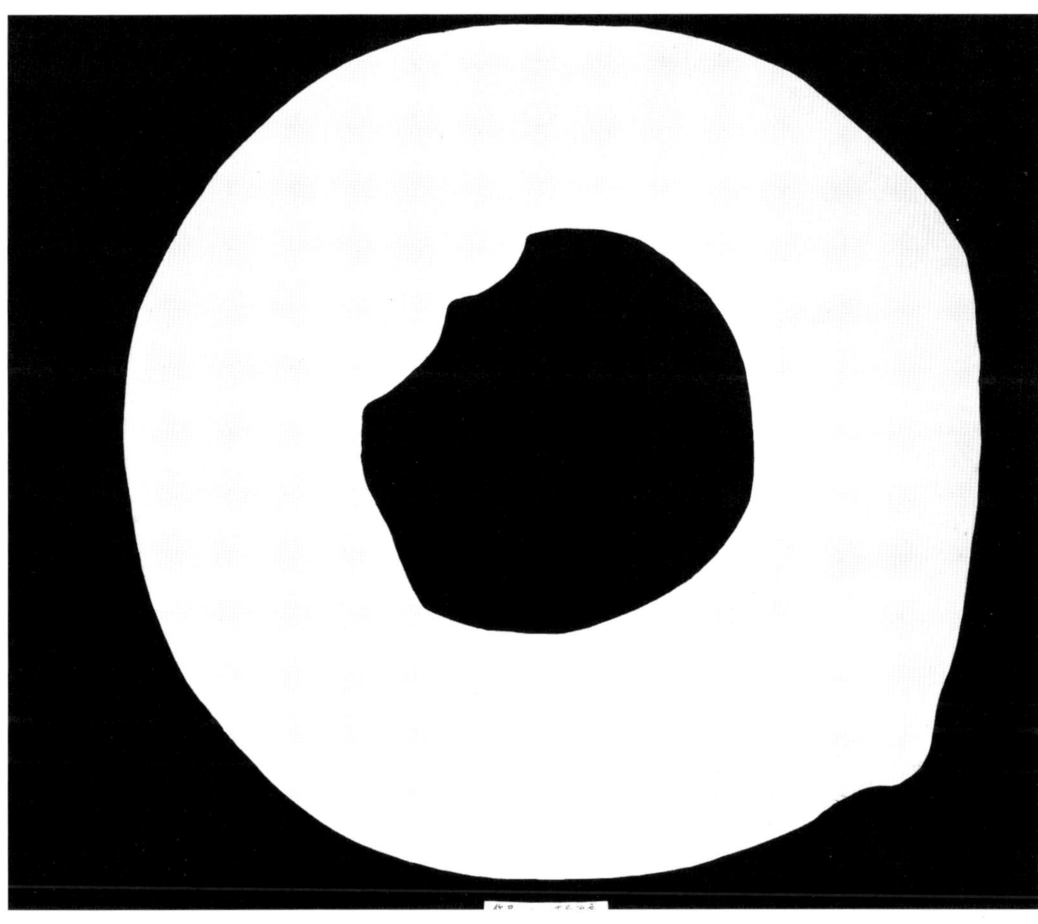

Ill. 18 Yoshihara Jirô, *White on a Black Ground,* Acrylic on Canvas, 1965, National Museum of Modern Art, Tokyo

war. It was apparently difficult to exhibit during the imperial era and the wartime years. "Independent artists" often had no opportunity to do so at all, and the increasingly strict rationing of painting supplies made it difficult for them to work. The term "degenerate art" never appeared, however. In fact, an international exhibition of Surrealist art was presented in Tokyo in 1937. Alluding to the signing of the Anti-Comintern Pact, Hamamatsu Kogenta painted a *Genealogy of the Century* (Ill. 16) in 1938, a painting in the Surrealist style in which a group of people is seen gazing up at a ragged swastika flag and an equally tattered Japanese flag. The message could hardly have been expressed more clearly. The painting was immediately placed on exhibit at the artists' society of the Imperial Japanese Army!

The situation quite naturally became more difficult after the attack on Pearl Harbor in 1941. Artists were accused of collaborating with the Comintern, but they continued to work. Many left-leaning artists became "reportage painters," depicting events realistically or with varying degrees of Surrealist alienation in the manner of Hamamatsu's *Genealogy of the Century.* In this way, artists forged a link between social phenomena and expression in art. This, by the way, was not a new development in Japanese painting. We find it, for example, in the illustrated scroll of the *Heiji-monogatari* presented by the soldiers to their superiors after the war in order to state their claims. It is also evident in the image of a poor Samurai who finally receives his fiefdom and in the detailed description of diseases in an illustrated scroll.

One of the painters most deeply concerned with social and political issues was Okamoto Tarô (1911–1996). One of his most famous paintings, *The Wounded Arm* (Ill. 17) was done in 1936 following the shocking experience of the war in Spain. The painter made use of Surrealist elements in this work, and it remains one of his most impressive paintings even today. After the war, Okamoto allied himself with several different groups and participated in many activities, none of which satisfied him. What he sought was a radical new beginning, the demolition of all existing structures. Thus in 1950, he began painting mostly large-scale tableaus with Surrealistic figural representations—aggressive snake-like monsters with zippers devouring the weak and other images of this kind—using loud pop colors long before the advent of Pop Art.

Although observers abroad found it difficult to believe, there were also painters in Japan who launched critical attacks against the war and its horrors—including those committed by the Japanese—and the misery that followed it. Abe Nobuya (1913–1971) was one of them. In 1949 he painted emaciated figures (Plate no. 43) that call to mind the spirits of famine in medieval scrolls. The remarkable feature of this painting is that, as moving as the gruesome subject may be and in spite of the simple parallel arrangement of the bodies, the artist employed a strongly diagonal approach to the composition of two-dimensional space—entirely in keeping with traditional Japanese aesthetics. Abe developed this diagonal composition to its logical culmination in his *Mankind,* a painting done in 1951. The convoluted body divides the picture, diagonally once again, into two triangles, the epitome of "classical" asymmetry. The refined aesthetics of the surface composition appear to diminish the horror of the subject.

In contrast, Furuzawa Iwami confronted the atrocities of war without defenses of any kind. In a series of etchings begun in 1960 and completed over a span of many years, he illustrated these horrors, often ruthlessly and using drastic means, in thirty prints entitled *Shuragai* (Plate no. 80–109). Only occasionally did he permit himself to transpose his images of bones and skulls into the genre of the still life in isolated prints. Formally speaking, they are realistic illustrations devoid of any particular aesthetic ambition; only rarely do we recognize an interesting asymmetrical subdivision of the pictorial surface.

Here it is the subject itself, the war, that is emphasized with clarity and consistency and without sacrifice of artistic quality.

At a number of different levels and in a range of different forms, Action Art had an invigorating effect upon Japanese art in the early 1950s. (It is interesting to note in this context that John Cage, the promoter of Action Art in the United States, was strongly influenced by East Asian philosophy and Japanese conceptions of art.) Of the many different groups and movements, the *Gutai* group, founded in 1952 and given that name in 1954, is probably the most memorable. The group attracted attention in Ameri-

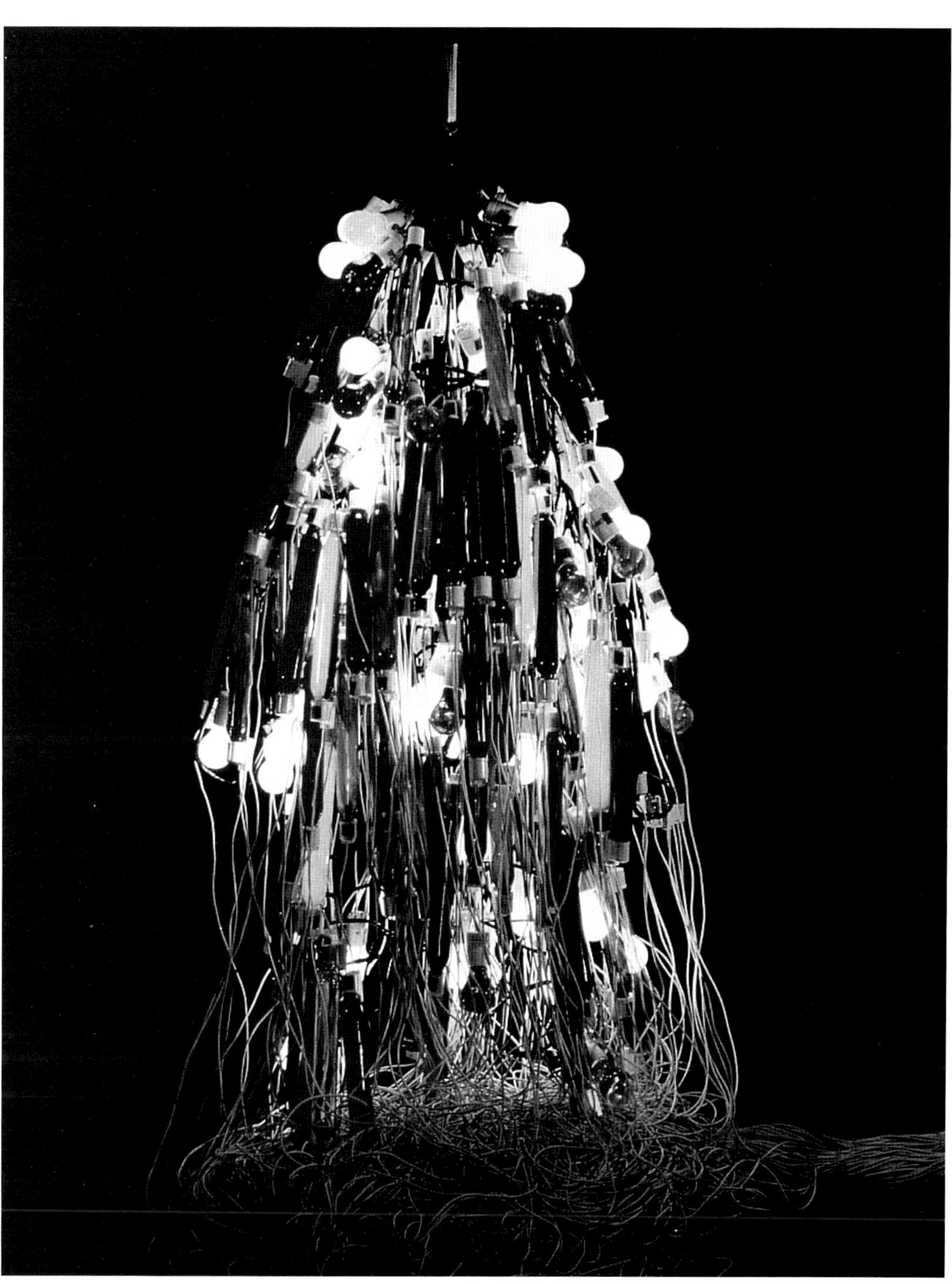

Ill. 19 Tanaka Atsuko, *Electrical Robe,* Light Bulbs, Fluorescent Tubes, 1956, City Museum of Art, Takamatsu

ca through its journal *Gutai,* a major feature in *Life* magazine and several exhibitions in the period preceding the advent of the Happening movement.

Under the leadership of Yoshihara Jirô (1905–1972), its members were less intent on destruction and provocation than on exploring the experience of material, on achieving new modes of access and expression. Material and the artist's use of it had always been regarded as aspects of essential importance in Japan. We are reminded of the thoughtful attention devoted to the individual stones, pieces of wood and roots placed in houses as objects of contemplation centuries ago. And we recall the art of tea-drinking in this context as well. The *Gutai* artists, however, were interested in ordinary everyday materials: paper, stones, water, mud, electric light, etc. Yoshihara's manifesto expresses this clearly: "*Gutai* artists do not alter material. Naturally in opposition to one another, the human mind and material reach out to each other in *Gutai.* One cannot subordinate material to the mind. If one leaves material as it is and in so doing calls attention to it, it begins to speak, calling out loudly" (*Gutai, Japanische Avantgarde,* Darmstadt, 1991, p. 103 ff.).

Shiraga Kazuo (born in 1924) was one of the most logically consistent of these artists. In his mud performances he immersed himself completely, with his whole body, in the experience of his material. A number of significant artists have emerged in the years since this group broke apart following Yoshihara's death in 1972. Although they have pursued more or less new directions with respect to technique, all of them have incorporated experiences gained in the actions of their early years into their more recent painting. Their painting developed, almost automatically, along the lines of aesthetic principles grounded in the Japanese way of seeing.

Yoshihara Jirô—the great seminal figure and promoter of this movement, dedicated to achieving a new approach to material and the conditions and feelings related to it—never organized actions himself. He stuck to painting. His most important theme was the sign-like, the sign in square (Plate no. 79) or circular (Ill. 18) form. Circles, closed or slightly open, have a profound philosophical significance in Japanese art and especially in *Zen-ga* painting. And this remains true even where they do not directly reveal the motion of the artist's brush, as in some of Yoshihara's circles with their almost smooth, strict outlines. Yoshihara never tired of dealing with the form of the circle. His concern with material, the material of everyday life, had no apparent effect upon his interest in the circle, nor did it influence his painting in general.

Ultimately, it was only to be expected that this focus on material would not last very long. Even Shiraga emerged from his mud and began to express his interest in material in broad, sweeping strokes of thick paint (Plate no. 61). Some of his paintings appear to come very close to the modern art of writing, which also relies upon broad, sweeping brushstrokes. But he painted with his feet, in order to integrate the whole body into the process. He undoubtedly learned how important this can be in the course of his mud performances. These powerful, richly textured bands of color, pushed together and superimposed on one another to form a densely woven pattern, can be regarded as a direct expression of color. Its distribution and rhythms evoke a mental image of the universe of the kind found, albeit in a totally different form, in the East Asian ink painting of past centuries.

The representation of a three-dimensional object on a two-dimensional surface presumably posed problems for some *Gutai* artists in the years following their action phase. Tanaka Atsuko (born in 1932), who exhibited her *Electrical Robe* in 1956 (Ill. 19), succeeded brilliantly in the attempt. The round, colored bulbs—like little pearls connected with dark electrical cords—enveloped her body like small cascades of light. She transposed them onto the flat surface in rhythmically ordered colored circles connected by lines (Plate no. 71), at times achieving a tension-filled asymmetry, to create pure surface images from her three-dimensional "electrical robe."

Despite the great diversity of styles and modes of expression that have emerged in the course of the century, one thing becomes clear: although artists did indeed become involved with European styles, an aesthetic, formal and philosophical foundation derived from a uniquely Japanese perspective continued to exist and retain its vitality. This foundation, in turn, had an appreciable influence on modern Western art, so that it is entirely appropriate to speak of a reciprocal relationship. Thus the growth of modern Japanese art contributed as much to the development of contemporary international art as it absorbed and reshaped into new and uniquely Japanese forms on its journey into the outside world.

This great diversity is also expressed—to the point of divergence—in general attempts to come to grips with the situation of art and the developments it spawned. The positions discussed here make this quite clear. But it is precisely in this diversity that we recognize the vitality of the culture and art of Japan. As a result, some things may remain inaccessible to Western viewers; yet the desire to understand everything can itself place obstacles in the way of understanding. Indeed, it can even be fatal. In the words of the Japanese art critic Kobayashi Hideo, "A picture teaches us nothing, and no one is capable of learning anything from a picture. It is enough for a picture to exist in the viewer's presence ... . All art retains its hold on life through silence, a silence that is full of the feelings from which the work was created. Whatever interpretation one may venture, one ultimately always encounters something that silences the voice, and that is precisely the reason why a *Manyôshû* poem from the eighth century is still alive today. It has resisted comprehension successfully until now. Were it ever to be fully understood, then it would have reached the end of its life" (*Das Kunstwerk,* 2XLI 1988, p. 12 ff.).

AN EXCEPTION

Sakai Tadayasu

I

In his book *Japan and its World—Two Centuries of Change,*[1] the renowned Japanologist Marius B. Jansen speaks repeatedly of the pronounced intellectual spirit of Japanese researchers. The theories of Galileo and Newton were known to the Japanese several decades before the opening of the country. Toward the end of the eighteenth century, the Tokugawa-Bakufu government assiduously collected foreign publications and in 1811 founded an institution that could be described as the "Translation Center for Foreign Books," which produced a large number of young, conscientious scholars.

Japan was indeed a "closed country," but it was nevertheless highly receptive to all information from outside. In my opinion, this bears witness, in a certain sense, to a high level of curiosity.

It was at the same time that modern Japanese art also emerged.

With the help of foreign books arriving in Japan (including many illustrated texts), it was possible to successfully produce copper engravings[2] and learn the technique of oil painting. From works of western art, the perspective of western landscape painting could be studied; moreover, a group of artists emerged whose pictures were referred to as *Ranga.* They represented a middle course between Japanese and western painting and were called *Ranga* ("Dutch painting") because the Japanese had adopted this kind of painting from the Dutch, their only link with Europe before the opening of their country.

As a result of this interest in western cultural commodities (including art), preoccupation with western painting further intensified during the so-called period of "cultural opening" after 1868, when the capital city Edo was renamed Tokyo. In this rather short space of time, public art schools were established, offering artistic training in the western tradition.[3]

At the same time, however, traditional Japanese painting continued to assert itself; similarly, the arts and crafts were influenced by the aesthetics of handicraft and promoted by the government for export. Thus modern Japanese art in fact developed within a complex web of differing schools. Strangely, a clear dividing line was drawn between these schools by designating traditional Japanese painting as *Nihonga* and oil painting as western painting or *Yôga*. Since then, these designations—which established a certain dichotomy between the two positions—have attained widespread use, up to and including contemporary art. The appropriation of western art did not take place along a straight path, but by way of various curves and detours.

For a time the encounter with such a different type of art took place against the backdrop of the opposing poles of "the west versus Japan." Regardless of which side was considered "orthodox" or "heretical," both provided artists with great incentive and unleashed as yet unknown creative stimuli. This applied in particular to traditional painting, which had become completely ossified and devoid of interest.

Yet as the social system consolidated itself with the advance of modernization and as living conditions began to change, the opposites "the west versus Japan" naturally changed as well. In place of a relationship of mutual co-existence, a kind of merger occurred; art adapted to the change in Japan's internal situation. As long as the opposing terms East and West clashed head-on, the window of curiosity to the world remained open. But as the modernization of Japan progressed, the interest in art converged with the "traditional and modern" mode of thought closely associated with the circumstances prevailing in the country. One example of this is the use of the designation *Nihonga* as a reinterpretation of the term "tradition." On the other hand, there were also links to tradition in the realm of *Yôga,* expressed in the choice of themes from history and mythology (the "conceptual images" of Western painting).

By this time, the difference between the intellectual worlds of eastern and western painting no longer provided any creative impulses; it was simply a difference in painting technique and theme.

Let us now shift our viewpoint slightly. In 1907, as a kind of national policy measure, the Ministry of Culture organized an exhibition entitled "Bun-ten" (Cultural Exhibition), aimed at resolving the internal turmoil in the world of art, which was embroiled in the complex division into *Nihonga* and *Yôga* and "traditional" and "modern." To a certain extent, the exhibition was successful, as it opened the door for new talent, imbuing the world of art with new vitality and promoting public interest. Yet the damage it did was far from negligible. In *Cultural Exhibition and Art* (1912), the only review he ever wrote of an art exhibition, the great poet Natsume Sôseki[4] criticised the exhibition's propagation of the authority principle, as it threatened to lead to academicism in art.

II

If we now move from the period around the turn of the century to the years between 1910 and 1920—the focus of this exhibition—the situation in Japanese art may be regarded as synchronous with the West. New ideas began to emerge; innovative intellectual trends gradually gained admission to Japan, and numerous small groups were formed, developing independent movements.

When examining the influence of these innovative intellectual trends on Japanese art, however, it appears that the more radical the views or ideas, the less headway they made. For this reason, the stimuli they provided for art were not very significant, but seem to have been confined to superficial phenomena; they were of more emotional than theoretical value, and in fact gained only very limited acceptance.

What were the primary reasons for this? One was that the innovative artistic trends came mainly from the intellectual world of the large cities and represented forward-looking pronouncements that established a precise rhythm for the future.

Yet the soil on which such modernist artistic trends might flourish was not yet sufficiently prepared in Japan. Modernity in painting meant not emphasizing the traditional artistic ambience, but striving for novel forms based on general ideas. In Japan, there was a great discrepancy between this modernity and a kind of sedentariness, which was expressed in terms like "oil painting by Japanese" and tended to result not so much in a unification of idea and form, but in their separation.

In Japan, "nature" as a kind of breeding ground had given rise over time to the traditional mode of thought and feeling; as western modernism gained a foothold in this traditional Japanese spiritual world, it was inevitable that (western) ideas on art would become transformed. And because this occasionally gave rise to something affective, indeed emotional, it became the subject of criticism. In actual fact, the efforts of Japanese artists—convinced they were heralding and working towards a new future—endeavored to let the eternal past live on through modernism in a truly innovative sense.

As examples, I would like to refer here to Yorozu Tetsugorô[5] (Ill. 1), who may be described as the first Japanese avant-garde artist, and Koga Harue (cf. Ill. 23),[6] whose manner of painting changed at a dizzying speed. In this context, the questions arise as to why Yorozu Tetsugorô, a Cubist for a time, developed a tendency towards *Nanga* painting,[7] and how Koga Harue's Surrealism was related to the Buddhist samsara.

III

In a speech entitled *I, from ambiguous Japan* given by Ôe Kenzaburô upon receipt of the Nobel Prize for literature, the author commented on the cultural and social situation in Japan in the context of a general assessment of culture:

"The modernization of Japan was the established course, to become like western Europe at all costs. But Japan is situated in Asia, and the Japanese have preserved their traditional culture uninterruptedly. This ambiguous course forced Japan into the role of invader in Asia. And Japanese culture, which was supposed to have completely opened up to western Europe, preserved its dark spots, which still remain unintelligible for western Europeans, or at least place obstacles in the way of understanding. Moreover, Japan occupies an isolated position in Asia, not only politically, but also socially and culturally."[8]

Perhaps this is even more difficult to understand when I summarize it, all too briefly: although modernism in Japanese art modeled itself on western painting, which had developed as a so-called iconology, in the final analysis it was unable to absorb it fully. Of course this was to be expected. And yet an understanding of art cannot simply ignore the fact that "ambiguities" remain, that they continue to exist as "dark spots"—as Ôe expressed it—that impede the development of understanding.

There seems to me to be a further problem, particularly from a western point of view. Without pleading objectivity, I doubt that in the final analysis, the Japanese avant-garde painters who represented differing positions with respect to modernism entertained the same sentiments as the Europeans (a fact for which this exhibition is a veritable touchstone). I recall the exhibition *Modern Western Painting in Japan: 19th and 20th Centuries,* shown at two European venues in 1985. There, examples of such "dark spots" could be seen and were subjected to criticism by westerners, yet without taking account of the situation in Japan. The exhibition, focused on a theme seldom seen even in Japan, was shown first in Italy and then at the Museum für Ostasiatische Kunst in Cologne.

Both positive and negative reviews appeared in German newspapers and magazines at the time; some articles accused the paintings of merely "aping" western painting. Nor was it only the Germans who were of this opinion. A few Japanese participants stated that the exhibition had received no attention in Italy. This reflects a view of art in which, even if sympathy for the work is presupposed, judgements based on criteria of good or bad quality are what determines its value. As they are unfamiliar with the background and state of the art scene at that time, the most these critics can do is to evaluate on the basis of easily accessible examples.

In my opinion, such a view of art is unreliable. I am aware that even among the Japanese there are intelligent people who proudly express the same sentiments. Such people, in particular, make use of these "old-fashioned" views. This has no direct connection with the content of this exhibition. Yet it is somehow strange to leave the evaluation of art and culture to a form of judgement based on the criteria of superiority and inferiority.

In their innovative, sometimes even militant approach, many of the artists who espoused modernist artistic ideas were aware of their status as a factor in the new creative force. In this sense, at least, there is no difference between east and west.

Between 1910 and 1920, young artists influenced by Futurism and Dadaism initiated a lively movement of their own. In the 1930s, avant-garde groups gradually emerged and pursued their activities under the influence of Surrealism and abstract painting. Just how these activities developed has been thoroughly evaluated, even from a contemporary viewpoint.

Unfortunately, the cultural activities of these groups were completely suppressed by the military during World War II. I will not comment on the subsequent events, as they are the theme of another essay.

The reference in my title to an "exception" is not intended to emphasize the modernity of modern Japanese art; my guiding concepts are not so narrow as to prevent me from seeing similar examples elsewhere in the world. I would like this word to be understood as expressing an awareness of the Japanese feeling of close proximity to nature, an awareness of an adherence to a "tradition" that has a constant impact, above and beyond the creation of the new and the "effects of time" recognizable in it.

I would like to see modernity in modern Japanese art as a concern for the cultivation of an awareness of beauty on the breeding ground provided to us by nature.

When a bud unfolds it becomes a blossom. But when a ship made of folded paper is unfolded, it returns to being a simple flat sheet of paper. Walter Benjamin[9] has referred to this double meaning of the word "unfold." I have forgotten the title of the text, but it seemed to me at the time that I recognized the very essence of the Japanese awareness of beauty in this "unfolding of the bud into a blossom." Perhaps this is putting it somewhat ambiguously, but I had the impression that the true aspect of those "dark spots which place obstacles in the way of understanding" is concealed there. As an exception ...

1 Marius B. Jansen, *Japan and its World–Two Centuries of Change*, Princeton University Press, 1980.

2 Shiba Kôkan (1717–1818) was the first to produce copper engravings in 1783.

3 The Kôbu Art School was founded in 1877 and was the first public art college in Japan. The school was closed in 1883.

4 Natsume Sôseki (1867–1916).

5 Yorozu Tetsugorô (1885–1927).

6 Koga Harue (1895–1933).

7 *Nanga* designates works painted by members of the wealthy educated class in Japan in the eighteenth century in imitation of Chinese painting of the southern Sung Dynasty. They are also referred to as *Bunjinga* (paintings by scholars).

8 Ôe Kenzaburô (*1935), speech given on December 7, 1994.

9 Walter Benjamin (1892–1940).

THE BURGEONING OF ABSTRACTION DIRECTIONS IN JAPANESE ART AFTER 1910

Mizusawa Tsutomu

The year 1910 was an extraordinarily decisive one for modern Japanese art, a time of change as the Meiji era approached its end. The first phase of rapid Europeanization—called "cultural renewal"—after the opening of the country in the mid-nineteenth century had reached its preliminary close after about half a century. In the face of this "renewal," outstanding young Japanese artists felt called not to persist in the mere imitation of some form or another, but to zealously seek within their own land what they had heretofore sought outside it, fired by lively curiosity and a sensitivity that both revealed and was heightened by the contradictions of that "renewal." The search within their own land also meant a search within themselves.

The year 1910 saw the founding of the literary magazine *Shirakaba (White Birch),* which also dealt with art and supported the cause of humanism; in the same year, the poet, artist, and sculptor Takamura Kôtarô (1883–1956) published *Green Sun,* a text which declared as absolute the freedom of expression of the individual artist. Furthermore, that same year Japan demonstrated its imperialist ambitions by annexing Korea, thereby turning an obviously distorted face toward its Asian neighbors; in the same vein, a case of high treason was followed by the onset of the suppression of the socialists within Japan itself. During that period, numerous artists reacted with great sensitivity to modernist western tendencies and sought a new and as yet unknown form of expression in the broad spectrum between tradition and innovation. After 1910, the distinction between *Nihonga,* or traditional form, and *Yôga,* the form introduced from the West, had been consciously regarded as something experimental and rather vague; it was also a reaction to the arbitrary subdivision of exhibitions undertaken by the Ministry of Culture, which had organized the first official exhibitions or "salons" since 1907. A large number of talented artists, often active in several areas—poets who were also painters, for example—swiftly came to the fore. Watercolors, which had ranked quite low in the realm of painting, came into fashion, followed shortly afterwards by the *Sôsaku-hanga* (creative woodcuts), prints that departed from the traditional division of labor typical of the *Ukiyoe* woodcuts. In this period, therefore, the number of artists in Japan suddenly increased quite considerably. After the Meiji era had run its course—preoccupied primarily with the establishment of a new state system—the Taishô era brought with it an enormous chaos, in a positive sense.

The poet and painter Murayama Kaita (1896–1919), for example, was typical of the years following 1910. He suggested that the votive picture halls in the Shintô shrines of the city of Kyoto, decorated with images donated to the shrines, be used as exhibition halls. He wrote: " ... In short, my wish for Kyoto is that instead of building inelegant western museums, new votive picture halls be built in the various Shintô shrines and devoted to art exhibitions. The age-old traditional style of the shrine is ideal for these exhibition halls. [A historicising, neo-Renaissance museum designed by Katayama Tôkuma had been built in Kyoto in 1885; it was officially opened in 1897, a year after Murayama's birth. Today it is the National Museum.] ... It is my sincere hope that one day, here in this old imperial city, it will be possible to see not only paintings in the Japanese style, but also woodcuts, oil paintings, watercolors or bronze nude statues in the votive picture halls of the Shintô shrines, that the wonderful, joyful, pious day will come when together with the lonely sound of the clap of hands, the sound of young voices discussing Matisse or Picasso will echo through the red enclosure of the shrines." ("A Respectful Look at the Votive Picture Halls," in *Asahi-shinbun,* Kyoto supplement, May 6, 1914). This suggestion by Murayama Kaita, not yet eighteen years old at the time, may seem strange on first reading. Yet his urgent desire to bring "bronze nude statues" (in the text quoted, Kaita had just spoken of Rodin's *Kiss*) or "Matisse or Picasso" into traditional Japanese venues such as the votive picture halls of the Shintô shrines can also be sensed in his self-portrait as a *Urinating naked Monk* (Ill. 20), daringly painted after Buddhist motifs in February 1915. The striking contrast between red and dark green shows his innate sense of expressionist color. Furthermore, a visionary, hitherto unknown plasticity emerges from the contrast between the strangely-shaped, fantastical mountains in the background—reminiscent of the mount Sumeru in Buddhist works—and the emaciated, naked body at the center of the painting, a rather brutal variation on the theme of the "Shakyamuni coming out of the mountains." The image manifests a force that seeks to unite opposites and is of the same quality as Kaita's conception of the mixing of different cultures, which caused him to see the votive picture hall as the ideal modern museum for Japan.

What Murayama Kaita initiated with the great open-mindedness of a "junger Wilde" was taken up in 1912 by Yorozu Tetsugorô (1885–1927), an artist ten years his senior. For a Japanese at that time, the amount of information at Yorozu's disposal was indicative of an incredibly pronounced sense of curiosity and a serious experimental spirit, with regard to both things in general and himself in particular. His examination piece for the Department of Western Painting at the Tokyo Art School, *The Naked Beauty* (cf. Ill. 12), shows the obvious influence of Matisse and Van Gogh, as the artist himself recalled in later years. The Japanese woman it portrays (the artist's wife) is wearing a red "loin cloth," a piece of traditional Japanese underwear. The natural scene around her, especially the red pines and the snow-covered peaks in the far distance, is said to correspond to the landscape visible at that time in the Tokyo suburbs, although Yorozu's hometown, Iwate in north-eastern Honshû, also comes to mind. At a time when the depiction of naked women in an academic salon style was gaining acceptance in the world of art, Yorozu Tetsugorô devoted enormous care to this large work, in which he dared to introduce Japanese elements into the traditional western form of painting. He thus communicates a very special type of humor in a strikingly different mood—it is this provocative "Japanese" *mise-en-scène* that makes his work so remarkable.

In 1912, the year he completed his studies, Yorozu Tetsugorô began to transgress the indifferent boundaries set up by the main trends in western painting. These boundaries, which in turn were marked by a compromise between academicism and Impressionism, were represented by Kuroda Seiki (1866–1924), director of the Tokyo Art School. (It should not be forgotten that Yorozu boycotted the gradua-

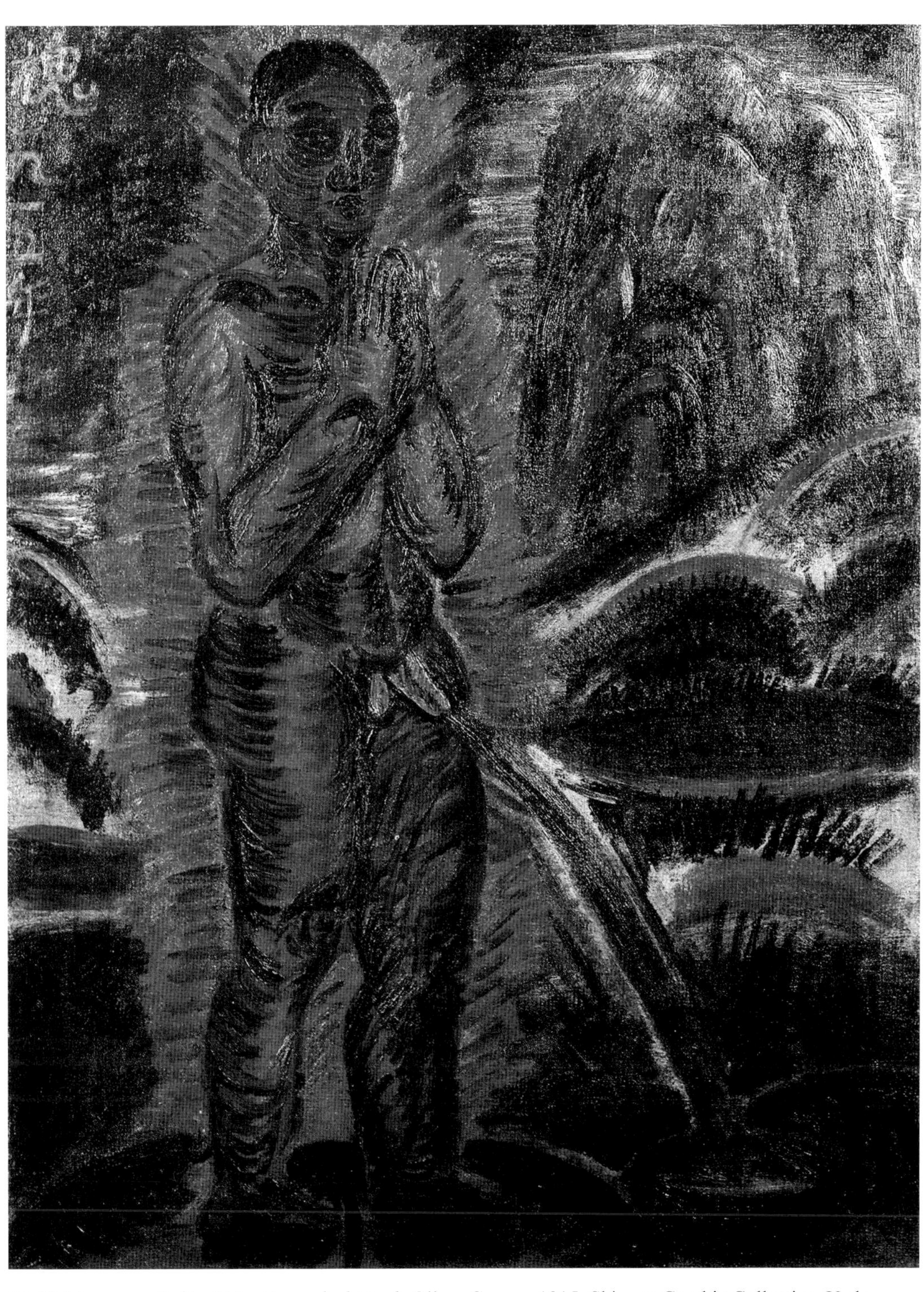

Ill. 20 Murayama Kaita, *Urinating naked Monk,* Oil on Canvas, 1915, Shinano Graphic Collection, Ueda

tion celebrations at that school.) *Naked Beauty* was an expression of this secession, and for Yorozu himself it signaled a creative and productive breakthrough. The modernist currents of the time—the late Impressionists, the Fauves, the Futurists, the Cubists, Kandinsky's abstraction, Munch's despairing view of man—presented a chaotic image. All of these modern elements can be found in Yorozu's works from the period around 1912, though without any chronological link. His artistic approach, which strove to liberate life through the simple expression of things, was perhaps closest to the early Ernst Ludwig Kirchner, should one wish to compare him to the modern German painters. Yet Yorozu also used a number of styles at the same time. For example, it is assumed today that his piece *Untitled,* of an almost abstract character that was to remain unique in his work, was done at the latest in 1912–13. Although Yorozu may have already understood Kandinsky's "inner necessity," the explanation given by Yamano Hidetsugus in the catalogue to the exhibition *Yorozu Tetsugorô* (National Museum of Modern Art, Tokyo, 1997), which regards this work as a landscape painting in an incomplete state, deserves our full attention. The painting bears neither a name nor a date, and neither the sky nor the earth are clearly distinguishable on the pictorial plane. In his explanation, Yamano makes no reference to the fact that beneath this painting, a half-length portrait shimmers through the layers of paint, with part of the lips still visible at the center of the pictorial plane. It would seem that the rather strong blue tone on the left edge of the picture has been influenced by part of the portrait painted beneath it. Yorozu, who sold few works during his lifetime, occasionally availed himself of old canvases for new paintings, integrating the color of the old work into the new one. Thus this example illustrates how the color of the clothing and lips of the human figure underneath gave rise to a new image by merging with the new motifs. Fragmentary figures hover at the lower left, possibly resembling flowers or leaves; at the top right, an almost futurist ray of light pours in. Yorozu's preference for colors is reflected in the spots of complementary green dispersed in the red in the upper part of the pictorial plane. The forms, on the other hand, are imprecise, although lines recall mountain ranges. The work *Landscape of Mental Conception* (Plate no. 3) from about the same period, considered typical for his work at the time, can be seen as a further example. It shows a more advanced stage in this process of the emergence of the "image." A shining yellow body resembles an ascending hill to which a small path leads. The work concentrates an imaginative force that facilitates this mode of seeing. The black lines forming a rectangle function as a frame for an imaginary image, which the artist, however, has painted over as an incomplete work. The effect is the discovery of another painting within it (one could perhaps speak of a meta-level, in view of the fact that one image conjures up another).

Unfortunately, Yorozu Tetsugorô did not further exploit his capacities for this organic, abstract form of expression. He never completely abandoned the representational function of painting, so that even in these largely abstract works, clear traces of figurative expression remain. What is most remarkable is that at the time, Yorozu deliberately avoided or to a certain extent alienated those motifs (such as the monumental groups of historicising western-style buildings built in Tokyo in swift succession during the Meiji era) whose depiction naturally demanded media introduced from Europe, such as oil painting. He achieved this by placing them into a non-original context. For example, the central motif in his *Gas Lantern* (Ill. 21) dating from the same period, is surely a symbol of modern Japan, yet the lamp-post seems crooked and makes an almost fragile impression. With its immediate surroundings omitted, this gas lantern is surprisingly and humorously combined with a small rendering of the large roof of a temple, a town stretching across the lower part of the painting, and a chimney which evokes association with a bath house; here too, deliberate alienation is evident. Perhaps the main focus of the composition of this small piece is the somewhat large, abstract foliage projecting into the picture from the edges as a kind of "pattern," lending expression to a particular rhythmic feeling. This rhythmic feeling corresponds exactly to the atmosphere in Tokyo shortly before it became a modern metropolis, at a time when a richly contradictory mix of Japanese and Western was something quite common. Here this atmosphere is captured in a strange and wonderful manner. The secret is that Yorozu strictly refused to apply western modernism as such to a depiction of Tokyo. To formulate it more boldly, one could say that Yorozu was imbued in his very unconscious with the spirit of a literary figure. It would seem that his very essence, his own contrary convictions, were challenged by the western modernism that had inundated the country like an avalanche. At the time, Yorozu discovered the "intellectual" within him, in the Japanese sense of a *Bunjin* (scholars), and developed his work in the 1920s on the basis of such a definite conviction.

Compared to the Japanese modernists who came after him, Yorozu's importance lies in the fact that as an artist, he grappled with what could be called the modernist breakthrough, and in so doing never faltered for a moment. Having been given the Zen name "Unshô-koji" at the age of nineteen by his teacher and Zen master Sôkatsu, he went to San Francisco in 1906 at the age of twenty-one in order to take part in missionary activities in North America. For Yorozu, this was a valuable confrontation with the West, although financial difficulties after the San Francisco earthquake forced him to cut short his sojourn after less than one year. Already harboring the wish to be an artist, Yorozu seems to have sought an opportunity to learn the fundamentals of oil painting in San Francisco. Yet one must not forget that at the time, he was a member of a religious group inculcated with a sense of spiritual leadership towards the West. When Yorozu signed the *Nihonga* paintings of his early years with his artist's name "Unshô," he was surely motivated by more than just the possibility of following western modernism. It must be remembered that the essence of this possibility was completely different from the ideology of a "return to the East" routinely propagated in Japan since the 1930s. For Yorozu, his spirit was not to "return" there, but to "go out" from there, and with this in mind, he challenged western modernism head-on, wholeheartedly, and in a grandiose manner.

The swift urbanization of Japan in the years after 1910, centered primarily in Tokyo, prepared the ground for the loss of cultural attachment that was to make the later "return to the East" inevitable. In other words, the 1920s saw the emergence of a large urban population with cosmopolitan ideas. (One could actually say that Japan also experienced what Heidegger referred to as a "falling away from authenticity.") Nishimura Isaku (1884–1964)—the inspiration for the novel *Beautiful City* of 1919 by Satô Haruo (1892–1964), in which the author dreamt of a utopian city on the delta of the Sumida river in Tokyo—belonged to more or less the same generation as Yorozu Tetsugorô, but represented a considerable contrast to him in his determination to adopt a completely westernized way of life. Nishimura Isaku, who, grew up in an extremely puritanical home in Shingû on the Kii peninsula, a remote place far removed from big-city life, distanced himself from Christianity under the strong influence of his uncle Ôishi Seinosuke (1867–1911), and for a time leaned towards socialism. When his uncle was arrested in connection with a case of high treason, Nishimura Isaku and his younger brother set out for Tokyo from Shingû on a motorbike to liberate his uncle, furtively carrying a pistol. Such an act might be viewed as the rash response of a young man willing to accept death, but the photograph taken in front of their house as a souvenir before they set out (at the time, Nishimura Isaku was an enthusiastic photographer) shows the two brothers dressed in astonishingly correct and totally western clothes. His uncle was later condemned to death, and although Nishimura Isaku escaped with his life after a period of detention, he distanced himself from the socialist movement and began with even more determination to pursue the new way of life that western modernism had introduced. He re-styled his house in Shingû as a Swiss chalet, based on his own design, studied landscape gardening, had his wife learn western tailoring in order to dress their children in western clothes, produced watercolors and oil paintings, made ceramics, invited important artists from Tokyo to Shingû, and turned his home into a kind of cultural salon. One could say that the circumstances surrounding the case of high treason motivated Nishimura Isaku not to a "reform" of society, but to an "improvement" in lifestyle. What this meant was the anticipation at an individual level the overall program of Japanese urban culture in the 1920s.

Only in 1997 was it discovered that Nishimura Isaku secretly painted a series of abstract works in oil on paper in 1916; this is not very surprising, however, when one considers his broad interest in the other arts and the fact that he had greedily absorbed knowledge of the West by privately studying western books. When Nishimura Isaku invited the artist Ishii Hakutei (1882–1958) to spend the summer in Shingû in 1913, the visit turned out to be a highly inspiring one for him. The previous year, Ishii Hakutei had completed a two-year sojourn in Europe before returning to Japan, where he was regarded by artists as a personality familiar with the latest European art trends. Nishimura Isaku took his visit to Shingû as an occasion to start a series of paintings, and in November of the following year he was able to mount an exhibition at the Hibiya Museum in Tokyo. (The Hibiya Museum, opened in 1914, was perhaps the first institution in Japan to refer to itself as a "museum." In fact, it was one of the smaller commercial galleries which emerged in swift succession in the early Taishô era. And like the other galleries, its had a short life-span, closing in late 1915.) Nishimura Isaku is sure to have known that in March, a good six months before his exhibition, the Hibiya Museum had shown an exhibition of woodcuts from the German magazine and gallery "Der Sturm." The composer Yamada Kosaku (1886–1965) and the designer Saitô Kazô (1887–1955) had exhibited and sold German expressionist woodcuts received from Herwarth Walden in Berlin, as the Tokyo branch of the "Sturm" gallery, as it were. Although the exhibition consisted mainly of woodcuts, the fact that original works of art arrived in Japan in early 1914 from the Berlin "Sturm" gallery is of great significance. If only for a short time, the Hibiya Museum exerted a great influence as a bastion of modernism in Tokyo in the first half of the Taishô era.

In 1916, Nishimura Isaku published two of his own attempts at abstract art (entitled *Attempt 1* and *Attempt 2;* their current location is unknown) in the magazine *Kagaku to bungei* (*Science and Art;* vol. 2, no. 5). In the accompanying text, "Movement of the Heart and Painting," he wrote: "The aim of my art is not, as it were, to reproduce nature as it exists outside me, but to express the movement of my heart. ... Furthermore I am convinced that even the kind of paintings in which I forget all nature's forms and colors and do not think of copying external nature, and which I complete by shaping forms, colors, lines and style in accord with my heart's desire, without copying or imitating, with the movement of my hand and the collaboration of tools such as canvas and brush, that these kinds of paintings too have a life as pictures and can possess the power to express the state of a man's heart and to move people's hearts. This is what I am trying to do." In view of such works and statements, it would seem possible that Nishimura Isaku had come into contact with the theory and oeuvre of Kandinsky. Even in those works by Nishimura Isaku to which we have access today, we discover the co-existence of pure abstraction and a suggestive vision of the end of the world or its genesis, such as is also found in Kandinsky.

The magazine *Kagaku to bungei,* in which Nishimura Isaku published these exemplary works along with his text, was almost private in character and did not exert the same influence as the magazine *Shirakaba.*

Nor was there opportunity for Nishimura Isaku to exhibit these new artistic attempts. Accordingly, scarcely any notice was taken of their existence, and they drifted into oblivion until only recently. On the other hand, the woodcut magazine *Tsukuhae (Reflections of the Moon),* published by Onchi Kôshirô and others, doubtless received great stimulus from the activities of the Hibiya Museum and at the right moment in time, just as the "creative woodcut" was experiencing an upswing, succeeded in drawing

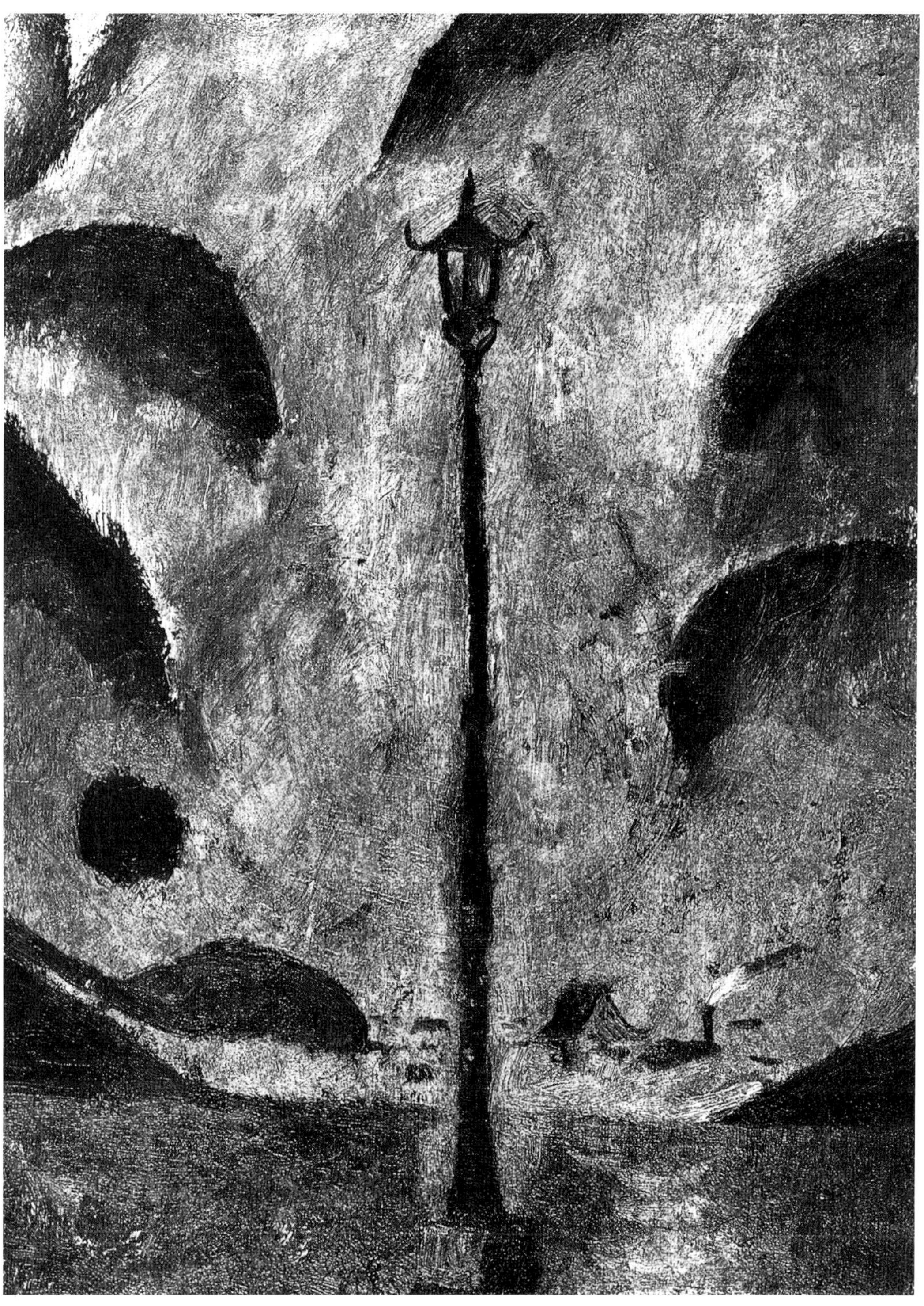

Ill. 21 Yorozu Tetsugorô, *Gas Lantern,* Oil on Canvas, ca. 1913, Private Collection

considerable attention to itself among a particular circle of artists. If many critics today honor the panel *Bright Time* (Plate no. 6)—the last work in the series *Five Types of Feeling,* published by Onchi Kôshirô in the no. 5 issue (March 1915)—as the "first abstract expression" in Japan, it is only because it enjoyed constant acclaim from the time of its first publication.

The composition of *Five Kinds of Feelings* is powerful, extremely clear and individual in character and might almost be described as a psychological revelation of, and liberation from, sexual obsessions. The title of the last work, *Bright Time,* was set in quotation marks when it was published, suggesting that this work was inspired by the title of a collection of poems by Emile Verhaerens. One poem from this collection, entitled *Joy,* had been published in Japanese translation as early as 1911 in the magazine *Zanboa* (*Soapwort,* vol. 1, no. 1, November 1912). When the work was later published by itself in the magazine *Kaze* (*Wind,* no. 3, March 1928), Onchi succinctly recalled in a poem the essential feeling he had experienced when completing the work:

Just like happiness
Like something joyful,
As when a totally unknown song
Becomes perceptible,
Bright light spreads out.
Bright bodies hover near
And rise up, just like vapor.

The print *Bright Time,* produced from two plates with bright pink for the center and a somewhat darker pink at the edges, expresses an undisguised feeling of sexual bliss, filled with "bright light" and "bright bodies" (female bodies, of course).

Onchi was a cosmopolitan who, as a modernist, supported the trends of his time and was guided by a strong inner feeling; his approach to things was highly subjective, though scrupulously thorough. If in the final analysis the rhythmical expression of feeling in Onchi's *Bright Time* shares certain qualities with the movements of the foliage in the *Gas Lantern* by the intellectual Yorozu, then this resemblance is extremely important. Onchi's *Human Body* and Yorozu's *Landscape* are both imbued with a similar quality. In order to facilitate the full unfolding of this common element and ensure its appropriate public acknowledgement, a suitable joint exhibition venue would have needed to have been found (possibly the "votive picture halls" mentioned by Kaita). Yet in Yorozu and Onchi's day, such spaces were not sufficiently available. The works created in the emerging style of abstraction in the early Taishô era did not fall on fertile soil; indeed, they remained sporadic, isolated achievements, a fact that boded ill for modern Japanese art. For Onchi, at least, the woodcut magazine *Tsukuhae (Reflections of the Moon)* was an indispensable little "votive picture hall." And if one follows the narrow stream that originated there, the importance of "modernism" in Japanese art comes to light from quite a different angle.

JAPANESE SURREALISM IN THE LATE 1930S: THE "SPACE OF FORMLESS MATTER" AND THE "SPACE OF MACROSCOPIC CREATURES"

Ozaki Shinzin

The sixteenth *Nika-ten* exhibition shown at the Tokyo Art Museum from September 3rd to October 4th, 1929, is generally regarded as the first exhibition of surrealist works by Japanese artists. The works on display included *Rien* and *Girleen* by Abe Kongô (1900–1969), *Sea, Cage, A Naive Moonlight Night* and *Fishermen* by Koga Harue (1895–1933), *Déclaration (A Surrealist Promenade)* by Tôgô Seiji (1897–1978), and *Feeling and Physics in the Air* by Nakagawa Kigen (1892–1972). At the time, these works were not only considered surrealist, but were also described by many art critics as exemplary of "Machinism."

As the works of art produced at the time show, Japanese Surrealism from the late Taishô to the early Shôwa era (around 1926) constituted not so much a real as a pseudo-Surrealism; yet it did embrace elements of modernism as well as individual factors

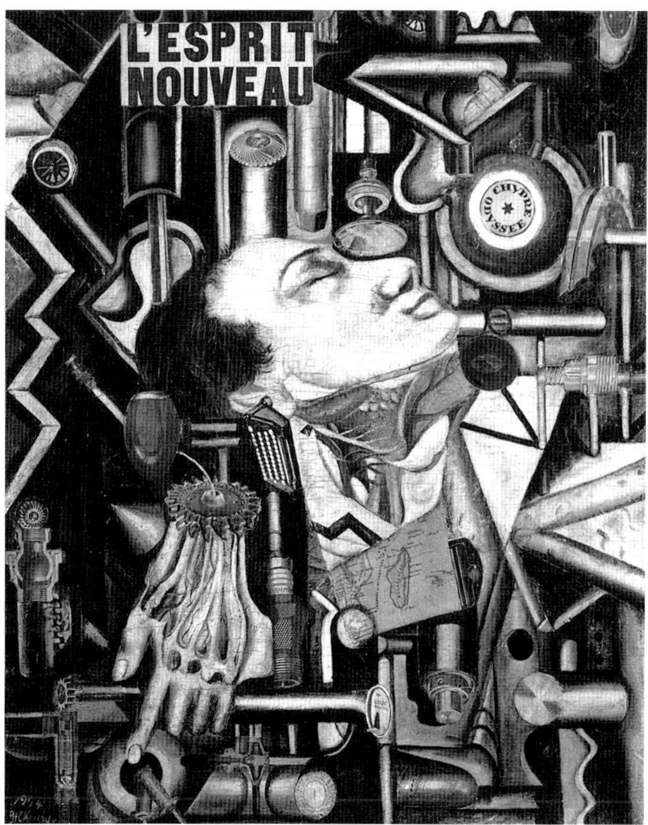

Ill. 22 Kawabe Masahisa, *Mechanism,* "Collage," Oil on Canvas, 1924, Itabashiku Art Museum, Tokyo

that exerted a considerable influence on the treatment of space in later Japanese surrealist works. My intention here is to elucidate the distinctive aspect of spatial construction in surrealist Japanese works from the pre-war period.

The Transformation of Machinism and Macroscopic Depiction

Machinism from the end of the Taishô to the beginning of the Shôwa era can be divided into the following three forms, illustrated by the works of three prominent representatives. The work *Mechanism* (Ill. 22) by Kawabe Masahisa (1901–1990) represents the first form of Machinism, largely dadaist in character, in the new art of the Taishô era. Later, in the early Shôwa era (1929), *Sea* (Ill. 23) by Koga Harue presented Machinism as a form of modernism. The Machinism in *Rotation Machine* (Ill. 24) by Kikuchi Seiji (1909–1973), which is treated in a fauvist manner, represents the third form. In the works representing the first and second forms, the artist used so-called "collages" or procedures comparable to collage. *Mechanism,* presented as such a collage, represents a "machine aesthetic" that glorifies the mechanical, an "aesthetic of being" conveying the

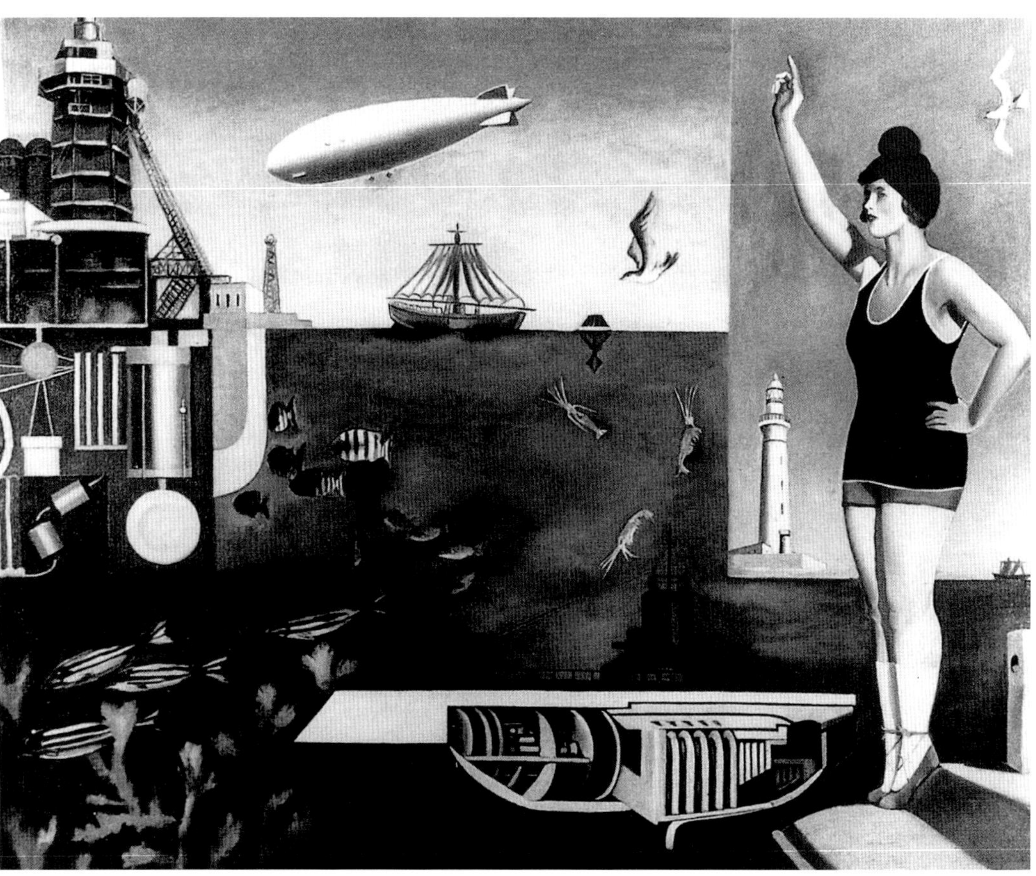

Ill. 23 Koga Harue, *Sea,* Oil on Canvas, 1929, National Museum of Modern Art, Tokyo

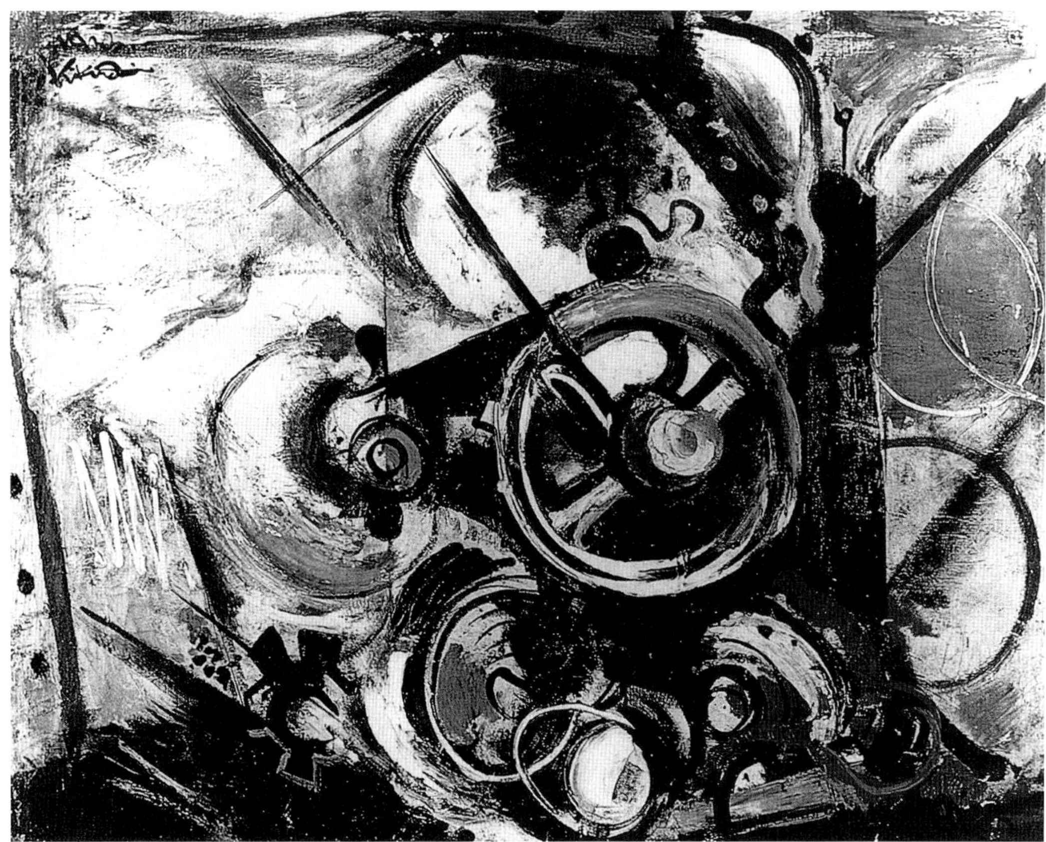

Ill. 24 Kikuchi Seiji, *Rotation Machine,* Oil on Canvas, 1933, Hokkaidô Prefectural Museum of Modern Art, Sapporo

reality of matter, a "state of being ahead of time" with regard to the motif, and an "aesthetic of destruction" that cancels out value. By contrast, the collage *Sea* can be equated with the above-mentioned "machine aesthetic," yet it also represents an "aesthetic of functionalism," concentrating on the use and construction of the motif, on a "contemporaneity" of the motif, and on an "aesthetic of syncretism" aimed at equivalence. In its third form, Machinism is not entirely regarded as such due to a thematic digression, but is still oriented to a "machine aesthetic." This aesthetic is characterized mainly by the "contemporaneity" of the motif, by an "aesthetic of construction" manifested in its composition and construction, by a "sense of speed" with regard to optical effect, and by the "symbol" of the state which opposes the great western powers. The Machinism recognizable in *Rotation Machine* takes the form of a "macroscopic depiction" in keeping with modernism. That is to say, the object appears "larger than life" on the pictorial plane. This fauvist, macroscopic form of depiction was later to exert an influence on surrealist painting through the work of younger artists who were members of the *Dokuritsu-bijutsu kyôkai,* or Independent Artists Association.

The "Dépaysement" of Fukuzawa Ichirô and the Space of the Young Artists' Quasi-"Dépaysement"

In 1930, when Louis Aragon (1897–1982) wrote *La peinture au défi (A Challenge to Painting)* as an introduction to the "Exhibition of Collages" at Galerie Goemans, Fukuzawa Ichirô (1898–1982) also completed *April Fool/Poisson d'Avril,* a work using the collage technique (Ill. 25). This work and 37 others by him were exhibited in the first *Dokuritsu-bijutsu* exhibition in January of the following year.

Fukuzawa's *April Fool* is based on illustrations cut out of the magazine *Gay Science,* assembled in collage form and finally copied in painting ("dépaysement"). This "dépaysement," in which selected cuttings on one theme provide the material for a new grouping, could be termed a "dépaysement that binds together."

The Surrealism that Fukuzawa Ichirô represented exerted an enormous influence on later young artists. The artists' association *Dokuritsu-bijutsu kyôkai* was their Mecca. Within the association, however, a strong confrontation developed between the representatives of Surrealism, led by Fukuzawa, and those of Fauvism, led by Satomi Katsuzô (1895–1981). This internal conflict led in 1934 to the formation of the first group in Japan totally devoted to Surrealism: *Shinzôkei-bijutsu kyôkai* (Society of New Fine Artists). Within the *Dokuritsu-bijutsu kyôkai* association, the collaboration had mainly been between the young artists and those oriented towards surrealist painting, with the intention of founding the École de Tokyo (1936). Despite its influence, Fukuzawa's "dépaysement that binds together" is to be found neither in the works of the *Shinzôkei* group nor in those of the École de Toyko. The young artists were obviously able to create a separate space for themselves.

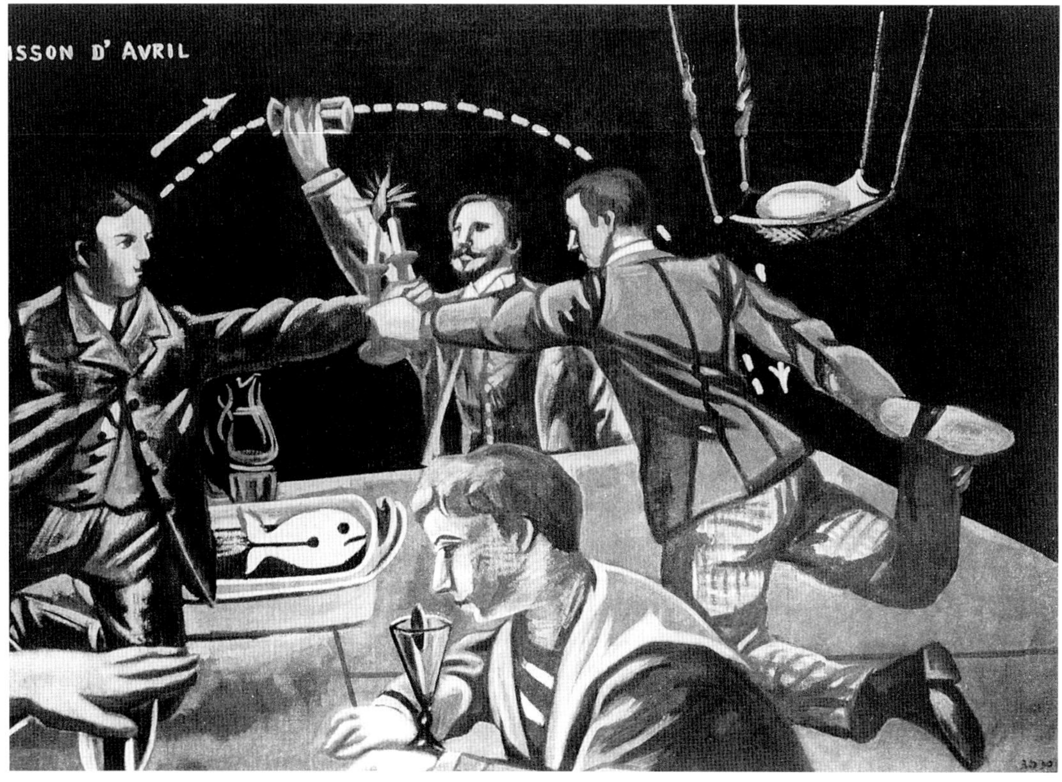

Ill. 25 Fukuzawa Ichirô, *April Fool/Poisson d'Avril,* "Collage," Oil on Canvas, 1930, National Museum of Modern Art, Tokyo

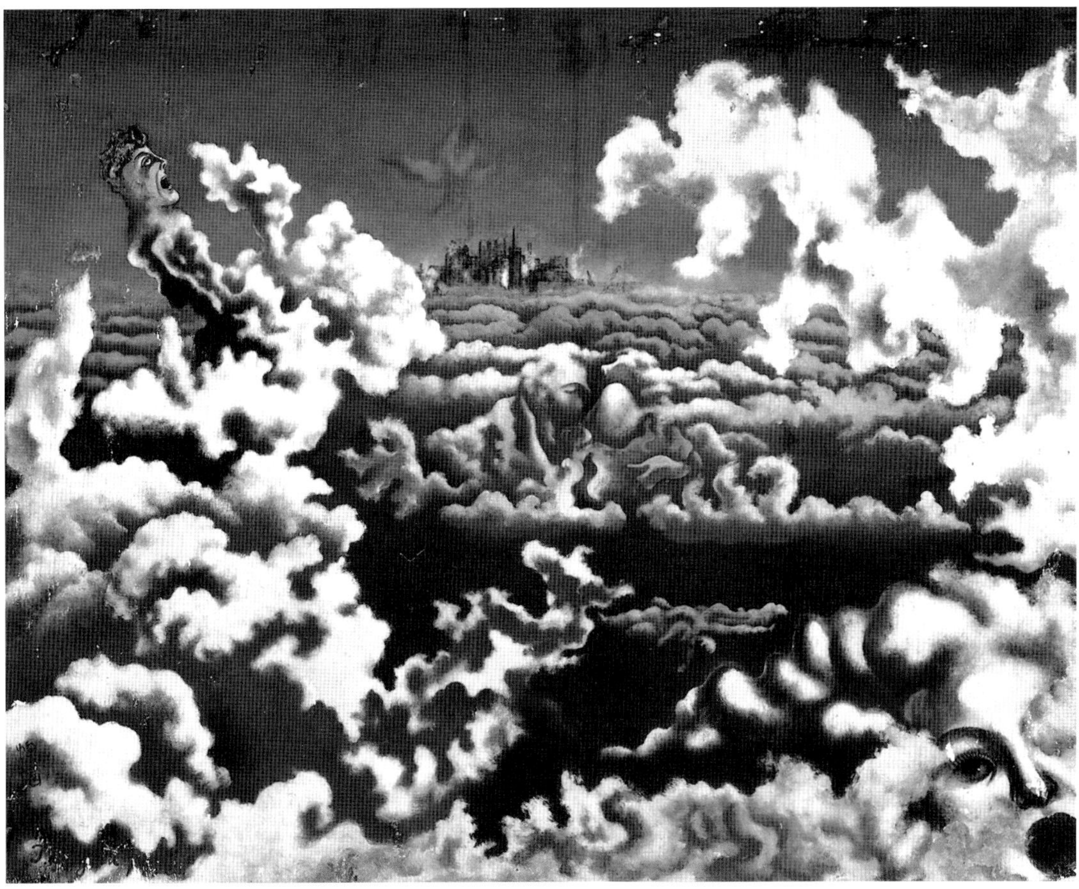

Ill. 26 Fujita Tsuruo, *Agony,* Oil on Canvas, 1926, Itabashiku Art Museum, Tokyo

"Formless Matter" and the Space of Quasi-"Dépaysement"

In the works produced within the *Shinzôkei* artists' association, space is often constituted using "formless matter" such as sand, clouds, and water. Examples of this are *Agony* (Ill. 26) by Fujita Tsuruo (1902–1952) and *Feminia Paranoia* (Ill. 27) by Shimazu Junichi (1907–1989). Around the same time, that is in 1937, an exhibition entitled "Surrealist Works from Overseas" was mounted by the critics Takiguchi Shûzô and Yamanaka Chiriu (1905–1977). The exhibition catalogue shows watercolors, drawings, prints and reproductions, 377 works in all. Most of these works were reproductions, and for the first time there was an extensive introduction to Salvador Dalí. Numerous Japanese artists also experimented with the paranoid-critical method Dalí had invented, i.e. the transformation of an image produced by staring at an object.

The genesis of *Feminia Paronoia* by Shimazu Junichi can be traced to the influence of Dalí's paranoid-critical method. In order to facilitate the transformation of the image through constant staring, a three-dimensional space is created out of "formless matter"; it is on this basis that the two-part painting, or more precisely two paintings in one, emerges. It should be noted that in Japan, the "formless matter" was produced first, so that the place from which the fantasy would emerge was laid down in advance or emanated from one's own fantasy; only then was the two-fold painting created by means of Dalí's paranoid-critical method. In European Surrealism, the main focus had been on the "dépaysement," the "re-ordering" by "linking unrelated things," as for example in Giorgio de Chirico. In the Japanese approach to fantasy, on the other hand, the linking of this three-dimensional "formless matter" with the transformation of the image produced the space of

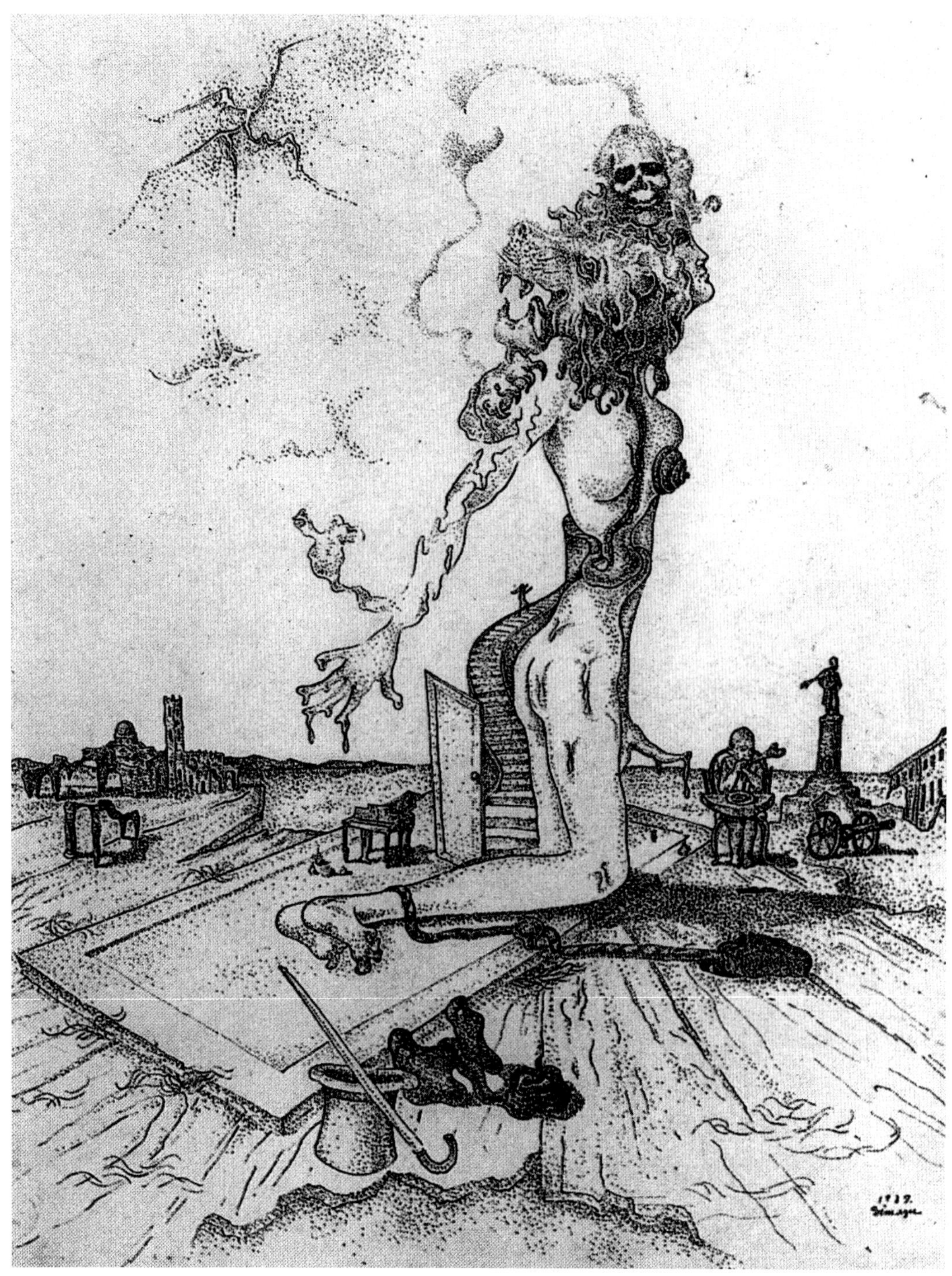

Ill. 27 Shimazu Junichi, *Feminia Paranoia,* Ink on Paper, 1937, Itabashiku Art Museum, Tokyo

quasi-"dépaysement" as a superimposition of various fantasies.

This space of quasi-"dépaysement" was adopted as a complex model by two other groups at the Imperial Art Academy: the groups "Jeune homme" and "Painting," referred to as "Dalí's Epidemic." Most of the artists in these groups produced works linking the space of quasi-"dépaysement" with real space, an approached they summarized with the term "passage." Both these groups were formed in 1938, at the time of the Nanking massacre and the start of the era of substitution.

In view of the contradictions inherent in the everyday reality of a society facing total destruction, "reality" could not be conveyed either by a liberalist mode of expression or by individualistic-aesthetic expression. In my opinion, once it became branded in public as a "flight from reality," Surrealism utilized the "passage" method in order to breathe new life into the work of art.

Macroscopic Depiction and Quasi-"Dépaysement"

Many of the artists in the Independent Artists Association *(Dokuritsu-bijutsu kyôkai)* macroscopically emphasized the size of objects in relation to one another in their works and thus rendered the spatial distortion visible. A fleeting glance at some of these works might suggest the influence of de Chirico, yet they lack his distorted perspective. The following members of the Association can be regarded as particularly influential: Kikuchi Seiji (1909–1973) depicted the machine macroscopically enlarged, once modernism had asserted itself in the Association; Hasegawa Zenshirô (1914–1996) was also preoccupied with macroscopic depiction. Above and beyond the influence of macroscopic depiction, the work *Sea and Lightning* (1934) by Migishi Kôtarô (1903–1934) also made an impact. There are numerous comparable works: *View of a Shell* by Komaki Gentarô (1906–1989), *View of a Shell* (Ill. 28) by Kitawaki Noboru (1901–1951), the *Sea's Petals*

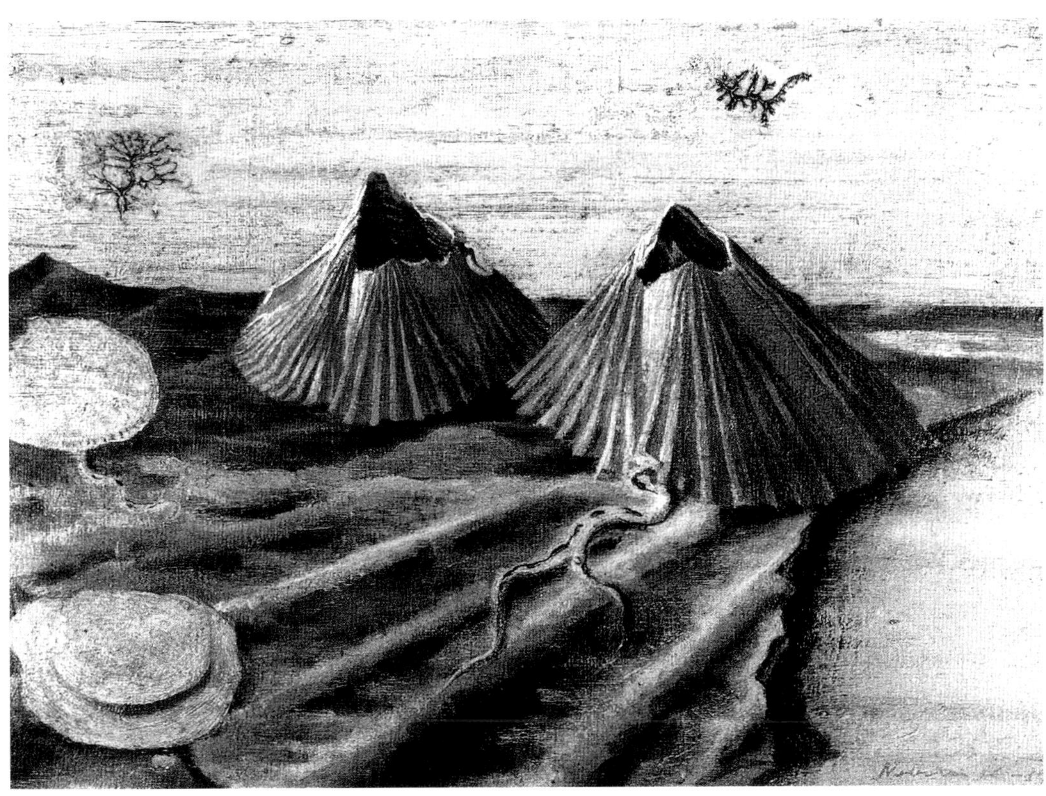

Ill. 28 Kitawaki Noboru, *View of a Shell,* "Collage," Oil on Canvas, 1937, Private Collection

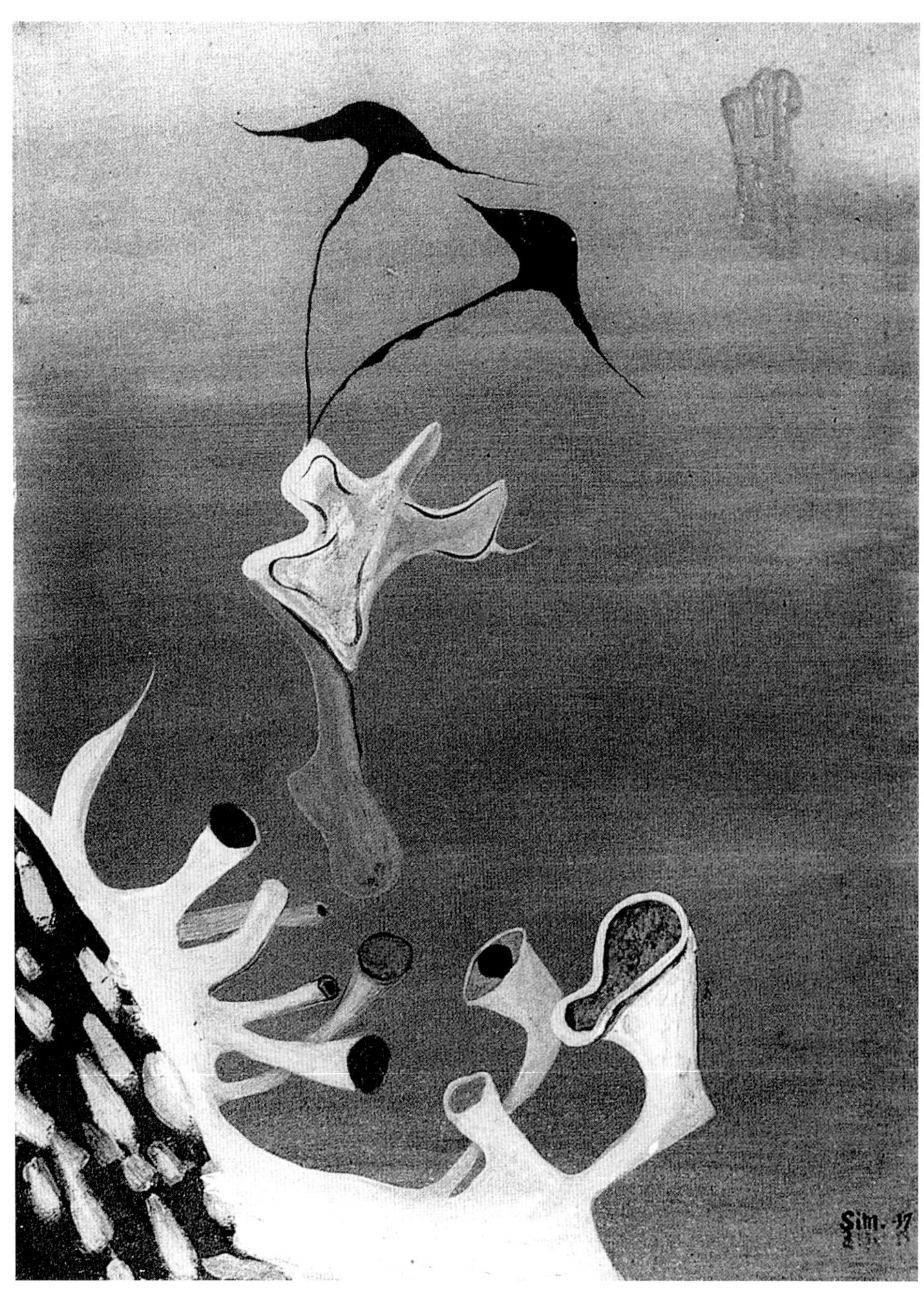

Ill. 29 Shimosato Yosio, *Sea at Izu,* Oil on Canvas, 1937, Municipal Art Museum, Nagoya

(1937) by Yonekura Hisao (1905–1993), the *Sea at Izu* (Ill. 29) by Shimosato Yosio (1907–1981), *Flowering Plant* (Ill. 30) by Abe Yoshifumi (1913–1971), *Flowers in a barren field* (1938) by Kakite Shunzô (1901–1951), *Bud* (1938) by Terada Masaki (1912–1989) and *Clay Figure* (Ill. 31) by Hamamatsu Kogenta. What these works have in common is their macroscopic depiction of living things.

Often the motifs depicted macroscopically are creatures that live at or in the sea, or wild flowers. Initially such works often showed shells and sea anemones. The location "at or in the sea" was intended to function as a no-man's land between the earth—the space of man—and the sea, the "mnemo-topos." Depicting living things macroscopically and in an unusual space linked with everyday life underscored the illusion. Among such paintings are also some with

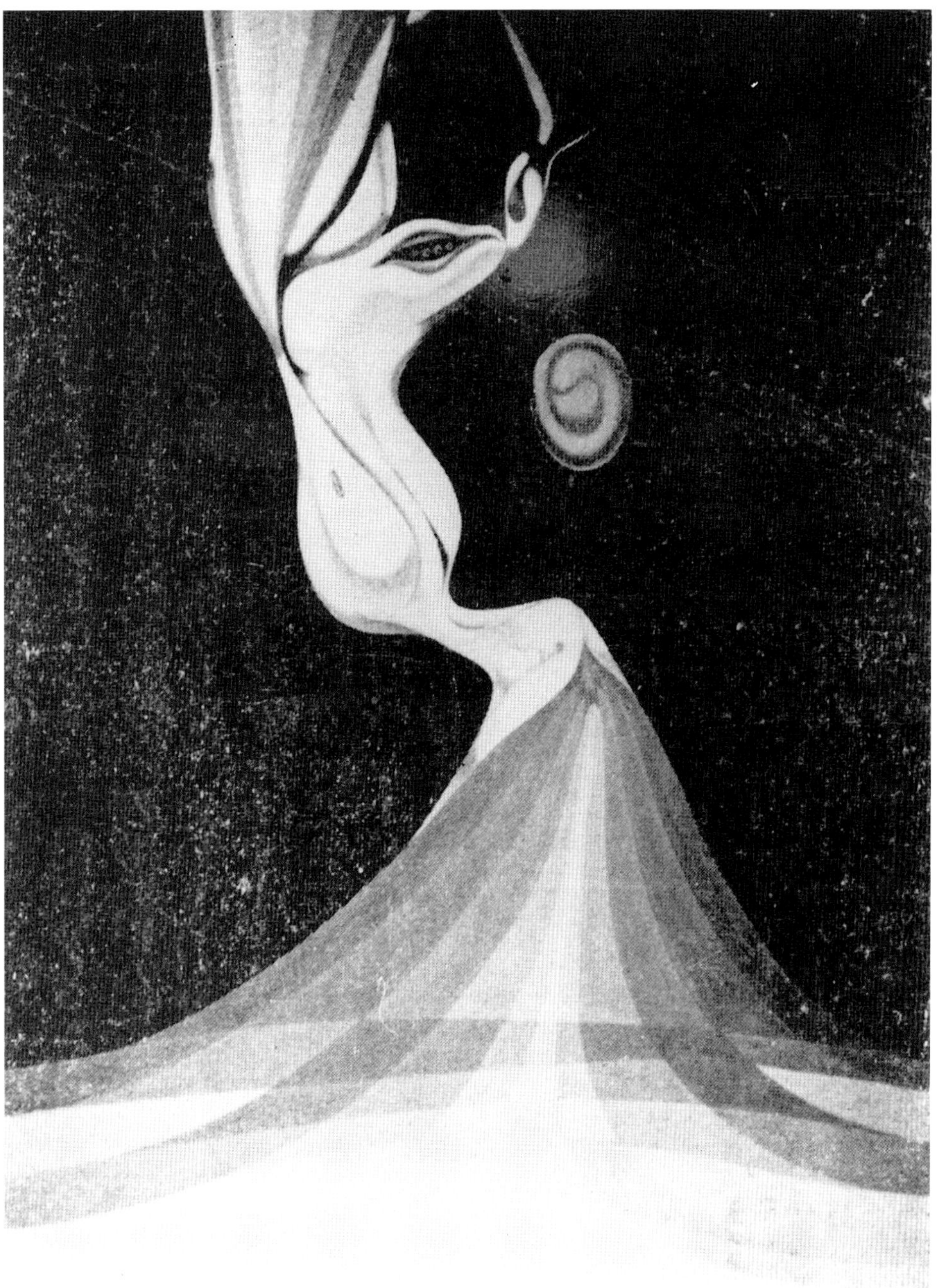

Ill. 30 Abe Yoshifumi, *Flowering Plant,* Oil on Canvas, 1937

a two-fold image—for example, Kitawaki Noboru's *View of a Shell,* where shells at the sea seem like mountains in a landscape. The macroscopic depictions of plants often include petals, filaments, and pistils. Thus Hamamatsu Kogenta's *Clay Figure,* obviously influenced by Max Ernst, shows the grotesque inside and outside of a growing plant. Other works focus on an interesting "repetition" in the pictorial composition, like Abe Yoshifumi's *Flowering Plant.* Such "macroscopic spaces" were created by the young artists of the *Dokuritsu-bijutsu kyôkai* school. In the course of time, they went on to found the École de Tokyo, and finally, through the surrealist group *Bijutsu-bunka kyôkai* (Society for Art and Culture), Surrealism became universally integrated.

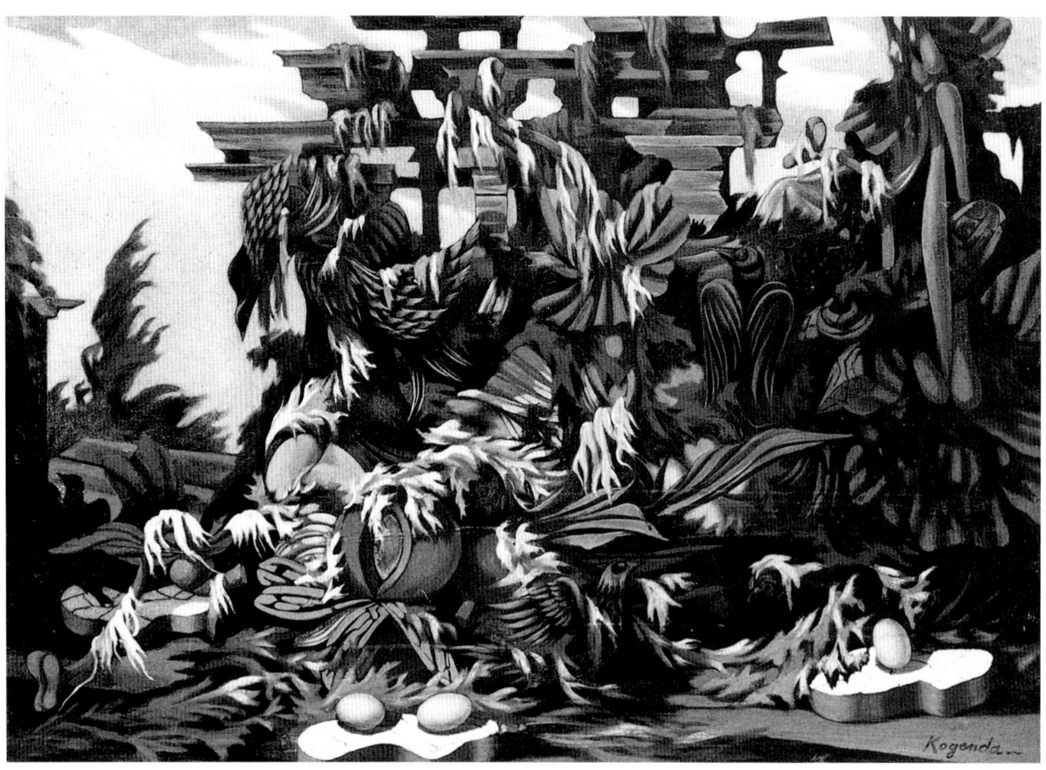

Ill. 31 Hamamatsu Kogenta, *Clay Figure,* Oil on Canvas, 1939, Itabashiku Art Museum, Tokyo

Quasi-"Dépaysement" as a "Temptation of Space" and the "Bestowing of Temporal Meaning on Space"

As mentioned above, Japan's reception of Surrealism was characterized by the fact that the artist first of all gave shape to "formless matter," a "space of macroscopic living things" or a space of quasi-"dépaysement," and thus spatially depicted a previous illusion. Japanese Surrealism was to develop as a stereo-typical depiction of an illusion in predetermined patterns. Does the attraction of the space of quasi-"dépaysement" not lie in a defensive attitude toward the real, everyday world? In the Japan of that era, from the resounding military boots of the prologue to the finale of the war, the instruments of Surrealism presented themselves sometimes in the form of humanism, sometimes of enlightened intellectualism.

In this respect, Japanese Surrealism differs from its European pendant, which was reputed to entail a liberation of the imagination and an uprising against rationalism. The intellectualism inherent in Japanese Surrealism may lack the political aspect of Louis Aragon, yet it still produced works that were highly critical of society. It exerted a considerable influence on works focusing on current events, for example the *Genealogy of the Century* (cf. Ill. 16) by Hamamatsu Kogenta, or *Still Life B* (Ill. 32) by Hayase Tatsue (born in 1905), which embraces the world of the unconscious and of Japanese spirituality. What it also contained was a new variation on the religious painting *Nigabyakudô-zu,* a depiction of a narrow white path leading between two streams of fire and water to paradise, a metaphor for the Buddhist teaching on paradise *(Jôdôkyô).* At the pinnacle of the intellectualism inherent in Surrealism stands Kitawaki's *Diagram of the Chinese Tshou Dynasty: Yin and Yang Divination (Heaven and Earth)* (Ill. 33), an example of a "diagram painting" constructed by the interplay of geometric abstraction and real landscape. The painting contains two signs, "*Ken,* i.e. *Yang*" for heaven or the ruler, and "*Kon,* i.e. *Yin*" for the earth or people. These signs are presented as

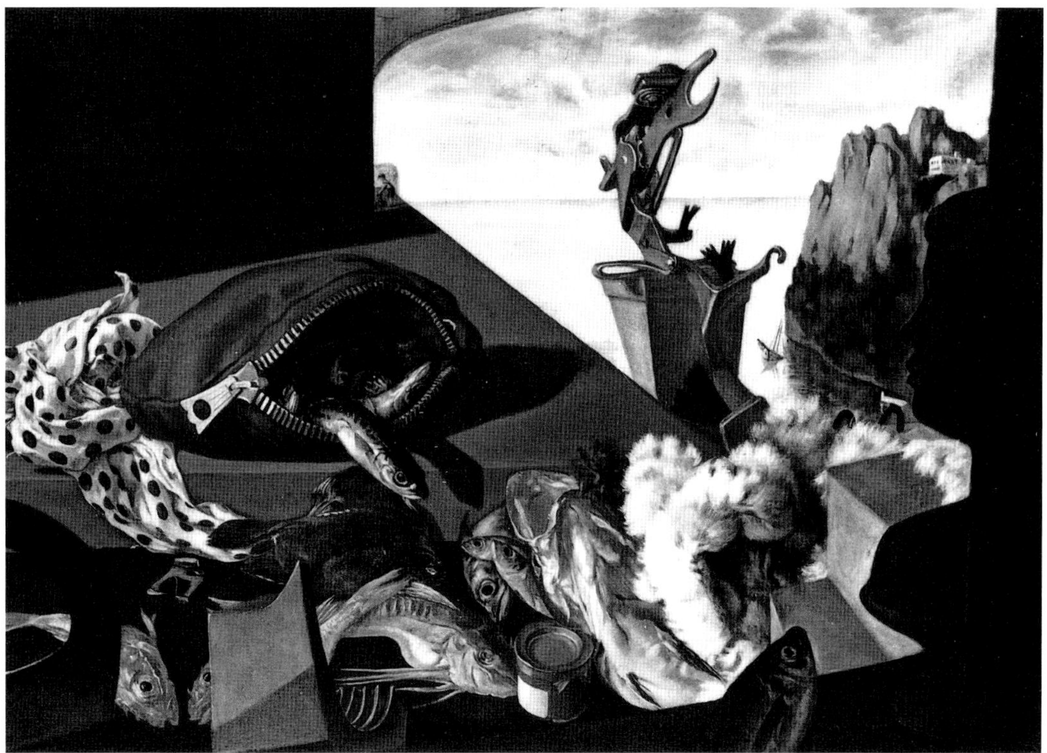

Ill. 32 Hayase Tatsue, *Still Life B,* Oil on Canvas, 1941, Itabashiku Art Museum, Tokyo

painted leaves and roots, so that the context mentioned above can be visualized.

This intellectualism, moreover, was already recognizable in the Machinism of the New Art and the modernism of the Taishô era (1912–1926). In Surrealism it emerged as one of that movement's specific, immanent motifs.

By creating a space of quasi-"dépaysement" in order to determine surrealist terms in advance, Japanese Surrealism with its inherent intellectualism was forced to pursue a stereotypical depiction of the "space of fantasy." On the other hand, it must be emphasized that the intellectualism inherent in that Surrealism was imbued with a critical spirit and produced not only surrealist paintings, but also works that engaged with Japanese culture.

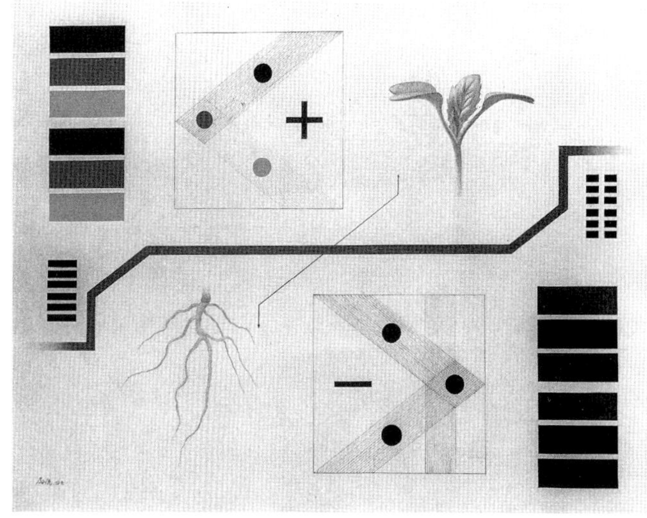

Ill. 33 Kitawaki Noboru, *Diagram of the Chinese Tshou Dynasty: Yin and Yang Divination (Heaven and Earth),* Oil on Canvas, 1941, National Museum of Modern Art, Tokyo

JAPANESE ART IN THE 1950S AND 60S: SURROUNDED BY A TRANSPARENT WALL

Matsumoto Tôru

More than half a century has passed since the days of the annihilating defeat. Yet the society and almost all the art movements of the post-war period are remembered as if they were only yesterday, even as they recede into the depths of history. "Is not 'history' simply the time when we were not yet born?" asks Roland Barthes. But if that is so, then the time in which I was already born would never become history, however long it lasted ...

One could say that the fundamental task of the historian of modern art is to observe past works from the viewpoint of the present and inquire as to their current value, as well as to observe current works of art as if confronted with historical objects and conjecture whether they might possibly have historical value in the future. Yet even for art historians, who move between past and present on a daily basis, it is no easy task to objectively discuss and evaluate art from their own country that has not yet become completely historical, and in so doing to abandon the characteristic mode of thought and feeling—one could also call it "tradition"—of the community to which they belong.

Yet it cannot be said that we have no measuring stick or compass for this purpose. Indeed, in modernism it is the artists themselves who, willy-nilly, cannot avoid engaging with the internal and external aspects of the tradition to which they belong. In a seeming paradox, modern artists regard it as imperative to constantly view themselves in the mirror of the "other" —whether the Japanese *Ukiyoe* polychrome woodcut, the culture of Tahiti, African carvings, or the dream and the unconscious—to lend their own works autonomy. For Japanese artists, it was above all the west and everything it produced that served as this kind of mirror. For them, the traditions of their own country were something to be opposed rather than adopted—or rather, something that could only be discovered in the "other," the "alien." Is the enjoyment of modern art, therefore, nothing more than a constant pendulum swing, an attempt, together with the artists, to at times pass beyond the borders of tradition, at times return within them?

Since the opening of the country under the emperor Meiji in 1868 and perhaps even to the present day, the overpowering "other" that has blocked the way for the Japanese is the sum total of the impact of European modernism, indeed of western civilization and culture. Thus with respect to the "other," there should now be no objection to dividing the history of Japanese art before World War II—from the Meiji to the Shôwa era—into two periods.

The first is the period of "modernization = Europeanization," which lasted from the Meiji era (1868–1912) to the Taishô era (1912–1926). Yet this dawning —the beginnings of which go back to the mid-eighteenth century, when oil painting and copper engraving were introduced as practical techniques equivalent to geodesy—was nothing more than an initial approach to modernism. Not until 1910 did we Japanese embark on our zigzag course toward "another modernism," different from that of Europe and other Asian countries. Only then did we fully understand what modern art really was, viewing ourselves in the mirror of that which came from the outside—oil painting, for example. Yorozu Tetsugorô, who lent expression to the discrepancy and range of oscillation between the radical tendencies in Europe at that time—above all Cubism—and our native, indigenous understanding of nature or feeling for life, deservedly stands at the beginning of this exhibition. Yorozu Tetsugorô and Kambara Tai—a self-taught artist and poet and an outstanding interpreter of the European avant-garde—and the graphic artist Onchi Kôshirô, who also wrote nature poems and united within himself the opposing poles of a modern rational mind and a deep, theoretically inexplicable sensuality, are the Japanese artists who established themselves most rapidly in the field of true abstraction.

The second period begins with the formation of the closed political blocs around the world, about the time of the world economic crisis in 1929. Finally, criticism was voiced even in Japan of the blind adherence ever since the Meiji era to the motto of "modernization = Europeanization." Now, the mood was reversed into a "rejection of modernization = Japanization." At that time, the catch phrase "Japanese oil painting" was brought into currency by the figurative artists (also known as the "Japanese Fauves" because of their sensitive color principles) who had returned to Japan after studying in Paris in the 1920s, where a whispered "return to order" was in the air. As masters of this style, Umehara Ryûzaburô (1888–1986) and Yasui Sôtarô (1888–1985) dominated a circle of artists oriented to the west *(Yôga)*. The fact that none of them is represented in this exhibition is evidence of the clear view of Japanese modernism held by Irmtraud Schaarschmidt-Richter, art historian and curator of the exhibition. As already mentioned, works of art require a fundamental comparison with their own tradition and a constant confrontation with the alien or the "other" —not only to gain autonomy and distance themselves from the regionalism and national characteristics of their countries of origin, but also to be able to address outsiders. At that time, the artists who had progressed to "Japanese oil painting" began to undertake stylistic refinements, some of them suffering a long and difficult battle, others advancing too fast. When they lost their sense of the "other" and the pendulum stopped swinging, their "modernism" came to an end as well.

Instead of their works, the exhibition shows works by artists of the next generation, including Ai-Mitsu, Ei-Kyû, Yamaguchi Takeo, Yoshihara Jirô, Matsumoto Shunsuke and others. Without exception, these artists made their debut on the public stage through free exhibitions organized by the "Nika" association—a group which, founded in 1914, may be described as the first "Secessionists"—or by the "Association of Free Artists," newly founded in 1937. These young artists began publicizing their works at a time when Japan was moving away from the Japanese-Chinese War towards the Pacific War. After a period during which war had forced them to interrupt work on their art and its presentation, many of them opted for participation in the process of reconstruction or for a new life.

On what basis therefore, did Japanese art develop during the post-war era, a period in which the country experienced, as it were, a "second opening"?

June 1948: start of the Soviet blockade of Berlin. August 1948: founding of the Republic of Korea. September 1948: founding of the Democratic People's Republic of Korea. May 1949: founding of the Federal Republic of Germany. October 1949: founding of the People's Republic of China and the German Democratic Republic. June 1950: outbreak of the Korean War. (In the wartime boom, Japan availed itself of the opportunity for economic reconstruction.) September 1951: signing of the peace treaty with Japan and the security agreement between Japan and the United States. April 1952: both treaties came into effect; Japan regained its sovereignty. Even this brief list of some of the historical events of the years preceding Japan's sovereignty shows that it came to pass under highly unique and dynamic political circumstances.

Japan's constitution, which came into effect in 1947 and thus preceded this series of events, contains a laudable article claiming that Japan as a country renounces the right to wage war. In reality, however, at the start of the Korean War in 1950, Japan had already established the "reserve troops of the police" (precursors of the "Jieitai" self-defense forces). (We Japanese have been unable to resolve this discrepancy between ideal and reality even to the end of the twentieth century.) Yet what is important here is that neither Japanese sovereignty nor its preservation came about through our own capacities—quite apart from the question of whether in this case, those capacities should immediately have been turned into military capacities. Despite its proximity to one of the most menacing fronts between east and west, Japan experienced neither a division of the country nor a repeated dispatch of troops to the front; nor did the country become a theatre of war. Yet peace, or the economic reconstruction under that peace, was something that came about without Japanese contribution, something that left Japan almost no scope for participation and was maintained by a balance of political and military forces. This may seem a childish standpoint, inadmissible in a discussion between adults, but the fact is that we always confronted the reality of the post-war world from a space as small as a greenhouse, surrounded on all sides by glass, by a transparent wall.

Yet the post-war era (the third period in modern Japanese art, following the first period of "modernization = Europeanization" and the second of "rejection of modernization = Japanization") cannot be neatly labeled as a period of "internationalization," for this reason: the question still remains as to whether, during the post-war era in Japan, the possibility of the "other" in any real sense would not have been forfeited if we Japanese had not confronted the reality of the world from within a transparent wall—until the present, with the collapse of the Cold War system.

Many of the works from the post-war era shown in this exhibition are by artists who, although active during the period of thought-control before the war, were moving toward a "second opening" of the country, though without abandoning the absolute identification of Europeanization with modernization. Already in 1947, Okamoto Tarô, one of the youngest of them, founded the "Club of Japanese Avant-Garde Artists" together with Abe Nobuya and others. The following year, together with Hanada Kiyoteru, Abe Kôbô and other avant-garde literary figures, he founded the "Yoru no kai" (Evening Society). In the public domain he appeared for a time as an opinion leader, who propagated his own form of "polarization" and broke through the narrow confines of the artistic and literary worlds.

Okamoto's "polarization" brought together the rationalism of abstract painting and the irrationalism of Surrealism. This is clearly reflected in Okamoto's own career during the pre-war era, when he took part in "Abstraction—Création" in the 1930s and later drew closer to the international Surrealist movement. He saw rationalism and irrationalism as the two main polarizing tendencies in the art of the twentieth century. Furthermore, he declared that identification with one or the other of the two camps should not represent an easy adherence either to "theoretical aesthetics" (in the case of the former) or the "dream and madness of the imagination" (in the case of the latter). And so he admonished artists to "come to grips with *reality*" (quoted from *Polarization,* 1948, emphasis M. T.).

A series of provocative essays by Okamoto dating from this period are imbued with an urgent concern with the problem of what is external and what is internal to art—whether in regard to artistic movements or particular styles. For this reason, I would like to focus more closely on the fact that what becomes "reality" through representation in art is also drawn to the center of consciousness. In the 1950s and 60s—independently of the differences between the abstract and the concrete schools—"becoming reality" (or "realism") developed almost into a kind of burden or obsession with which Japanese artists were constantly preoccupied. On the other hand, was it not also true that they themselves—at a time when food and clothing (to say nothing of paint and canvas) were in short supply and when, with the start of the Cold War, the reconstruction of the Japanese economy was ironically being put on the right track—were continually plagued by insecurity and nervousness, as if confronted with "reality" from behind a transparent wall?

It was Yoshirhara Jirô from the Kansai region, who, like Okamoto and to a certain extent even more thoroughly than he, compared and contrasted the differences between the art schools and styles and refuted the position that the arts are a place where spirit and matter (the inside and outside of art) meet and enter into a kind of alchemical bond. By reversing this idea, the artists' association *Gutai,* founded by Yoshihara in 1954, attracted an incredible number of differing talents (above all Shiraga Kazuo and Tanaka Atsuko), battled with groups such as *Informel* from France or later *Nul* from the Netherlands, and carried on a whole range of activities that can be regarded as early performances or happenings. Through exhibitions mounted in many American and European cities in the 1950s and early 60s, this group was the first association of Japanese artists to overcome the "walls" of their country's borders.

When one considers Japanese art of the post-war period, it is significant that many artists overcame this transparent wall, travelling overseas never to return. Abe Nobuya, for example, spent seven months in India in 1953; beginning in 1957, he traveled to Europe and the United States, but also to Asia, the Middle East, and eastern Europe, finally settling in Rome in 1962, where he later died. Hasegawa Saburô was another such figure. Before the war, he had devoted himself to the famous fifteenth-century ink painter and priest Sesshû, and had also been active as a zealous mediator of modern art (above all Mondrian). After the war and following his first solo exhibition in New York in 1953, he traveled throughout America more or less as a missionary for the traditional Japanese arts (not only ink painting and drawing, but also Zen, Sho-calligraphy, and Ikebana). Sugai Kumi, on the other hand, who went to Europe in 1952, took the reverse course: in the late 1950s, when from beyond the wall he may even have wished to be behind it, his expressive brushstrokes—obviously similar to those of Japanese calligraphy—were full of nostalgic emotions and memories of home. Once he gained recognition as an artist, he turned to a newly developing style in the early 1960s, in which no hint of any state of mind is ascertainable.

Among the artists who were too naive or who regarded an uncritical return to tradition as undesirable, yet were no longer young enough to simply allow themselves to be influenced by trends from abroad, some attained artistic maturity in the 1950s and 60s by silently tilling their fields like peasants, sowing seeds and awaiting the harvest. Such figures include Yamaguchi Takeo, Onosato Toshinobu or Murai Masanari, although the latter should hardly be compared with a peasant, as he had something very metropolitan about him.

Let us take the example of Yamaguchi Takeo. In the late 1940s, his works from the pre-war period began to show landscape-like forms painted in simple, colorful strokes and a series of figures whose strange movements and gestures were far removed from any natural figurativeness. These figures on the ground of the painting clearly convey the impression of living movement. In the 1950s, he developed them further in various ways, and in the early 1960s, figure and ground began to merge. This so-called "reciprocal relation" between figure and ground constitutes a problem that has repeatedly preoccupied artists in this century since Cubism. Here reference should be made to a characteristic awareness of the quality of the red earth tones in the ground/figure, as they appear in Yamaguchi's most mature works (e.g. Plate no. 78). When speaking of abstract painting, it is inappropriate to place too much trust in comparisons. Yet are not the finely expressive nuances in Yamaguchi's reddish (or yellowish) earth tones, applied in a number of layers, his warm-heartedness, and his tolerance reminiscent of the earth, from which the meadow flowers sprout and the newly hatched insects emerge in spring? This is the earth, in a modern, minimal form, and at the same time the earth which we, both Asians and Europeans, have tilled since time immemorial and on which we have built roads and erected power stations.

PLATES

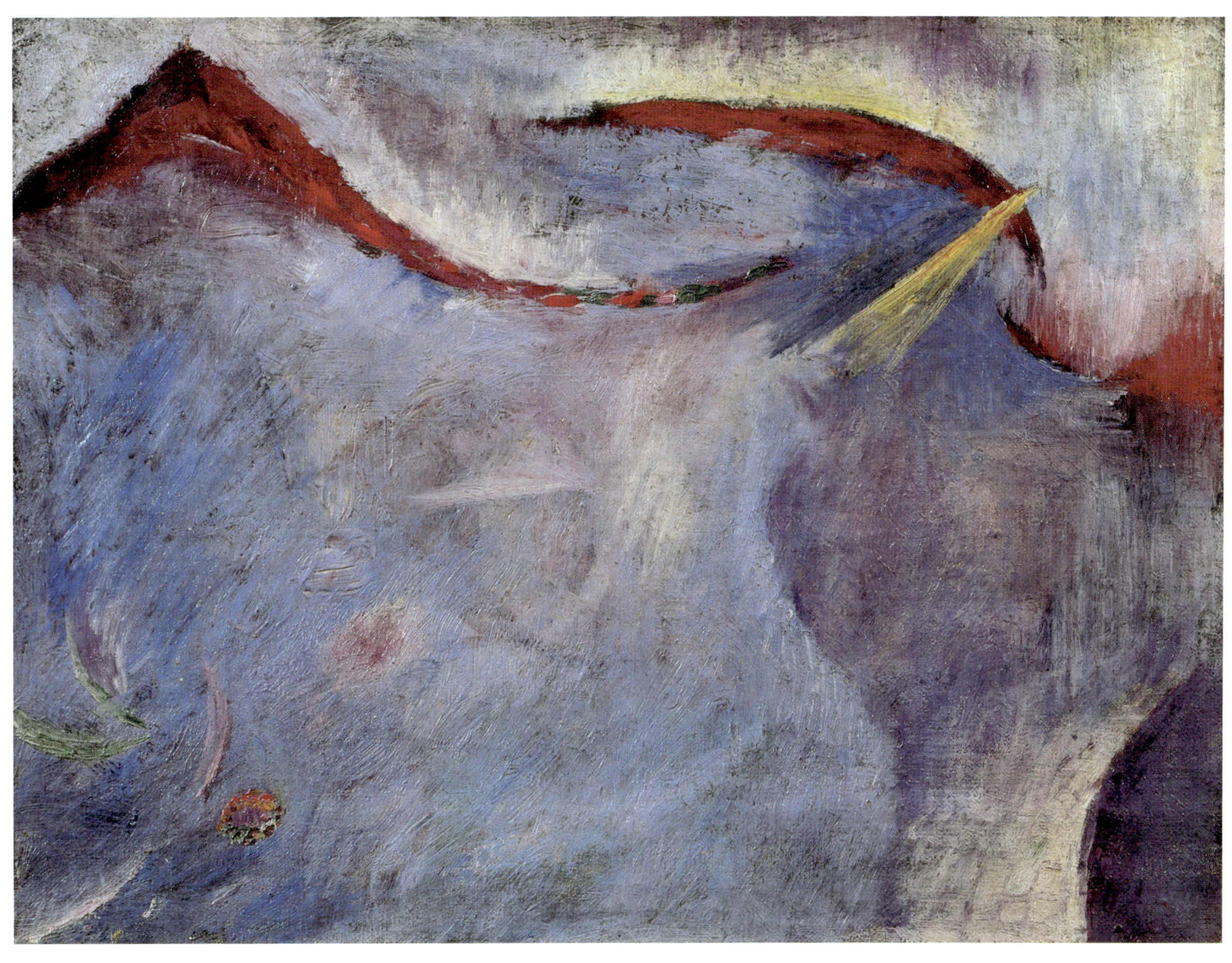

1
Yorozu Tetsugorô, Mu dai (Untitled), 1912–1913
Oil on Canvas, 24.5 x 32.8 cm, Iwate Prefecture Museum, Morioka

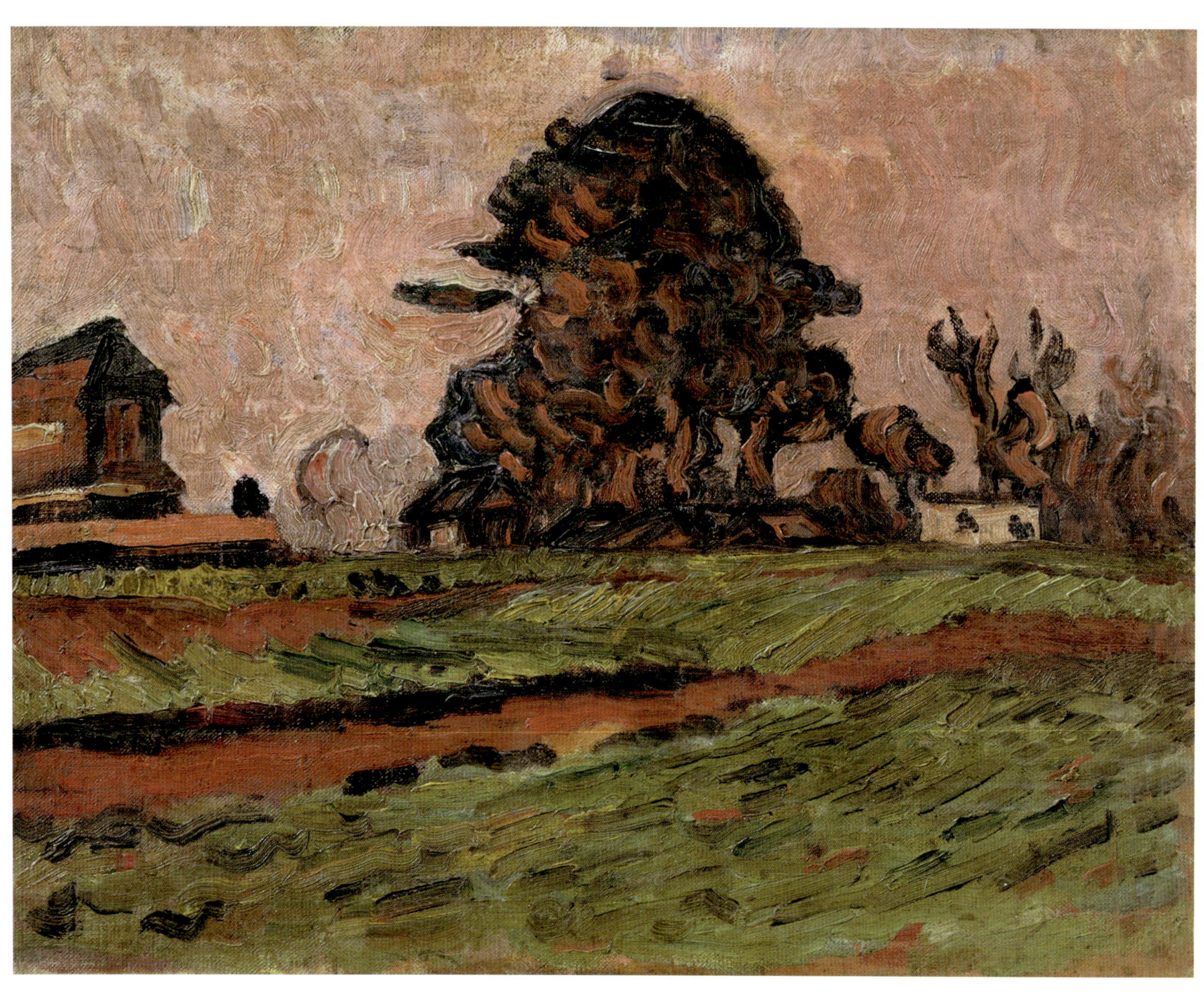

2
Yorozu Tetsugorô, Rustic Landscape, 1912–1913
Oil on Canvas, 30.7 x 40 cm, Kanagawa Prefecture Museum of Modern Art, Kamakura

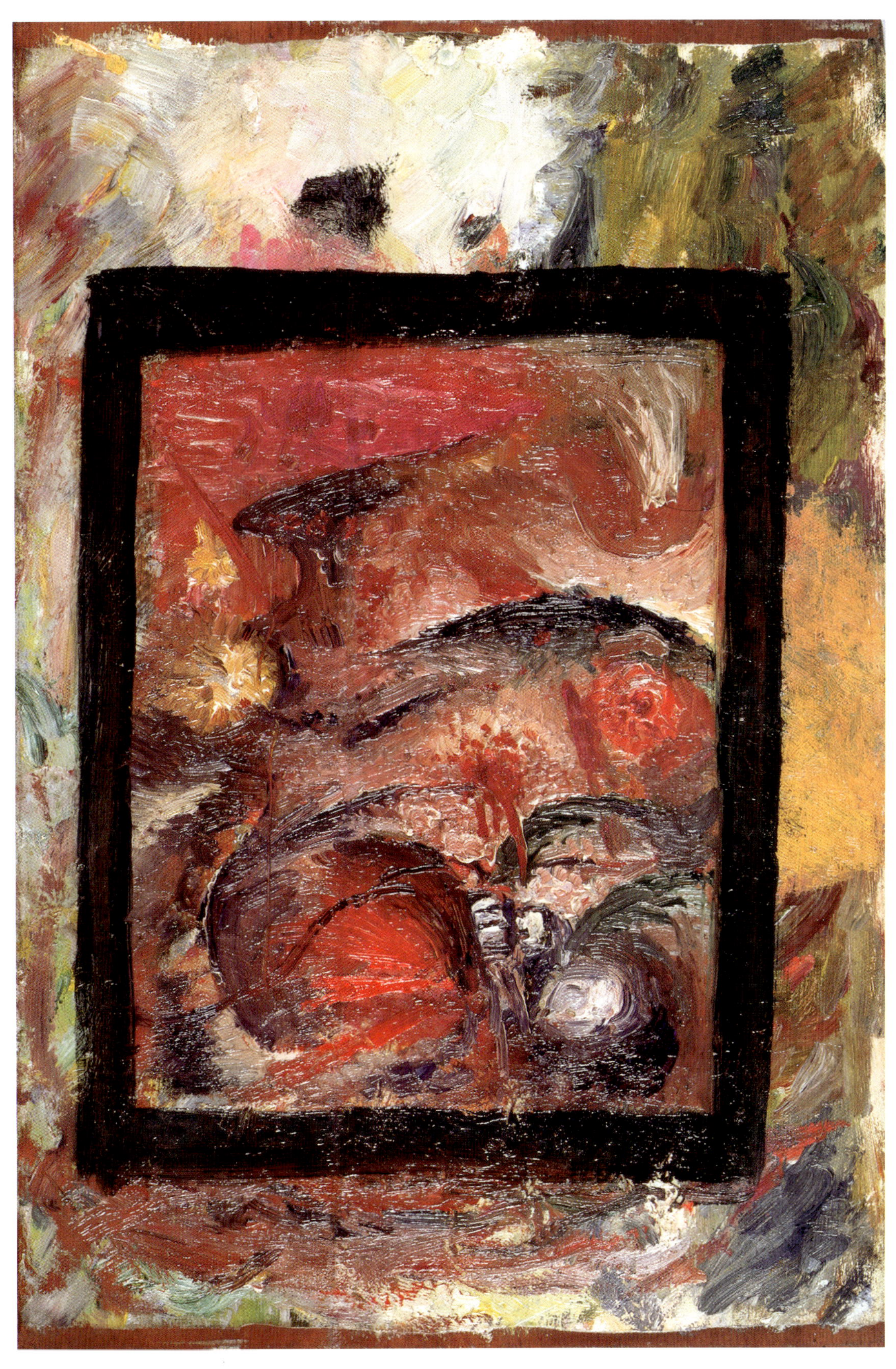

3
Yorozu Tetsugorô, Landscape of Mental Conception, 1913
Oil on Board, 32 x 23 cm, Yorozu Tetsugorô Memorial Museum, Tôwa

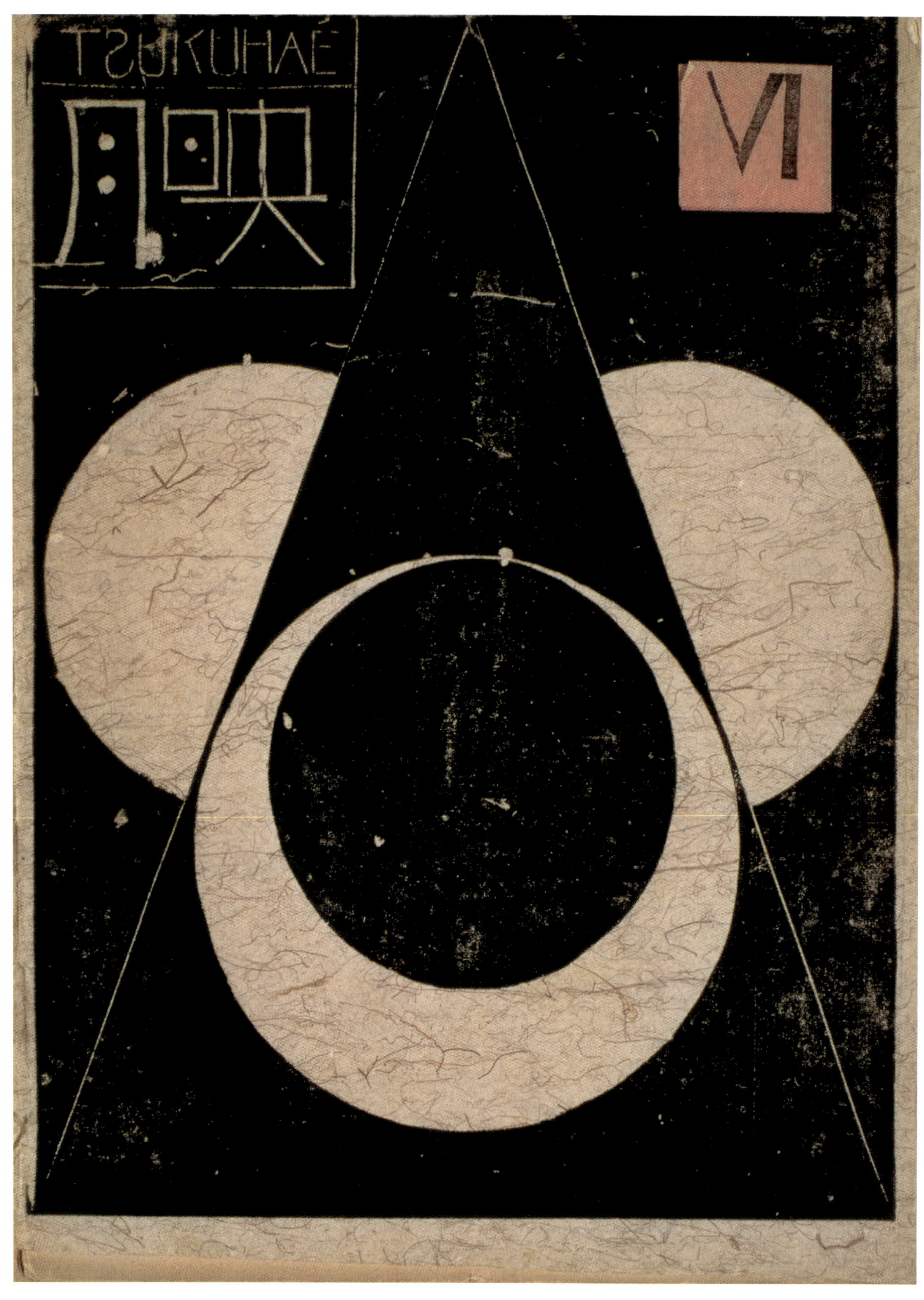

4
Onchi Kôshirô, Reflections of the Moon VI, 1914–1915
Wood Engraving, 27 x 20.3 cm, Ono Tadashige Museum of Graphic Art, Tokyo

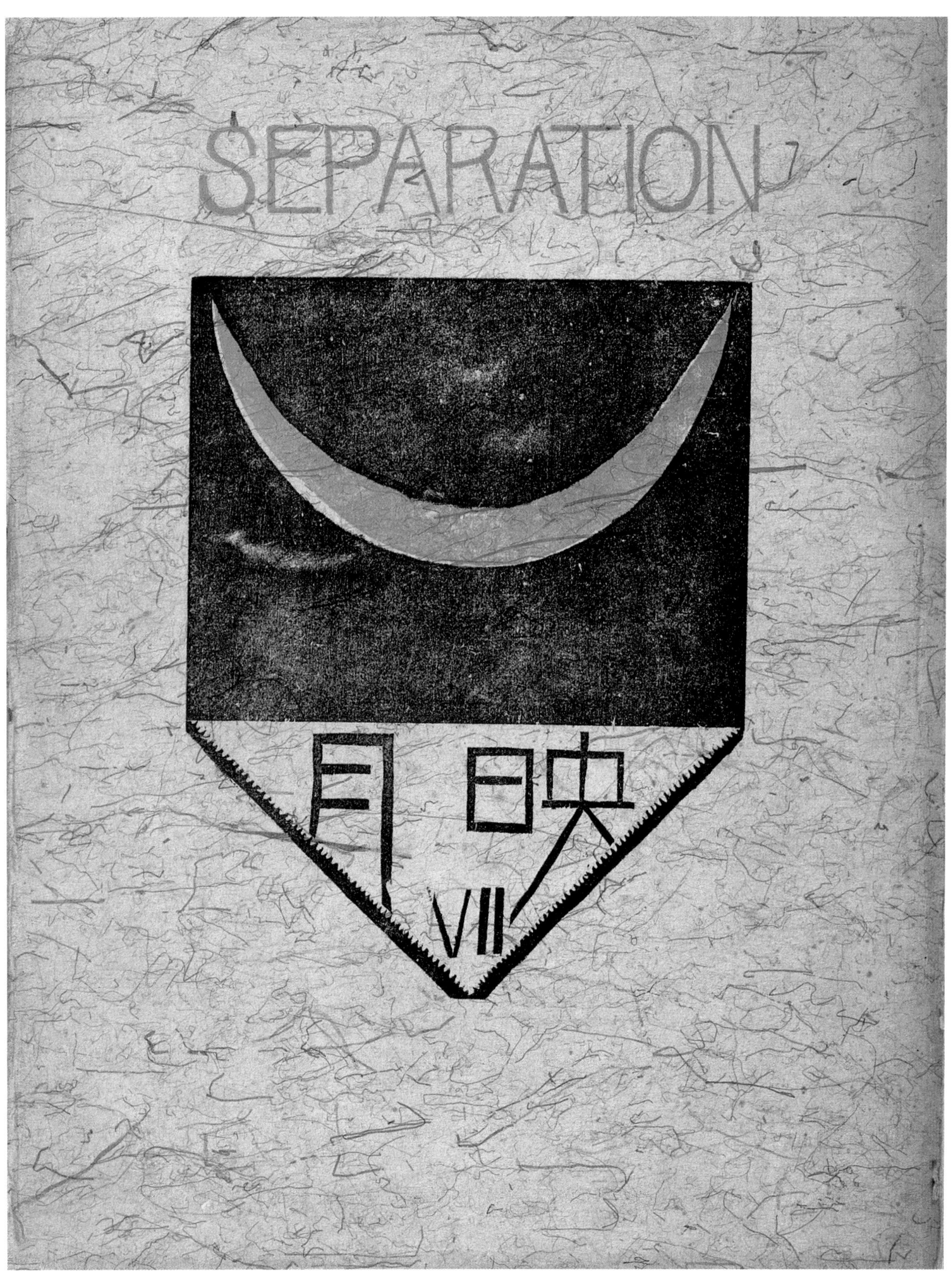

5
Onchi Kôshirô, Reflections of the Moon VII, 1914–1915
Wood Engraving, 26.6 x 20.4 cm, Ono Tadashige Museum of Graphic Art, Tokyo

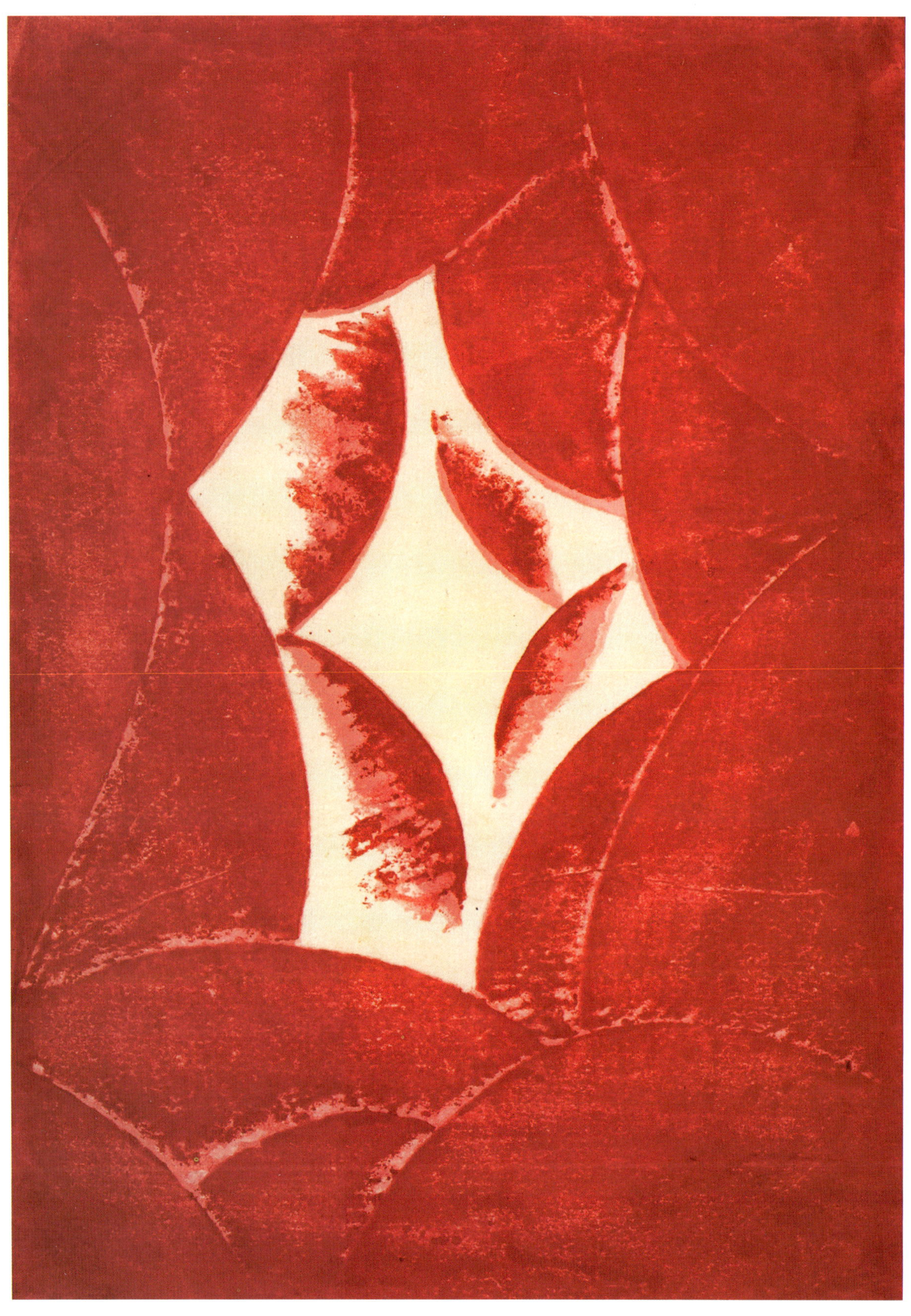

6
Onchi Kôshirô, Bright Time, 1915
Colored Wood Engraving, 13.5 x 10 cm, National Museum of Modern Art, Tokyo

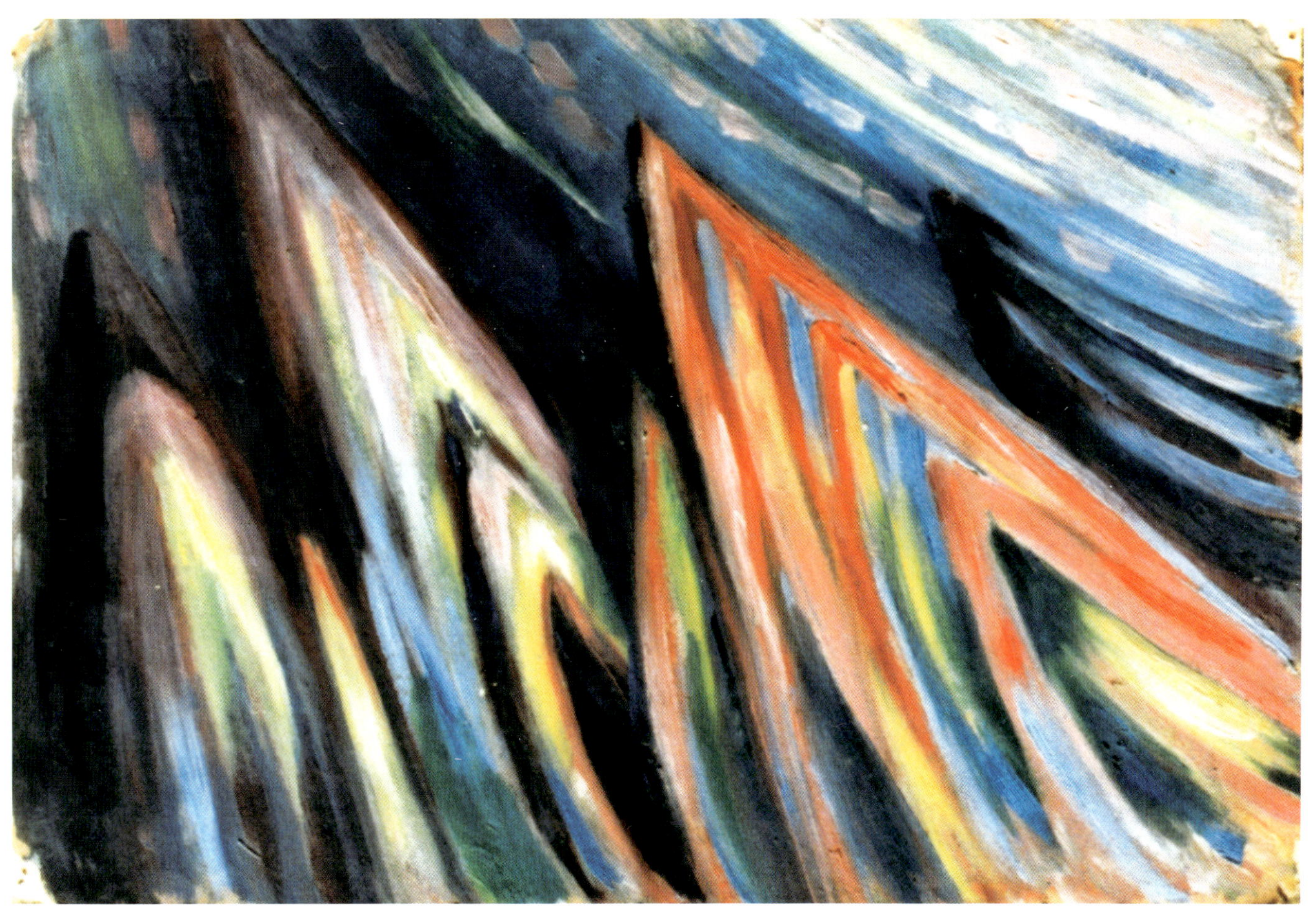

7
Nishimura Isaku, Abstract Image (Wave-shape), 1916
Oil on Canvas, 18.9 x 29 cm, Nishimura Hatch, Bunka Gakuin

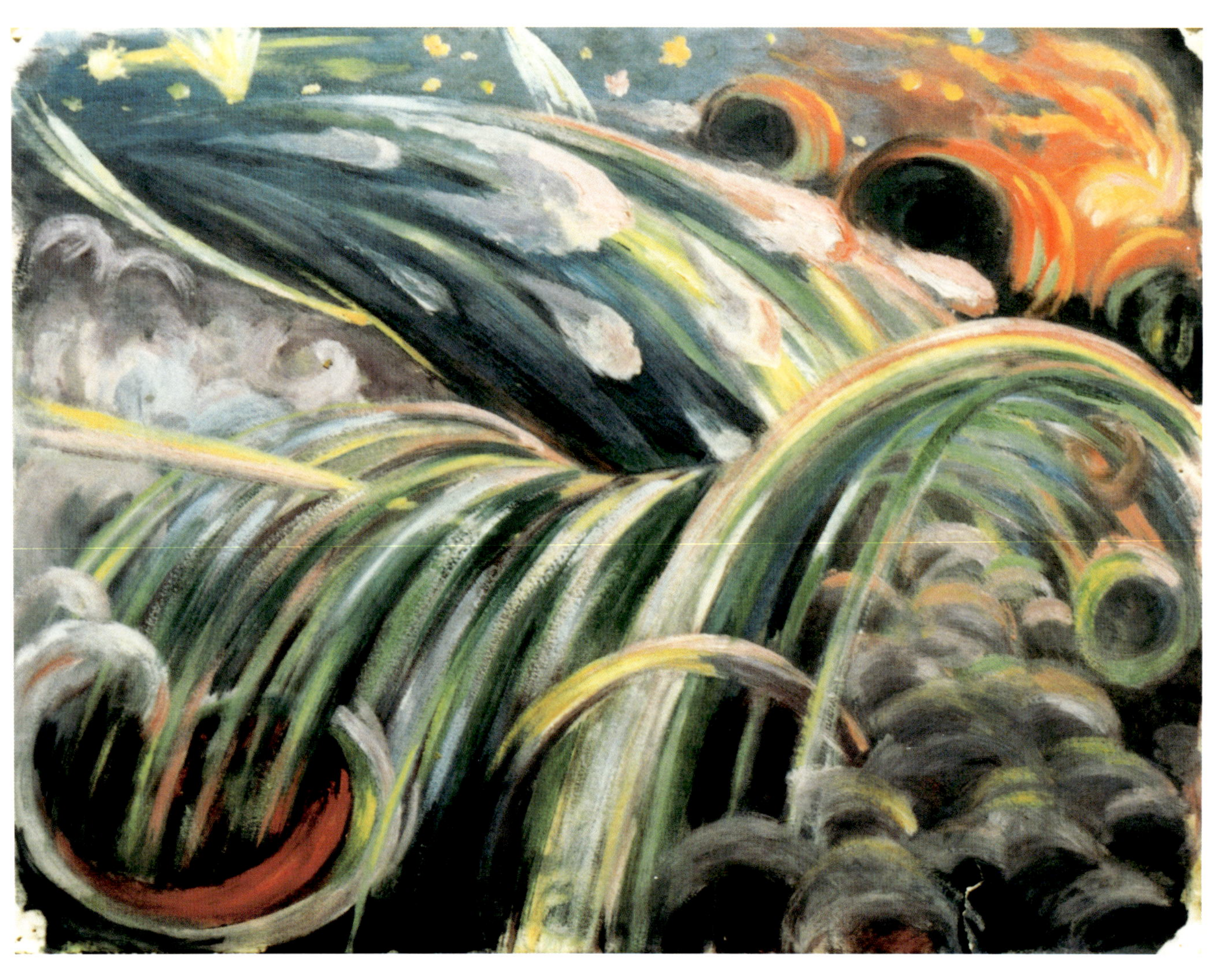

8
Nishimura Isaku, Abstract Image (Cosmos), 1916
Oil on Canvas, 29.4 x 38.3 cm, Nishimura Hatch, Bunka Gakuin

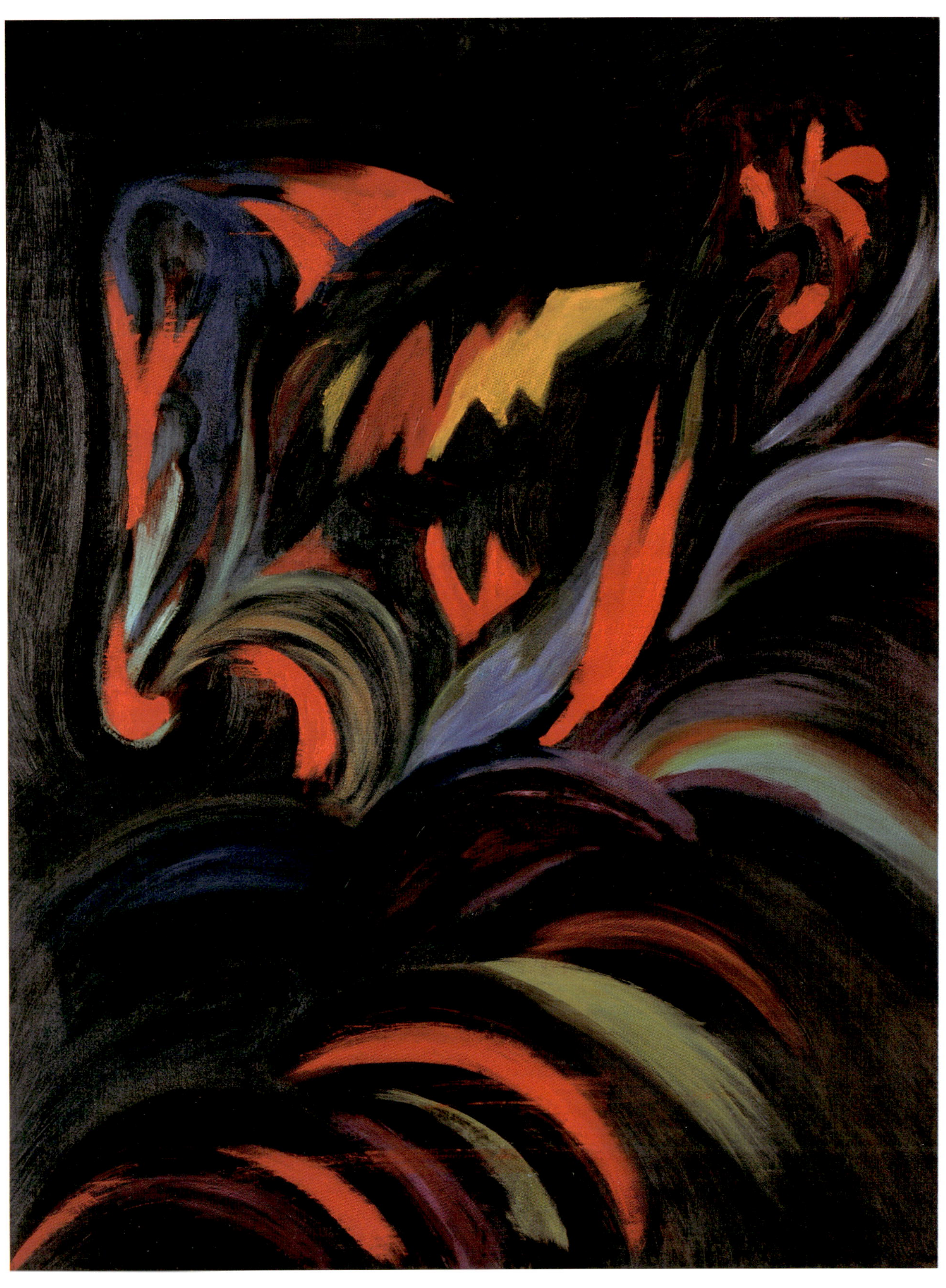

9
Kambara Tai, Currents of Life, Musical Creation, Symphony No. 35, 1919
Oil on Canvas, 116.7 x 90.9 cm, Municipal Art Museum, Tokyo

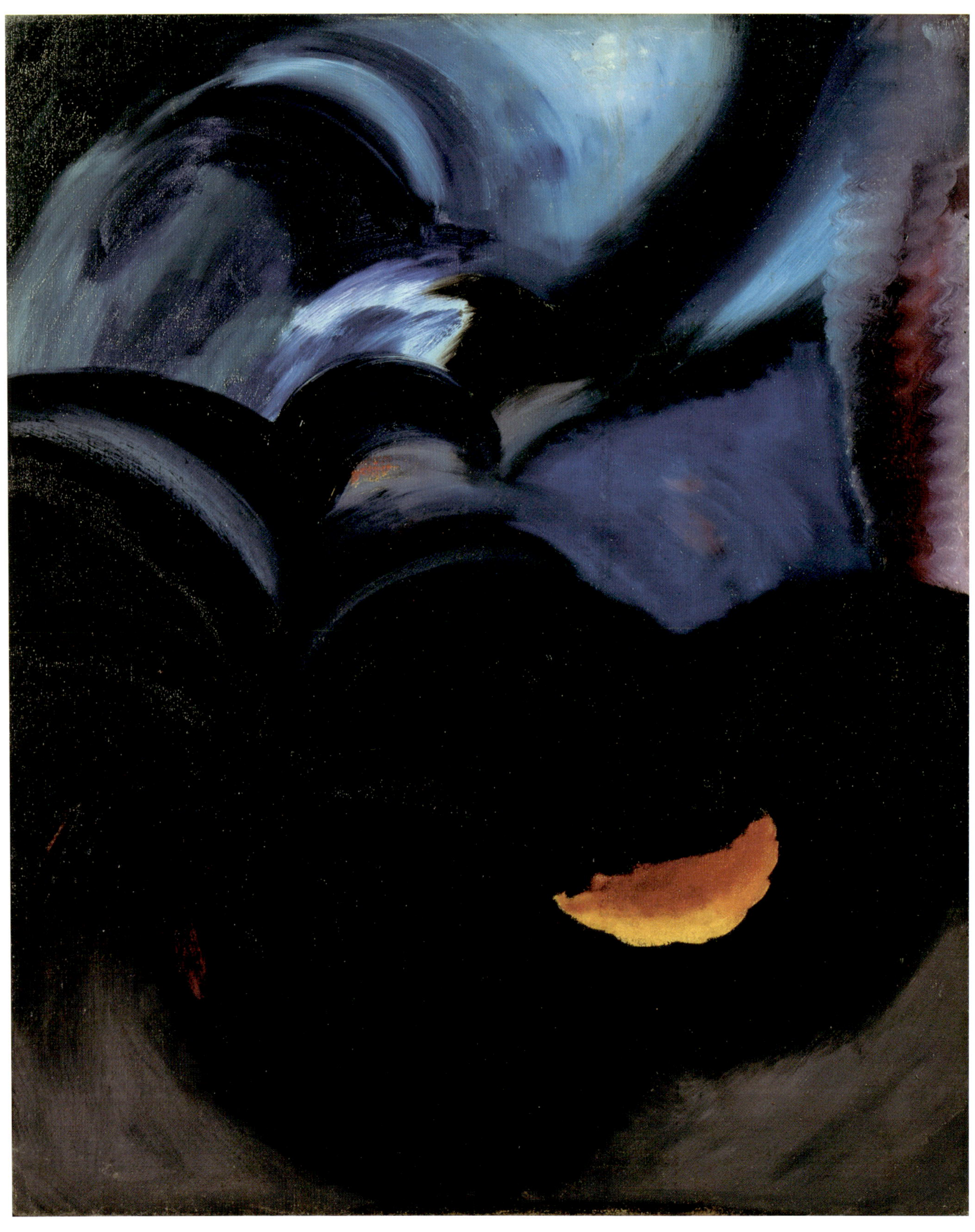

10
Kambara Tai, A Pessimist's Notes C, 1923
Oil on Canvas, 60.6 x 50 cm, National Museum of Modern Art, Tokyo

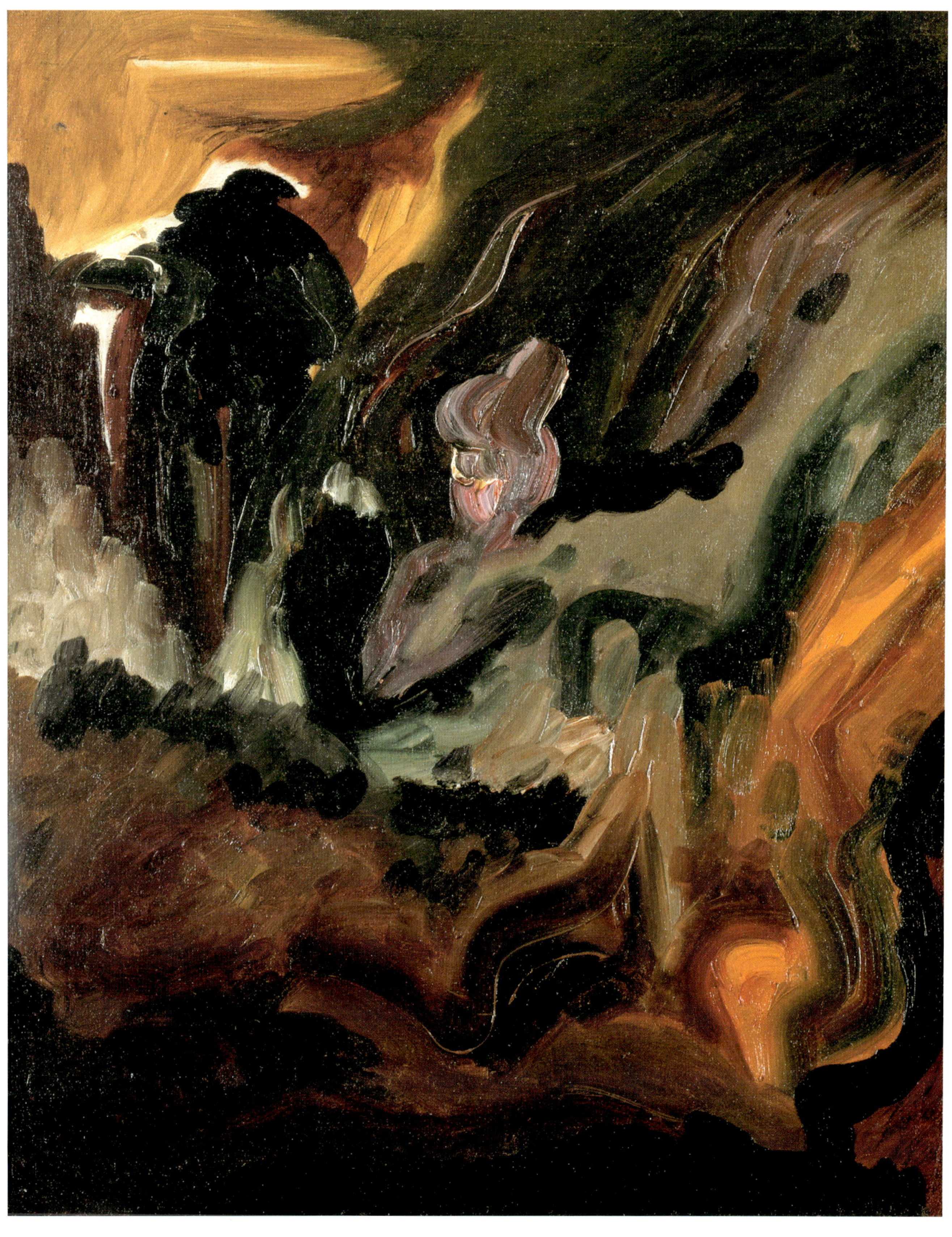

11
Kambara Tai, A Pessimist's Notes D, 1923
Oil on Canvas, 60.6 x 50 cm, National Museum of Modern Art, Tokyo

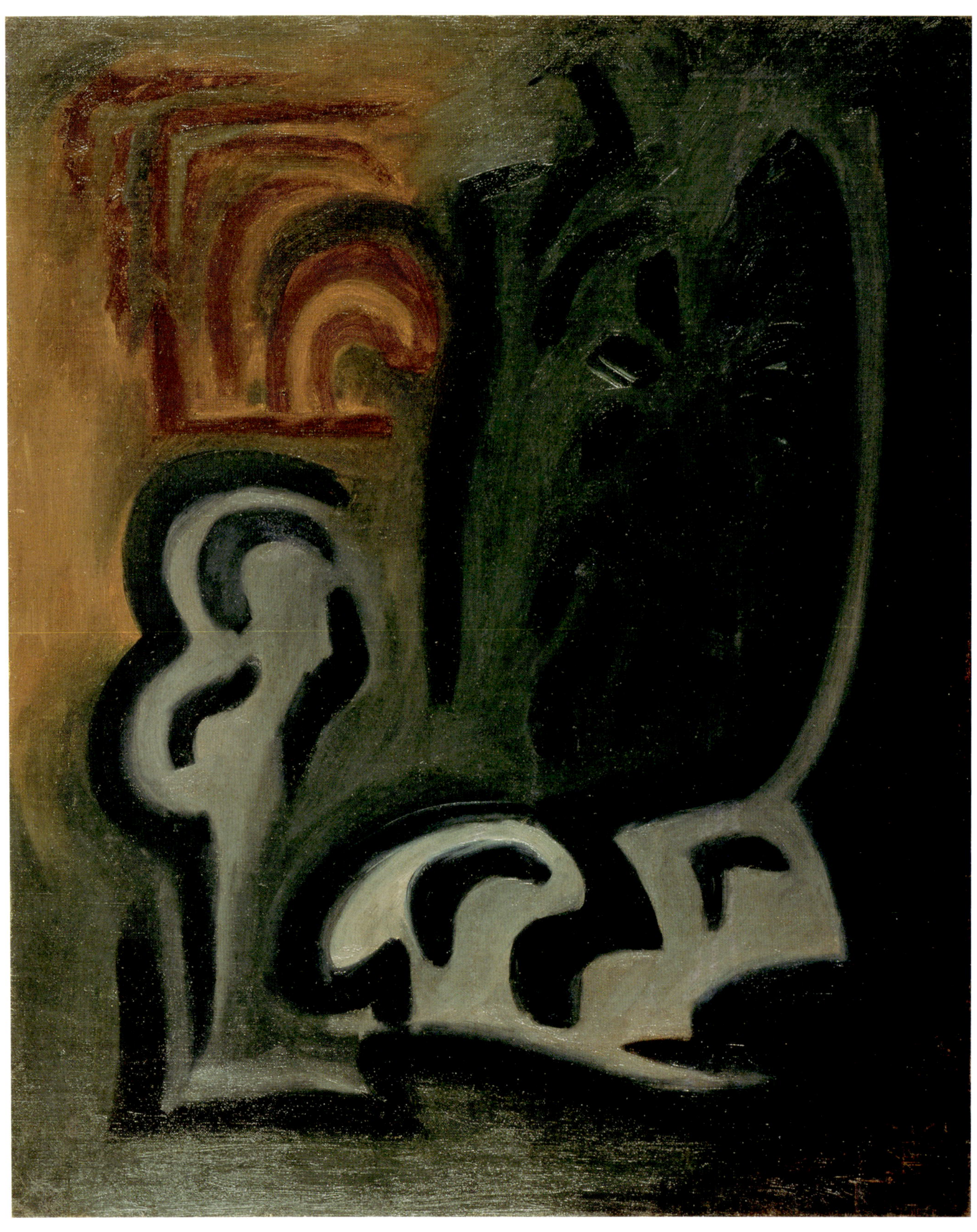

12
Kambara Tai, A Pessimist's Notes E, 1923
Oil on Canvas, 60.6 x 50 cm, National Museum of Modern Art, Tokyo

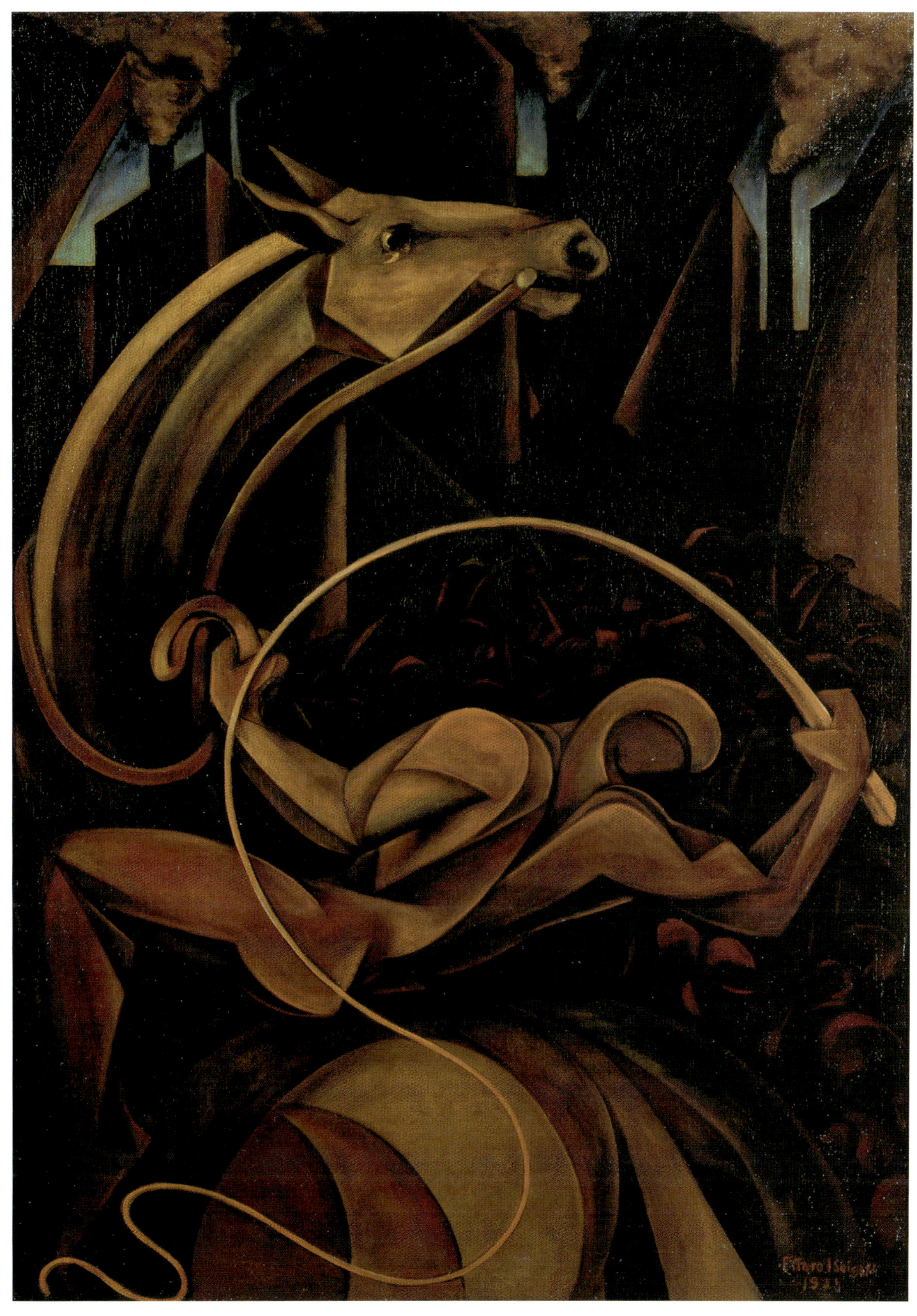

13
Ishigaki Eitarô, Whiplashes, 1925
Oil on Canvas, 145.5 x 106.5 cm, National Museum of Modern Art, Kyoto

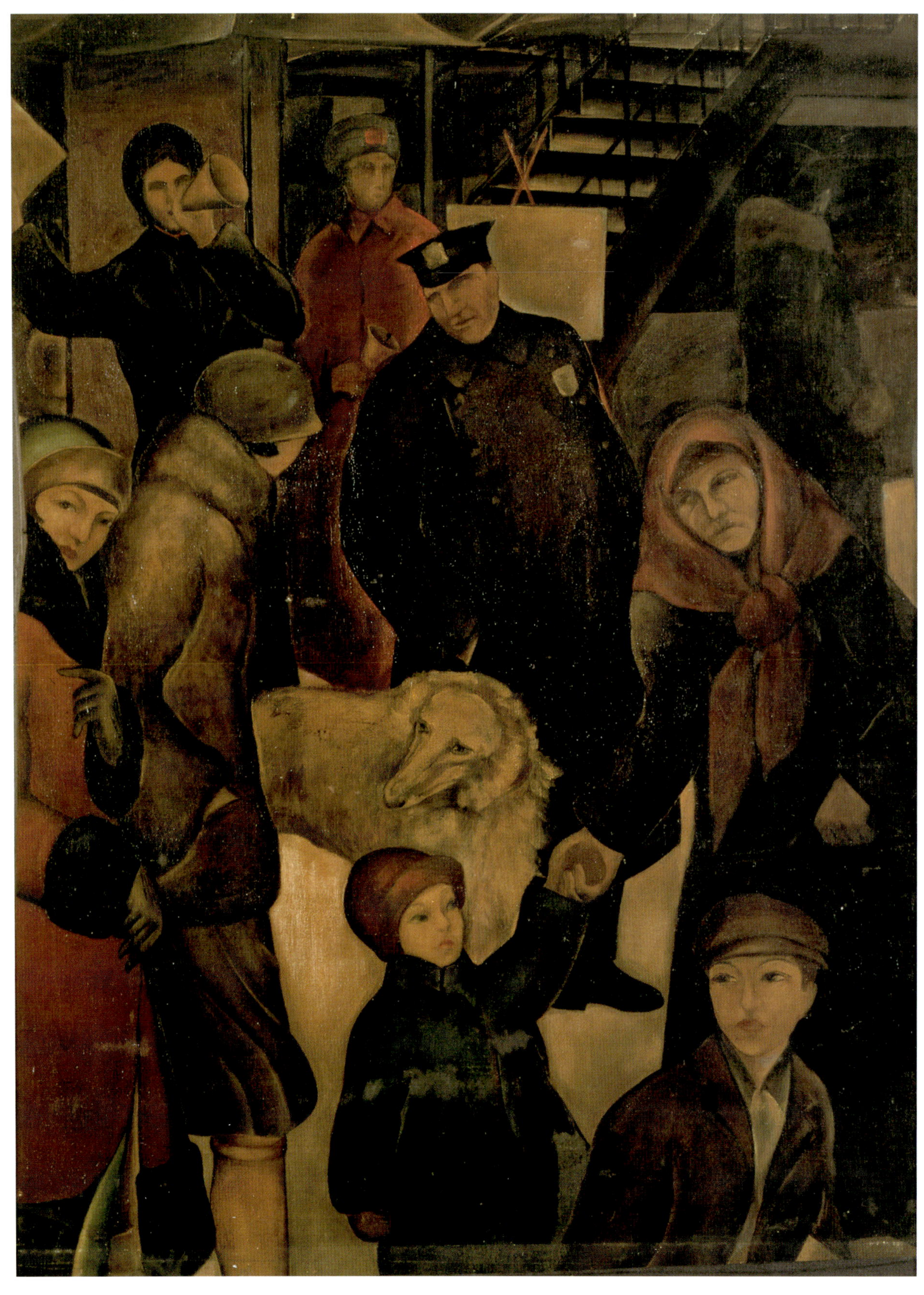

14
Ishigaki Eitarô, Street, 1925
Oil on Canvas, 113.5 x 86.5 cm, Kanagawa Prefecture Museum of Modern Art, Kamakura

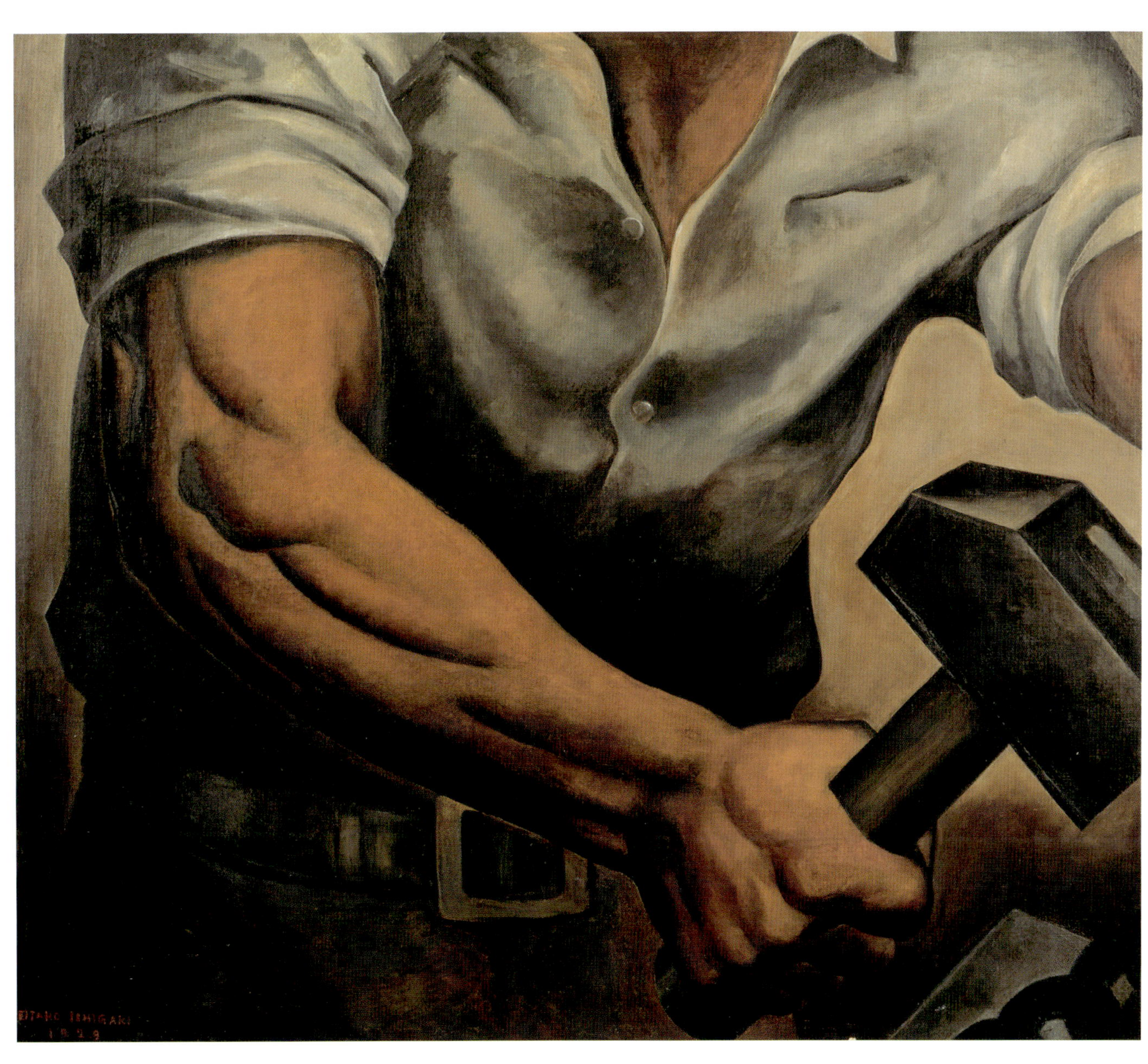

15
Ishigaki Eitarô, Arm, 1929
Oil on Canvas, 91 x 86.5 cm, National Museum of Modern Art, Tokyo

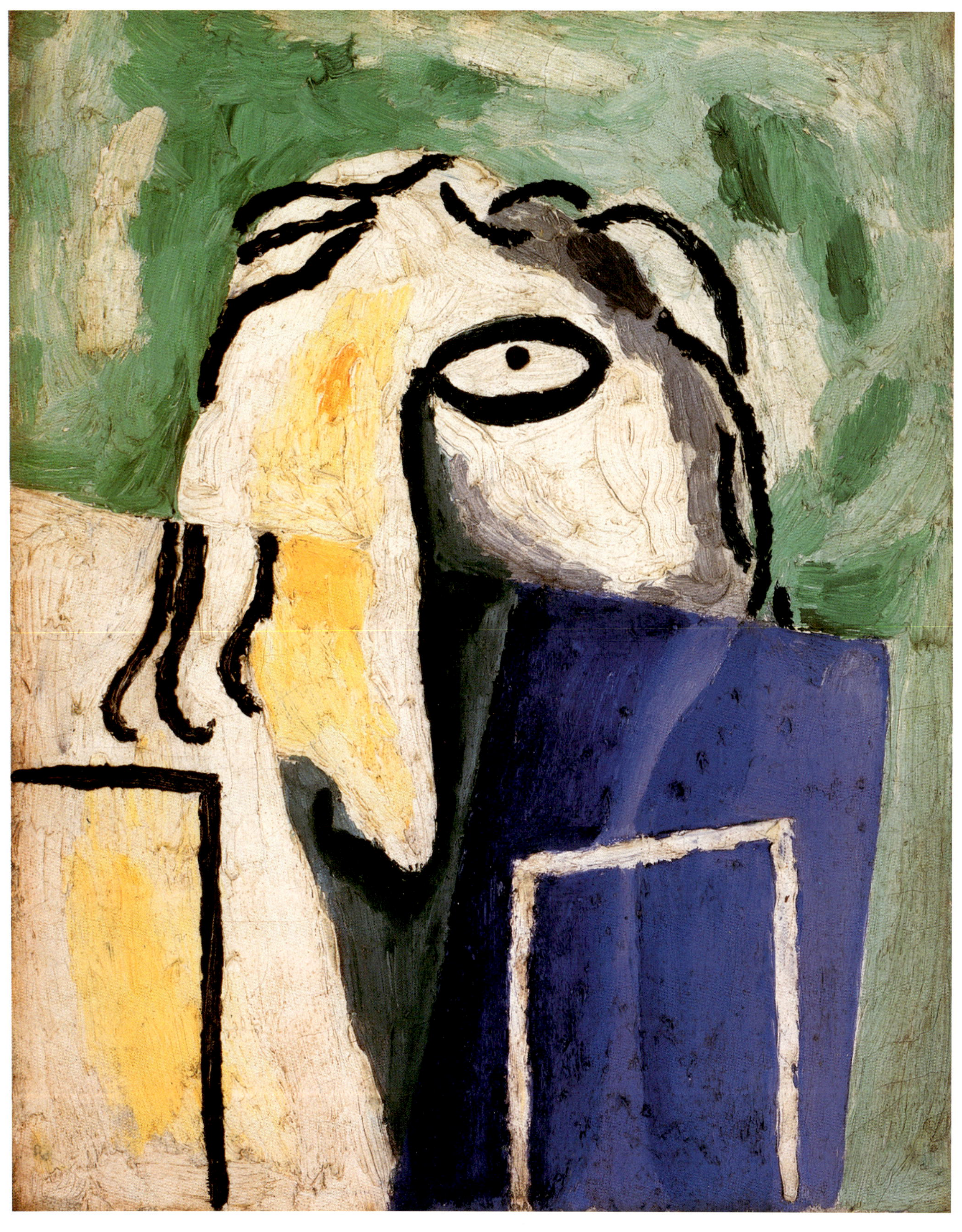

16

Yamaguchi Takeo, Head, 1930

Oil on Canvas, 40.8 x 32.8 cm, Itabashiku Art Museum, Tokyo

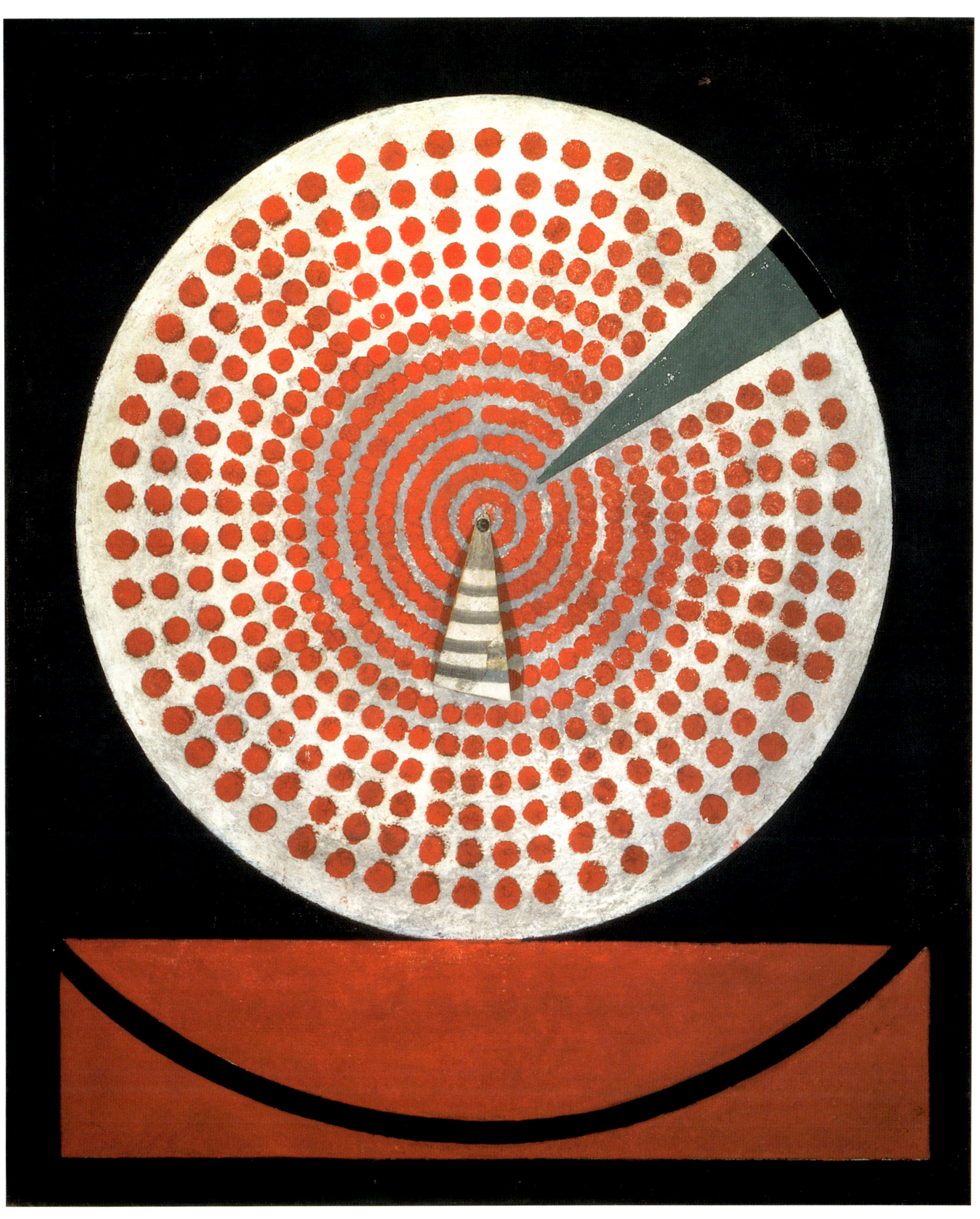

17
Yoshihara Jirô, Work, 1934
Oil on Canvas, Paper, 73 x 60.8 cm, Itabashiku Art Museum, Tokyo

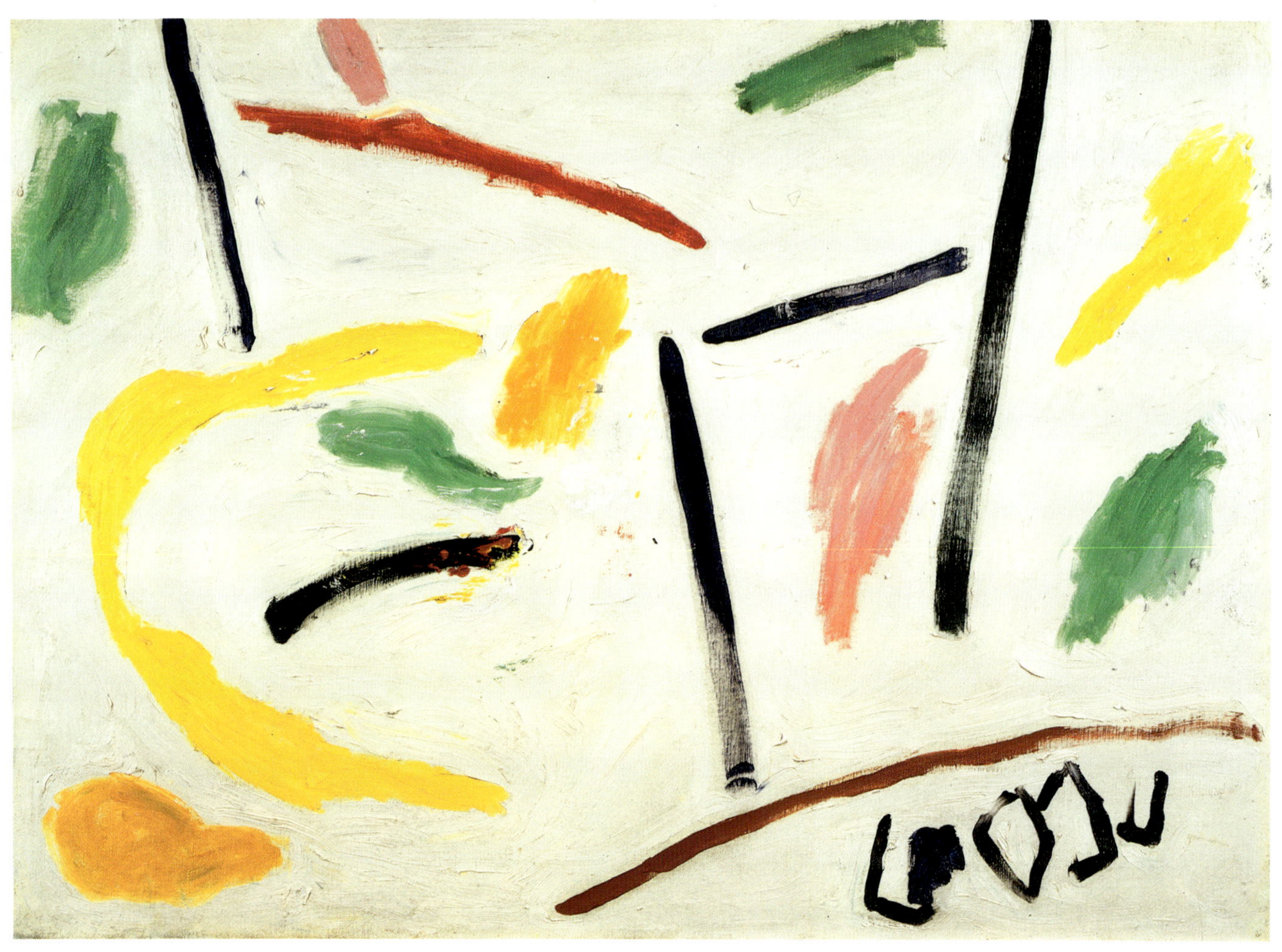

18
Yamaguchi Takeo, Pond, 1936
Oil on Canvas, 65.3 x 92 cm, National Museum of Modern Art, Tokyo

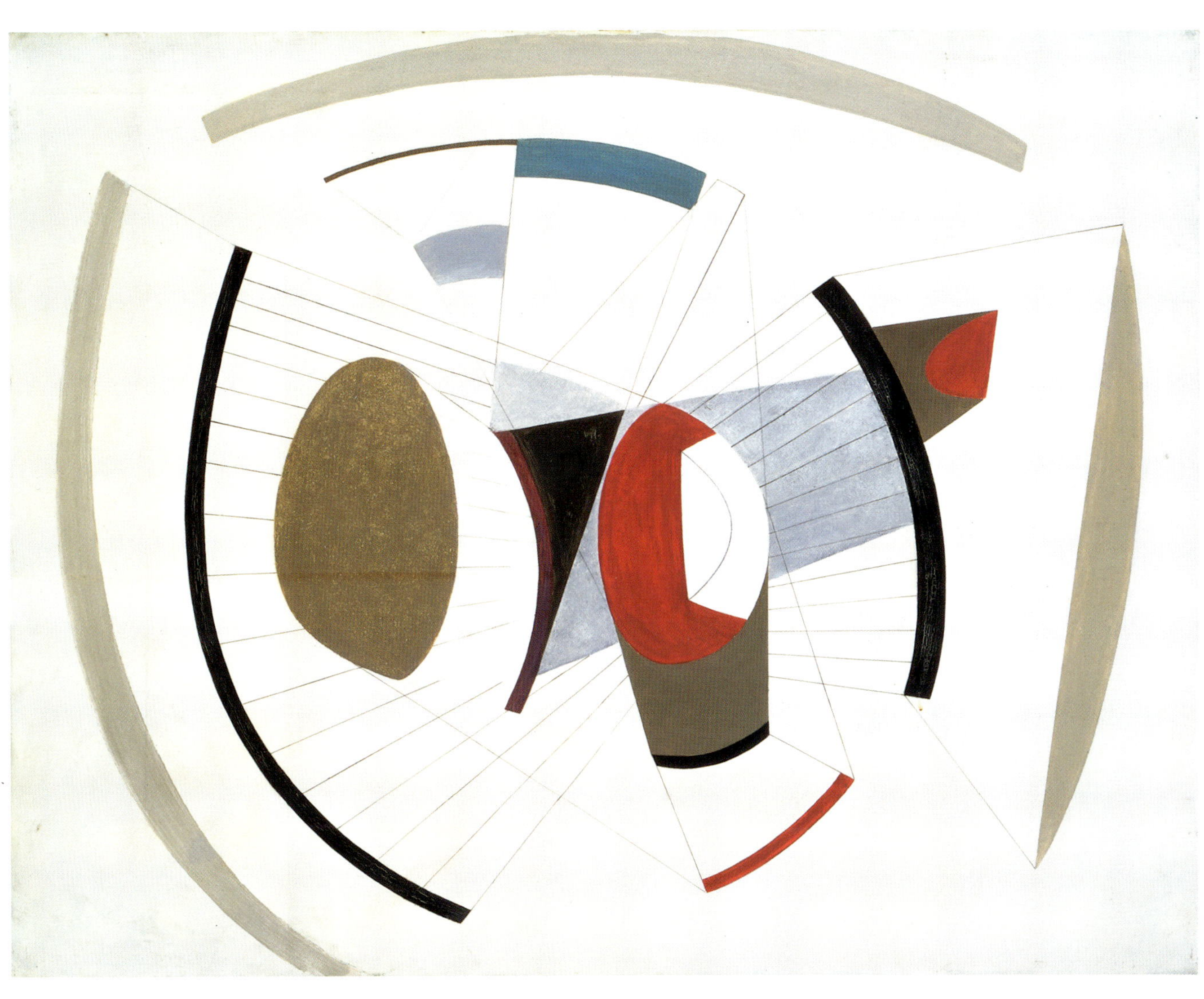

19

Yoshihara Jirô, Work, 1936

Oil on Canvas, 145.5 x 162 cm, Kanagawa Prefecture Museum of Modern Art, Kamakura

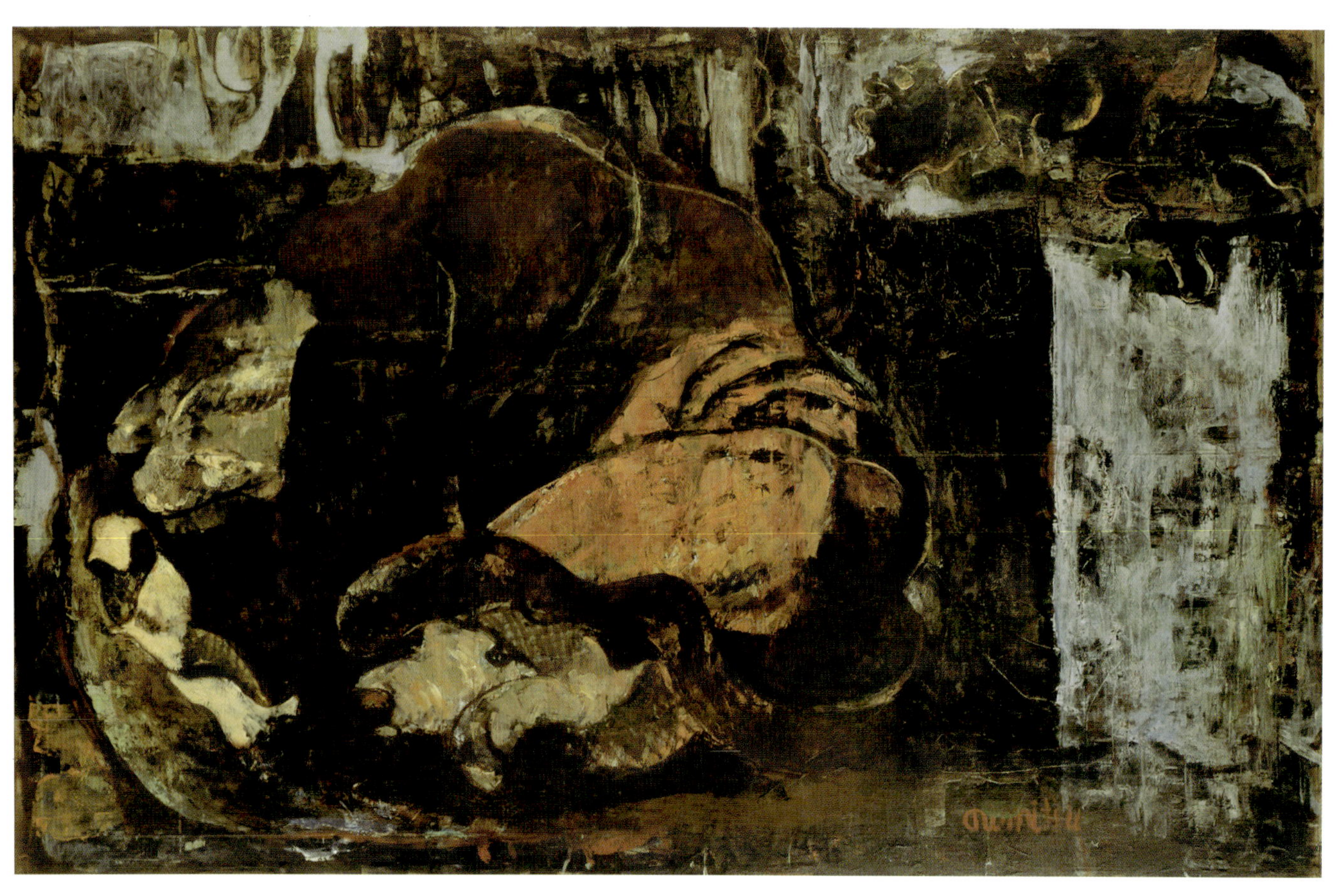

20
Ai-Mitsu, Lion, 1936
Oil on Canvas, 144.5 x 228 cm, Private Collection

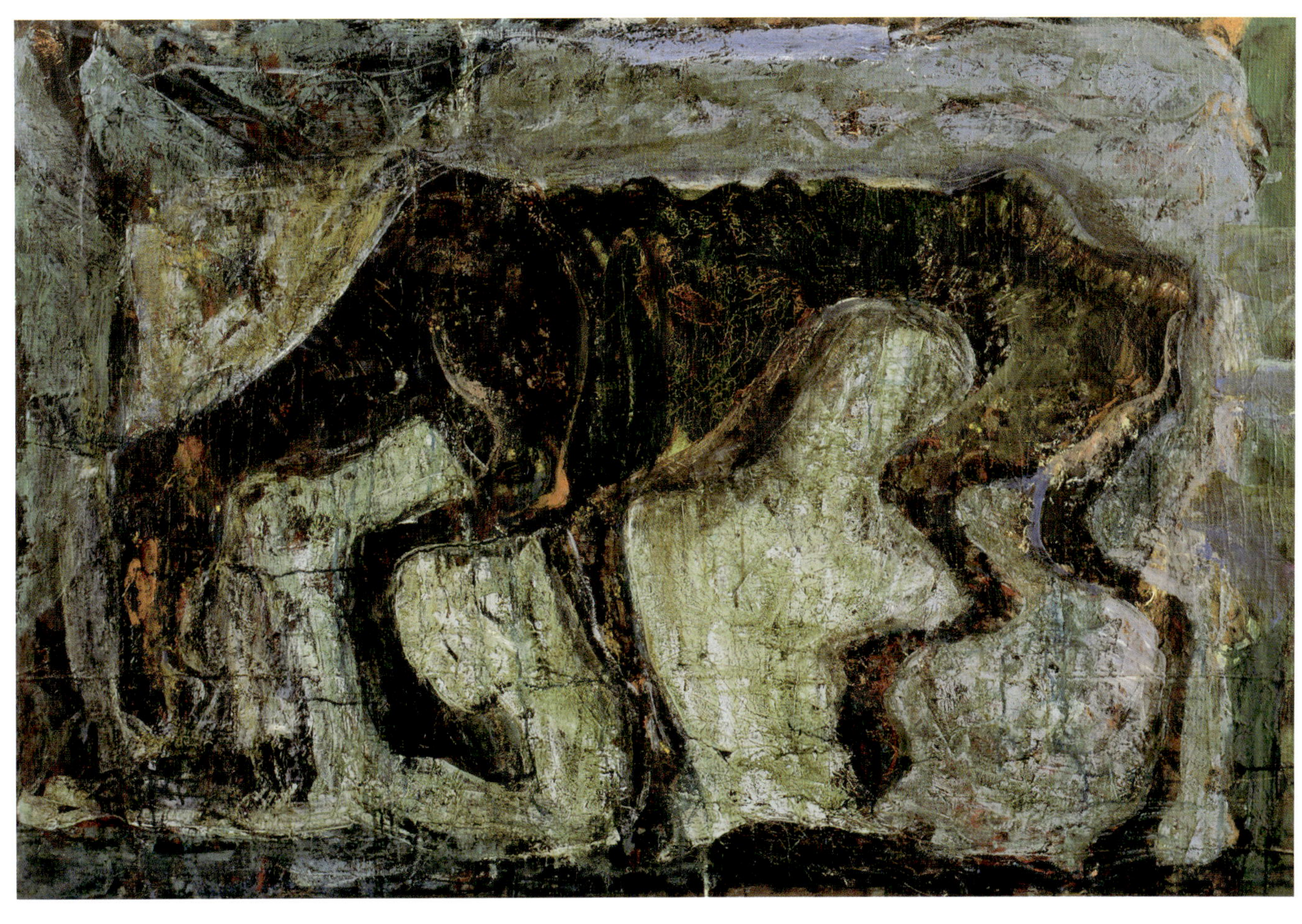

21
Ai-Mitsu, Horse, 1936
Oil on Canvas, 96 x 141 cm, National Museum of Modern Art, Tokyo

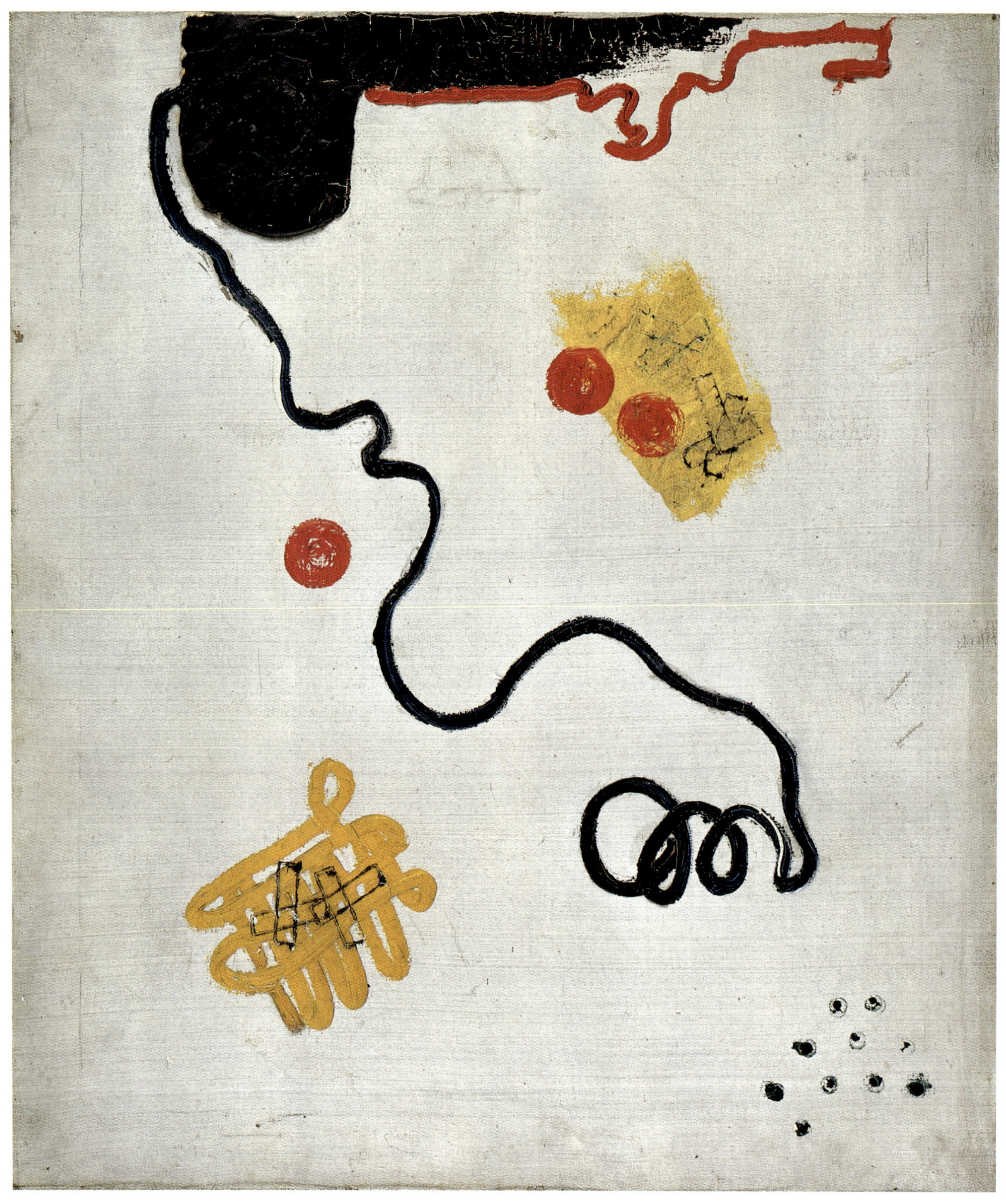

22
Ei-Kyû, Matchstick Marks, 1936
Oil on Canvas, 53.2 x 45.7 cm, Miyazaki Prefecture Museum, Miyazaki

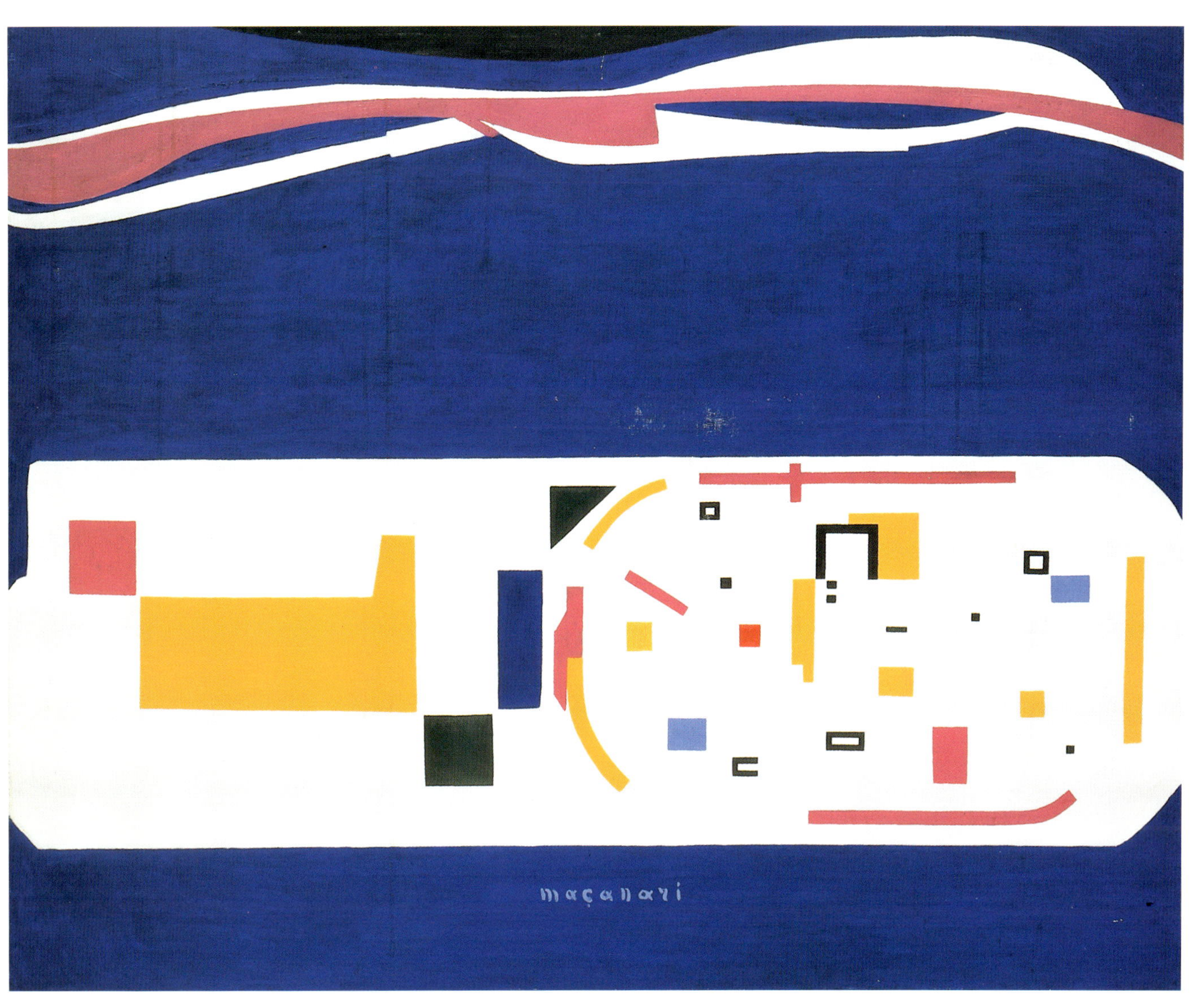

23
Murai Masanari, Urban, 1937
Oil on Canvas, 130 x 162 cm, Kanagawa Prefecture Museum of Modern Art, Kamakura

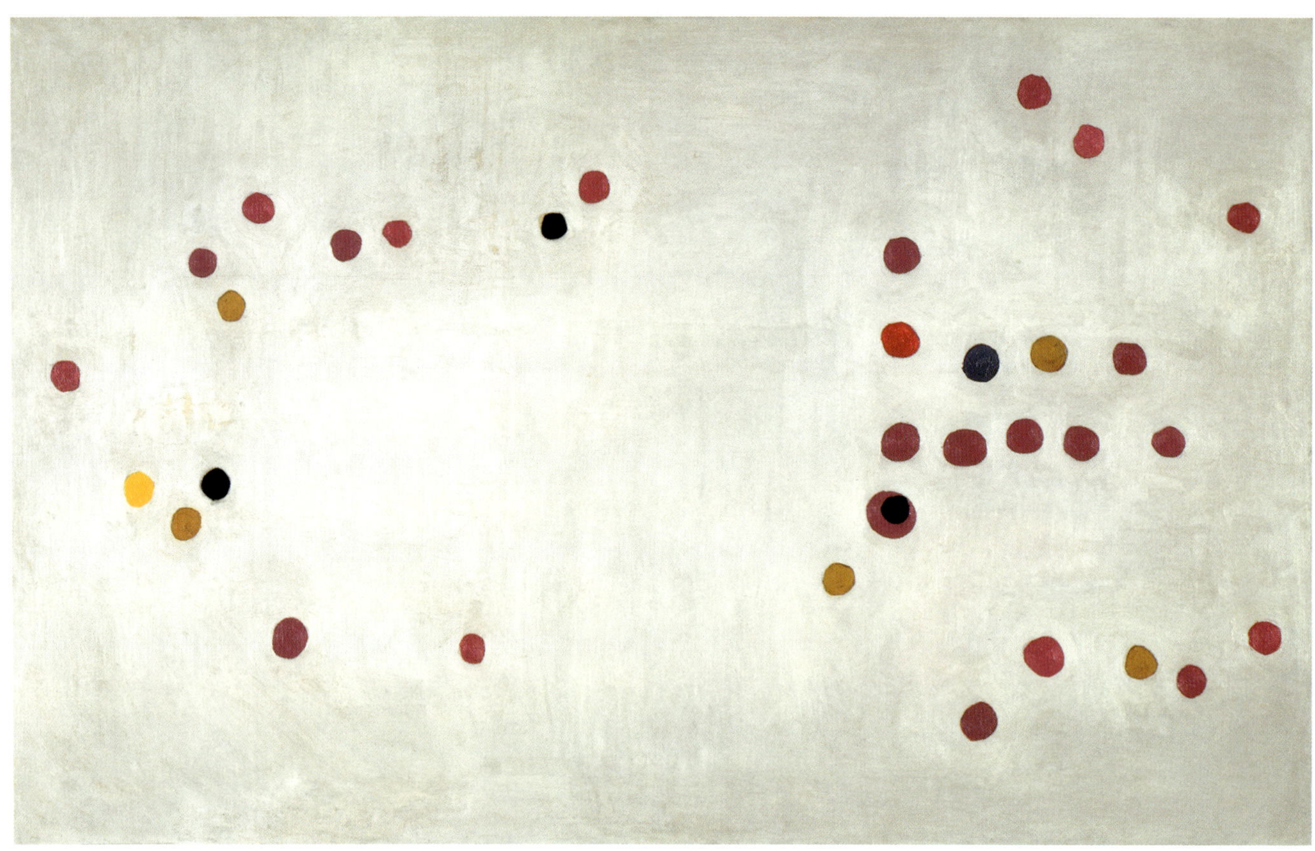

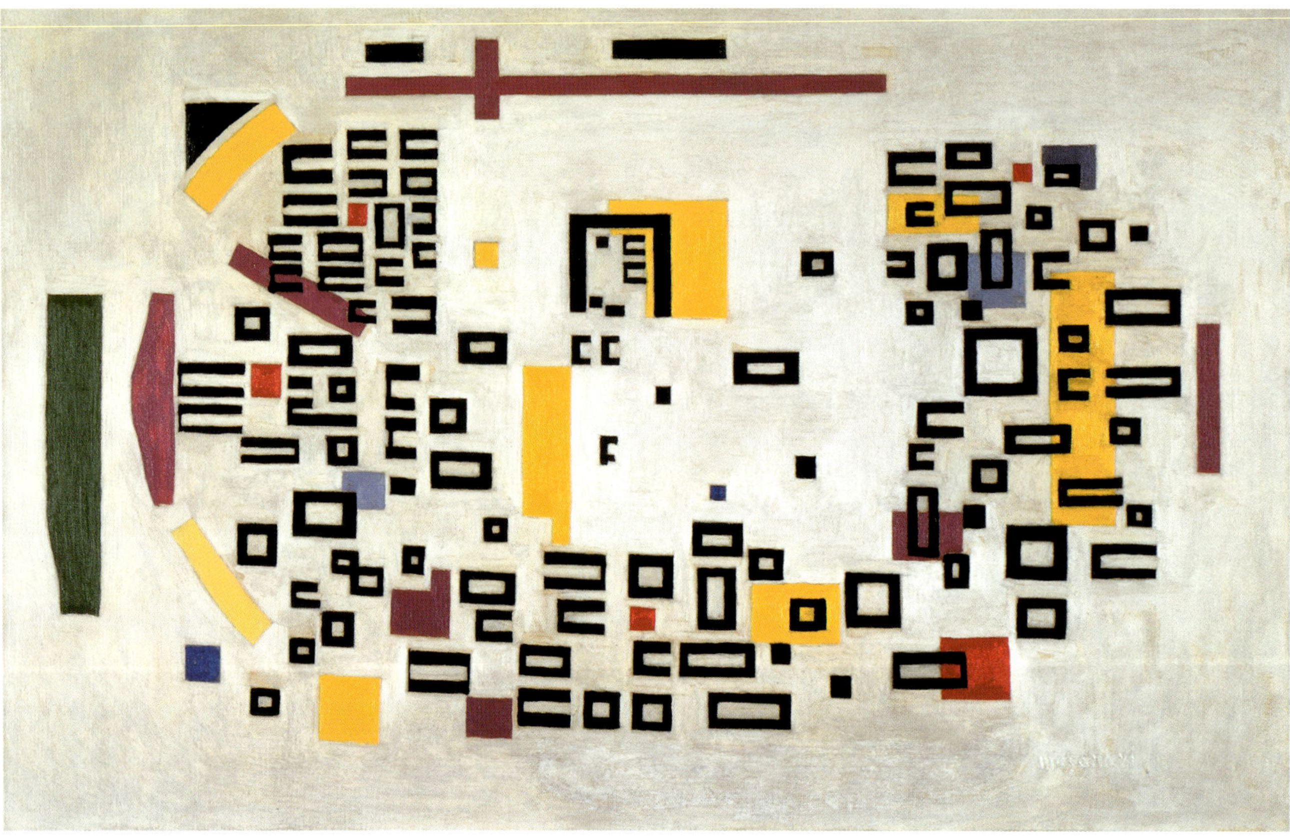

24a/b
Murai Masanari, Urban, 1937
Oil on Canvas, each one 72.5 x 233.5 cm, National Museum of Modern Art, Tokyo

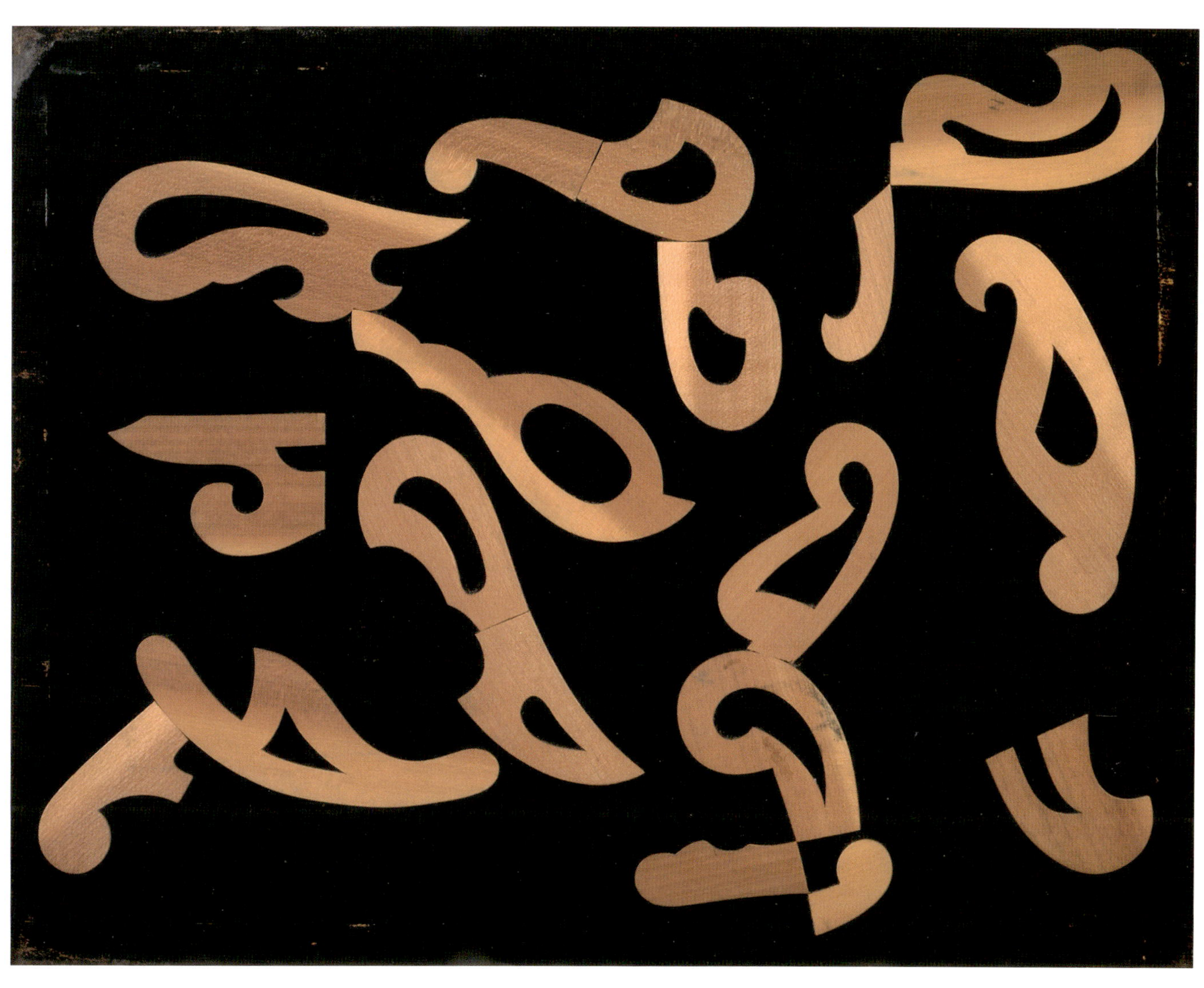

25
Hasegawa Saburô, Shapes, 1937
Oil on Canvas (Collage), 39 x 50 cm, Konan Gakuen

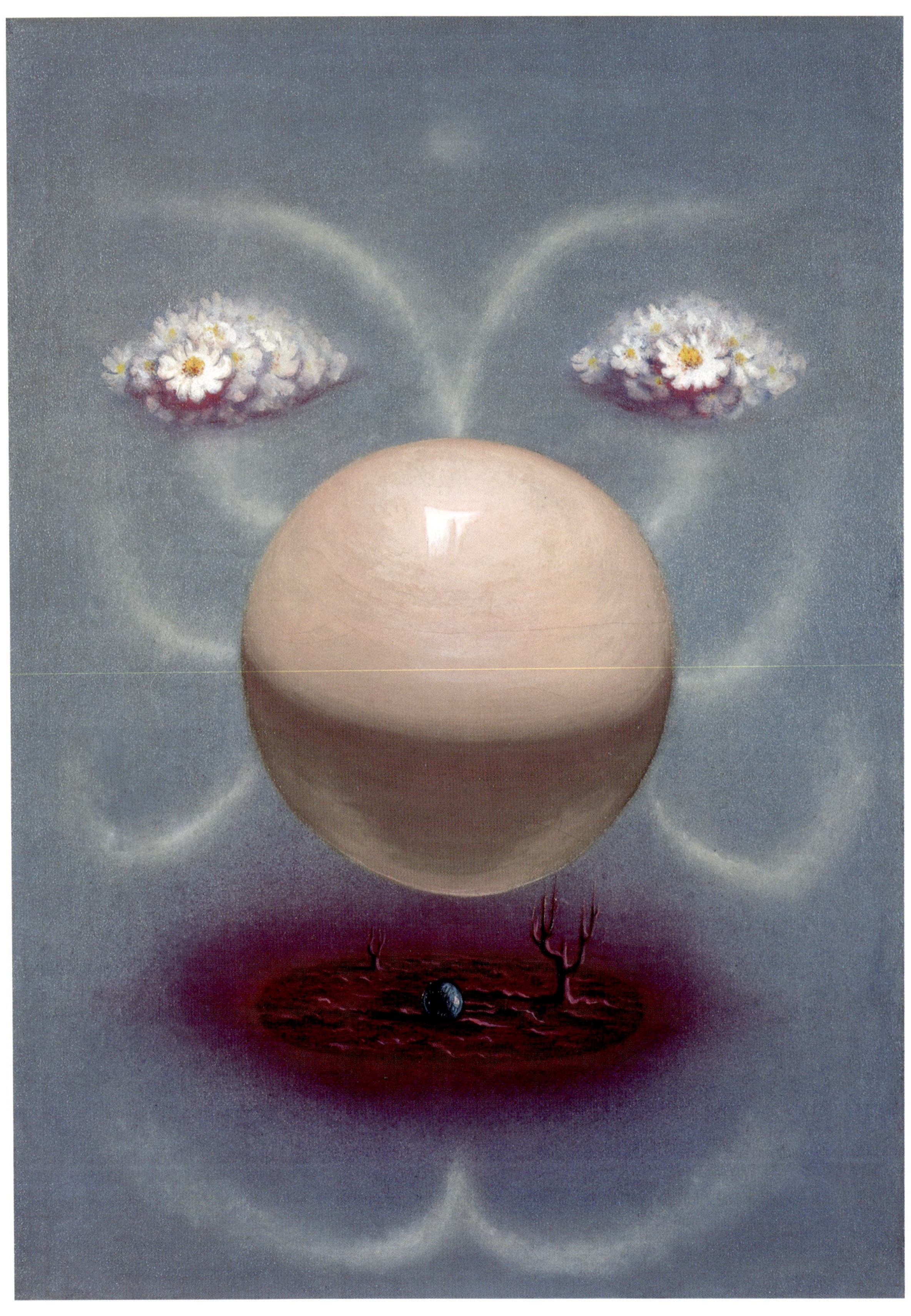

26
Kitawaki Noboru, Metamorphosis of Life (Physiognomy Series), 1938
Oil on Canvas, 72.7 x 53.4 cm, National Museum of Modern Art, Tokyo

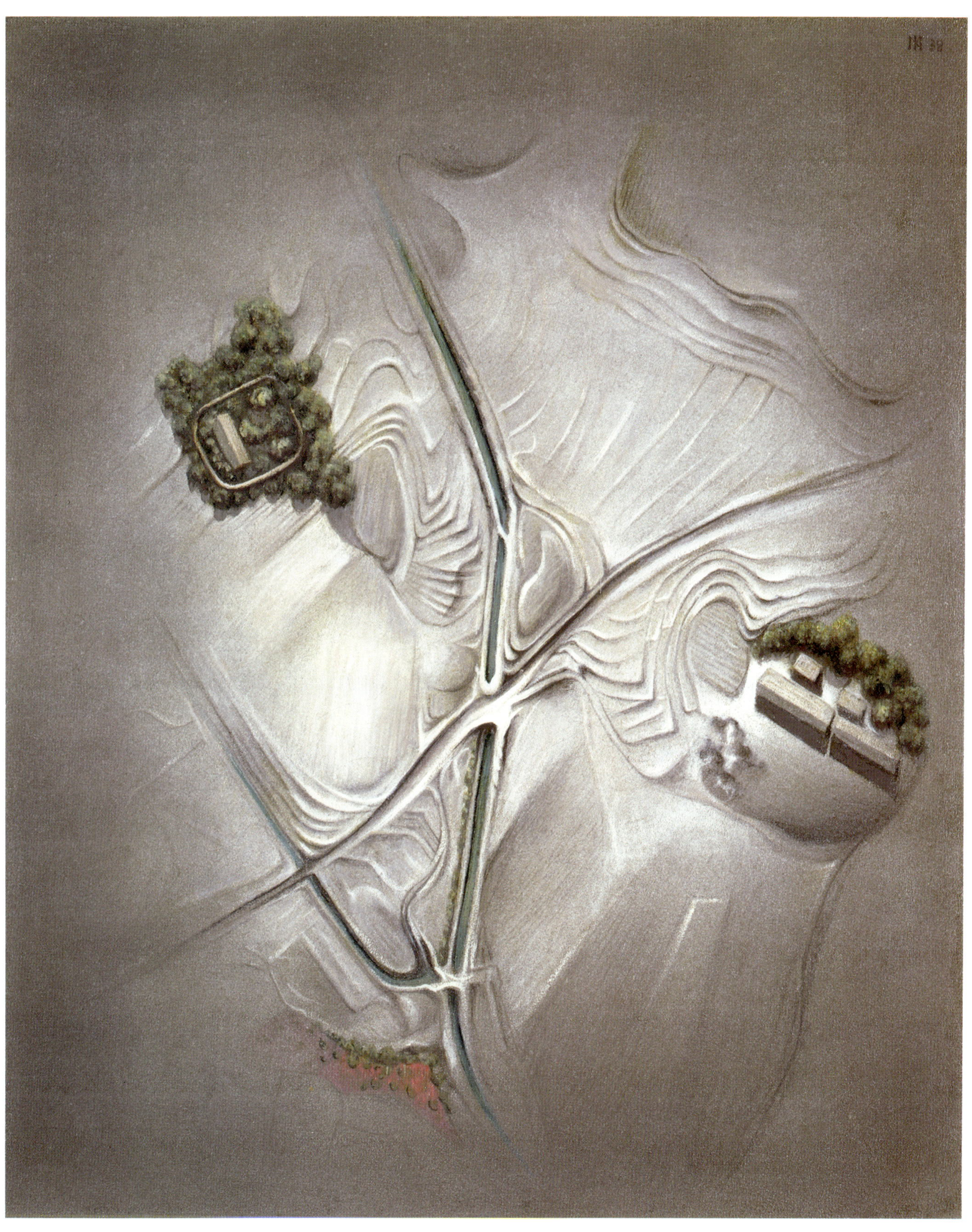

27
Kitawaki Noboru, Cities and Villages (Physiognomy Series), 1938
Oil on Canvas, 72.8 x 60.8 cm, National Museum of Modern Art, Tokyo

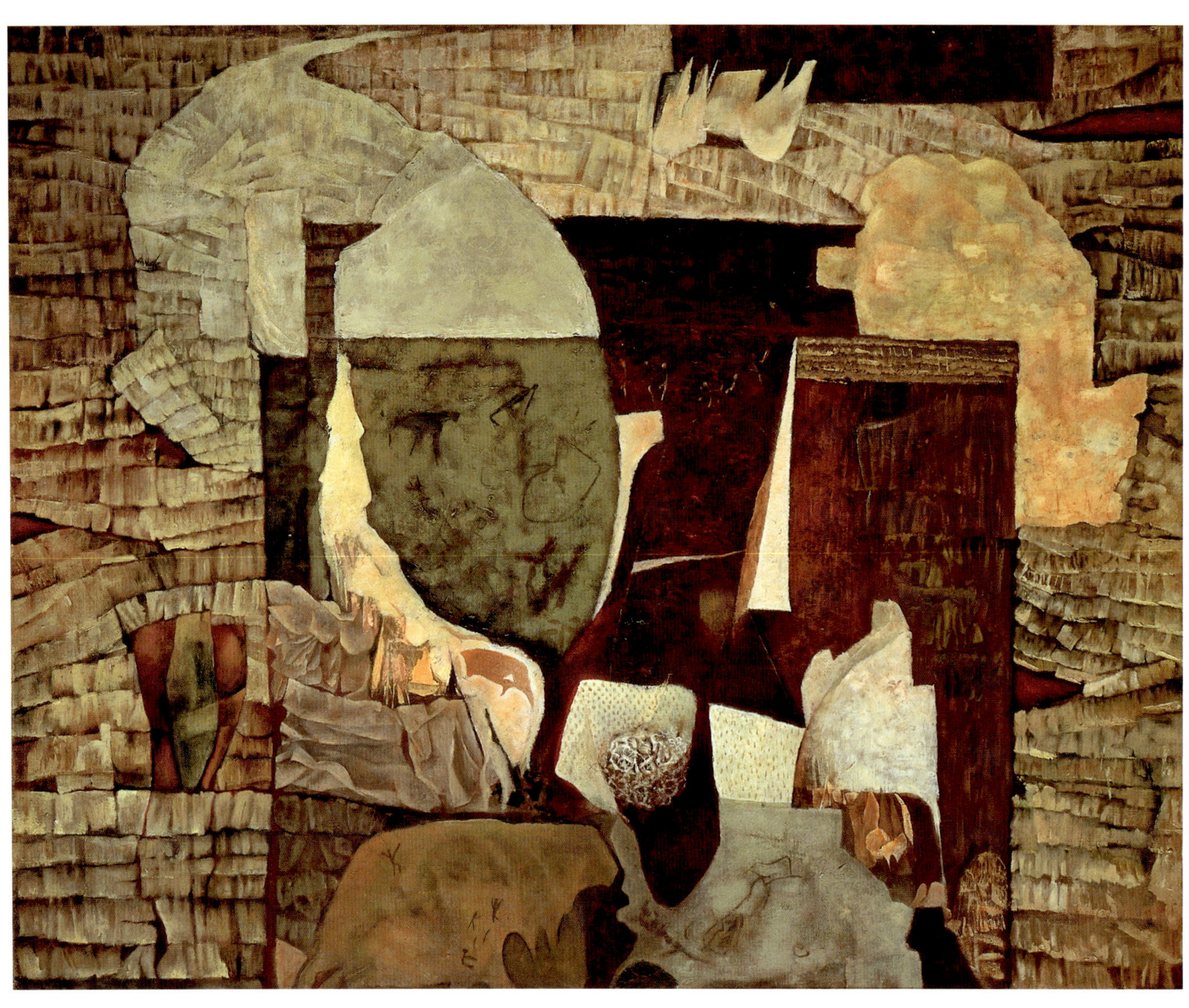

28
Katsura Yuki, Genji, 1938
Oil on Canvas, 130.8 x 162 cm (reconstructed 1979), Itabashiku Art Museum, Tokyo

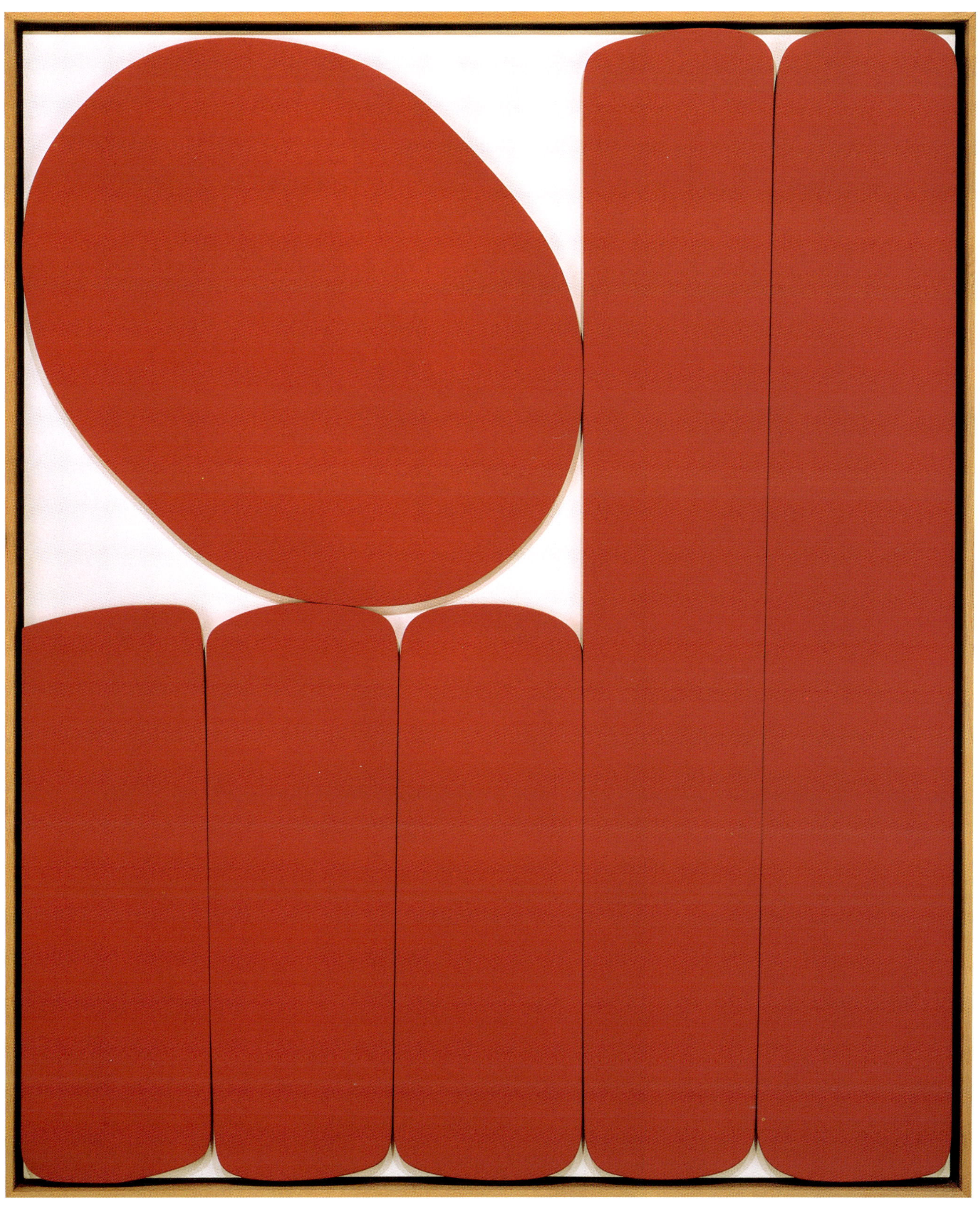

29
Saitô Yoshishige, Toro-wood, 1938
Oil, Casein on plywood, bas-relief (reconstructed 1973, acrylic on plywood), 120 x 100 cm, Yokohama Art Museum, Yokohama

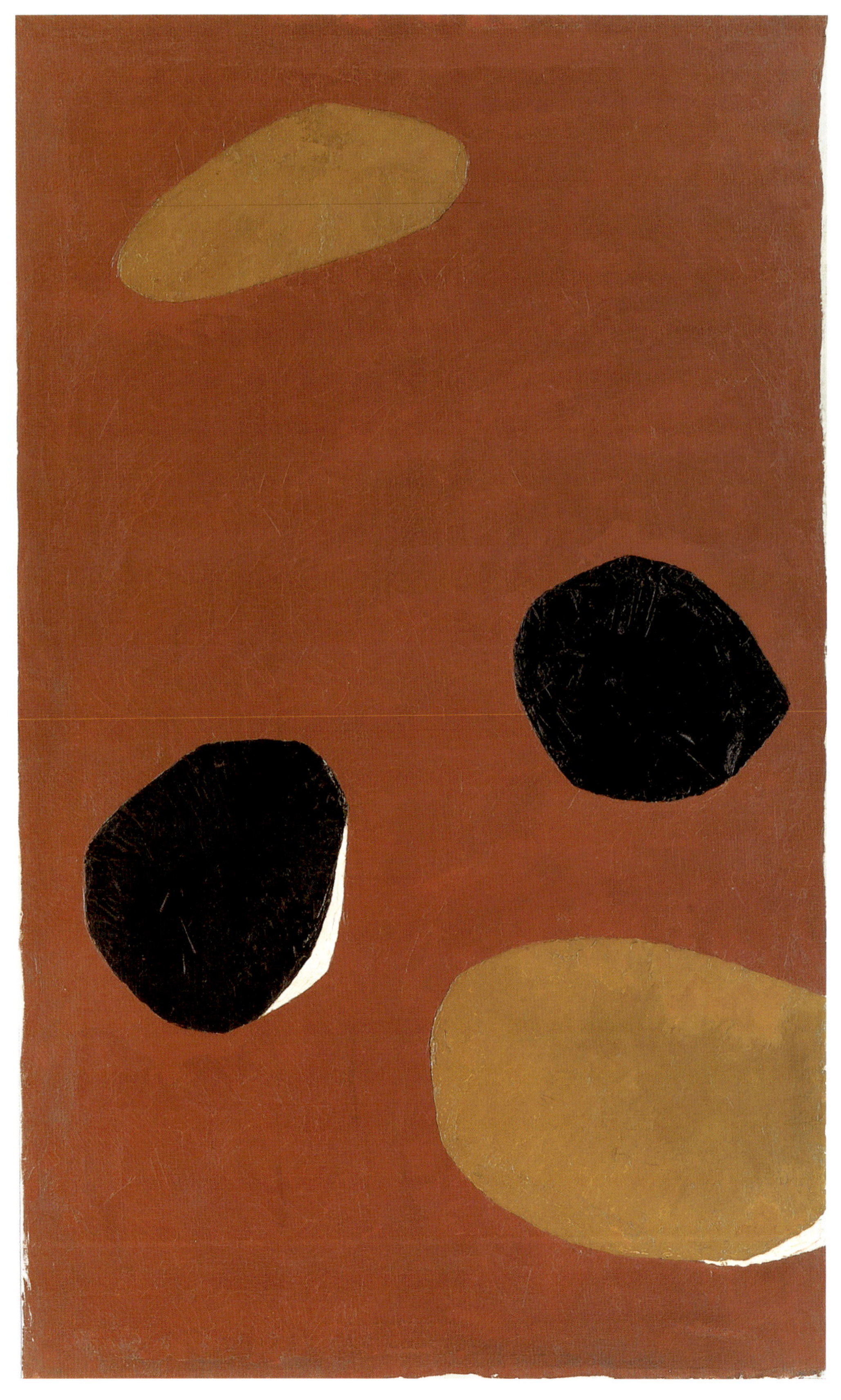

30
Yamaguchi Takeo, Work, 1940 (–1950)
Oil on Canvas, 129.8 x 79.1 cm, Nerimaku Art Museum, Tokyo

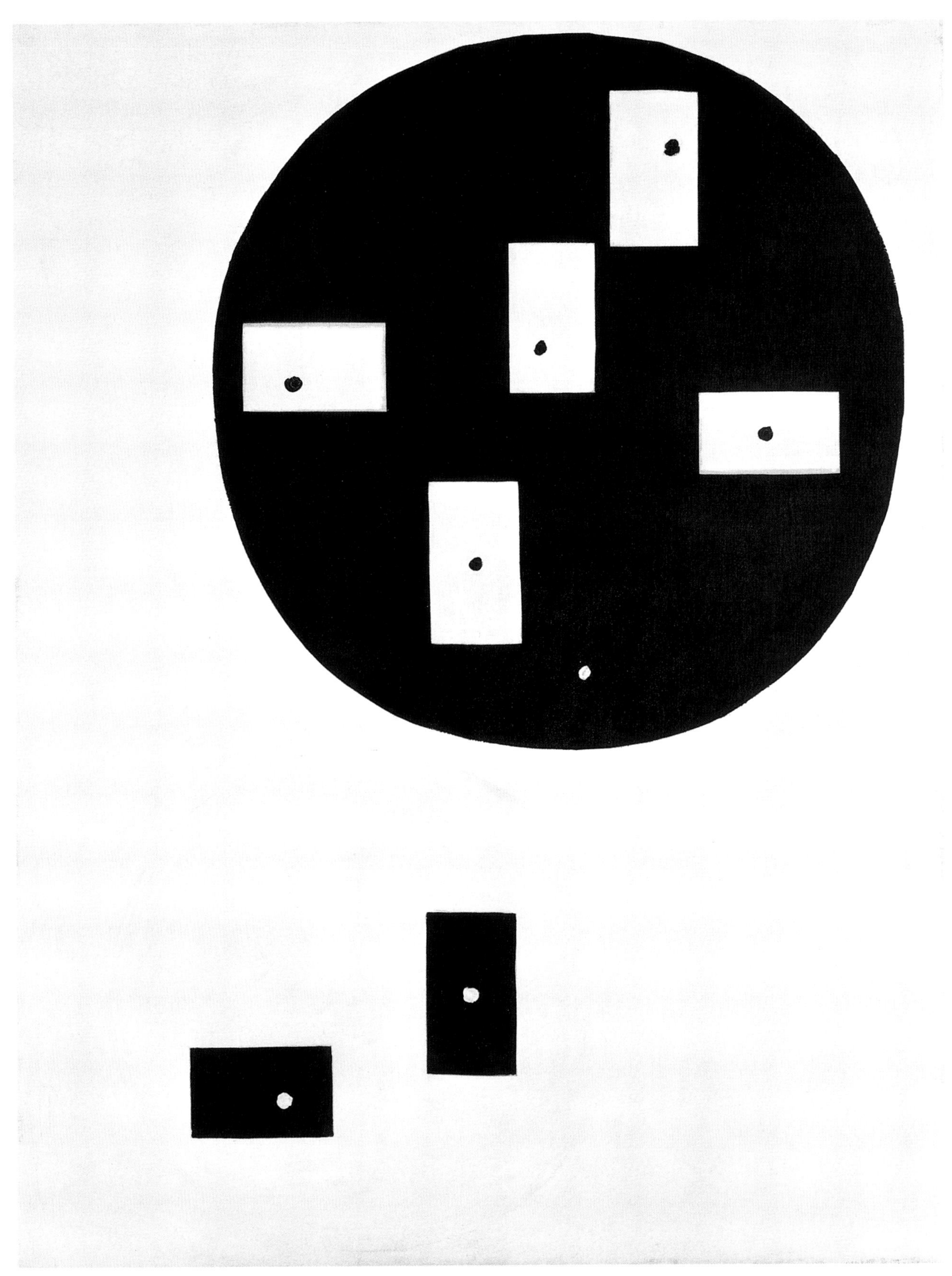

31
Onosato Toshinobu, Black and White Round, 1940
Oil on Canvas, 116 x 89.3 cm, National Museum of Modern Art, Tokyo

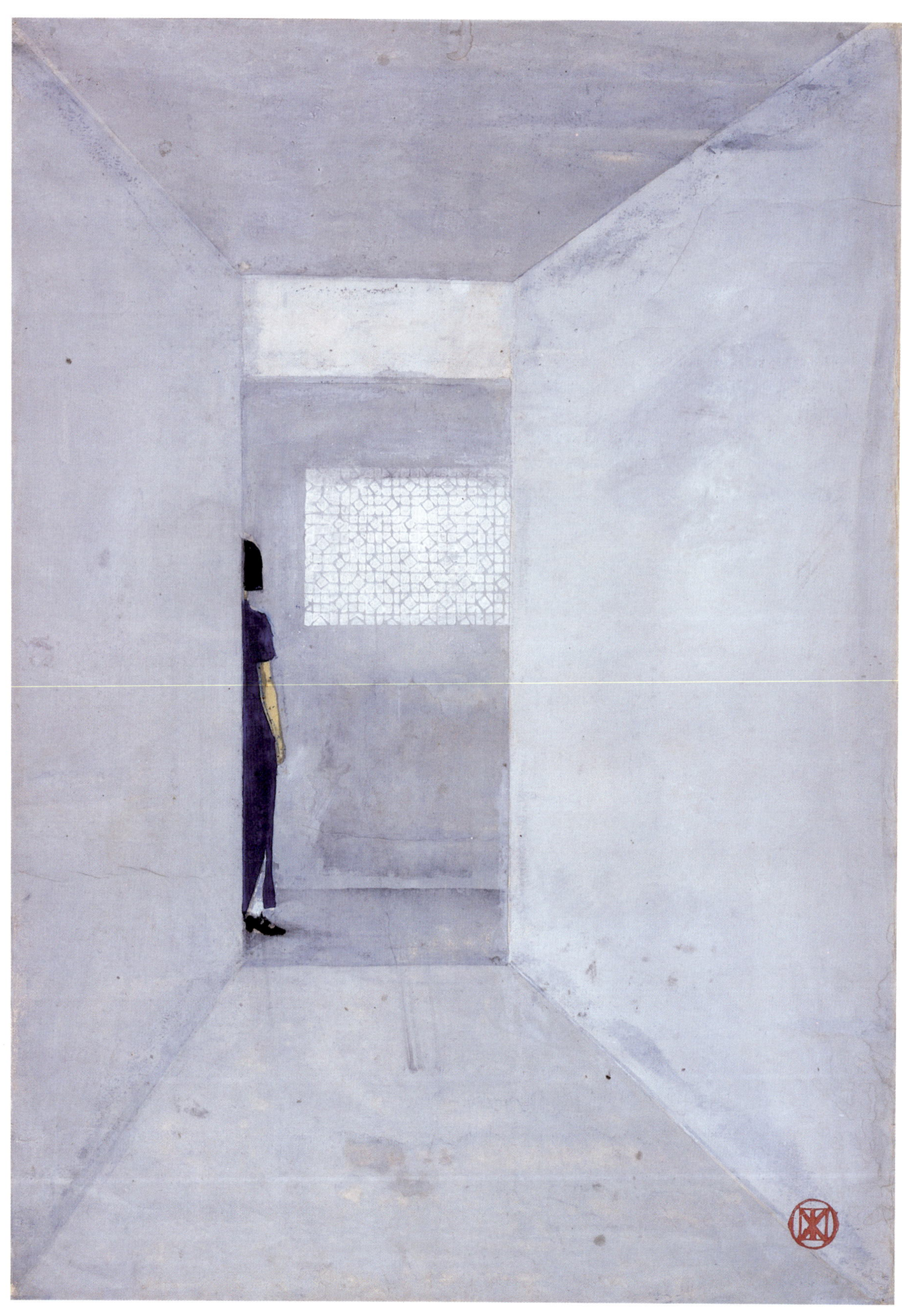

32
Onchi Kôshirô, White Walls (Scene in Suchuo), 1940
Wood Engraving, 83 x 58 cm, Municipal Art Museum, Chiba

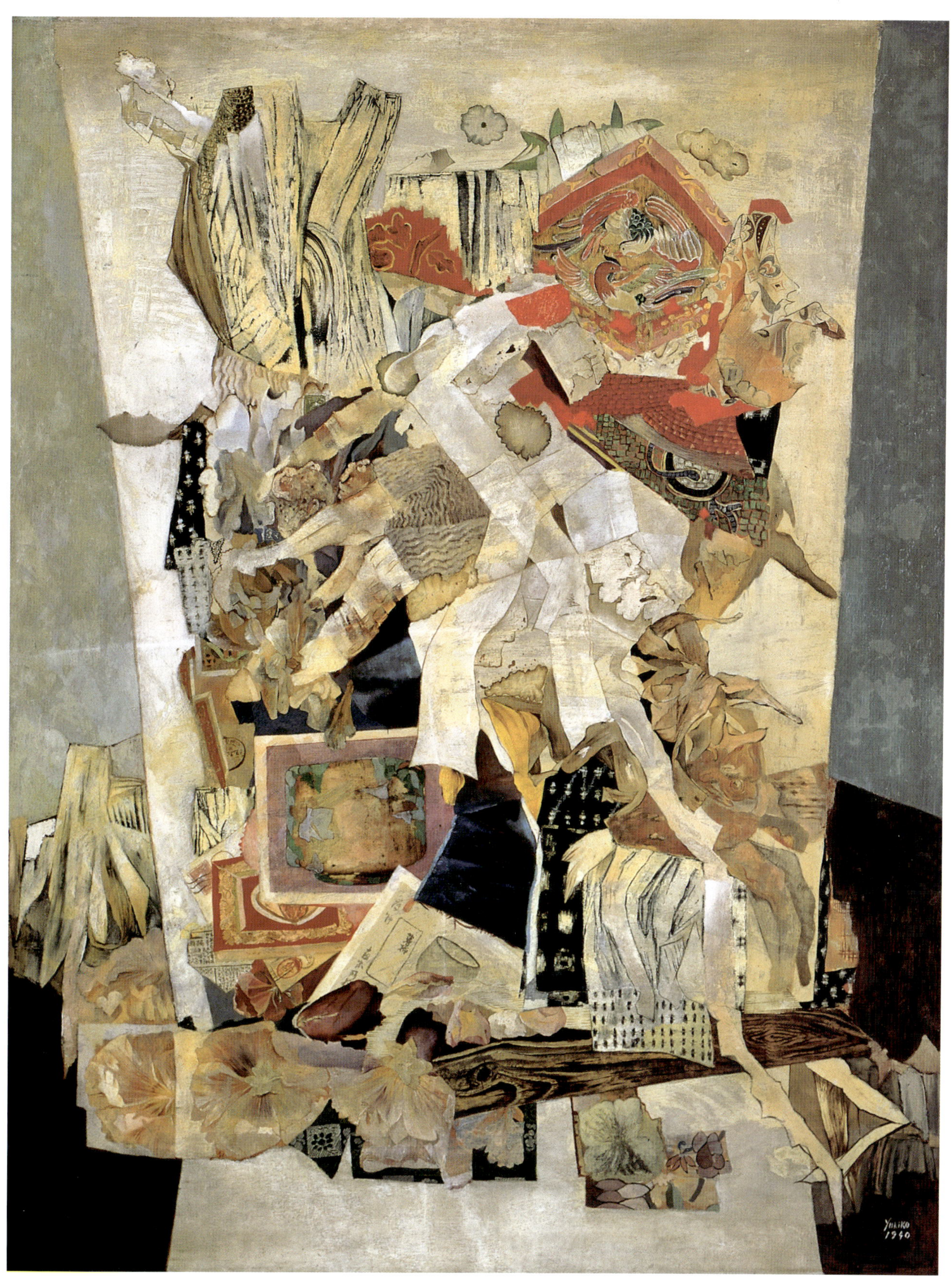

33
Katsura Yuki, Work, 1940
Oil on Canvas, 116.7 x 91.4 cm, National Museum of Modern Art, Tokyo

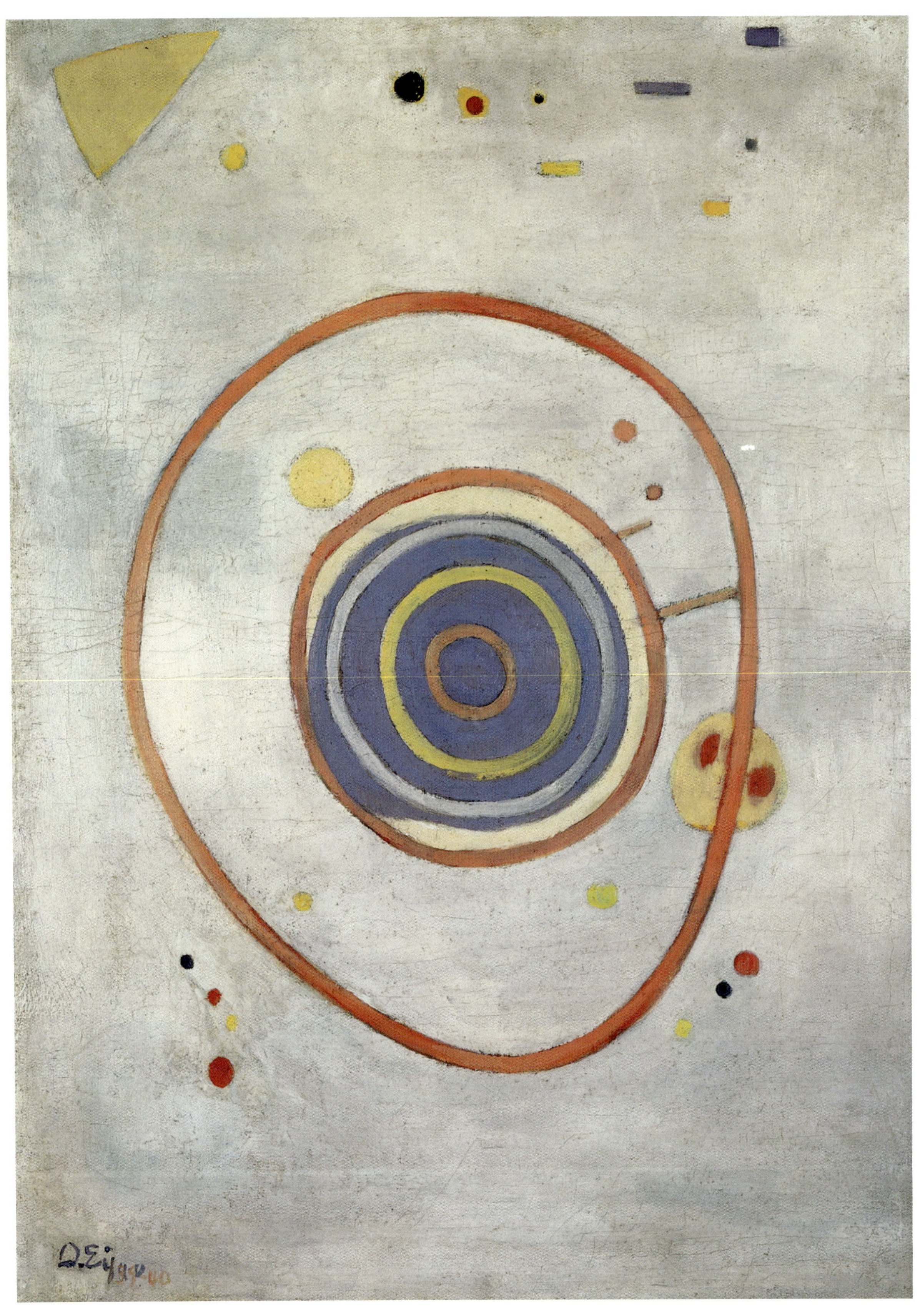

34
Ei-Kyû, Eg, Gentle Balance, 1940
Oil on Canvas, 72.5 x 52.3 cm, Municipal Art Museum, Kitakyûshu

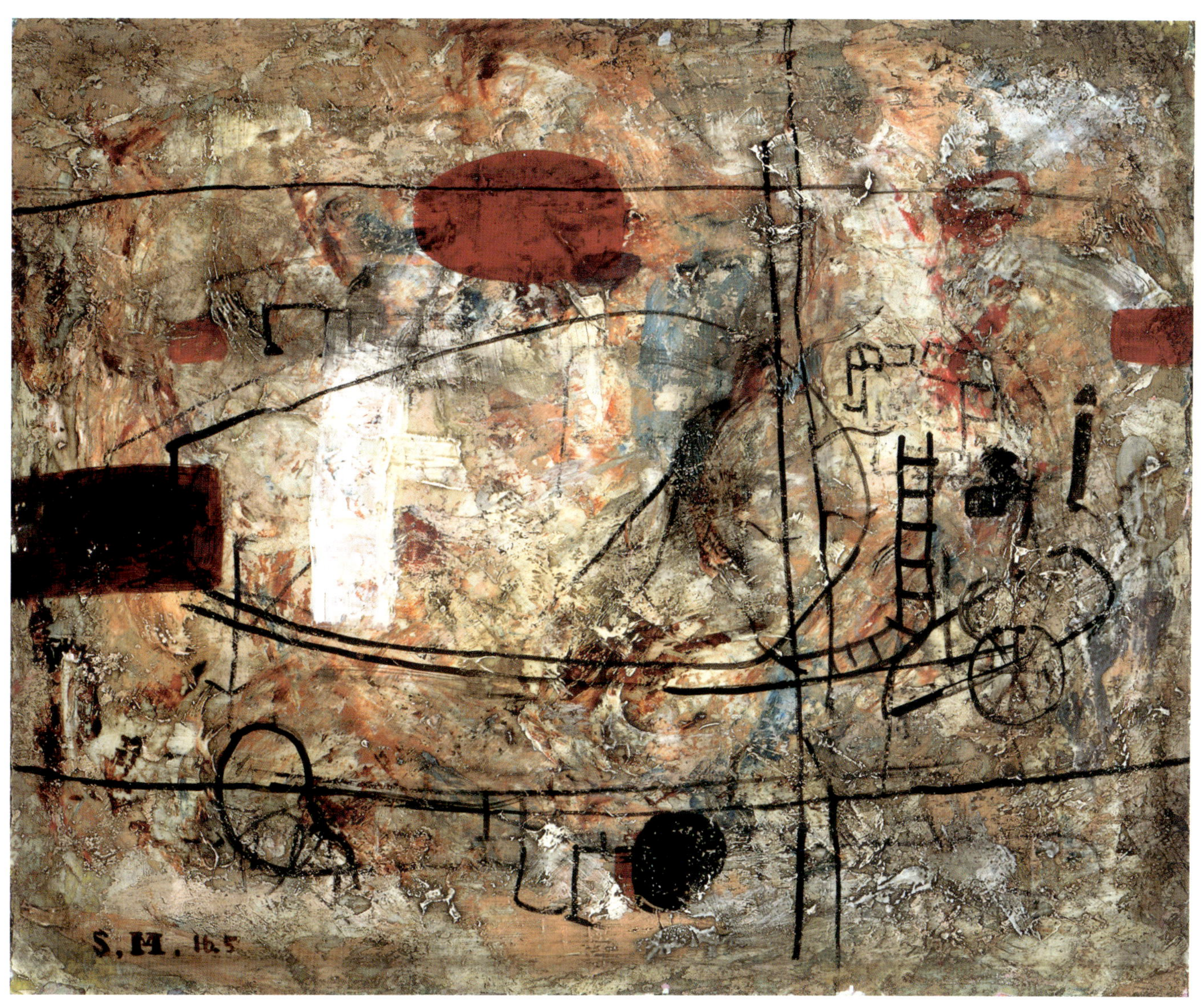

35
Matsumoto Shunsuke, Composition, 1941
Oil on Board, 45.5 x 60 cm, Kanagawa Prefecture Museum of Modern Art, Kamakura

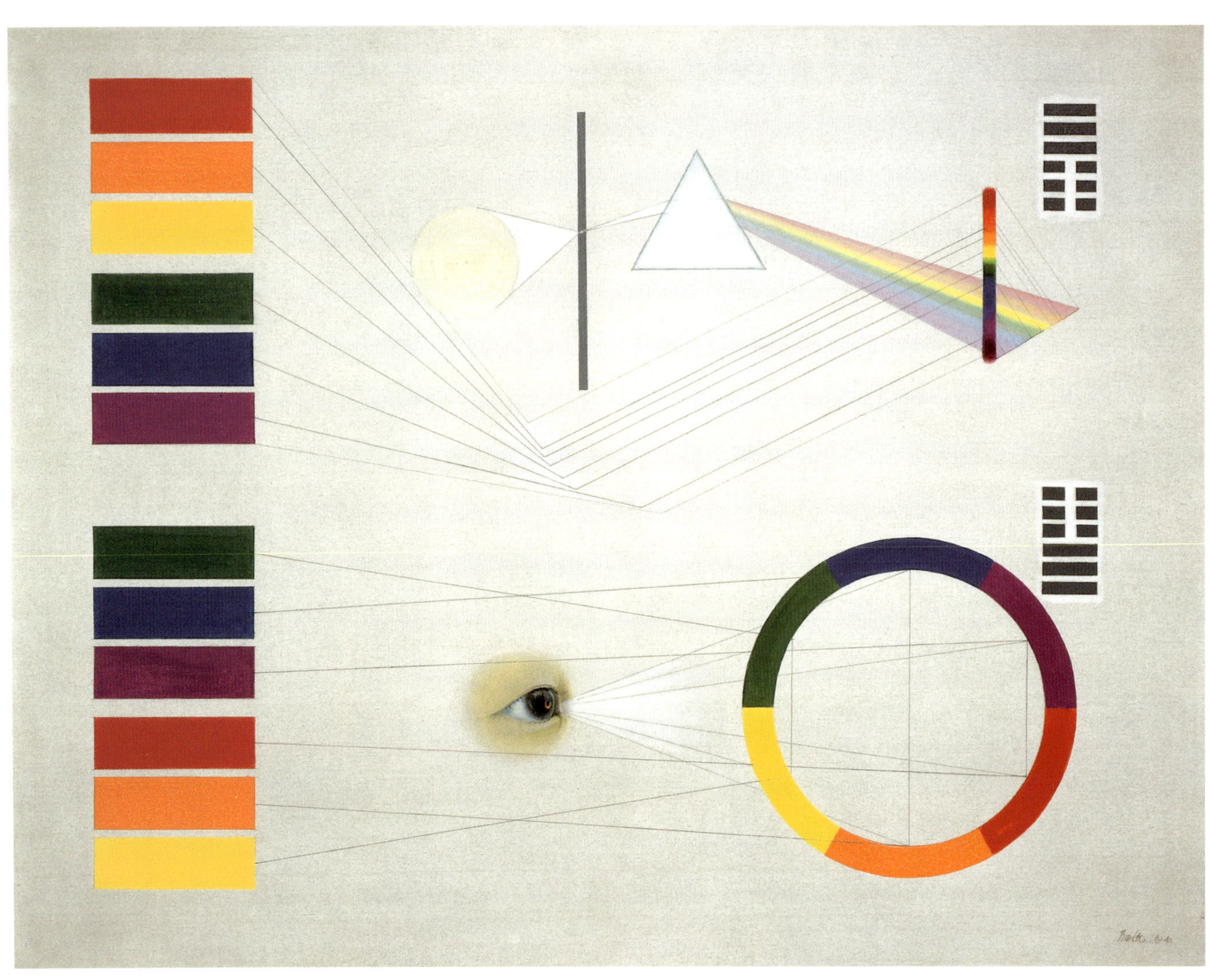

36
Kitawaki Noboru, Analysis of the Chinese Divination Sign from the Chou Period, 1941
Oil on Canvas, 90 x 116 cm, Municipal Art Museum, Kyoto

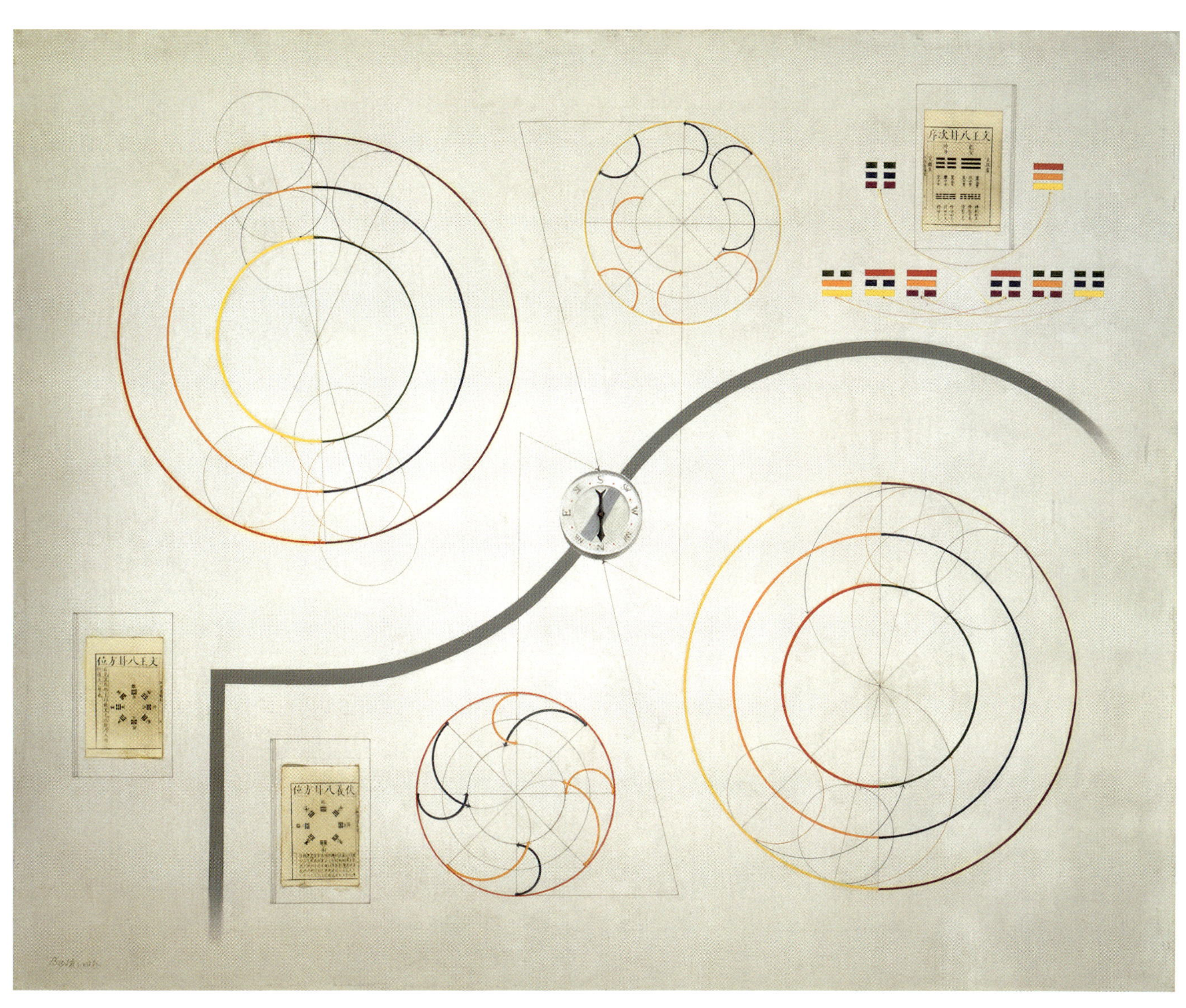

37

Kitawaki Noboru, Diagram of the Chou Divination (Eight Phenomena), 1941
Oil on Canvas, 129.5 x 162.1 cm, National Museum of Modern Art, Tokyo

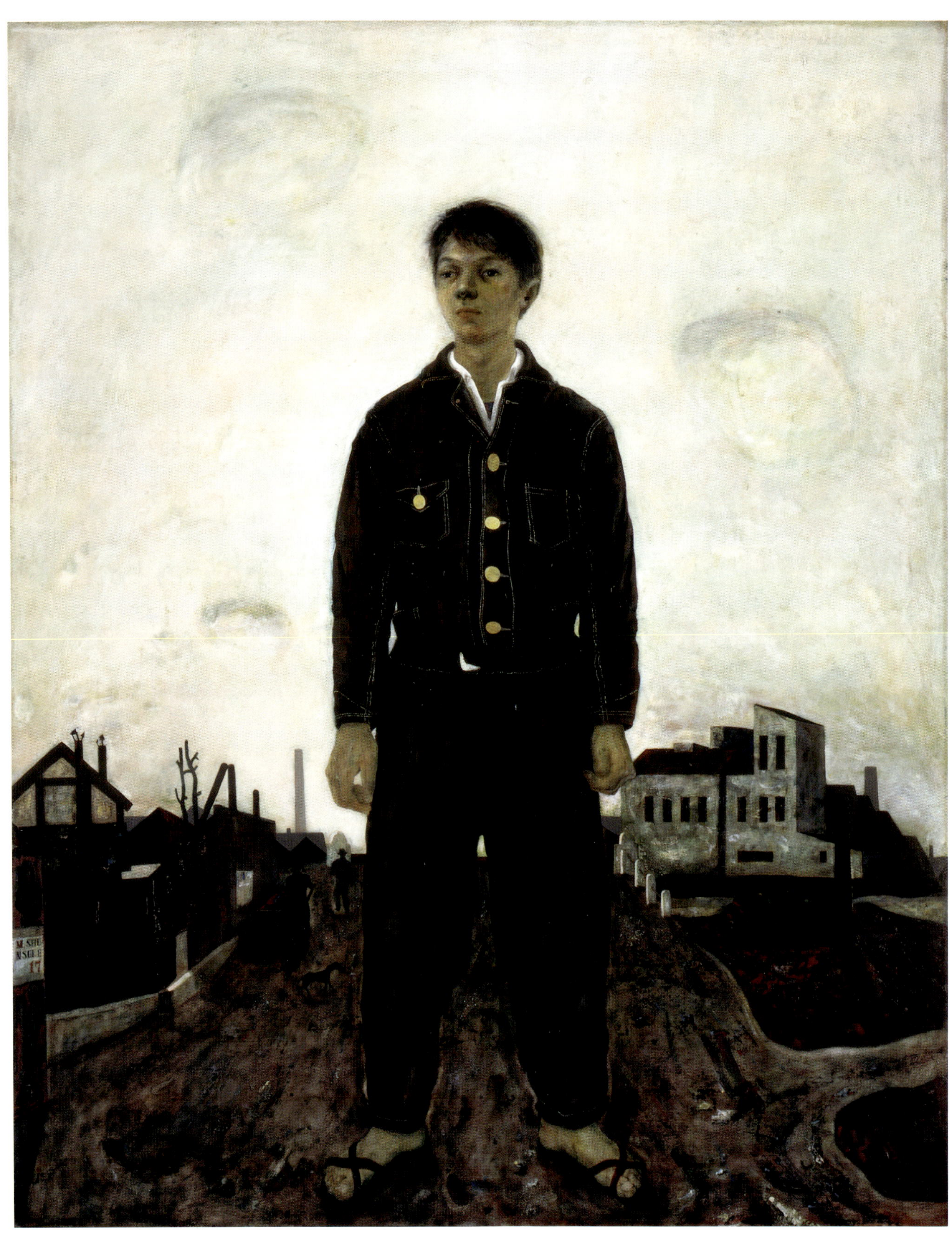

38
Matsumoto Shunsuke, Standing Figure, 1942
Oil on Canvas, 162 x 130.5 cm, Kanagawa Prefecture Museum of Modern Art, Kamakura

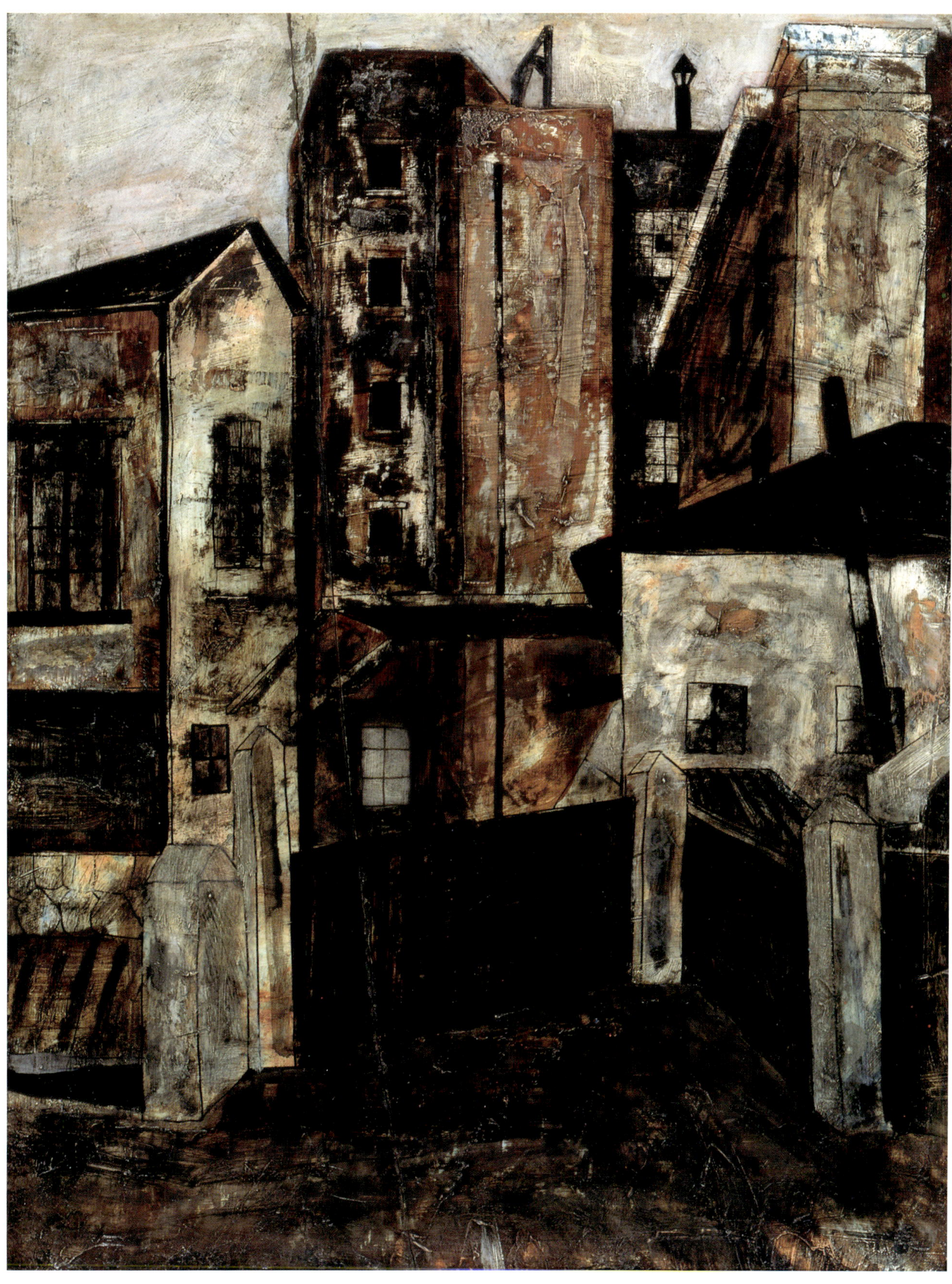

39
Matsumoto Shunsuke, Workshop, 1942
Oil on Board, 41 x 31.5 cm, Kanagawa Prefecture Museum of Modern Art, Kamakura

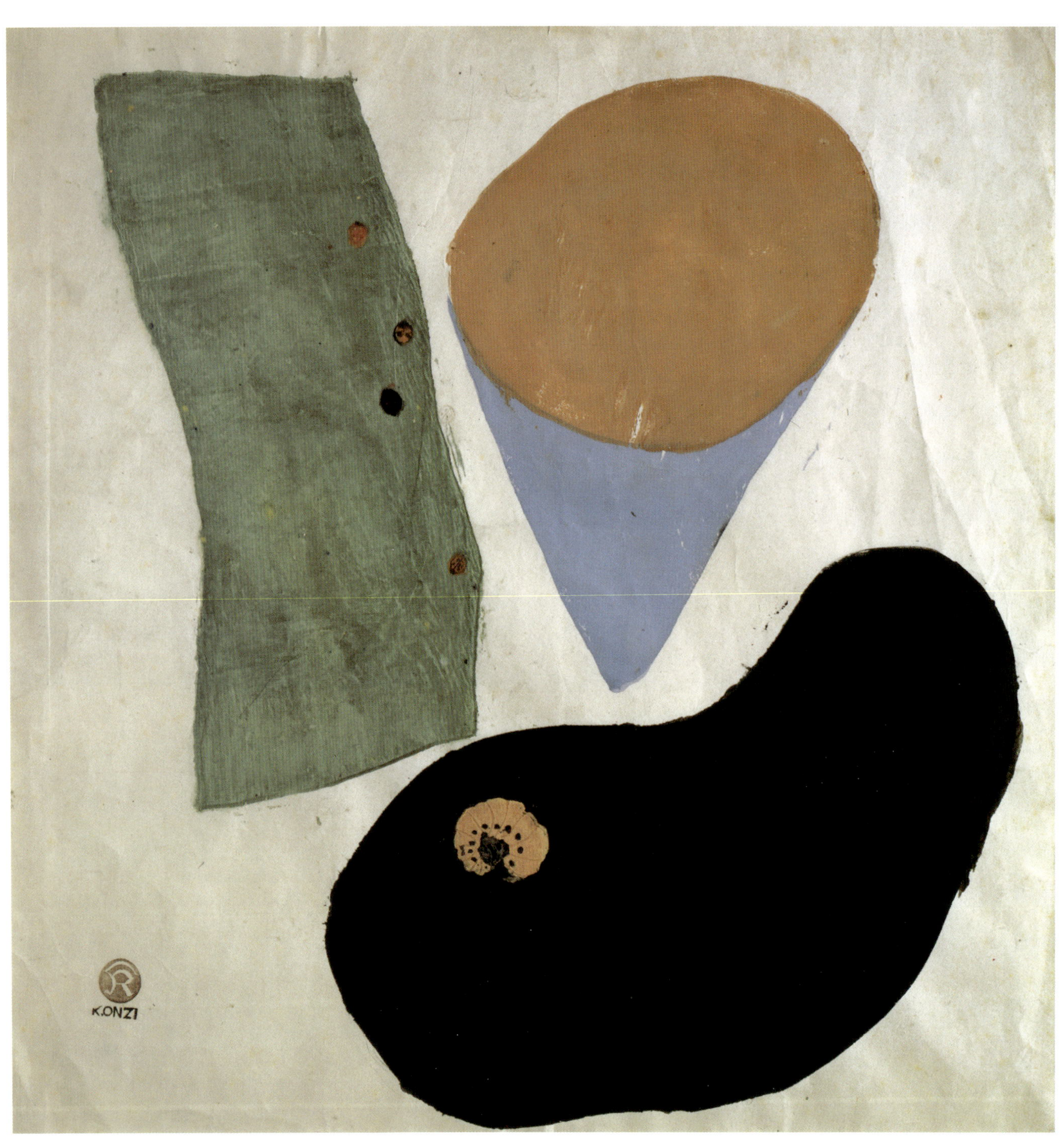

40
Onchi Kôshirô, Spring Etude, Poem No. 3, 1944
Colored Wood Engraving, 41.6 x 37.5 cm, National Museum of Modern Art, Tokyo

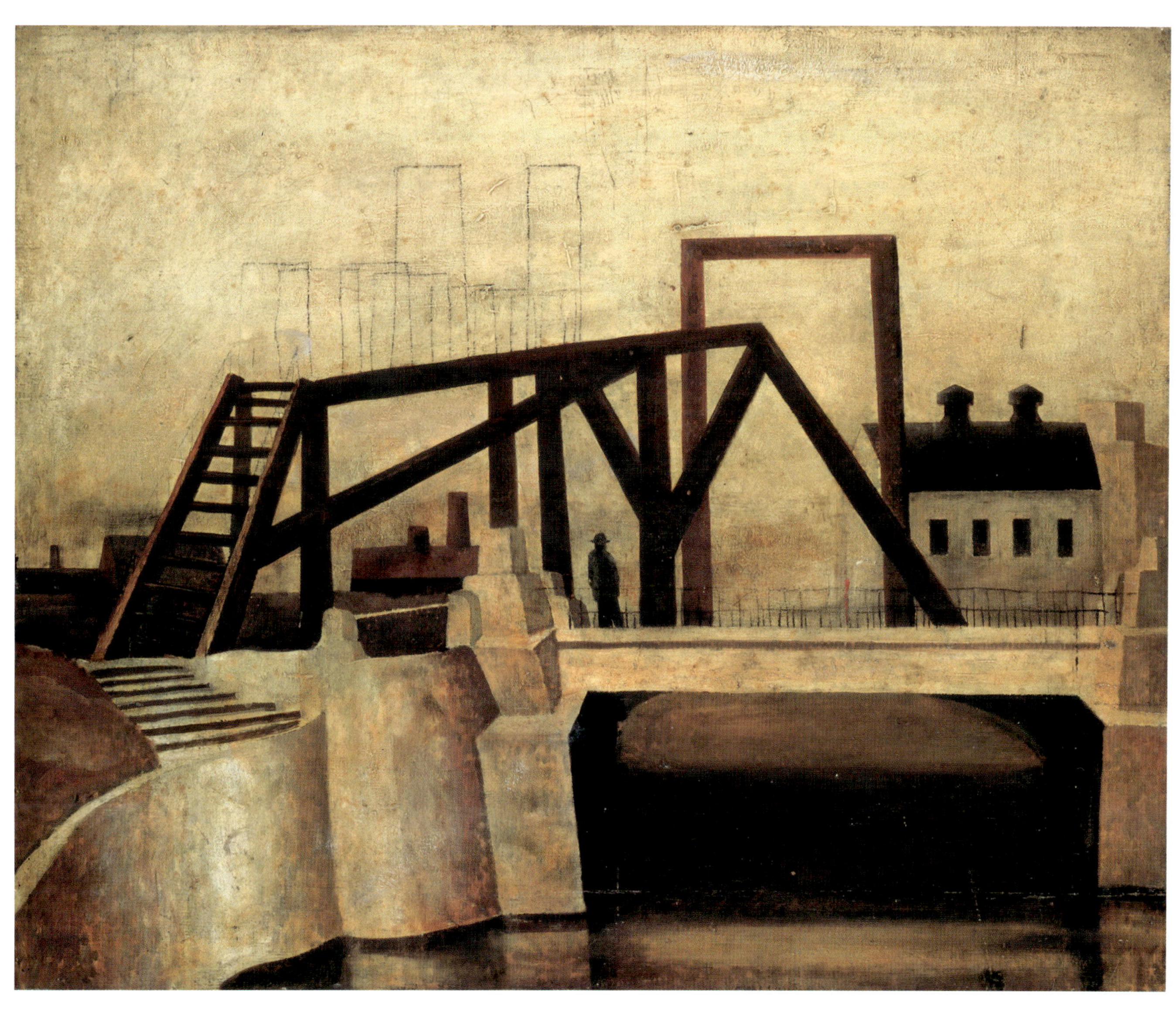

41
Matsumoto Shunsuke, Bridge in Y City, 1944
Oil on Canvas, 65 x 80.5 cm, Matsumoto Kan

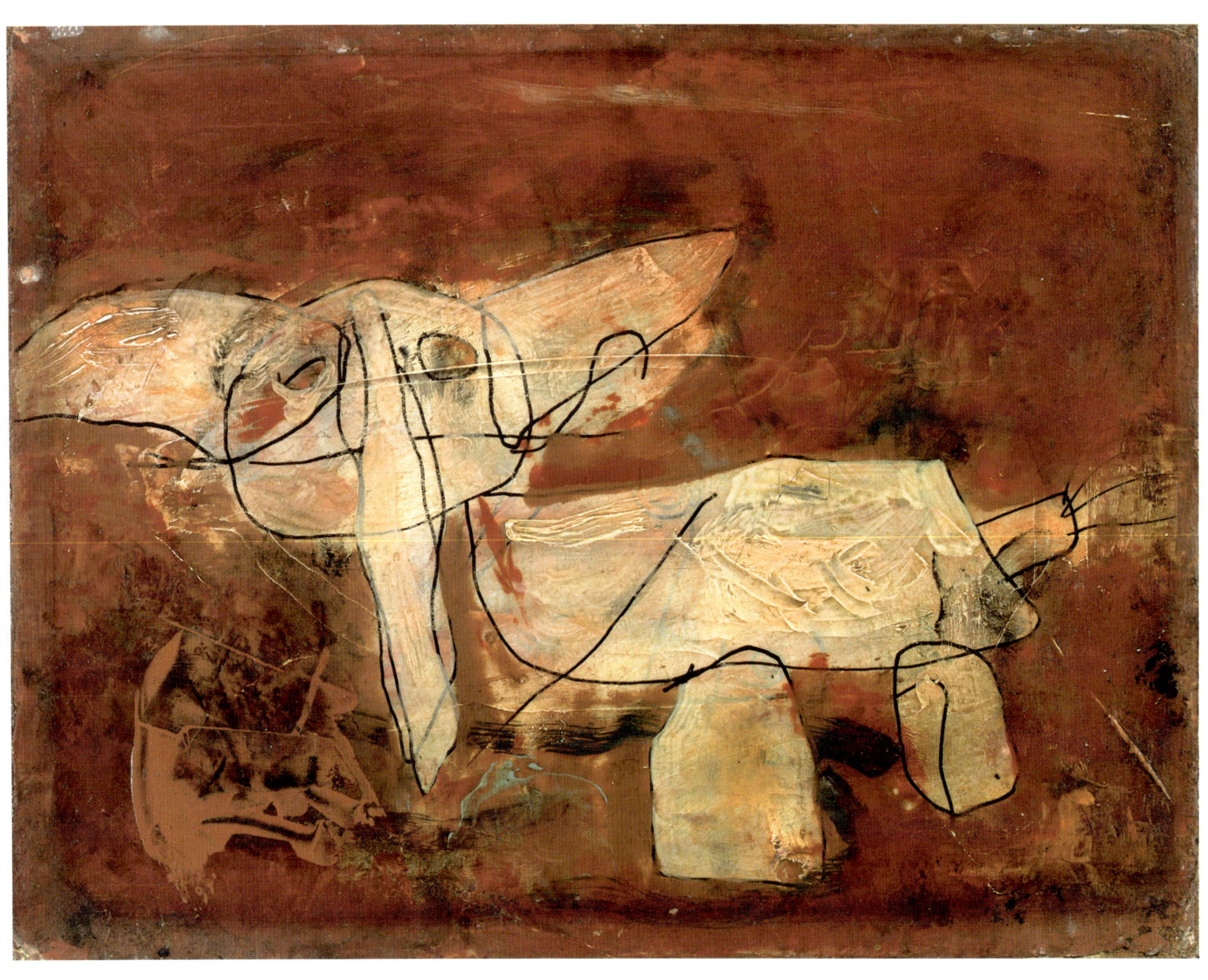

42
Matsumoto Shunsuke, Elephant, 1943–1946
Oil on Canvas, 14 x 31.5 cm, Kanagawa Prefecture Museum of Modern Art, Kamakura

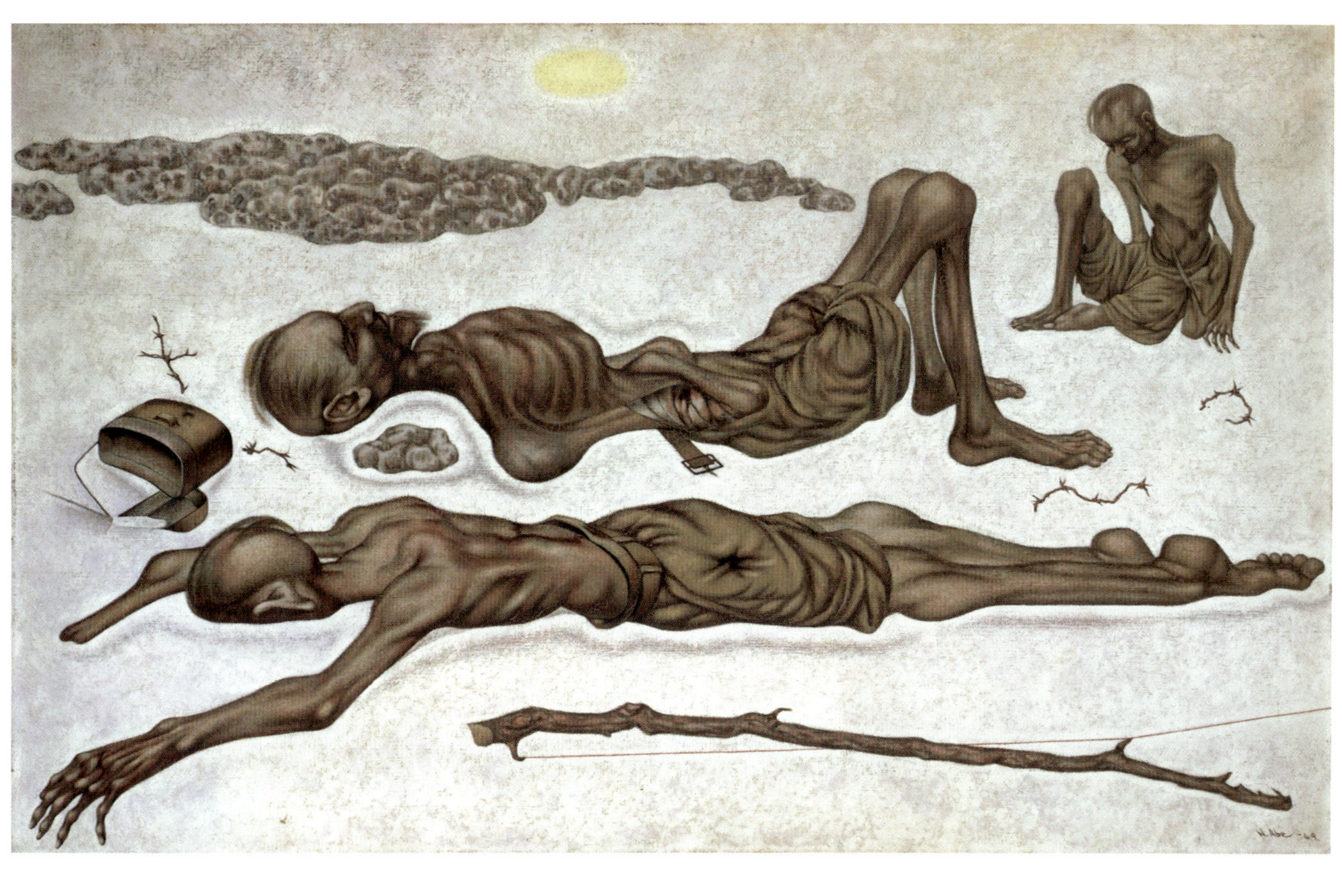

43
Abe Nobuya, Hunger, 1949
Oil on Canvas, 80 x 130 cm, Kanagawa Prefecture Museum of Modern Art, Kamakura

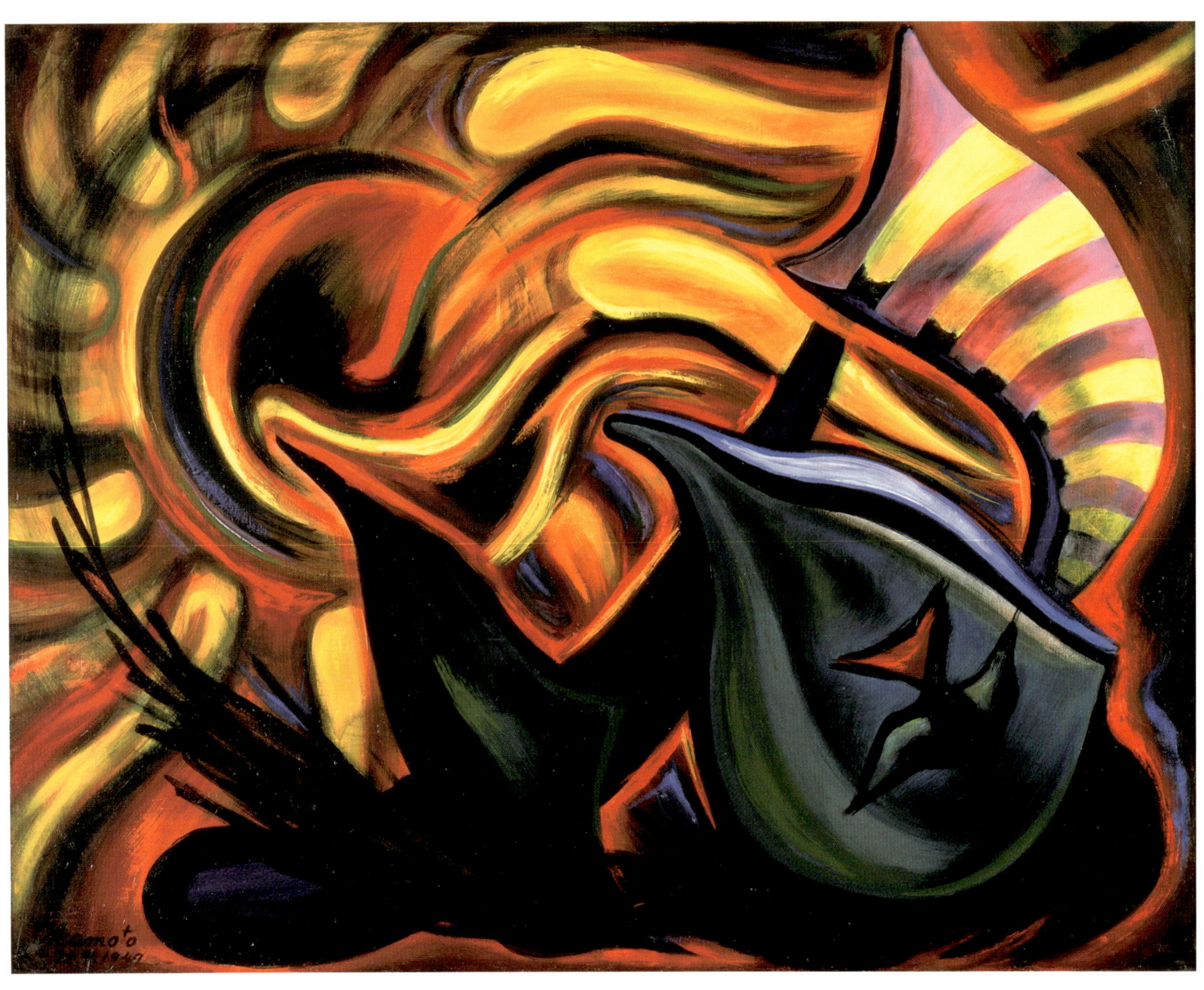

44

Okamoto Tarô, Black Sun, 1949

Oil on Canvas, 91.3 x 117 cm, Okamoto Tarô Art Museum, Kawasaki

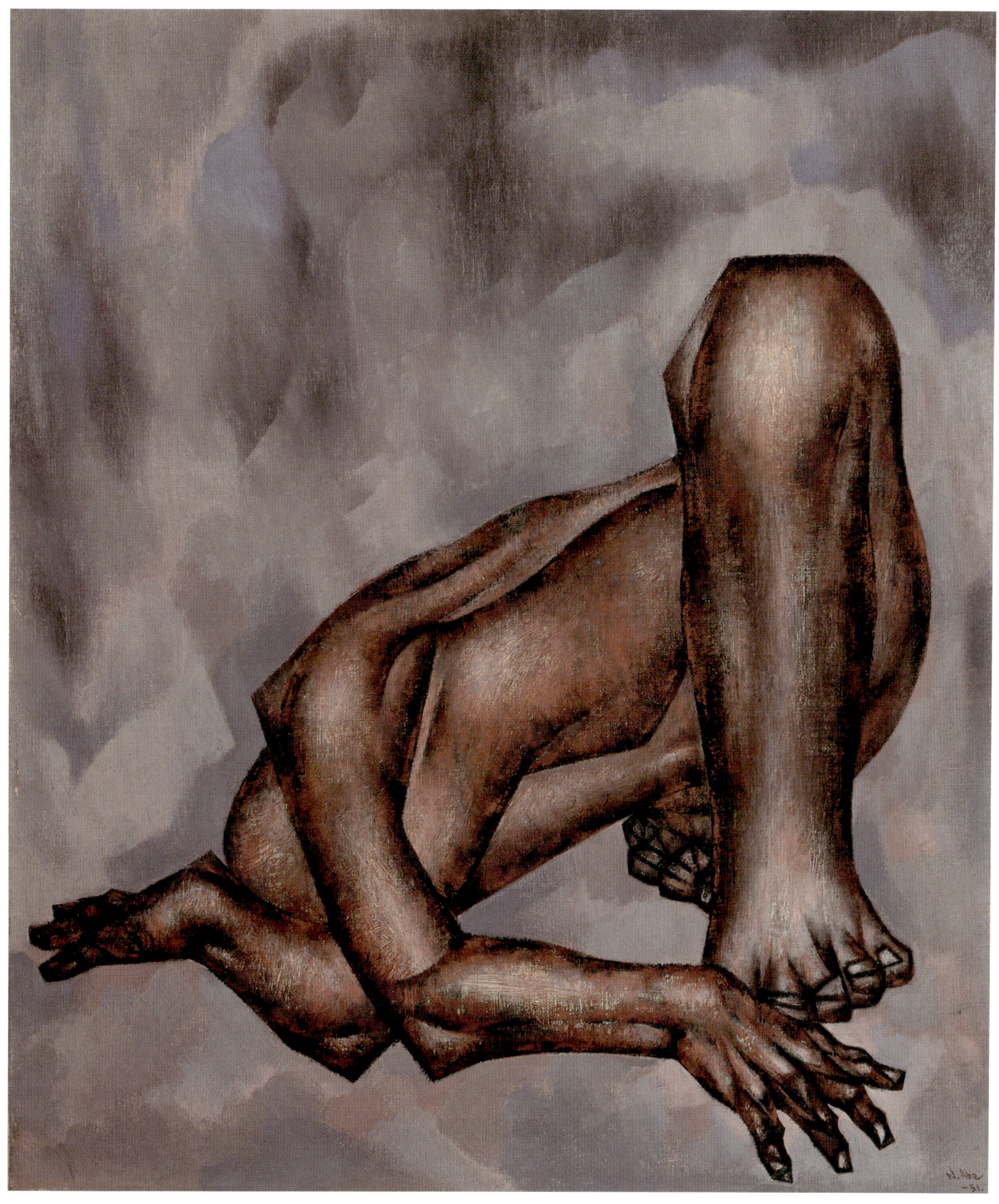

45
Abe Nobuya, Human Figure, 1951
Oil on Canvas, 72 x 61 cm, Niigata Prefecture Museum for Modern Art, Nagaoka

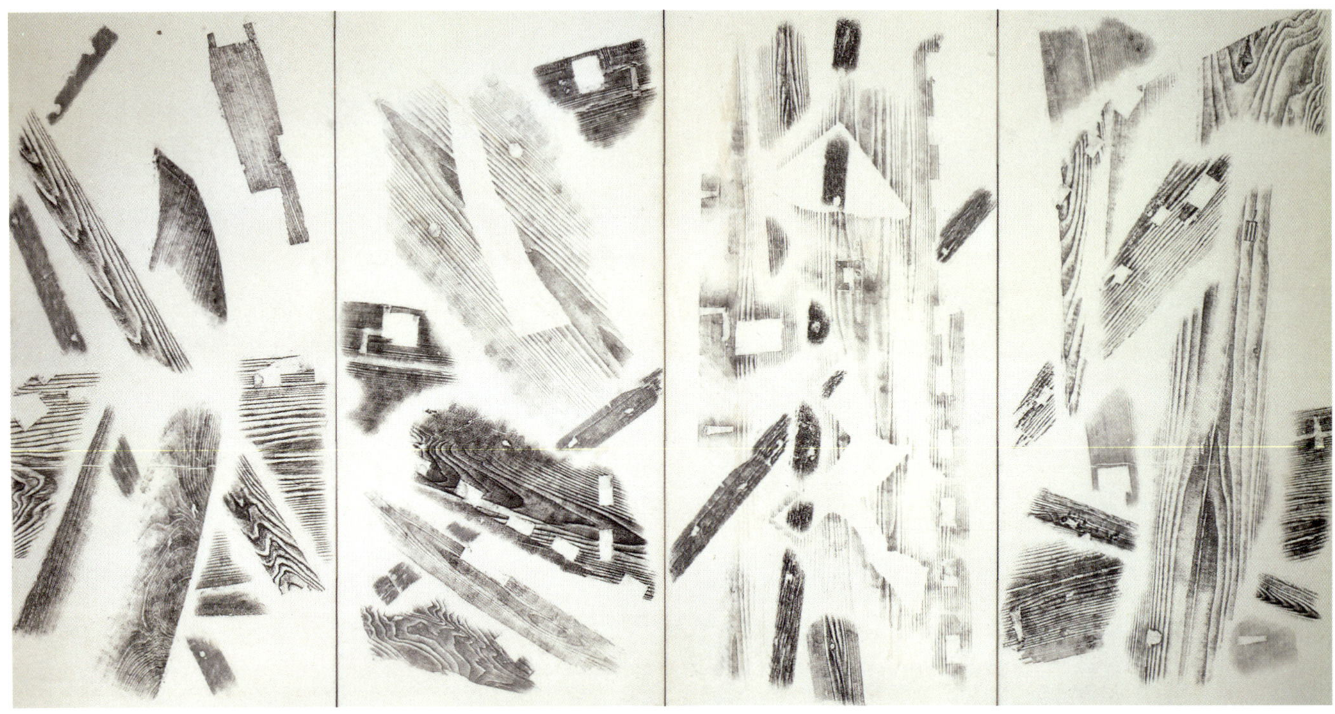

46
Hasegawa Saburô, Rhapsody in a Fishing Village, 1952
Four-part Folding Screen, Frottage, 167.8 x 266.4 cm, National Museum of Modern Art, Tokyo

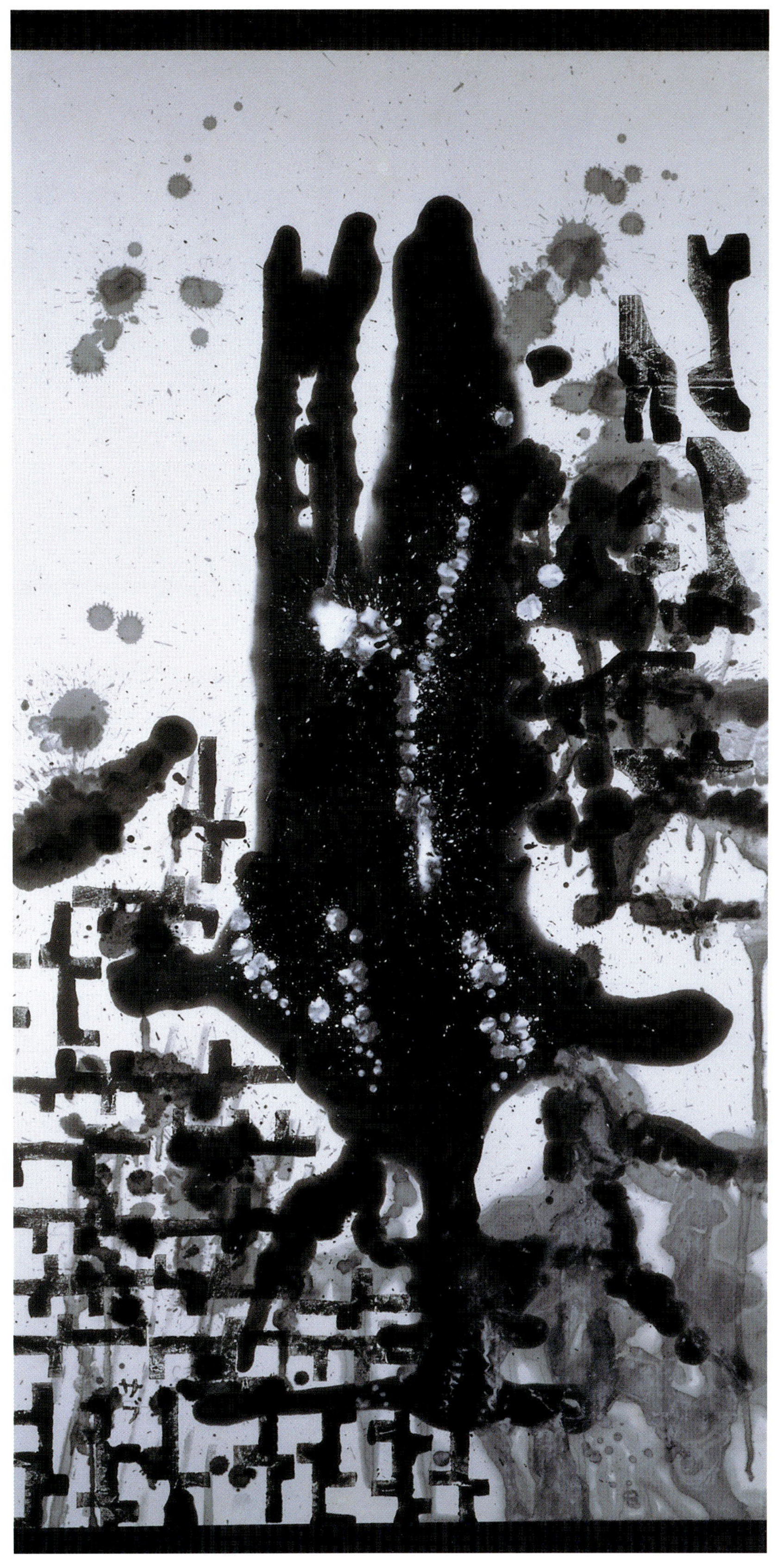

47
Hasegawa Saburô, Non-Figure, 1953
Indian Ink on Paper, 129.5 x 69.7 cm, Hyôgo Prefecture Museum of Modern Art, Kobe

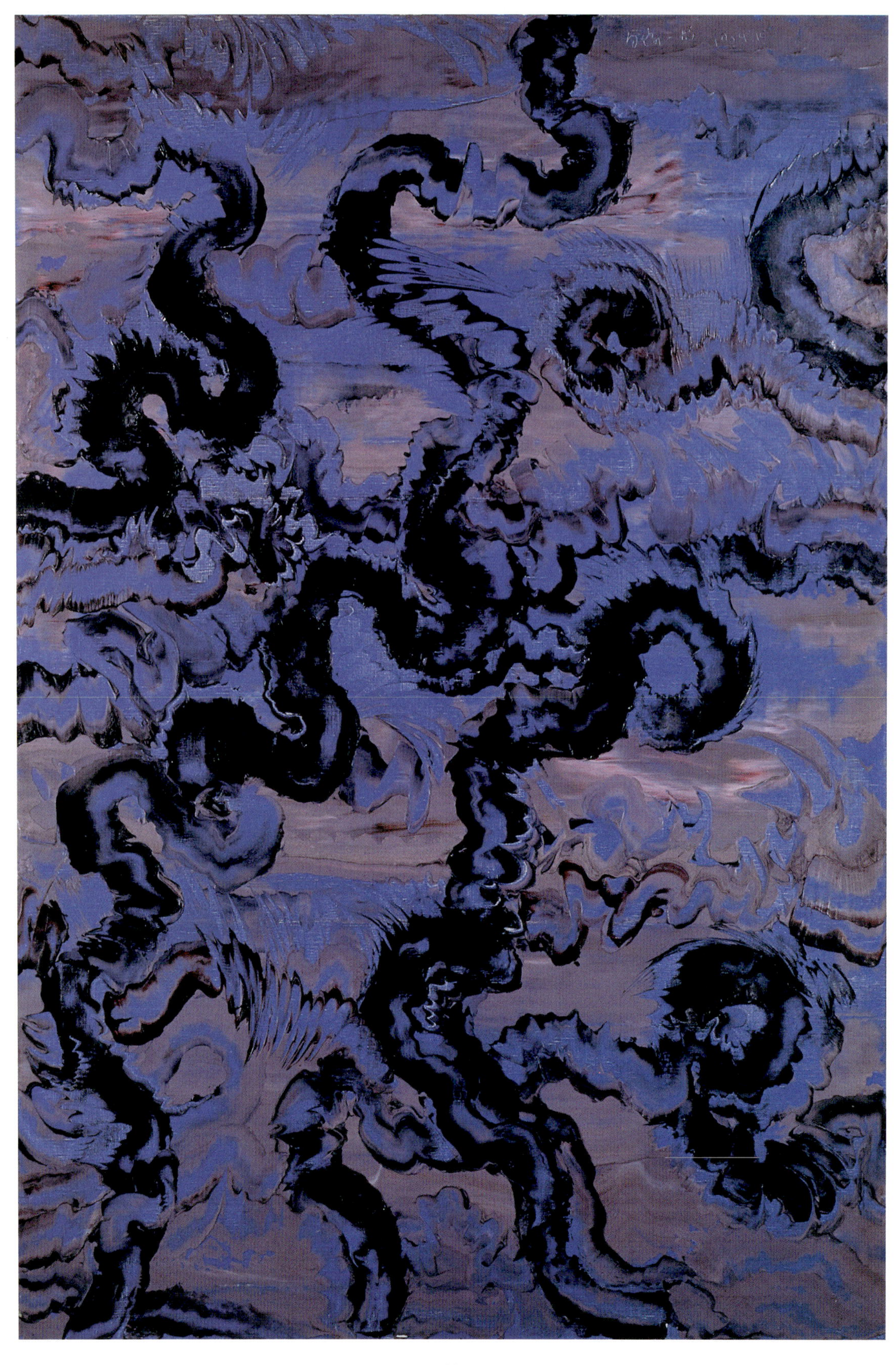

48
Shiraga Kazuo, (Worm's) Crawl, 1954
Oil on Canvas, 116 x 80.5 cm, Hyôgo Prefecture Museum of Modern Art, Kobe

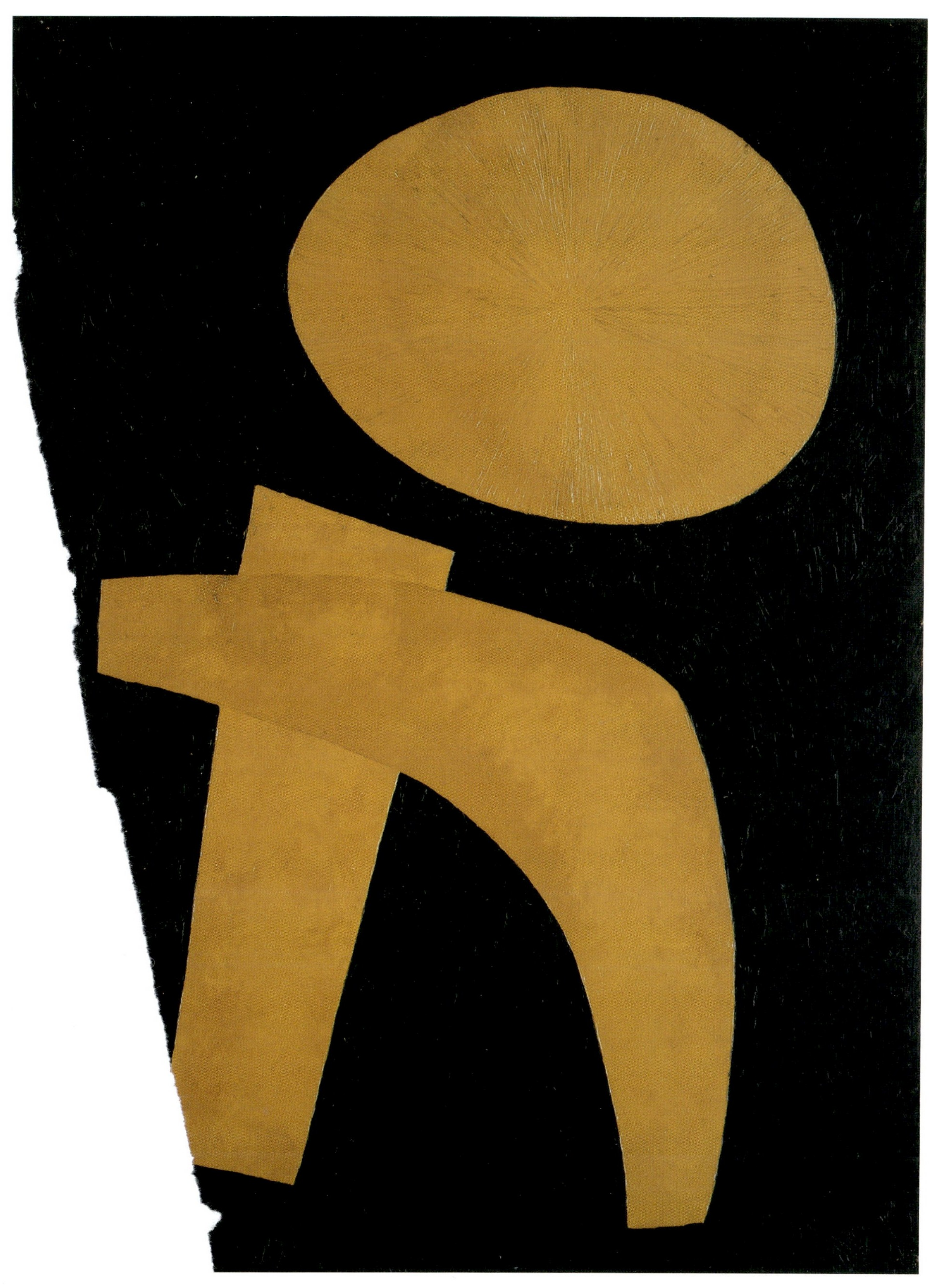

49
Yamaguchi Takeo, Work (Form), 1954
Oil on Plywood, 121 x 91.5 cm, Mainichi shimbun Newspaper

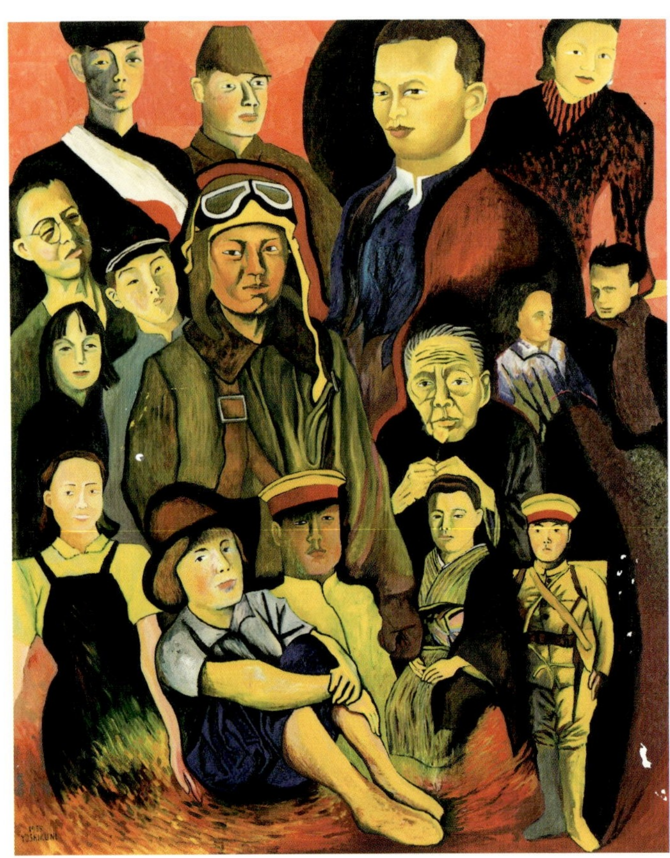

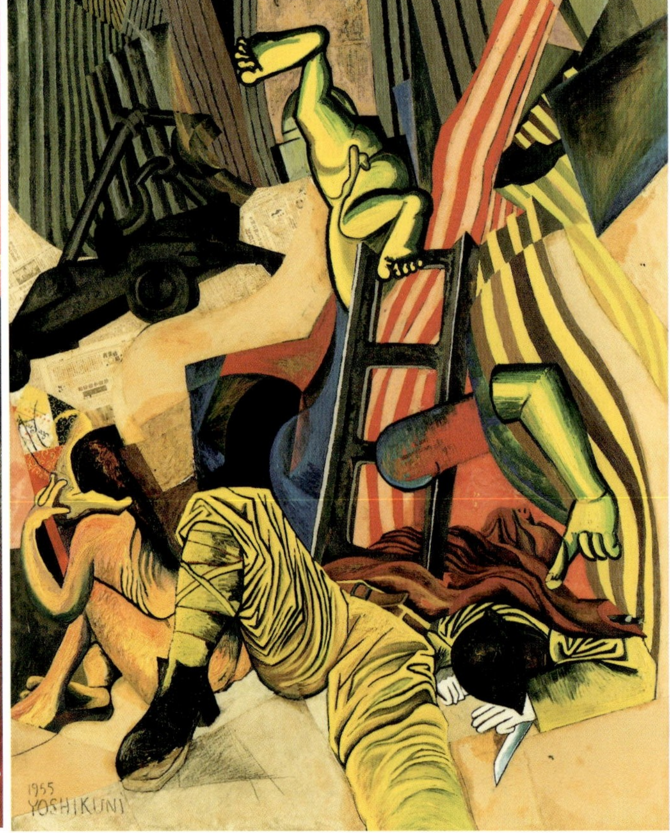

50a/b
Iida Yoshikuni, War A & B, 1955
Oil on Canvas, each one 162.8 x 130.5 cm, Meguroku Art Museum, Tokyo

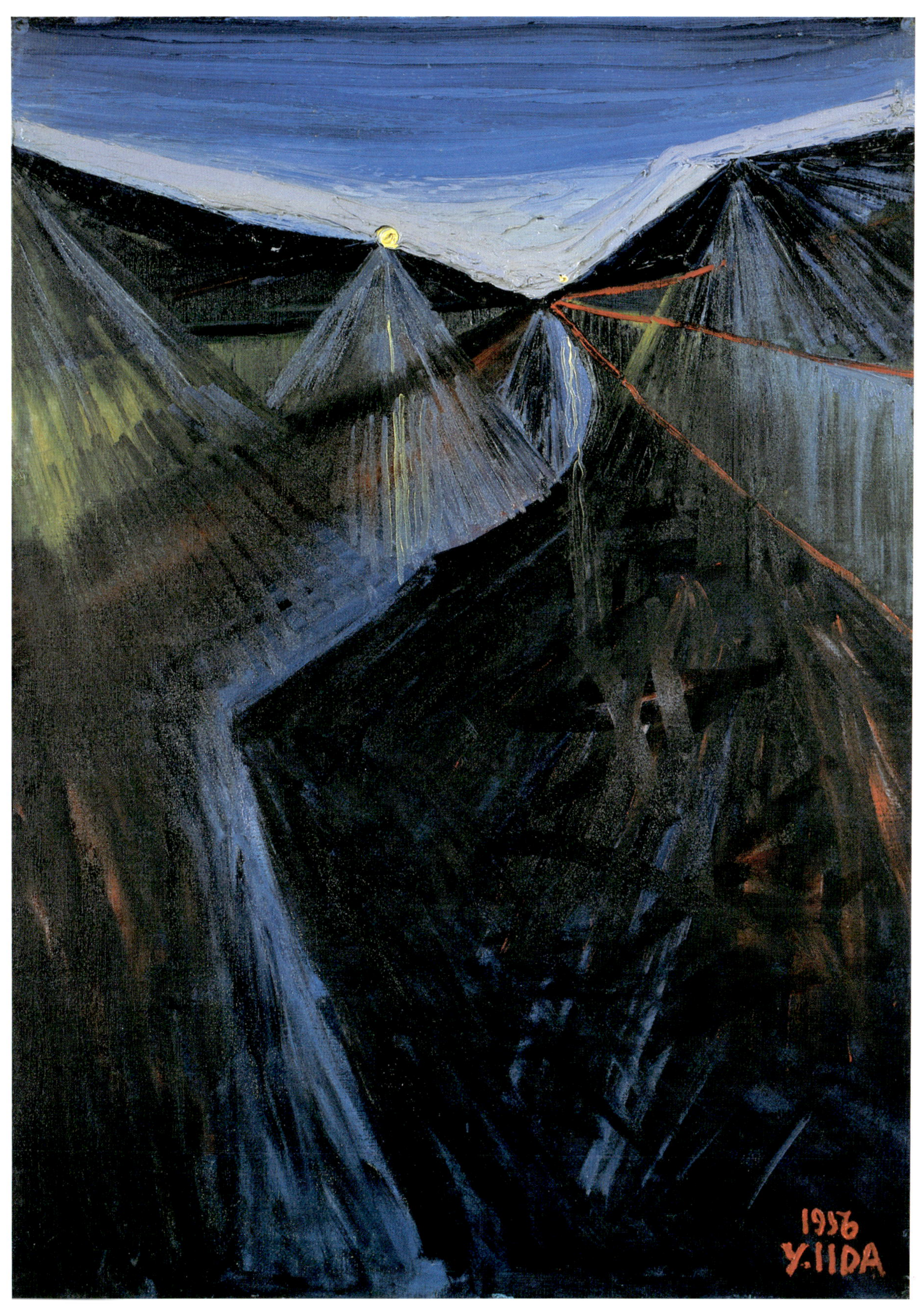

51
Iida Yoshikuni, The Meguro River by Night A, 1956
Oil on Canvas, 100 x 73 cm, owned by the artist

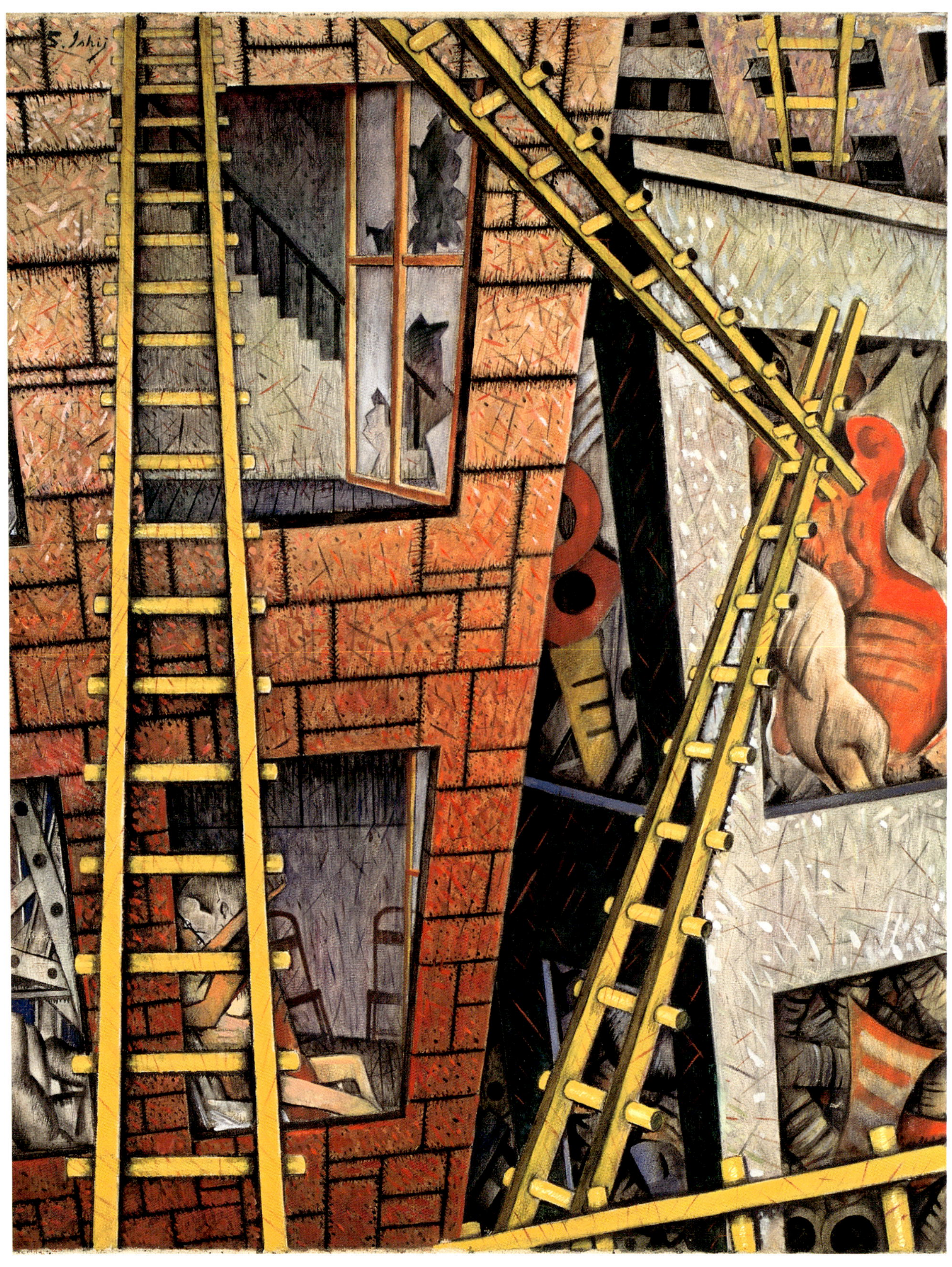

52
Ishii Shigeo, Insecure City—Insecure Steps, 1956
Oil on Canvas, 116.8 x 91 cm, Itabashiku Art Museum, Tokyo

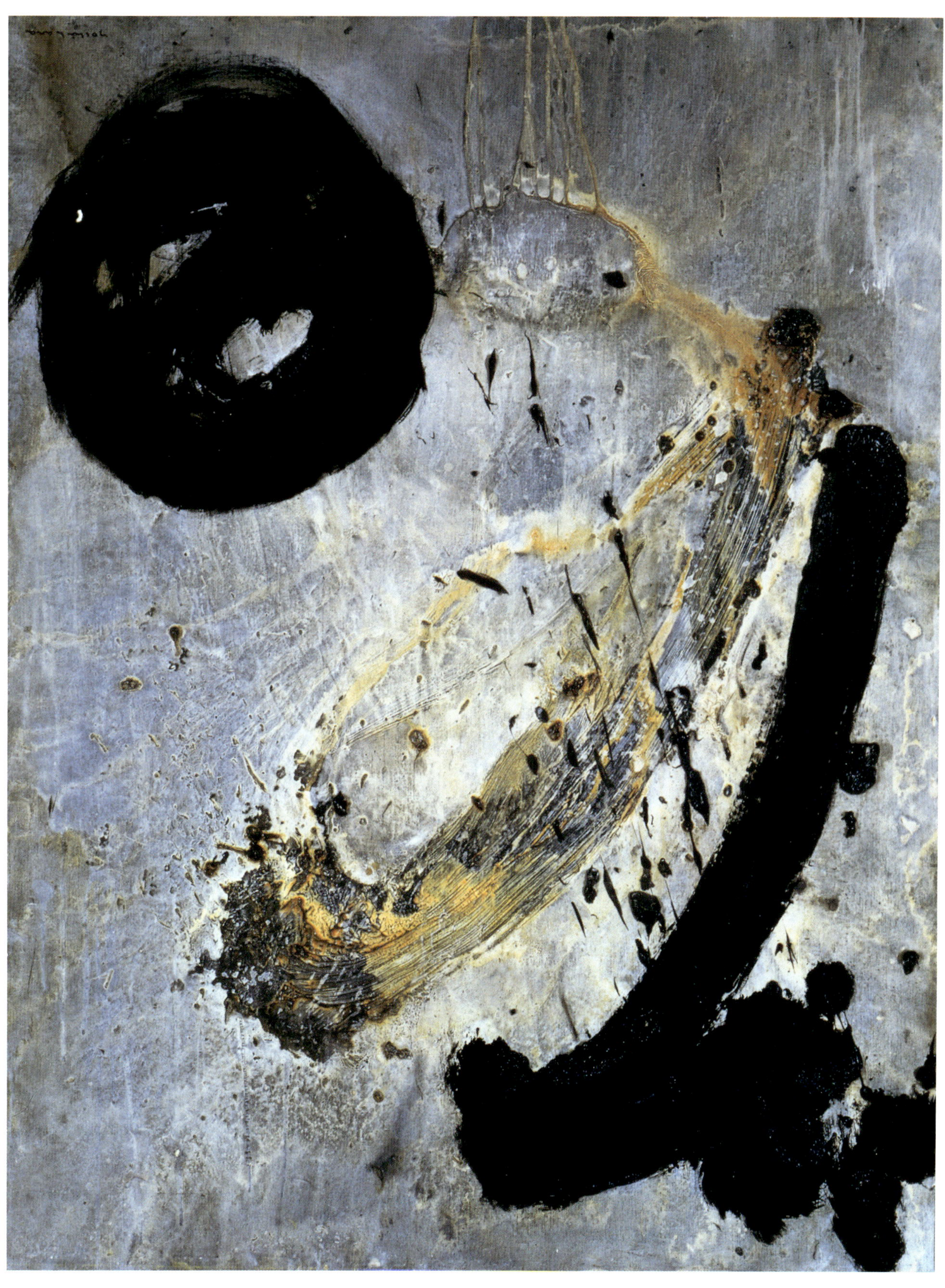

53
Yoshihara Jirô, Work, 1957
Oil on Canvas, 116.5 x 91 cm, Hyôgo Prefecture Museum of Modern Art, Kobe

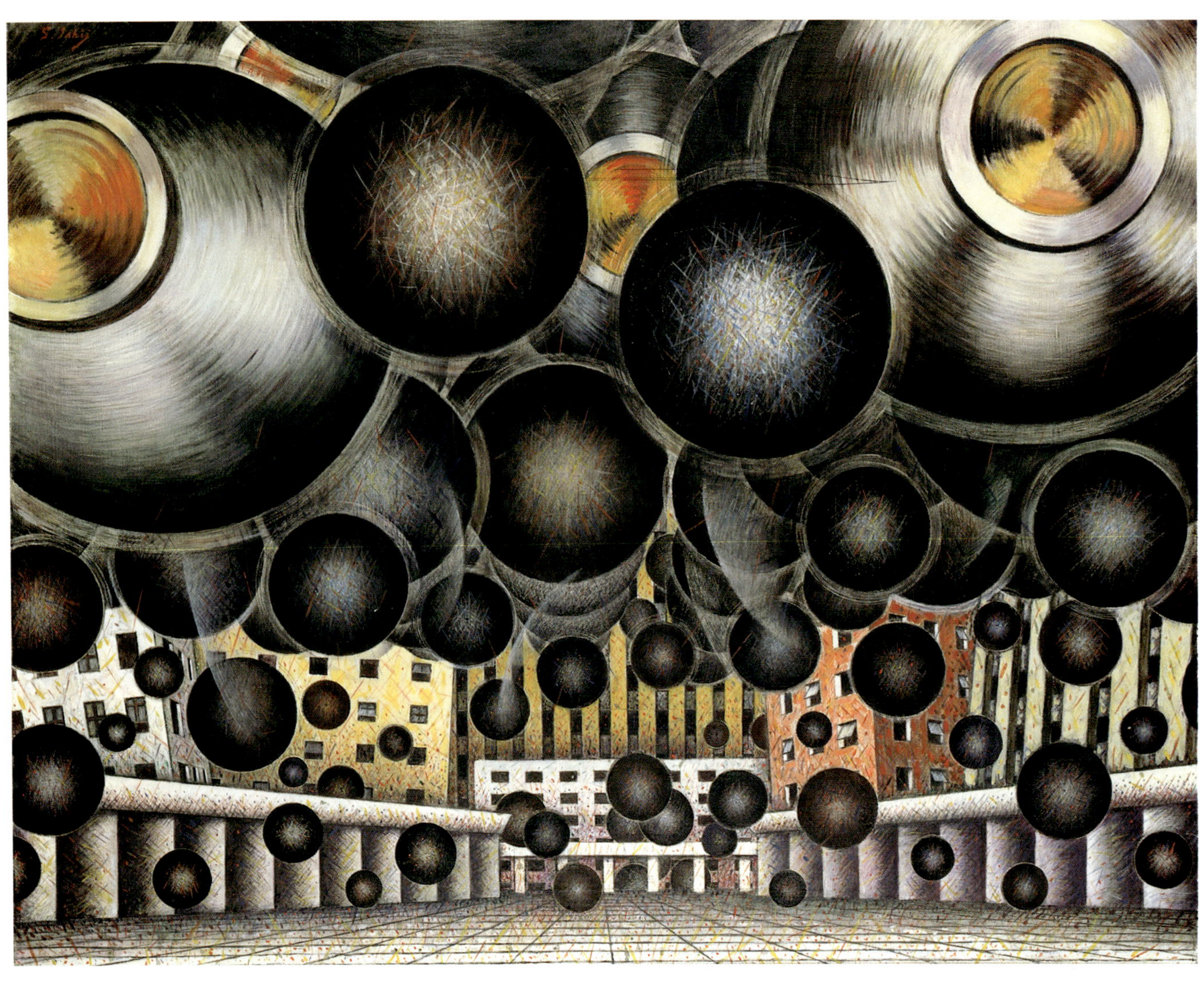

54
Ishii Shigeo, State of Siege, 1957
Oil on Canvas, 91 x 116 cm, National Museum of Modern Art, Tokyo

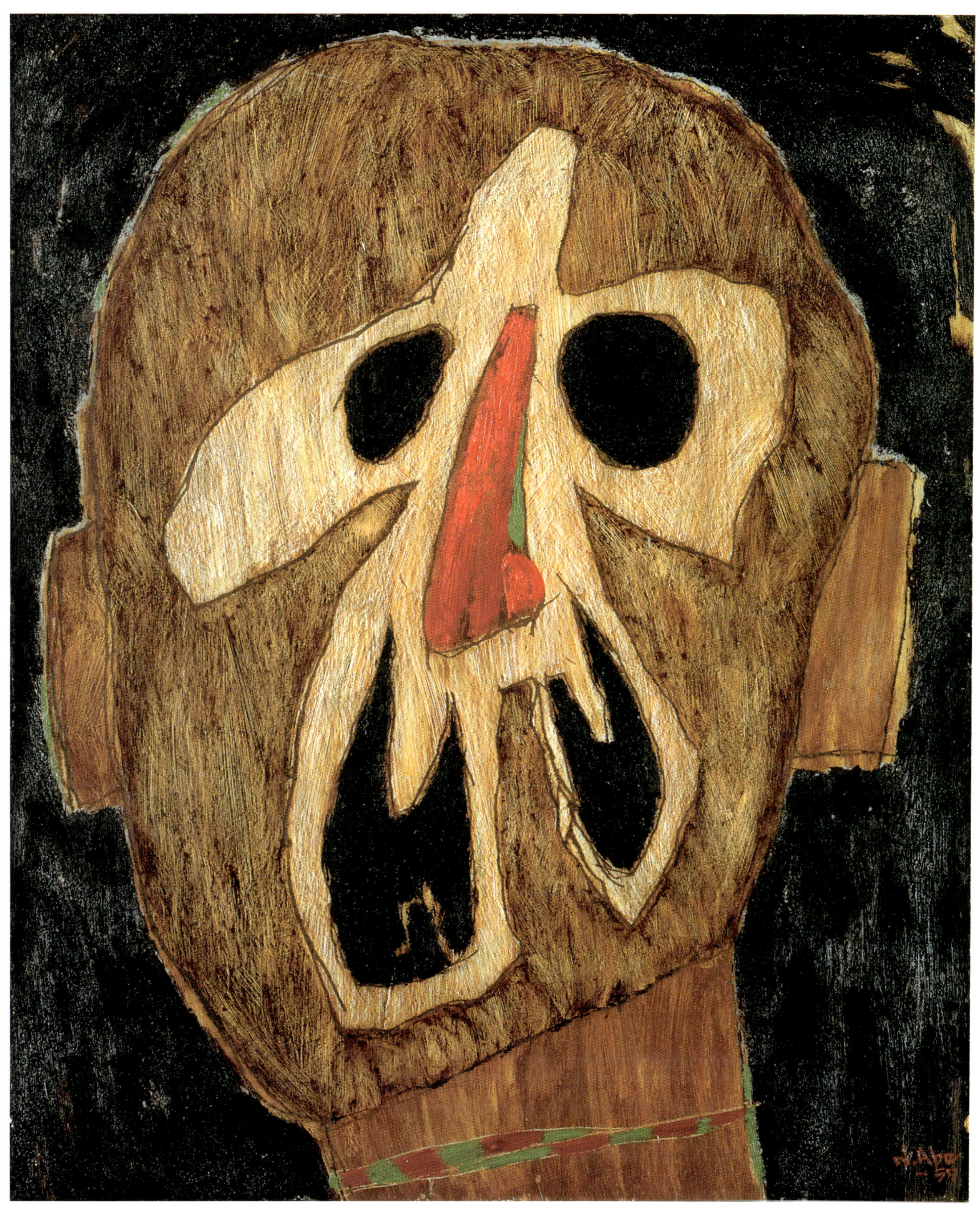

55
Abe Nobuya, The Face of the Face Behind, 1957
Oil on Board, 72.7 x 60.3 cm, Itabashiku Art Museum, Tokyo

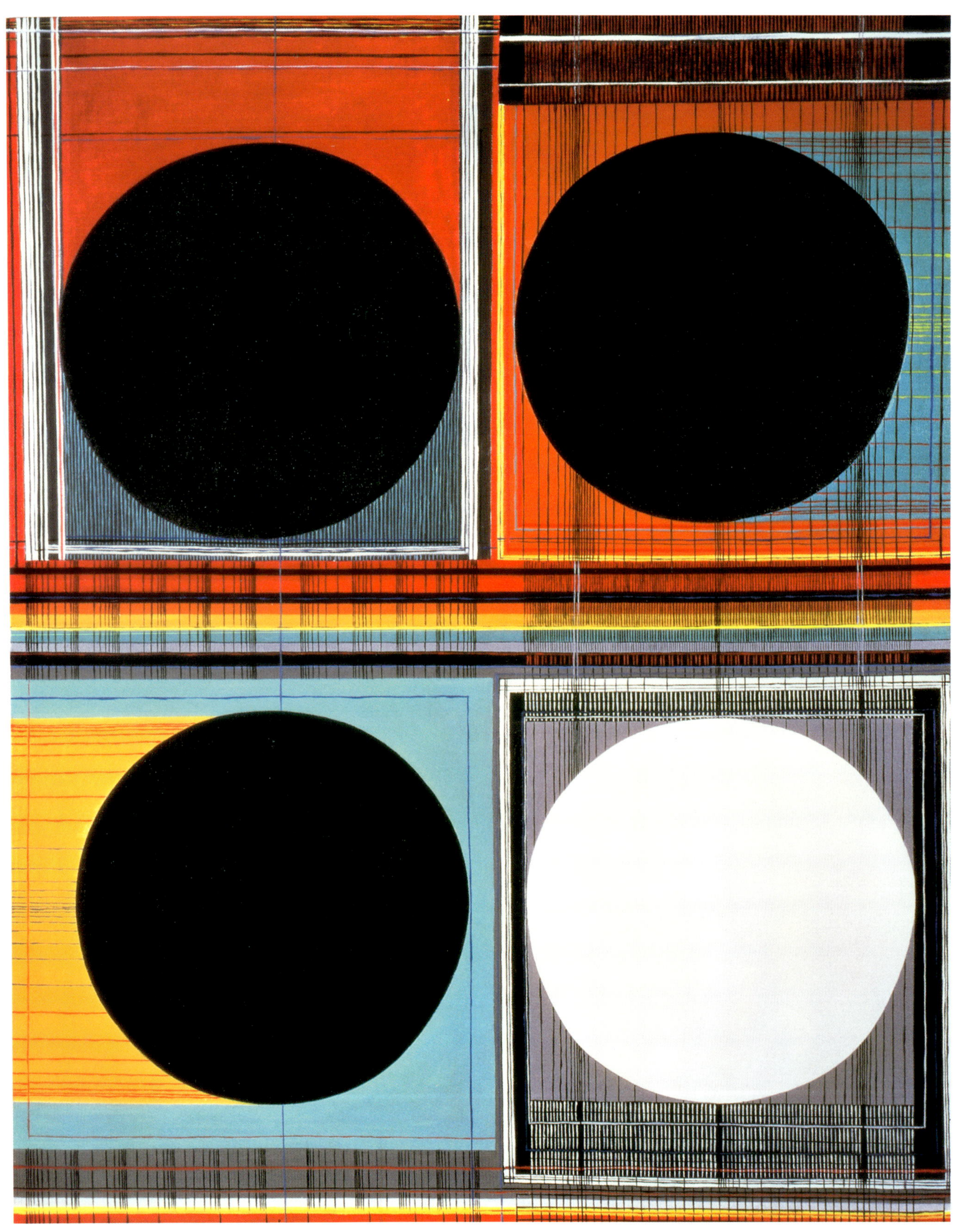

56
Onosato Toshinobu, Three Blacks, 1958
Oil on Canvas, 162 x 132 cm, Aichi Prefecture Art Museum, Nagoya

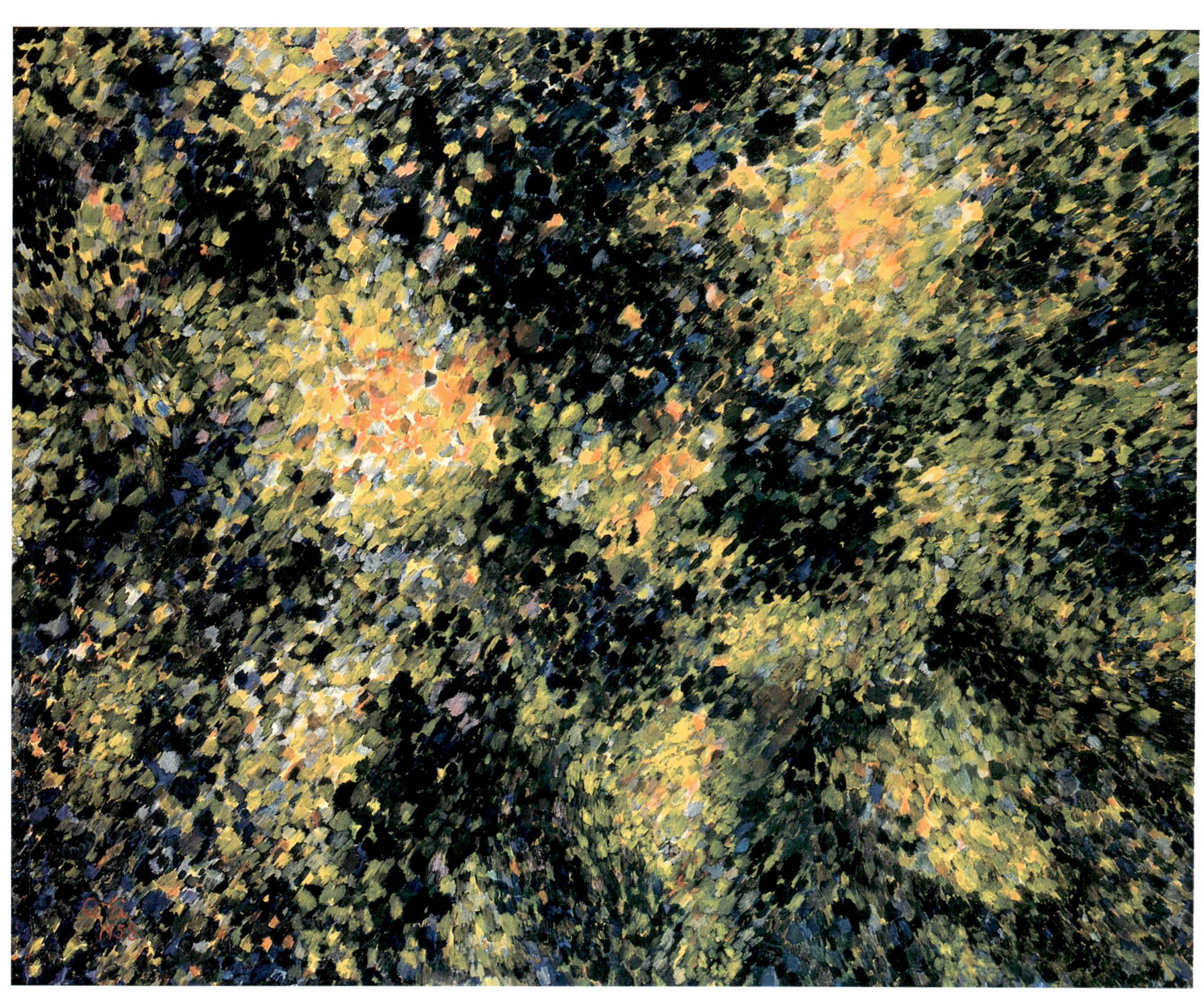

57
Ei-Kyû, Afternoon (The Absence of Insects), 1958
Oil on Canvas, 130 x 162.5 cm, National Museum of Modern Art, Tokyo

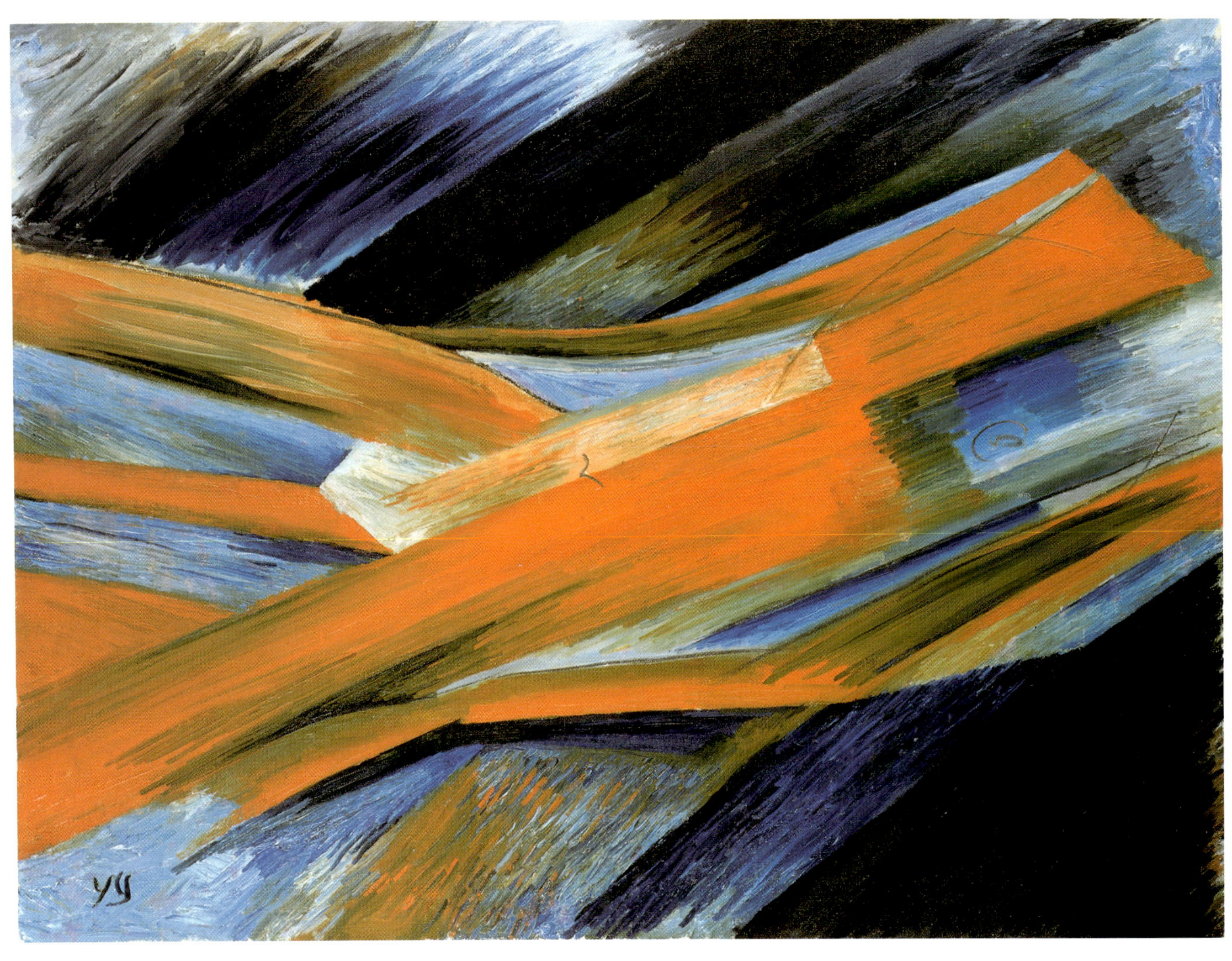

58
Iida Yoshikuni, Untitled (Nude in the Cosmos), 1959–1961
Oil on Canvas, 97 x 130 cm, The Ito Mitsumasa Collection

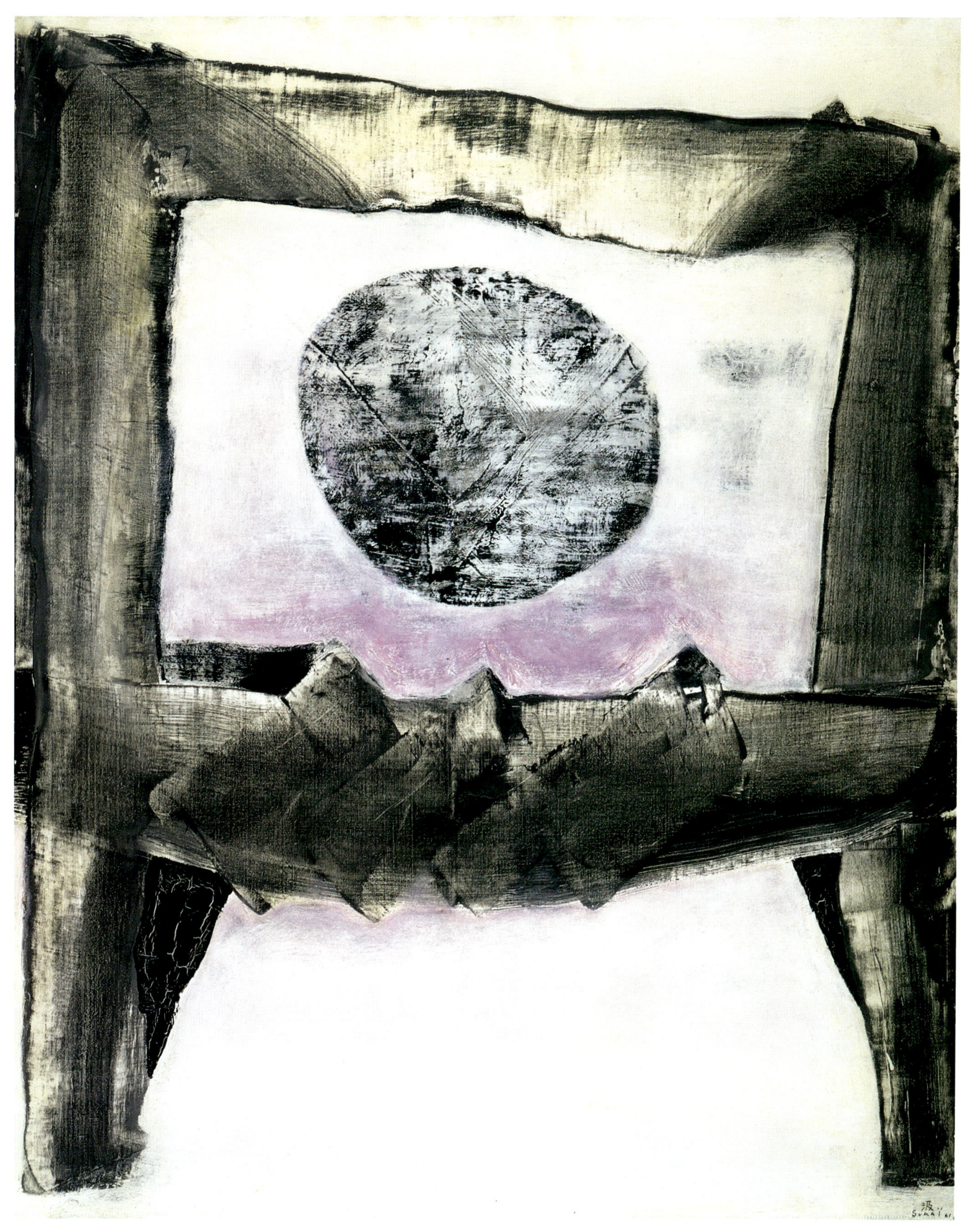

59
Sugai Kumi, Hill, 1960
Oil on Canvas, 100.3 x 81.3 cm, Yonetsu Gallery

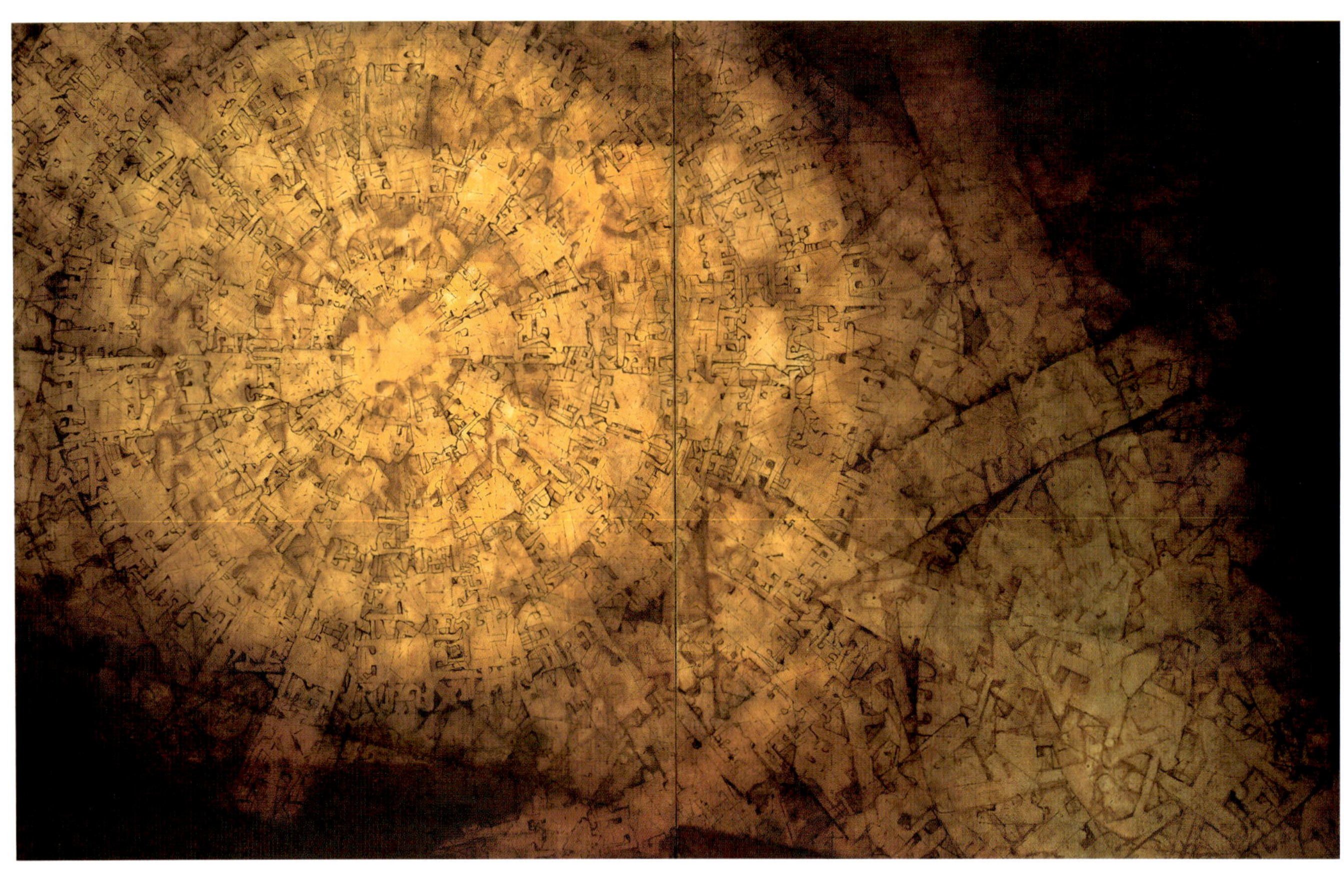

60
Maeda Josaku, Landscape with People II, 1960
Oil on Canvas, 162 x 260 cm, National Museum of Modern Art, Tokyo

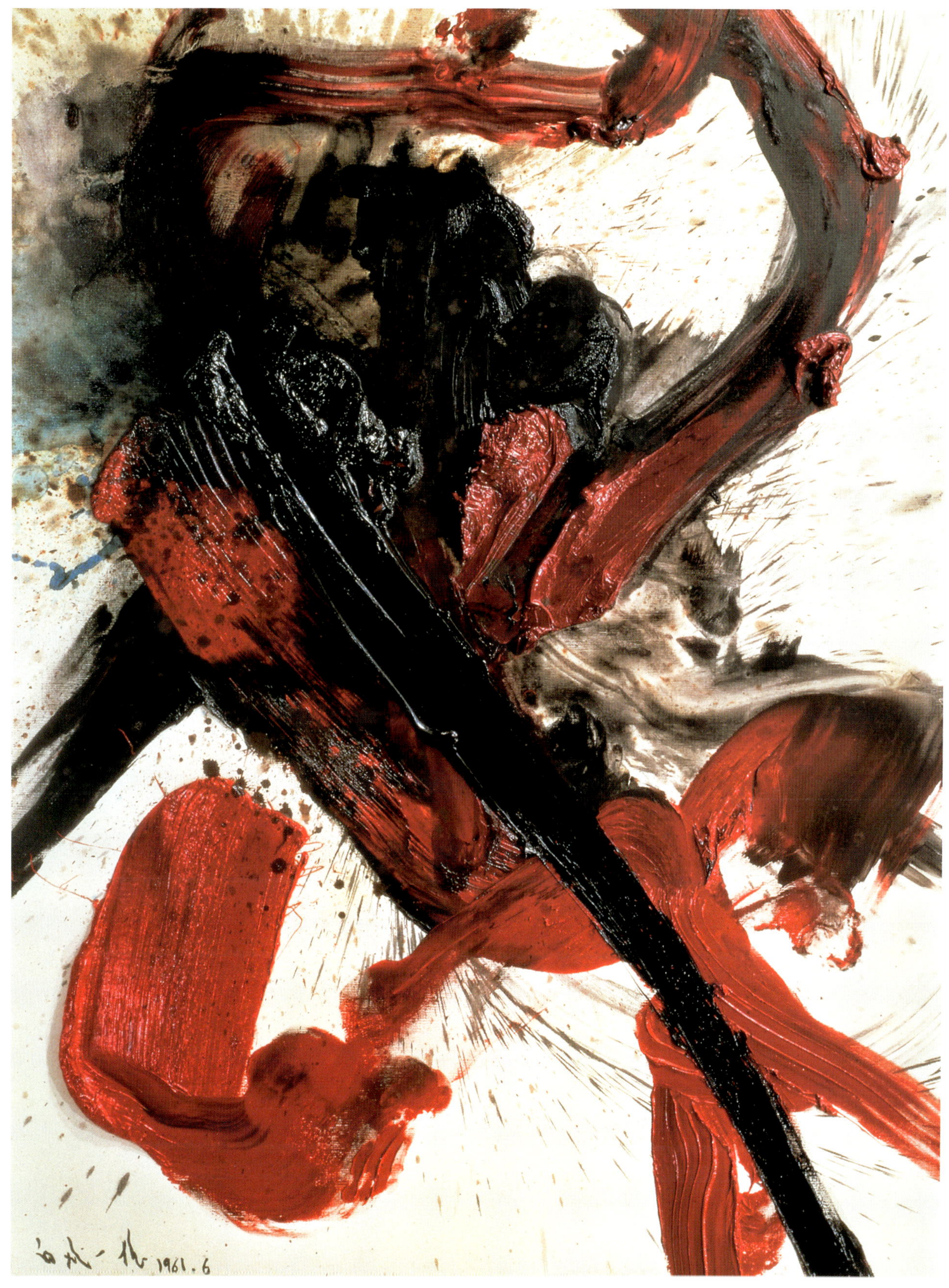

61
Shiraga Kazuo, Chibôsei Imon-shin, a Chinese Hero, 1961
Oil on Canvas, 170 x 130.5 cm, Hyôgo Prefecture Museum of Modern Art, Kobe

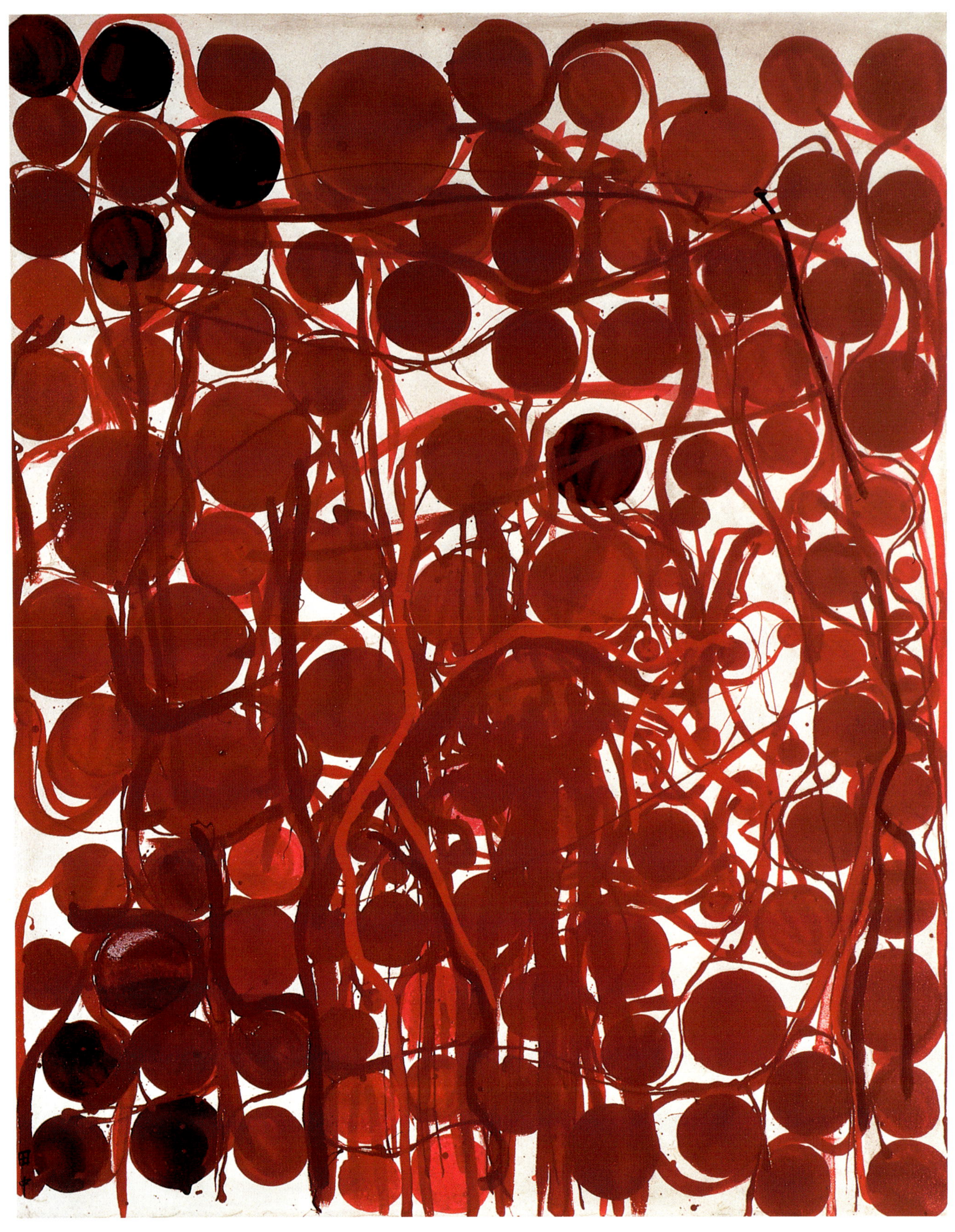

62
Tanaka Atsuko, Work, 1961
Acrylic on Canvas, 162 x 130 cm, Ham Gallery, Nagoya

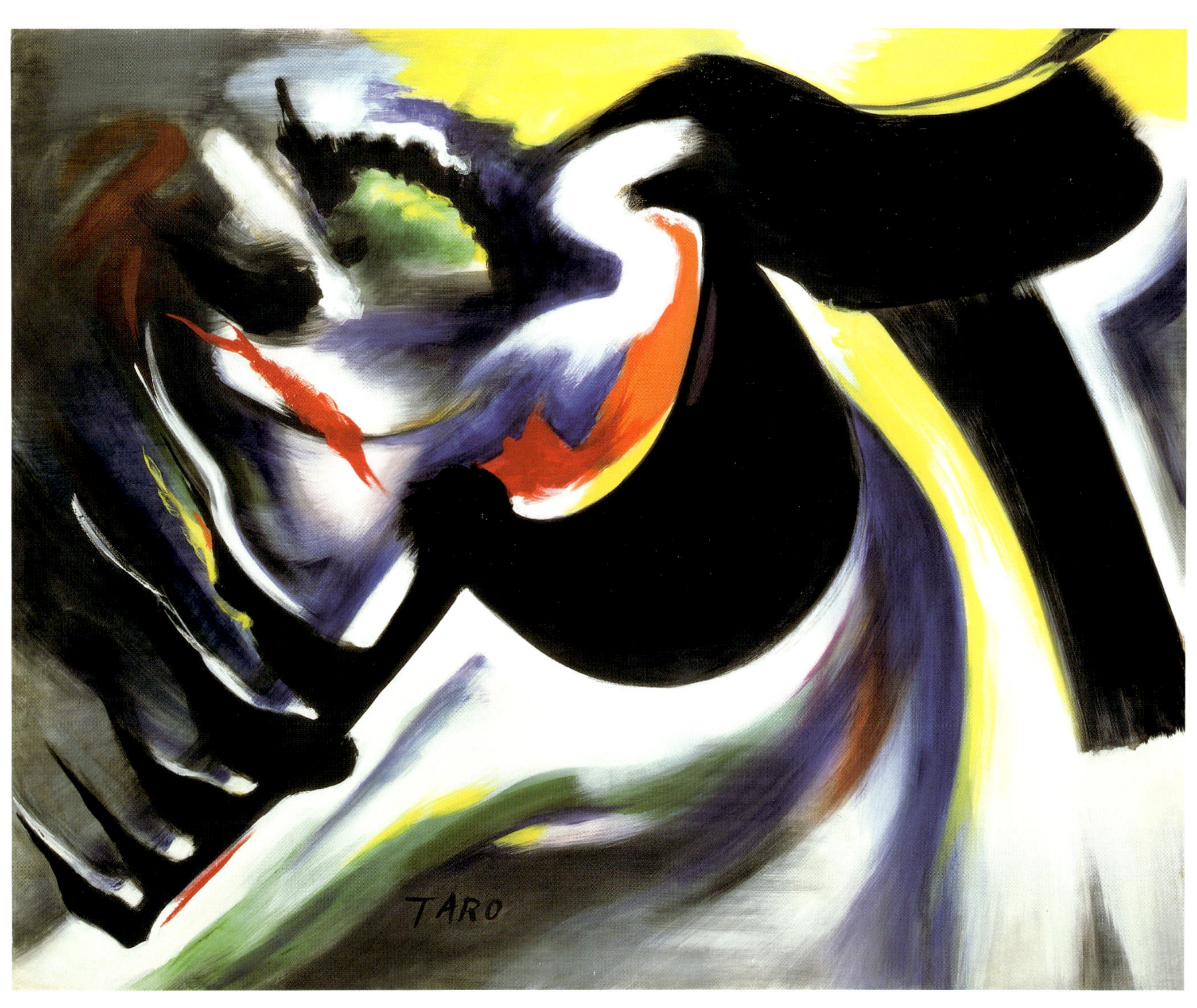

63
Okamoto Tarô, Playing, 1961
Oil on Canvas, 182 x 226.5 cm, National Museum of Modern Art, Tokyo

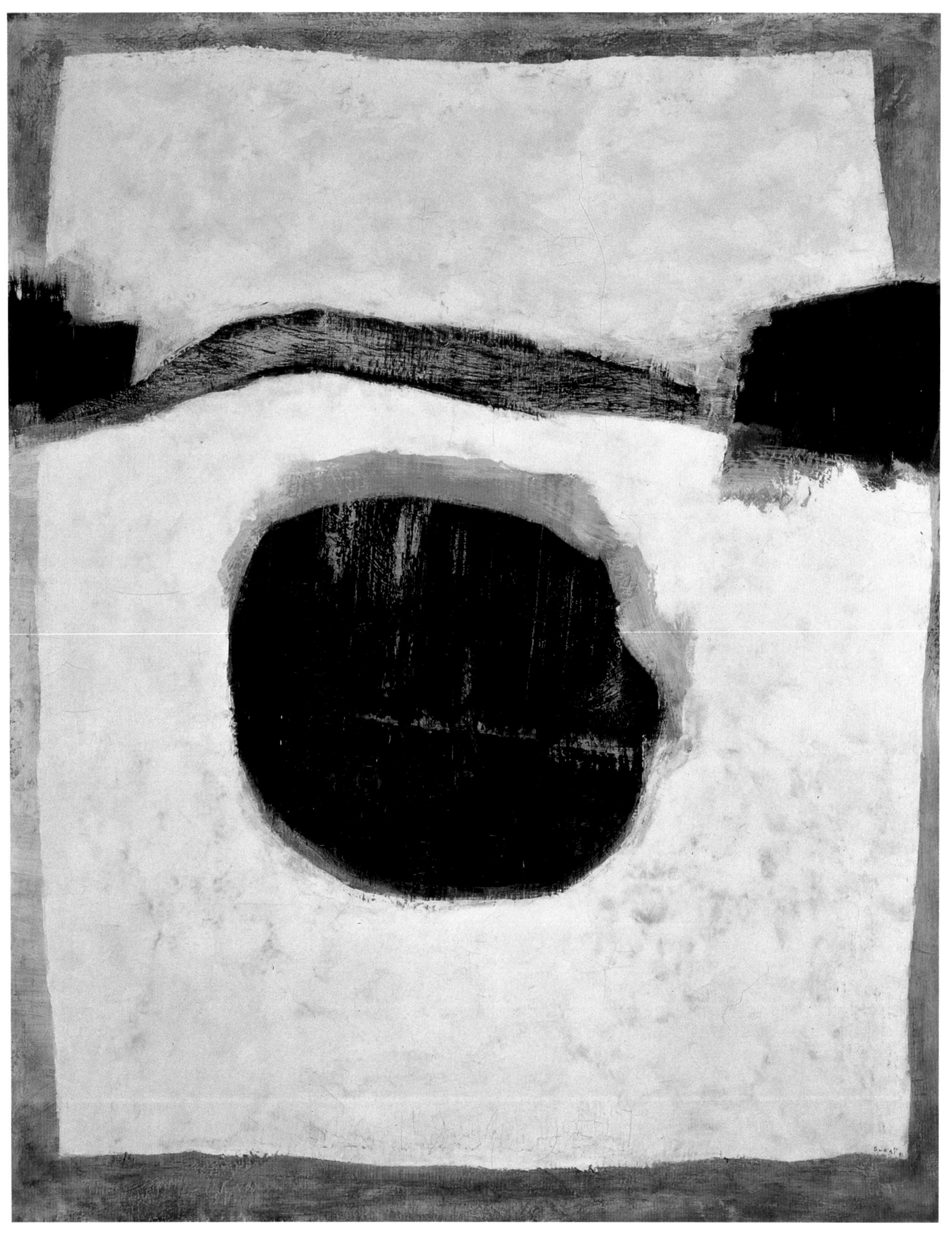

64
Sugai Kumi, Black Moon, 1961
Oil on Canvas, 161.3 x 130 cm, Yonetsu Gallery

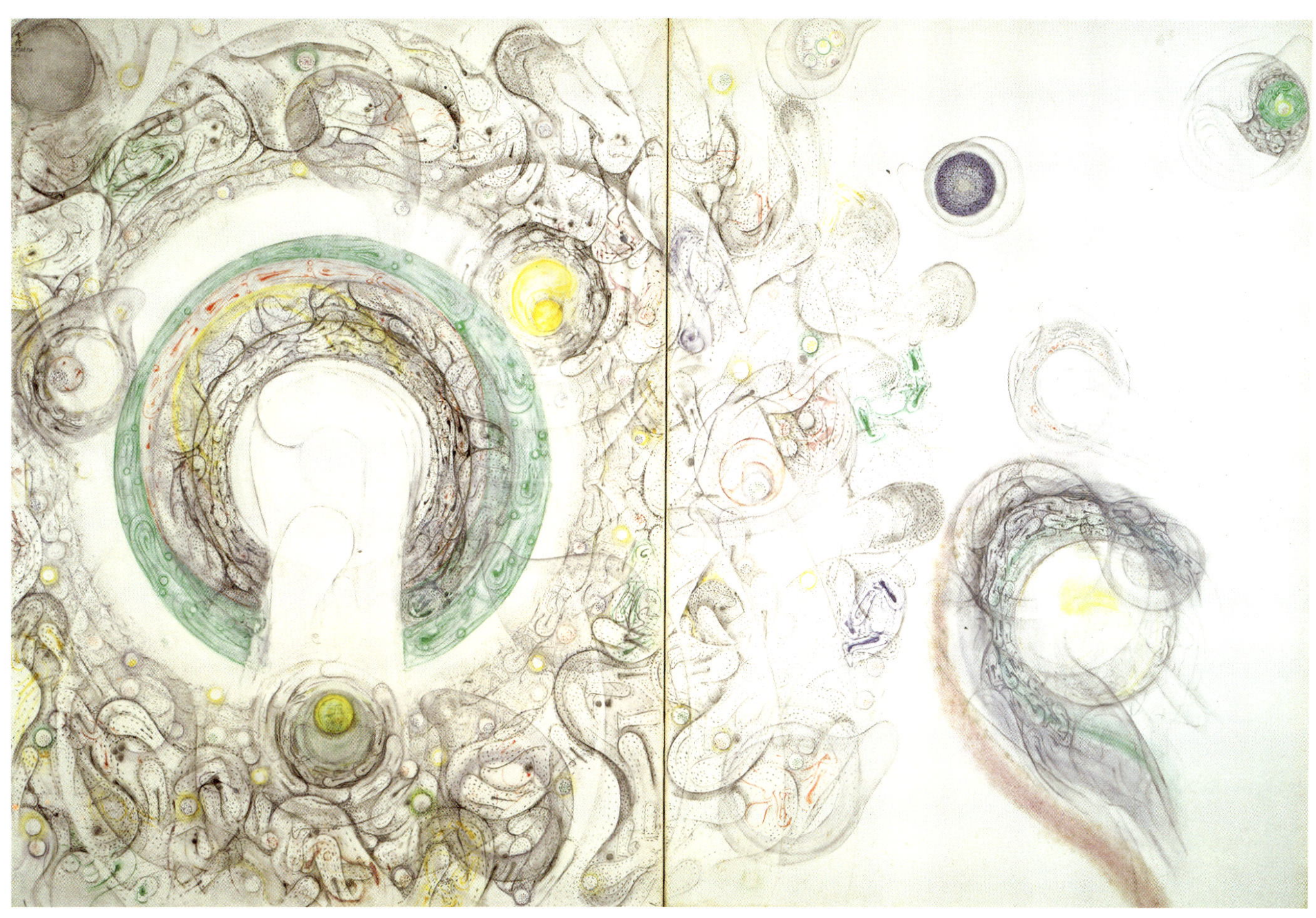

65
Maeda Josaku, The Birth of Mankind 5, 1962
Oil on Canvas, 130 x 194 cm, Prefecture Museum of Modern Art, Toyama

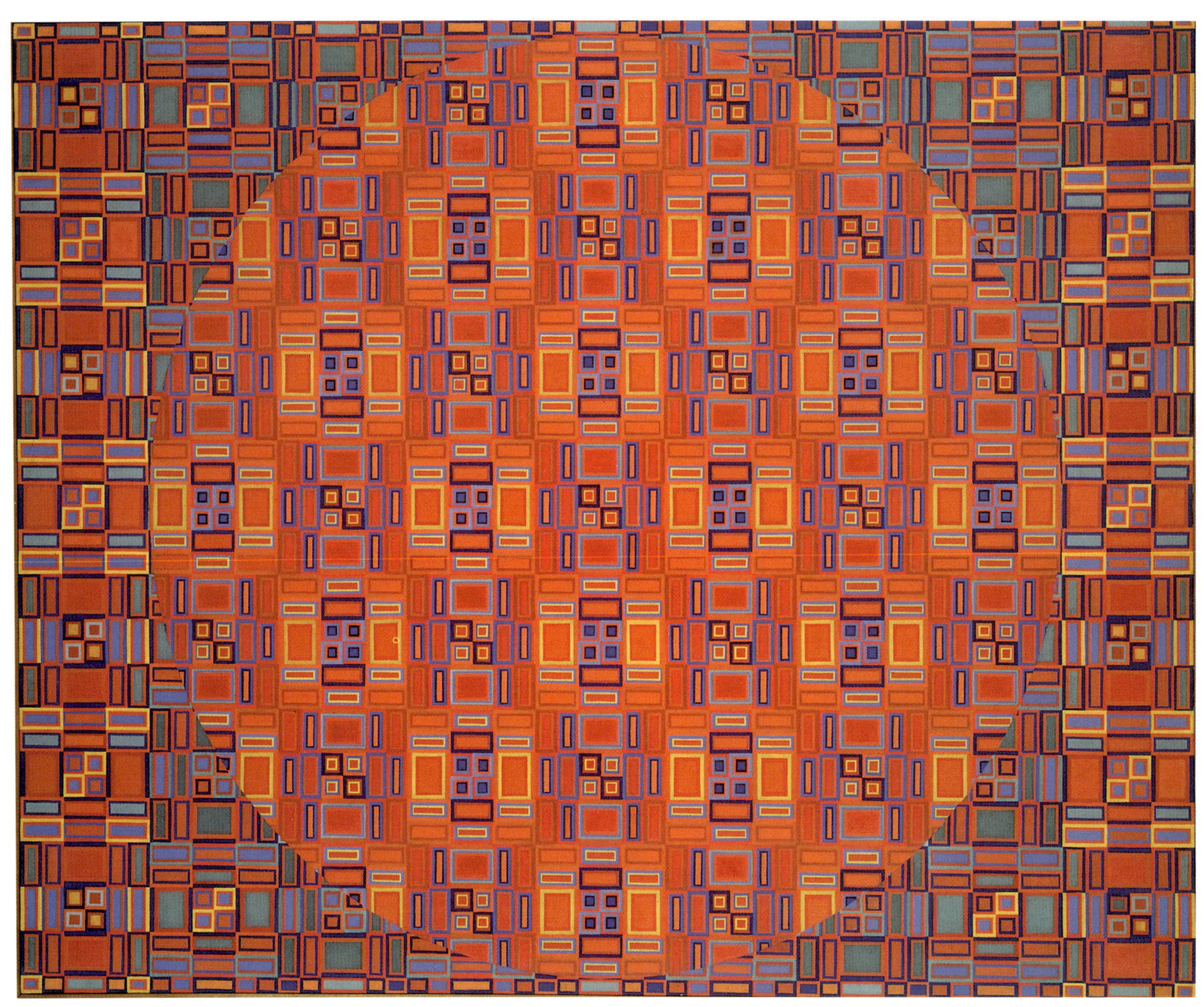

66
Onosato Toshinobu, Work 100-B, 1963
Oil on Canvas, 130.8 x 162.3 cm, National Museum of Modern Art, Tokyo

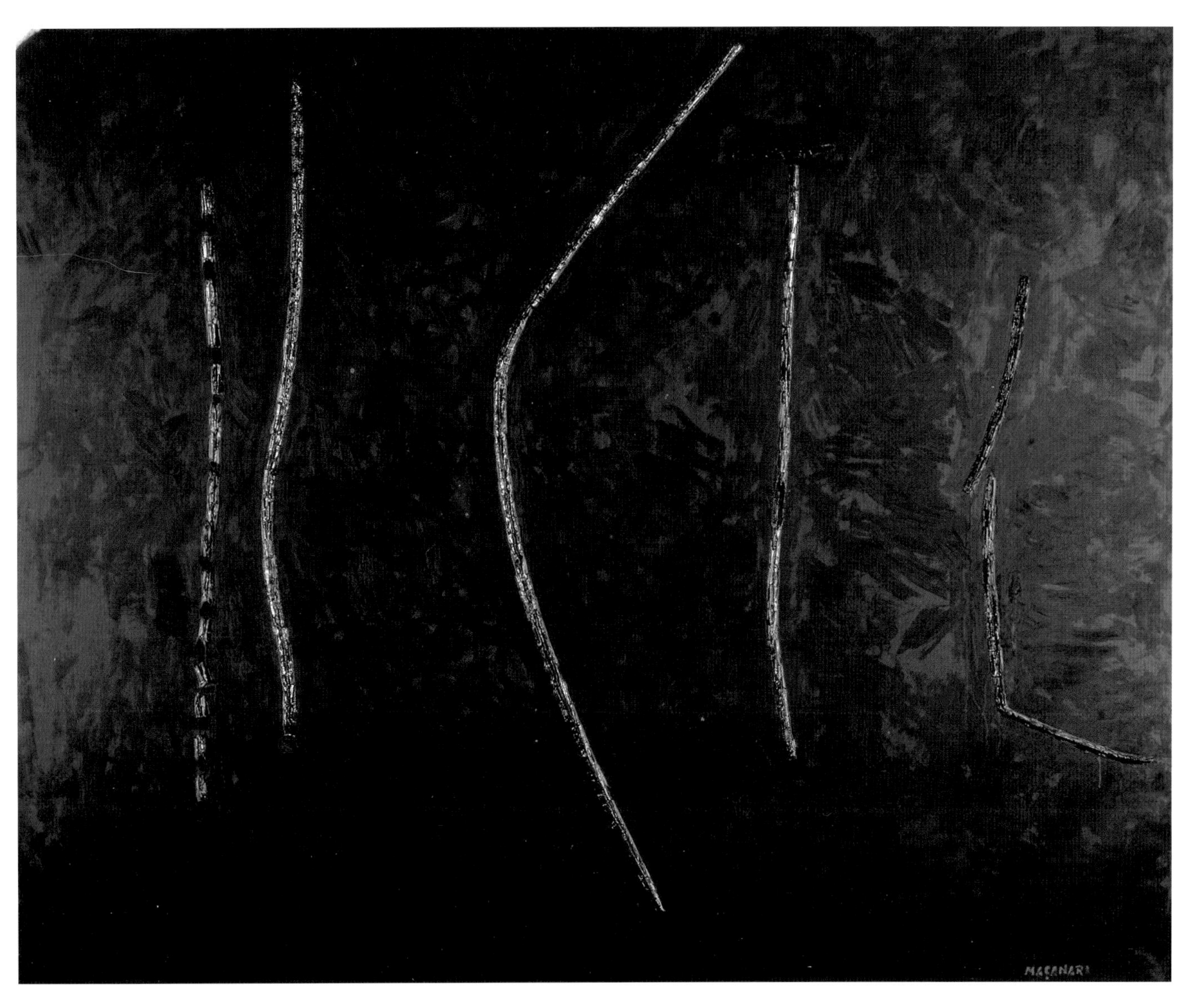

67
Murai Masanari, People on the Beach, 1964
Oil on Canvas, 182 x 230 cm, Kanagawa Prefecture Museum of Modern Art, Kamakura

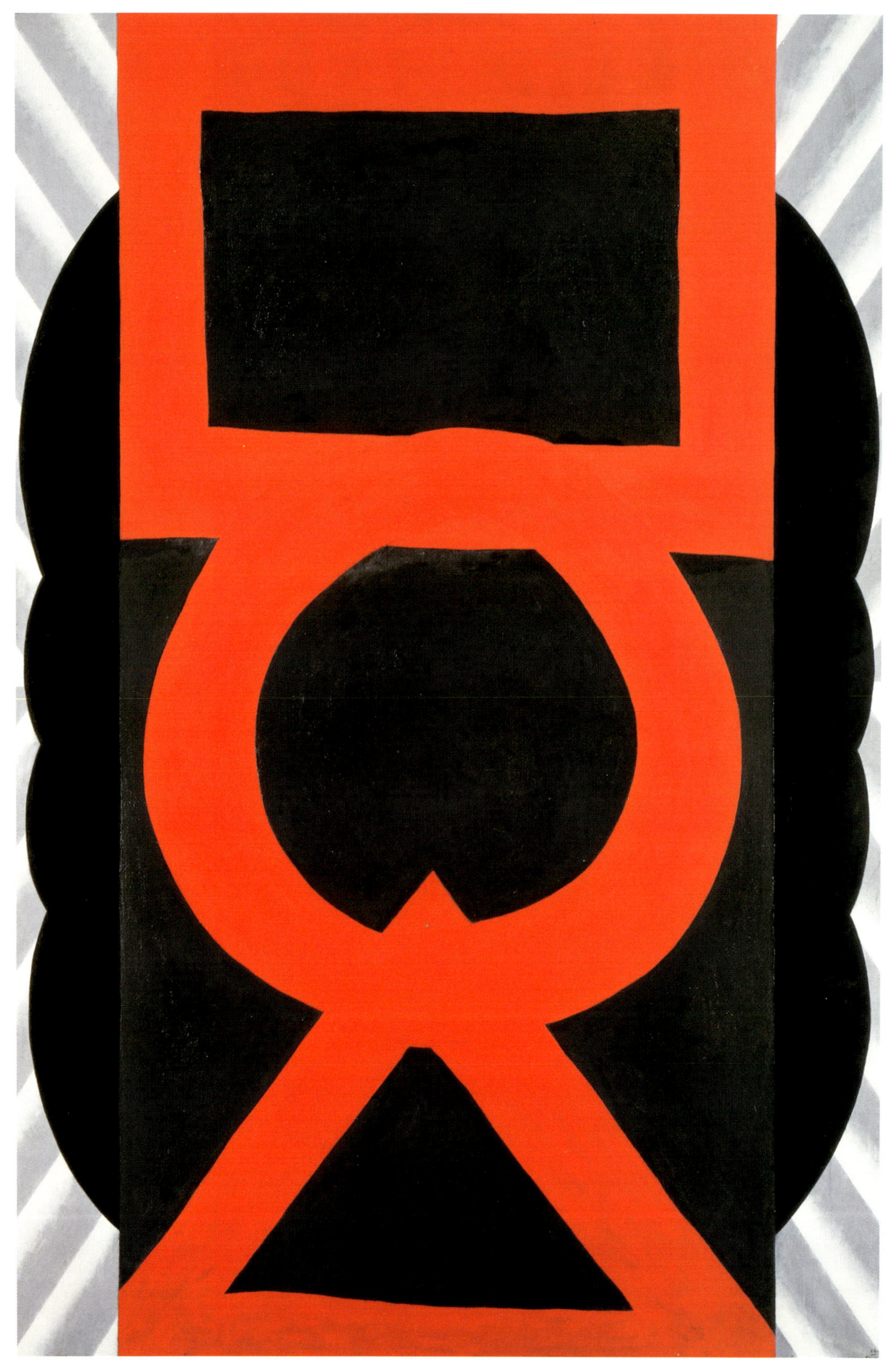

68
Sugai Kumi, Red and Black, 1964
Oil on Canvas, 195 x 131 cm, Kanagawa Prefecture Museum of Modern Art, Kamakura

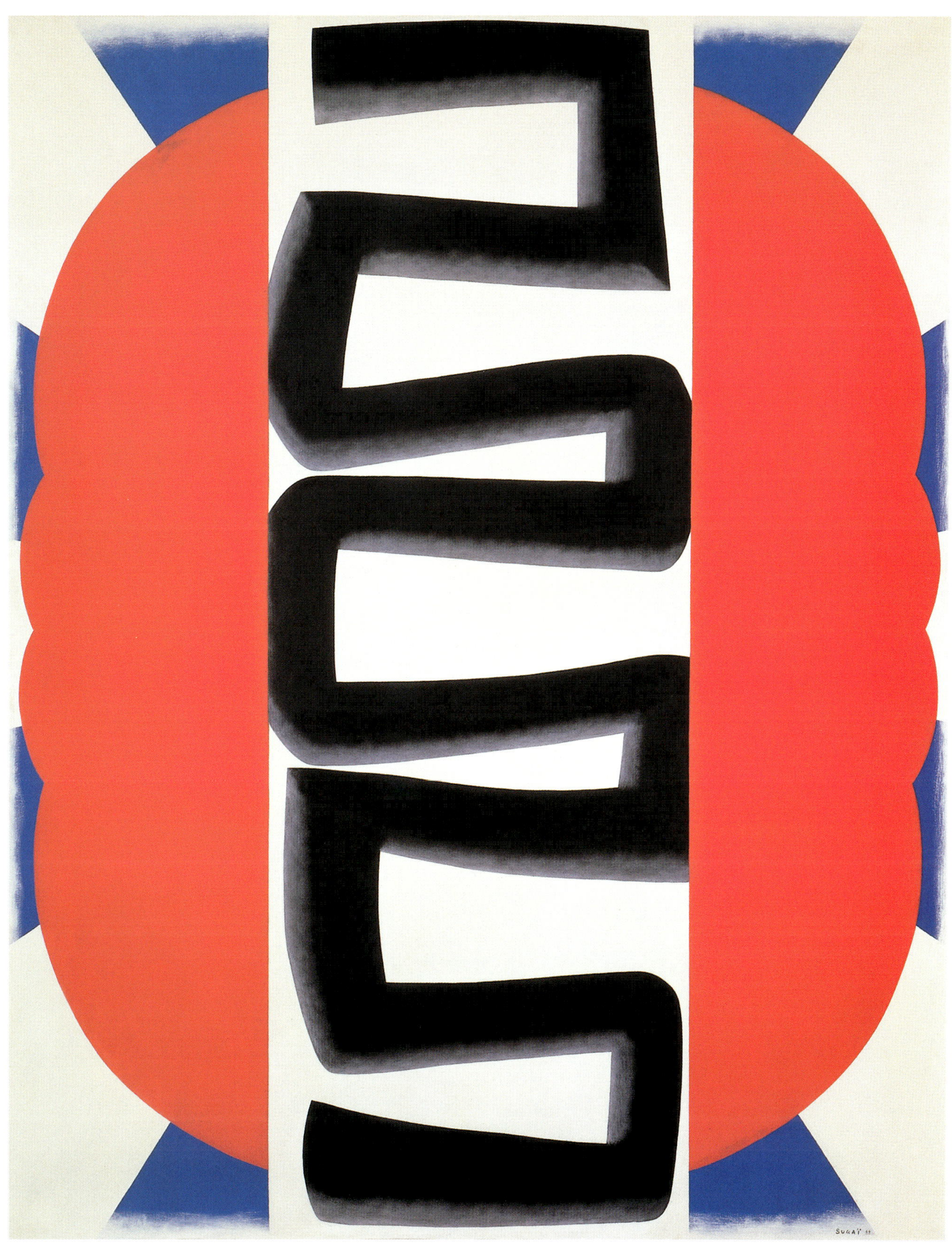

69

Sugai Kumi, Freeway in the Morning, 1964

Oil on Canvas, 195 x 154.5 cm, National Museum of Modern Art, Tokyo

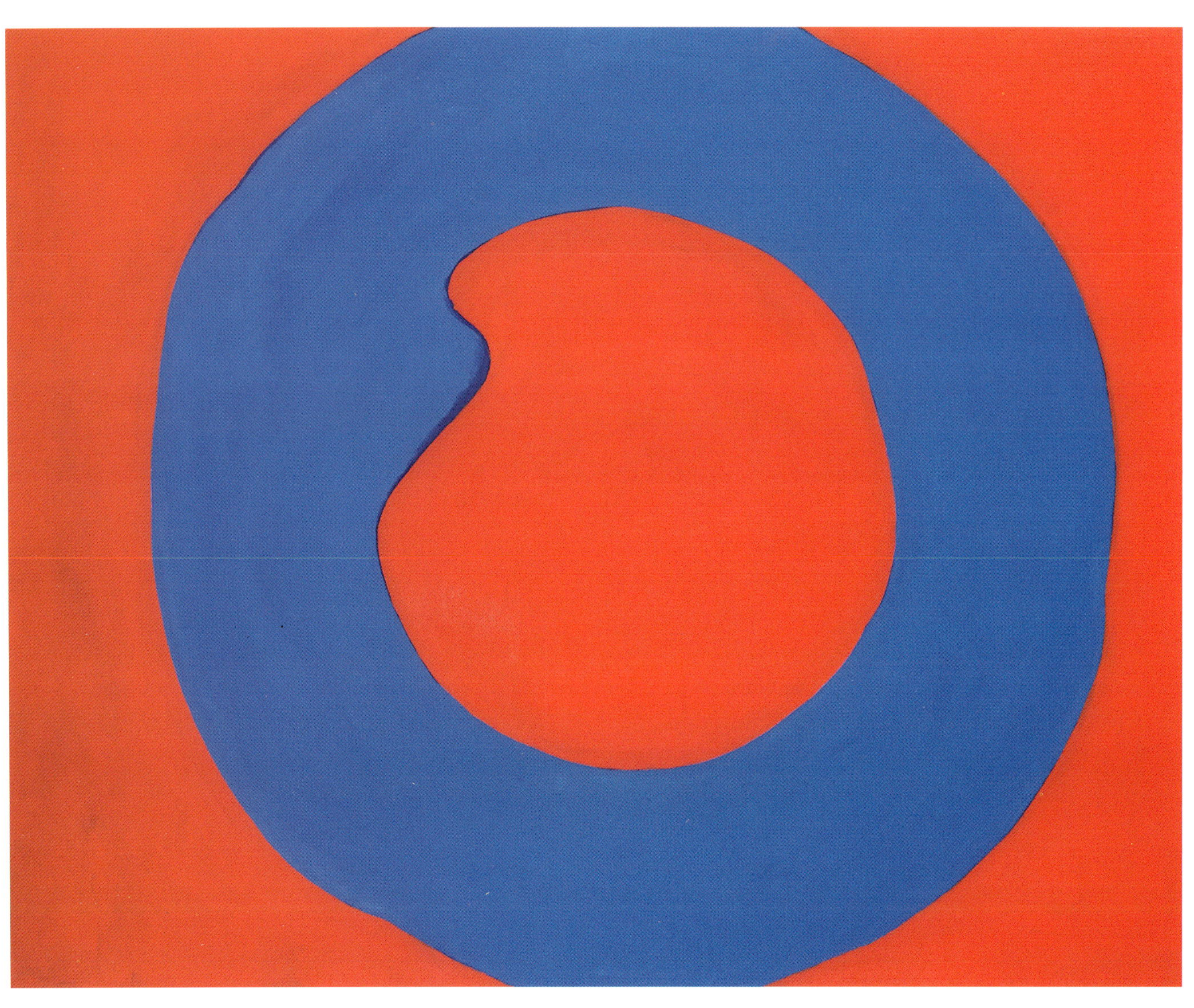

70
Yoshihara Jirô, Work, 1966
Acrylic, Oil on Canvas, 130.5 x 161 cm, Hyôgo Prefecture Museum of Modern Art, Kobe (The Yamamura Collection)

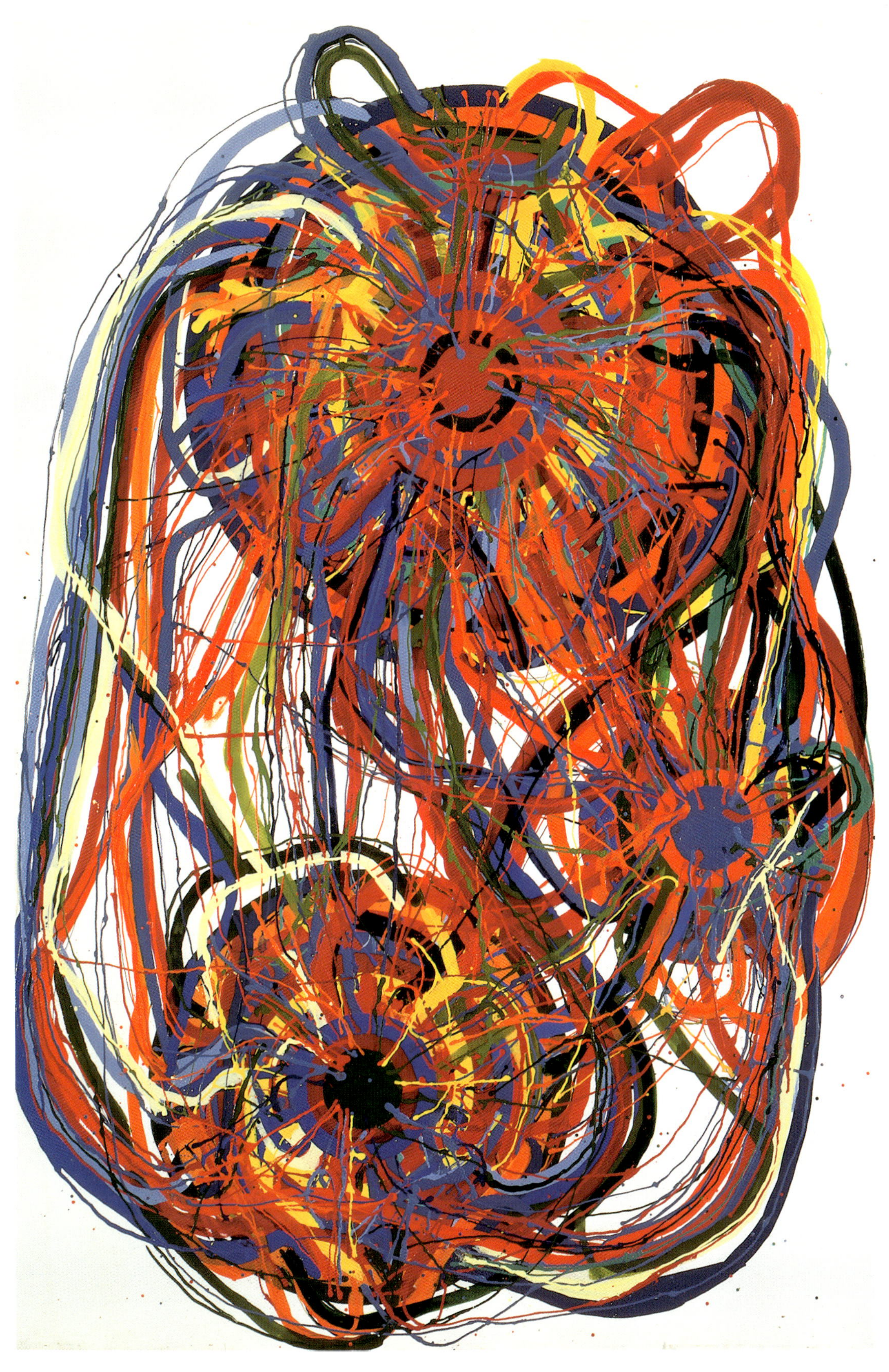

71
Tanaka Atsuko, Work 66 SA, 1966
Vinyl Resins on Canvas, 193.8 x 130.8 cm, National Museum of Modern Art, Tokyo

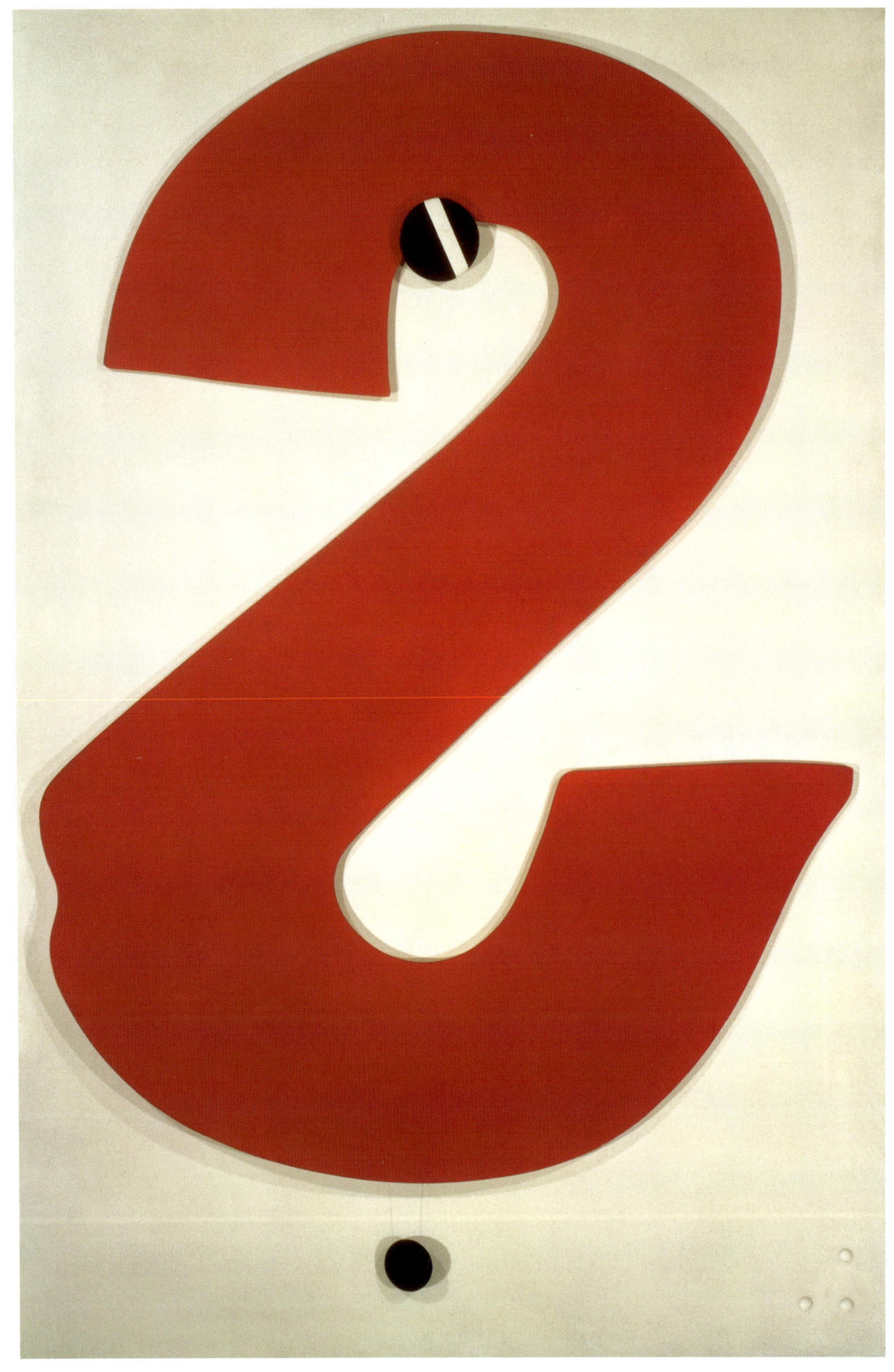

72
Saitô Yoshishige, Crane (Hook), 1967
Enamel on Plywood, 183 x 122 cm, Yokohama Art Museum, Yokohama

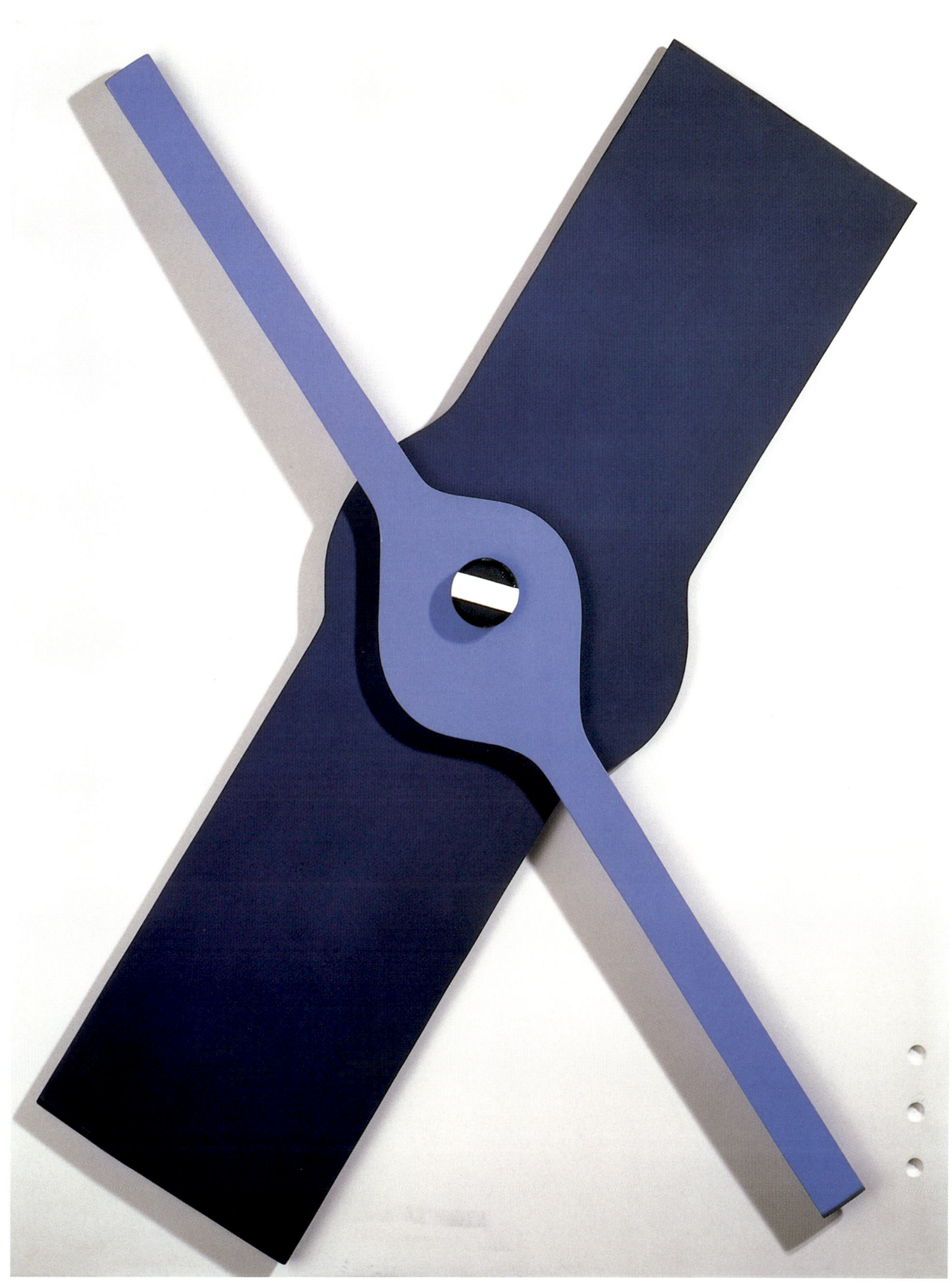

73
Saitô Yoshishige, Hanger, 1967
Enamel on Plywood, 110.5 x 68 cm, National Museum of Modern Art, Kyoto

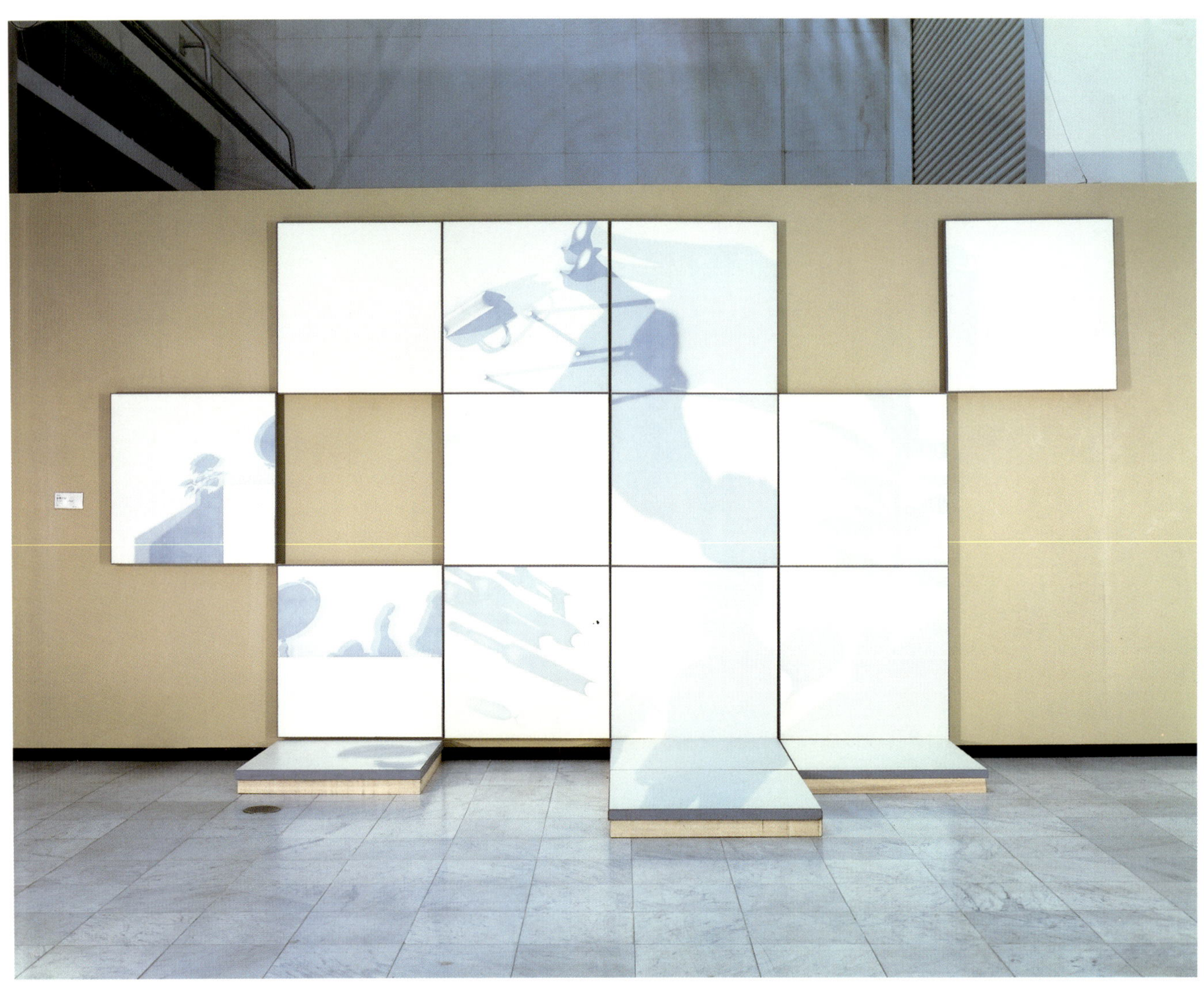

74
Takamatsu Jirô, The Wall of the World, 1967
Acrylic on Wood-Panel, 264 x 486 cm, Kanagawa Prefecture Museum of Modern Art, Kamakura

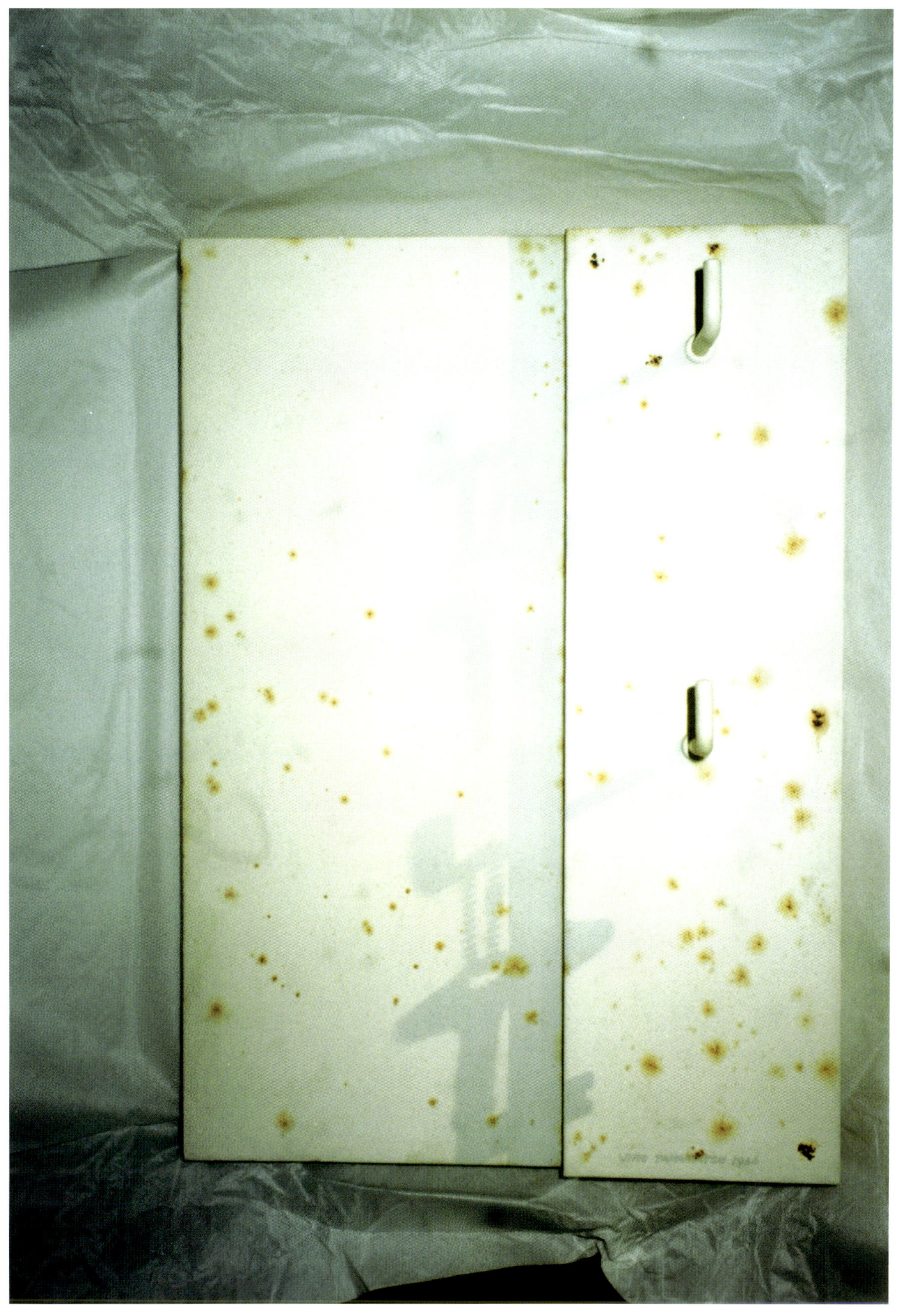

75
Takamatsu Jirô, from the Series: Shadow of the Key, 1968
Enamel on Wood, 33 x 24 x 7.5 cm, The Nakajima Hiroshi Collection in conjunction with the Tokyo Gallery

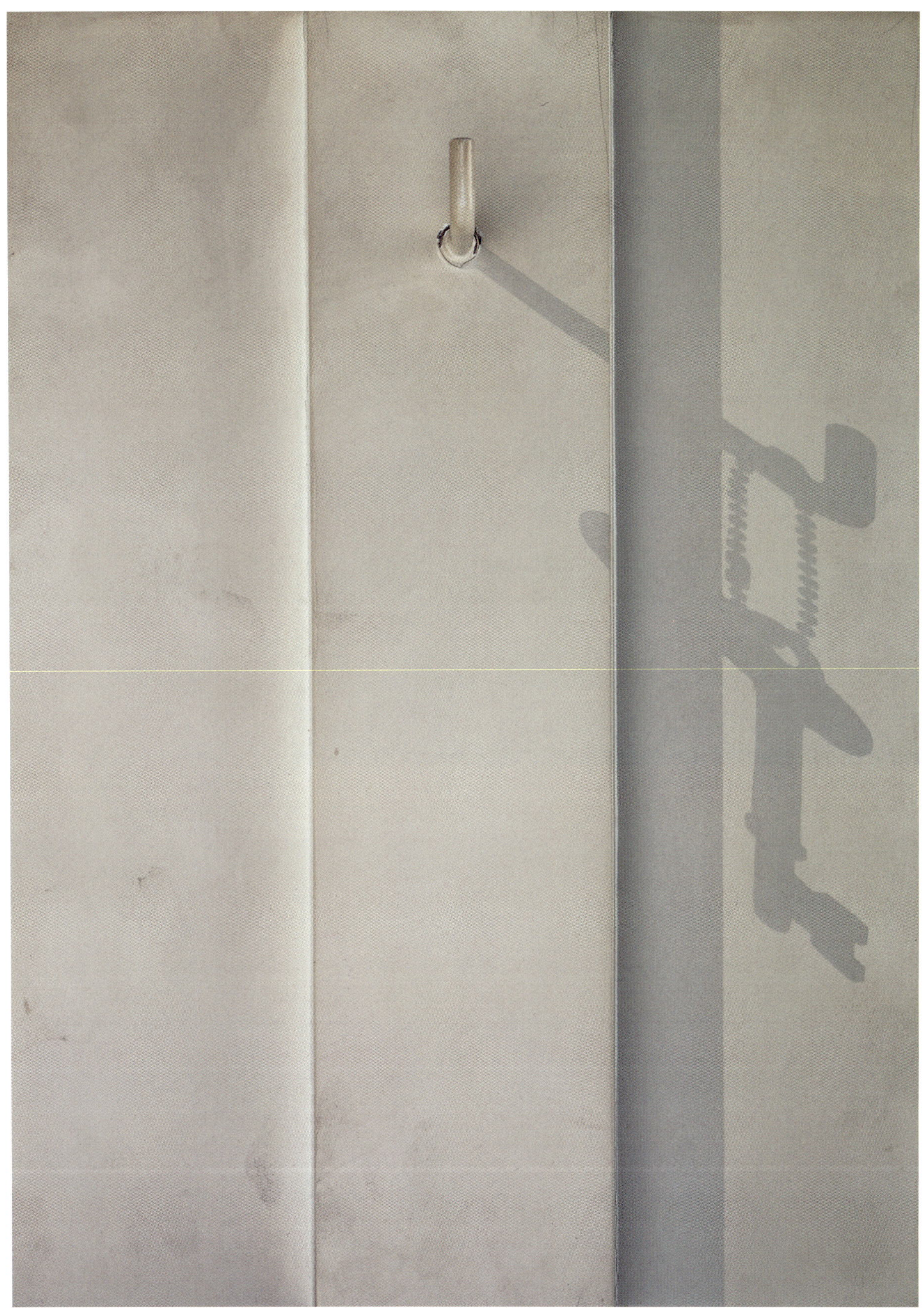

76

Takamatsu Jirô, from the Series: Shadow of the Key, 1966

Acrylic, Hook on Wood-Panel, 33 x 24 x 7.5 cm, The Takamatsu Yasuko Collection in conjunction with the Yumiko Chiba Associates

77
Takamatsu Jirô, from the Series: Shadow of the Key, 1968
Acrylic, Hook on Wood-Panel, 33 x 24 x 7.5 cm, Niigata Prefecture Museum, Nagaoka

78
Yamaguchi Takeo, Parallel Rows, 1968
Oil on Plywood, 182 x 182 cm, National Museum of Modern Art, Tokyo

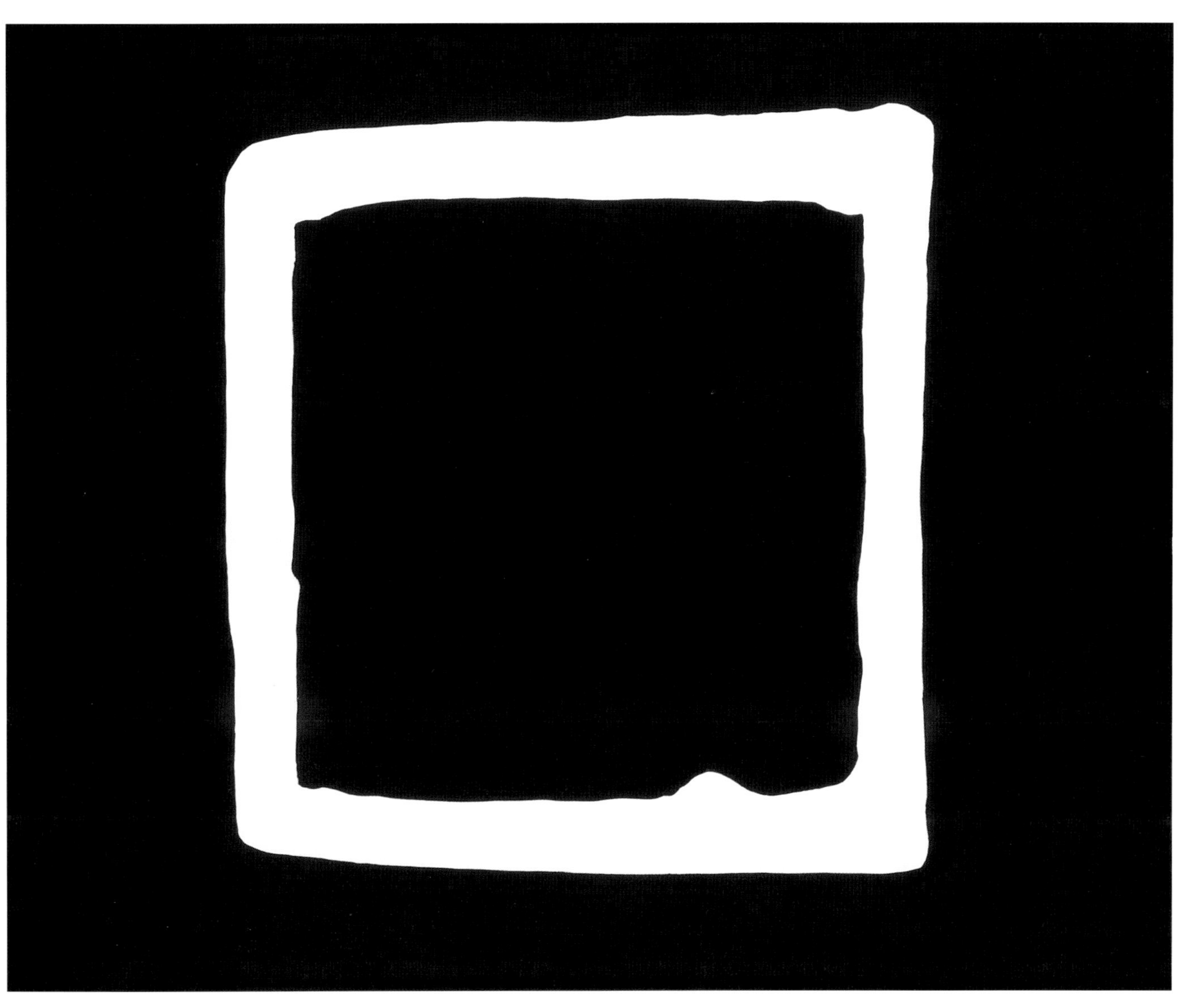

79

Yoshihara Jirô, Work (White Square on Black), 1971
Oil on Canvas, 162 x 145.5 cm, Kanagawa Prefecture Museum of Modern Art, Kamakura

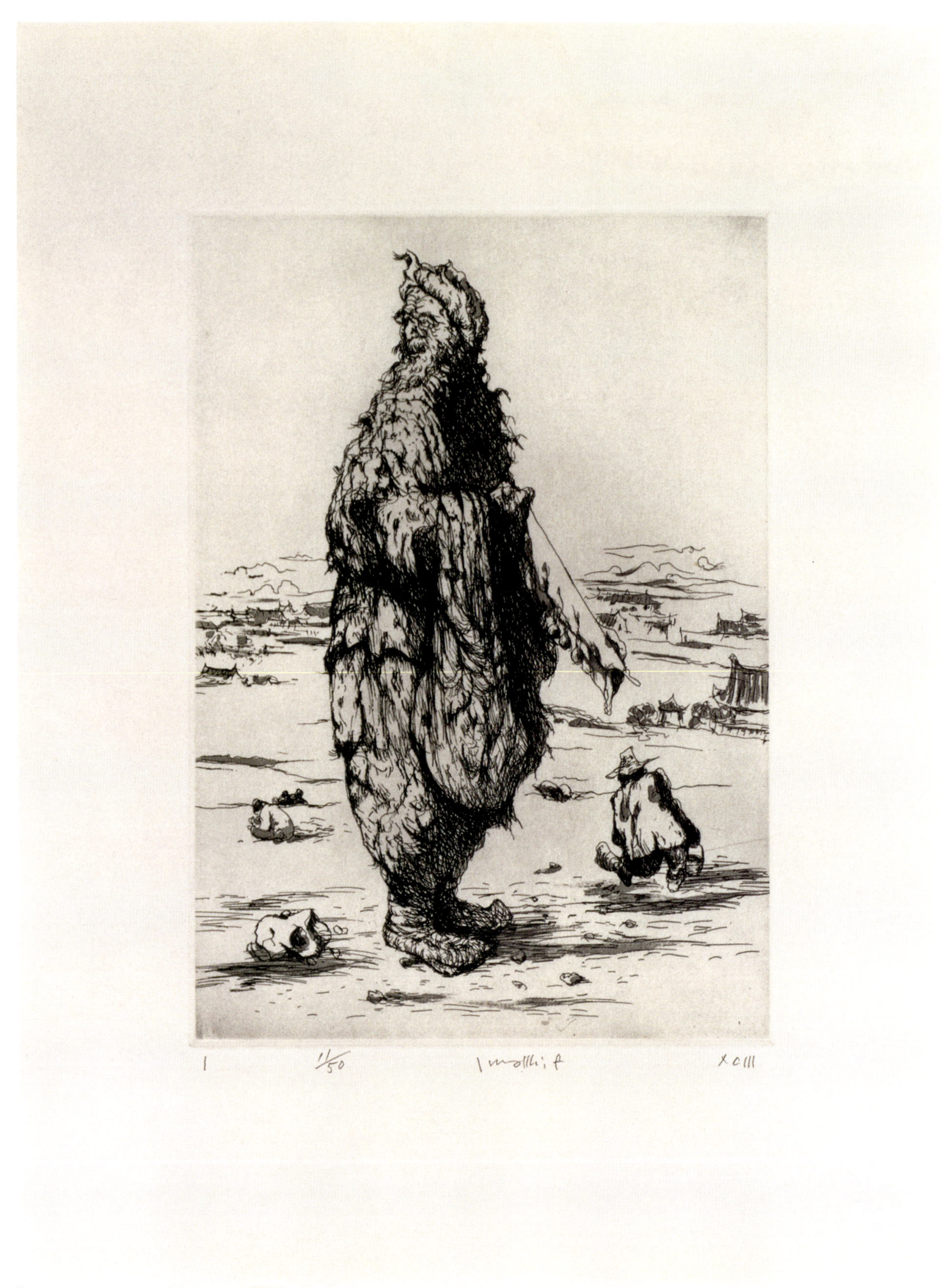

80

Furuzawa Iwami, Begging Saints, from the Series: Shuragai, Scenes of Bloody Conflicts between the Famine Devils in Hell, 1960–1993
Etching, Series of 30 sheets, each one 25 x 18 cm, Itabashiku Art Museum, Tokyo

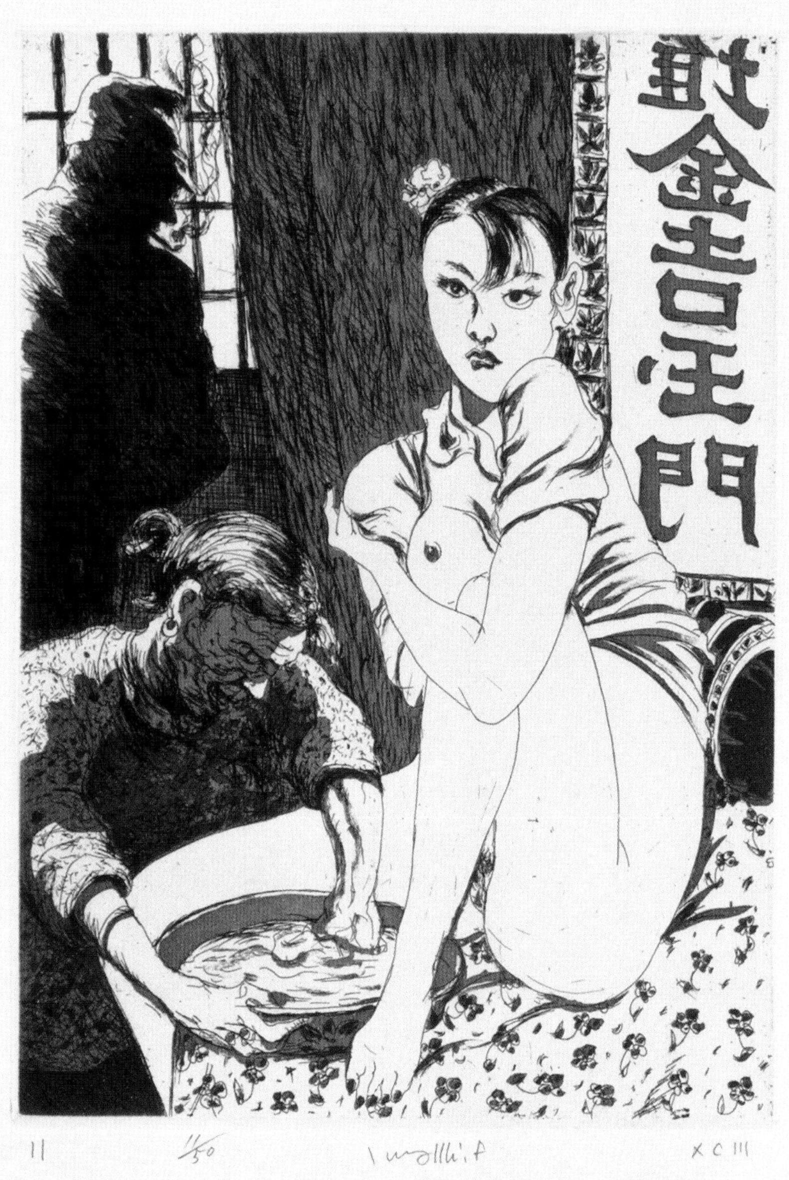

81
Rape

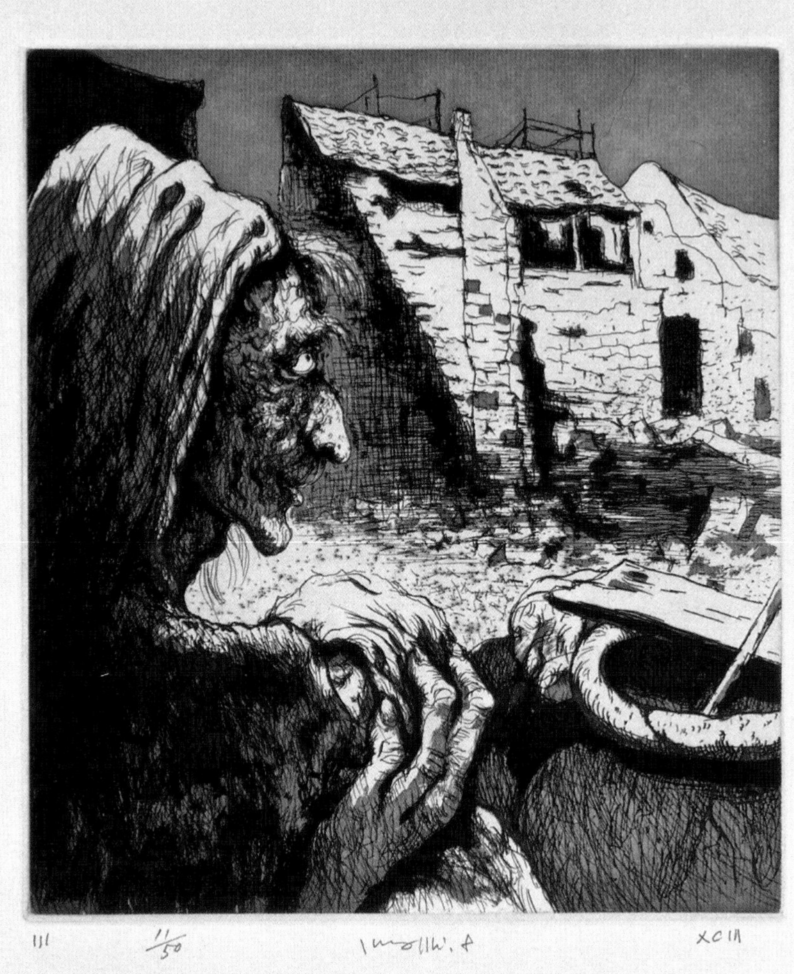

82
Insane Woman

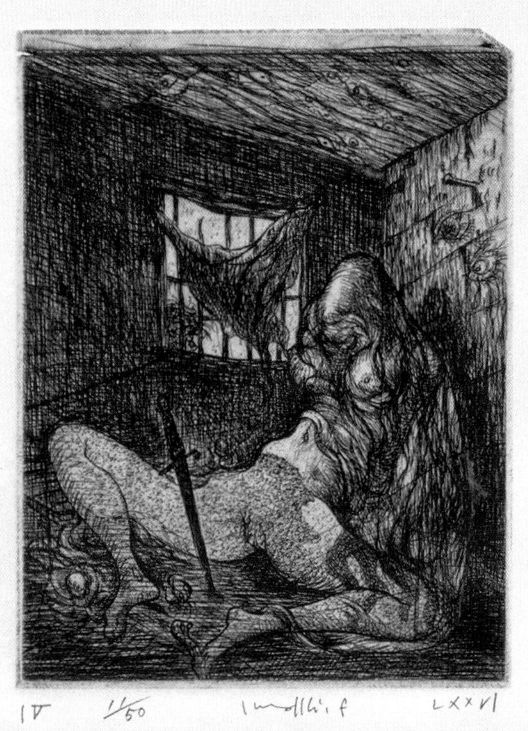

83
Rape

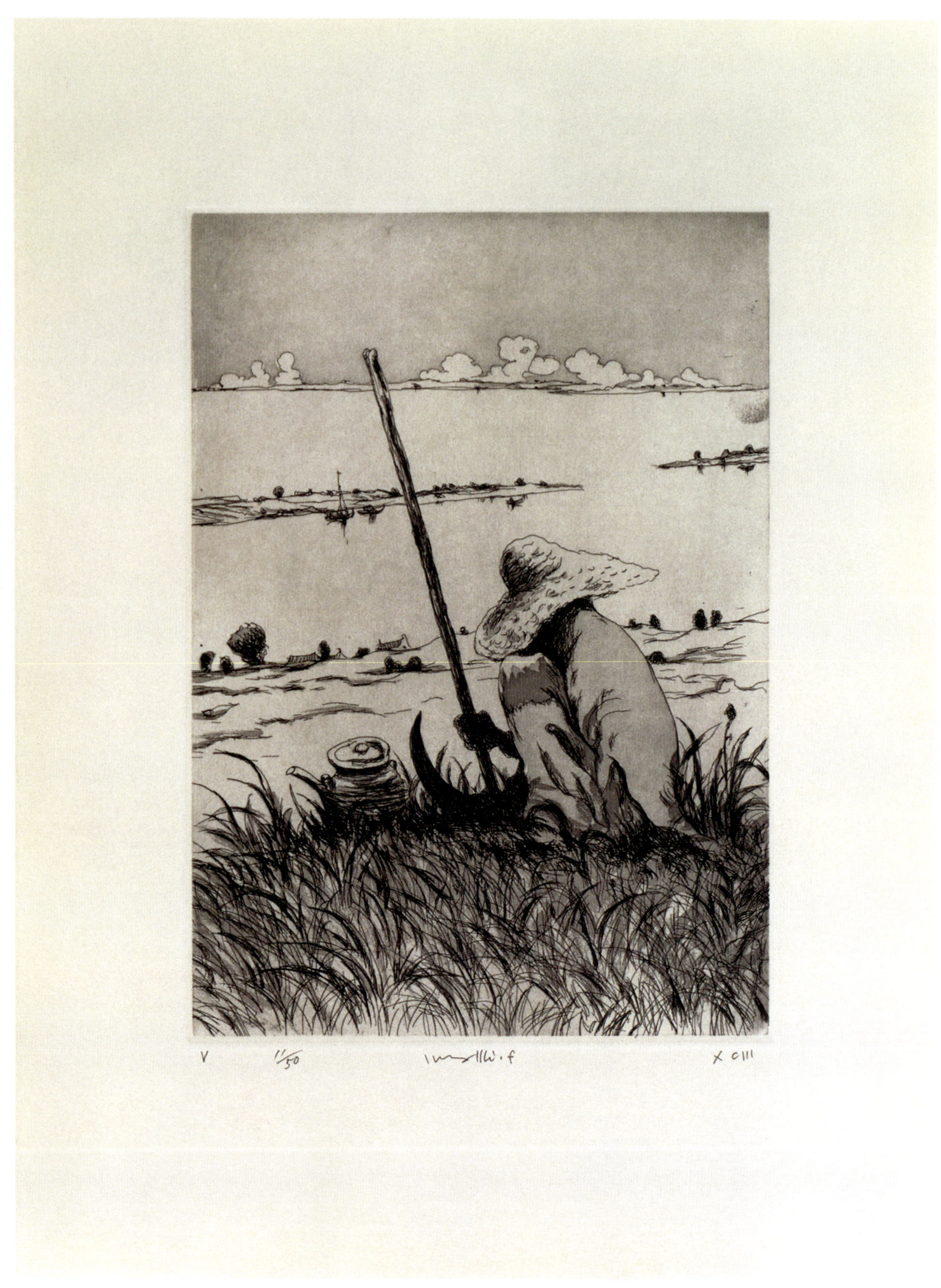

84
Old Woman Cutting Grass

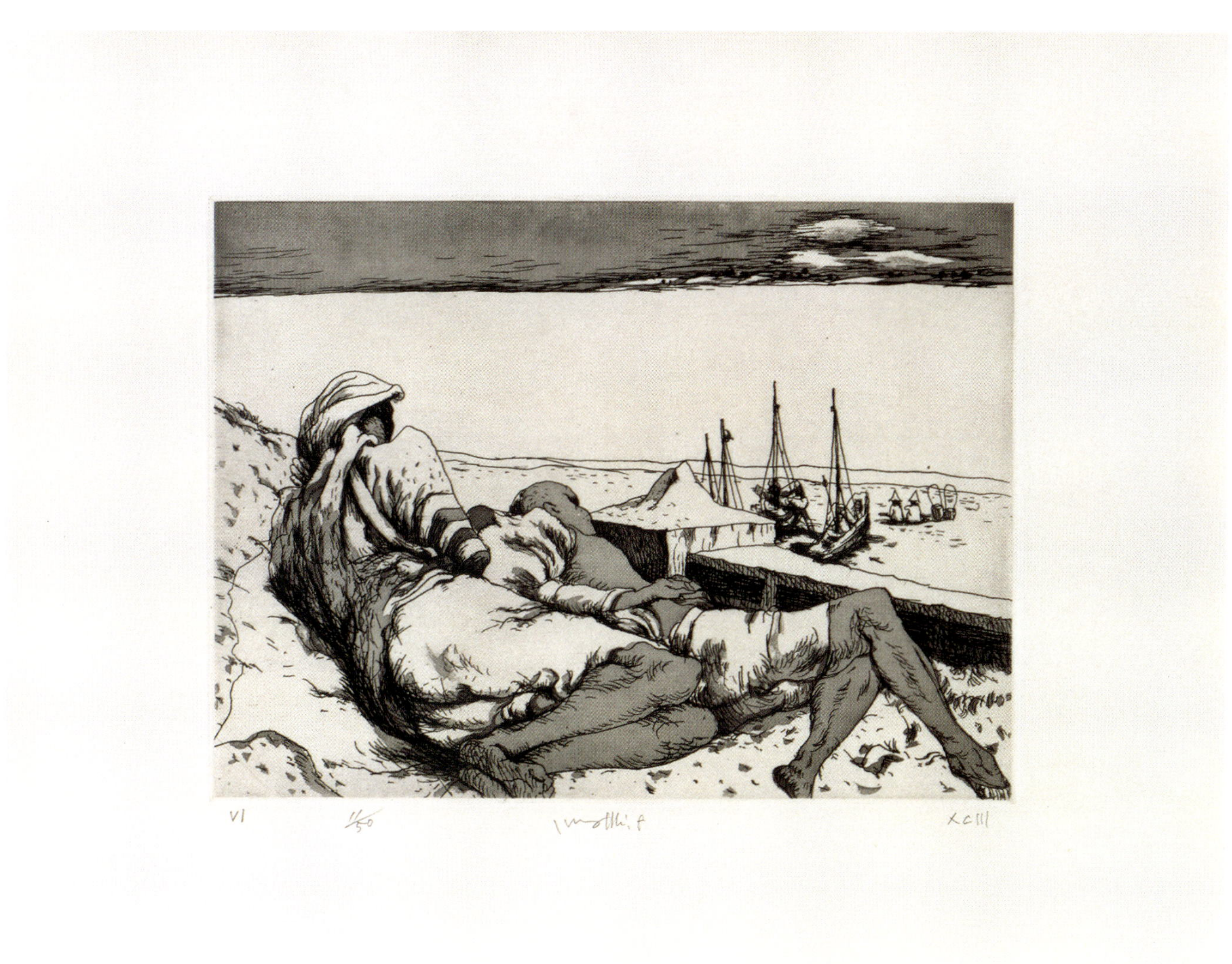

85
The Chang River

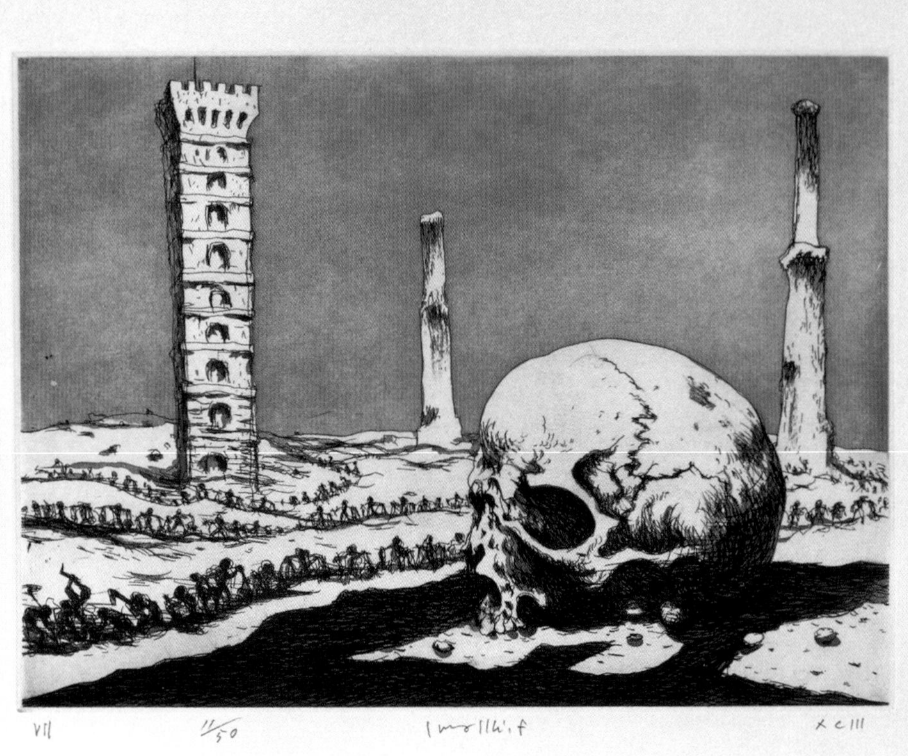

86
Forced Labor

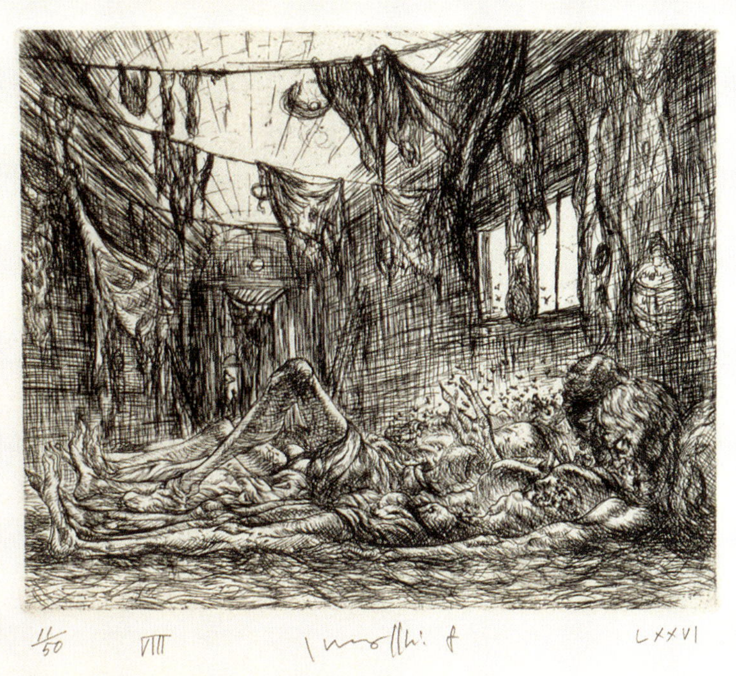

87
Return of the Freight Cars

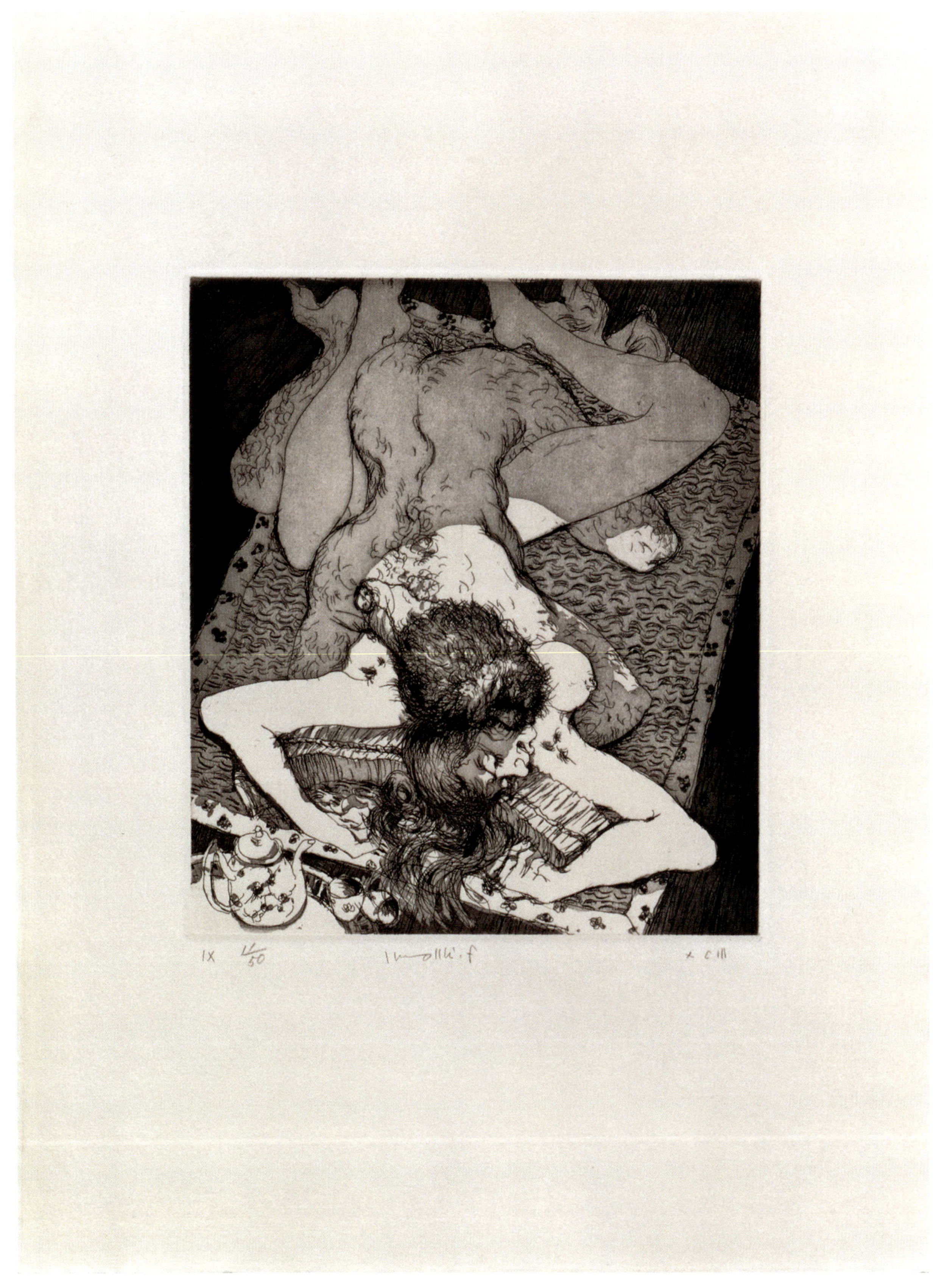

88
Be a Man!

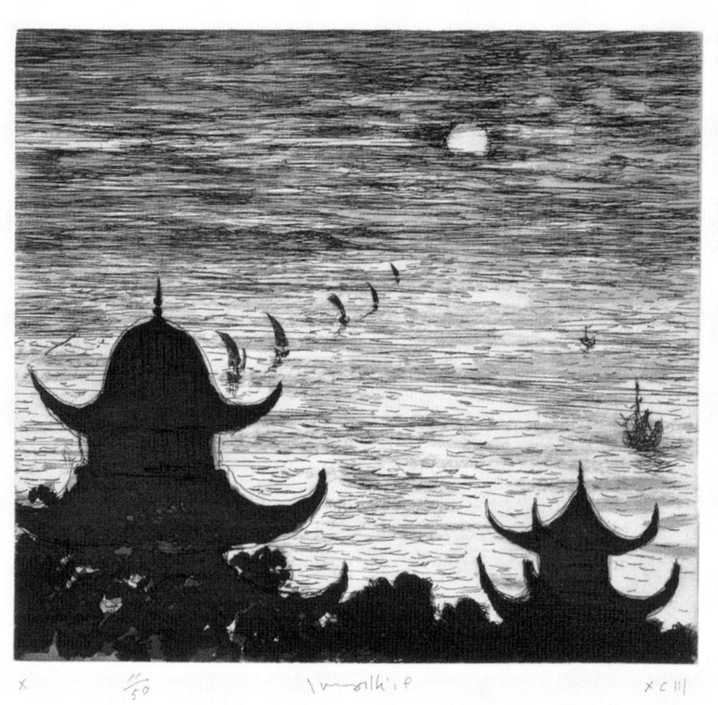

89
Dongtingu-hu Summer Moon Garden

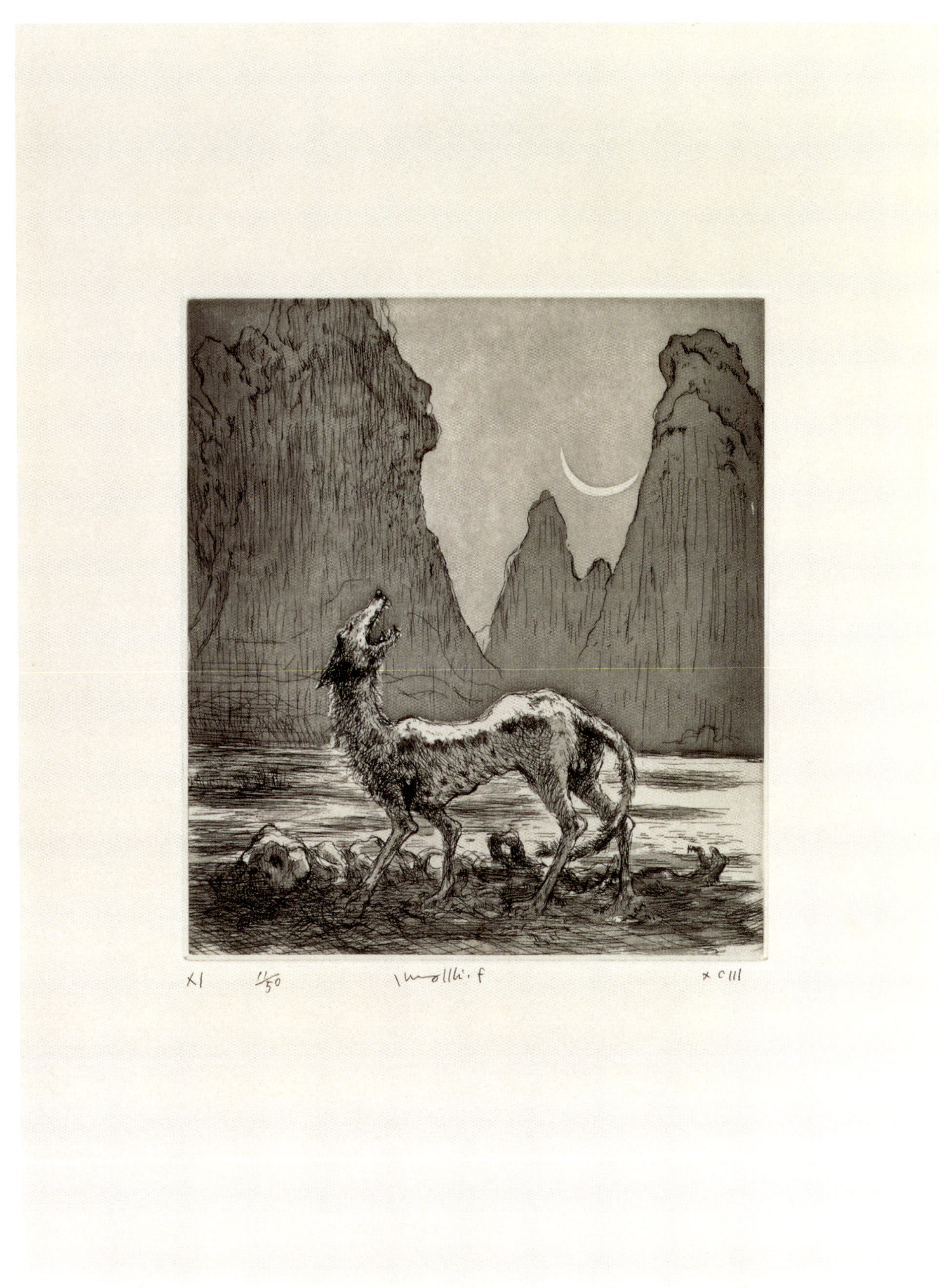

90
Barking Moon

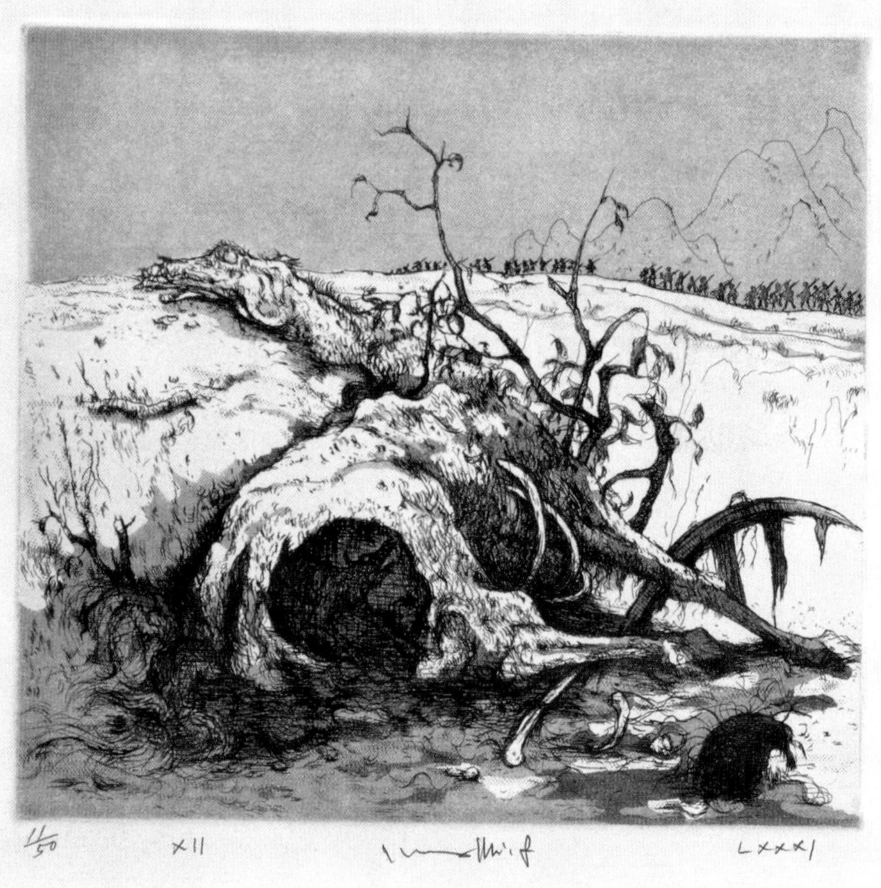

91
Wretched Military Horse

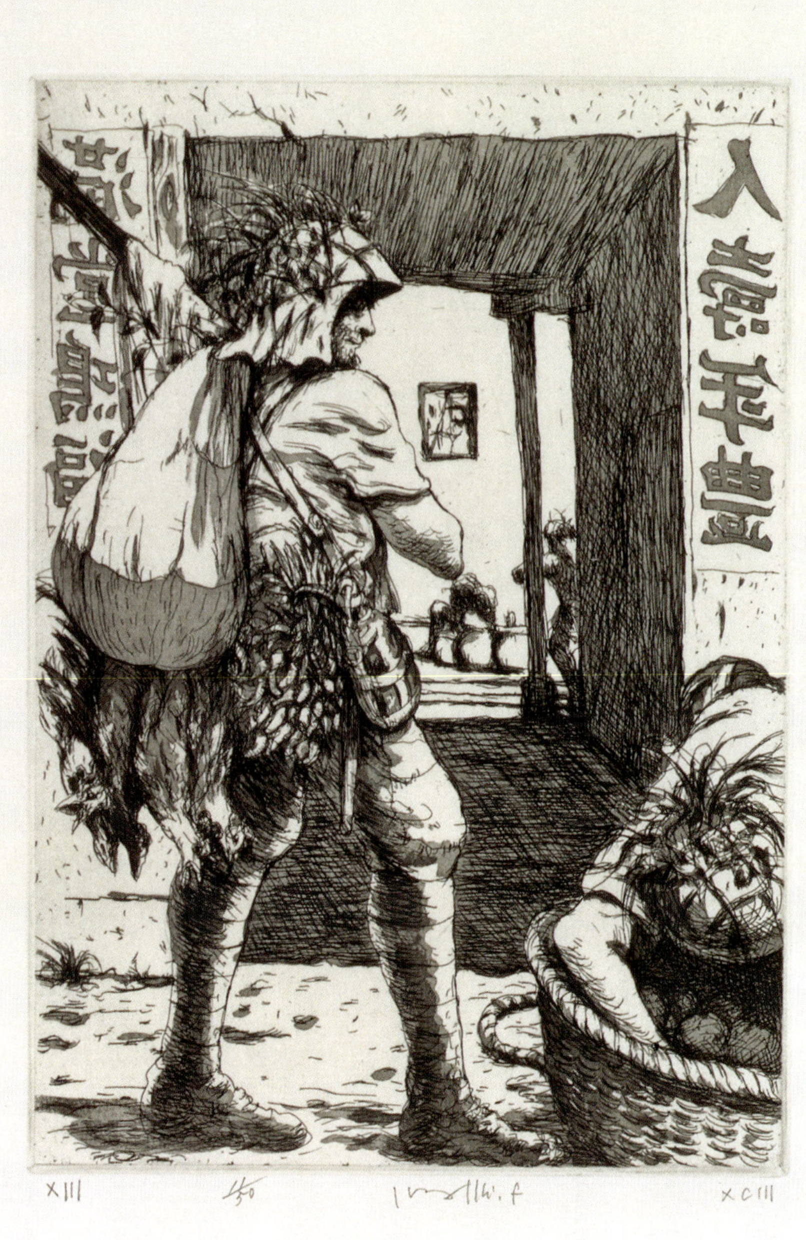

92
Looting

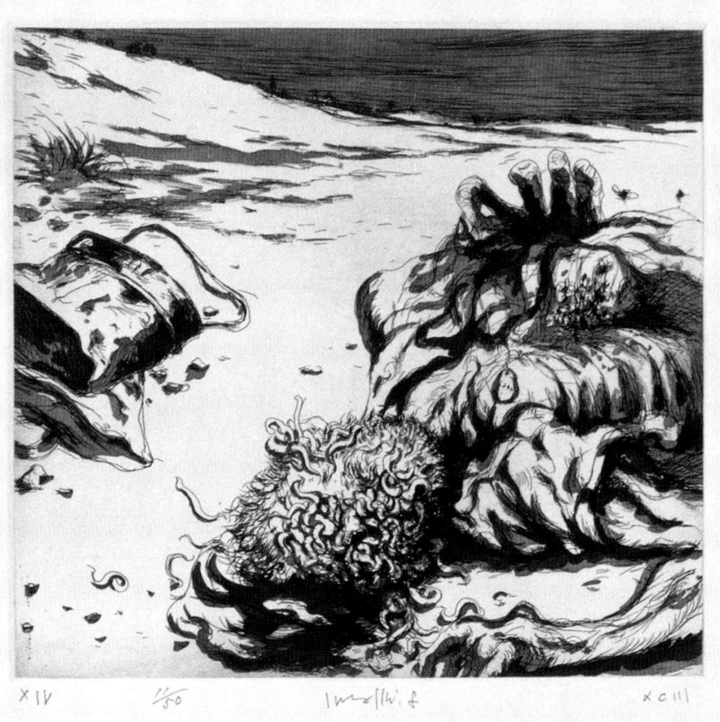

93
Die for Nothing like a Dog (a Disgraceful Death)

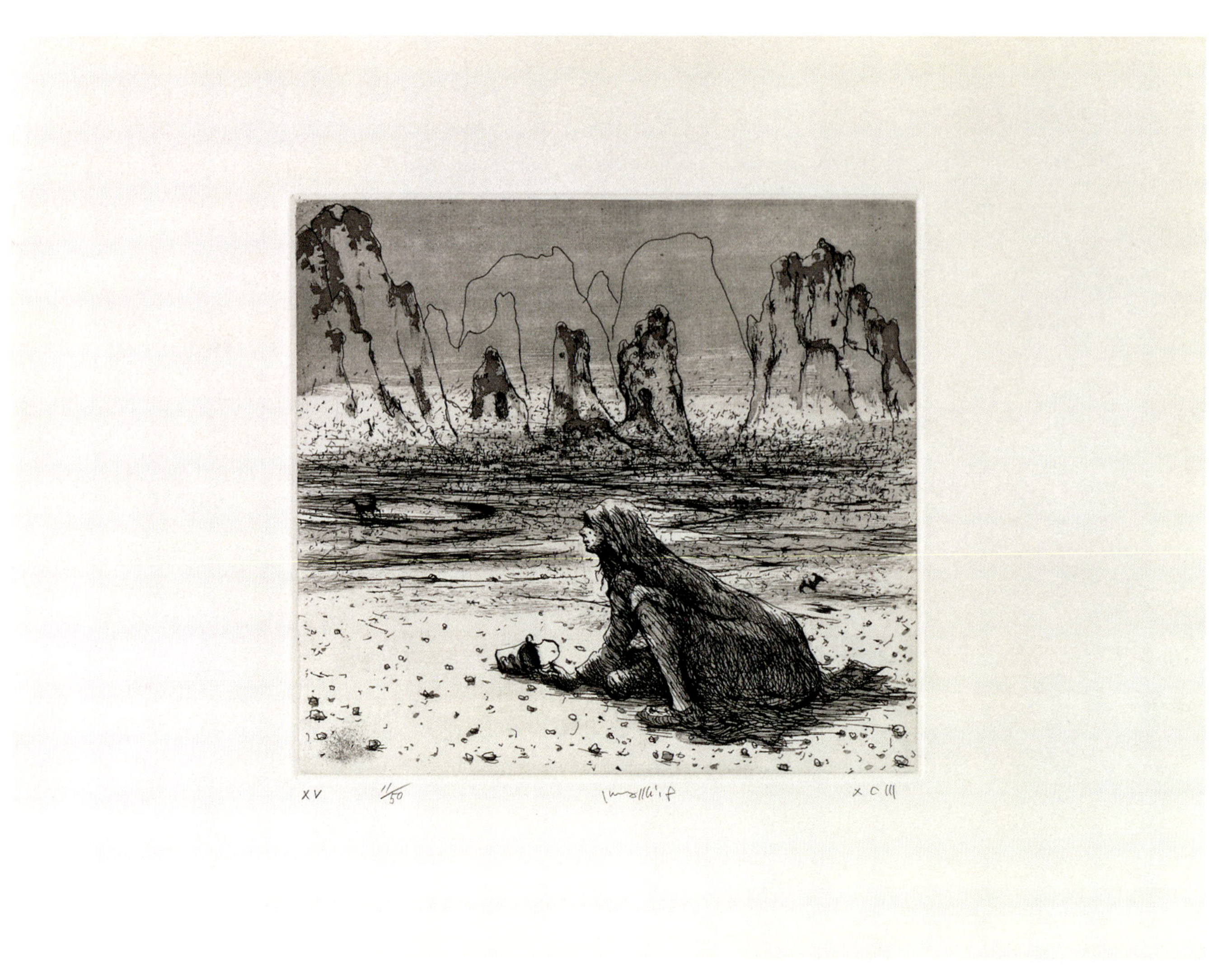

94
Wailing in the Depths of the Mountains

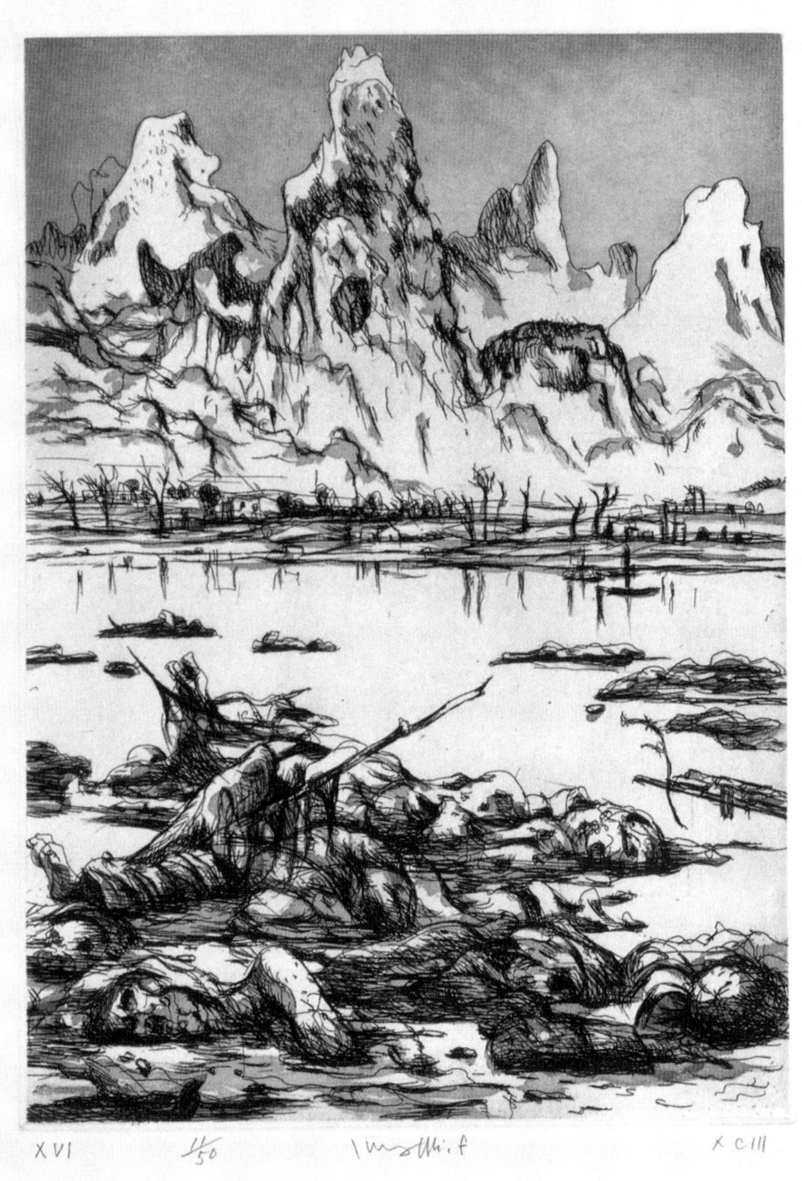

95
Wailing of the Devil

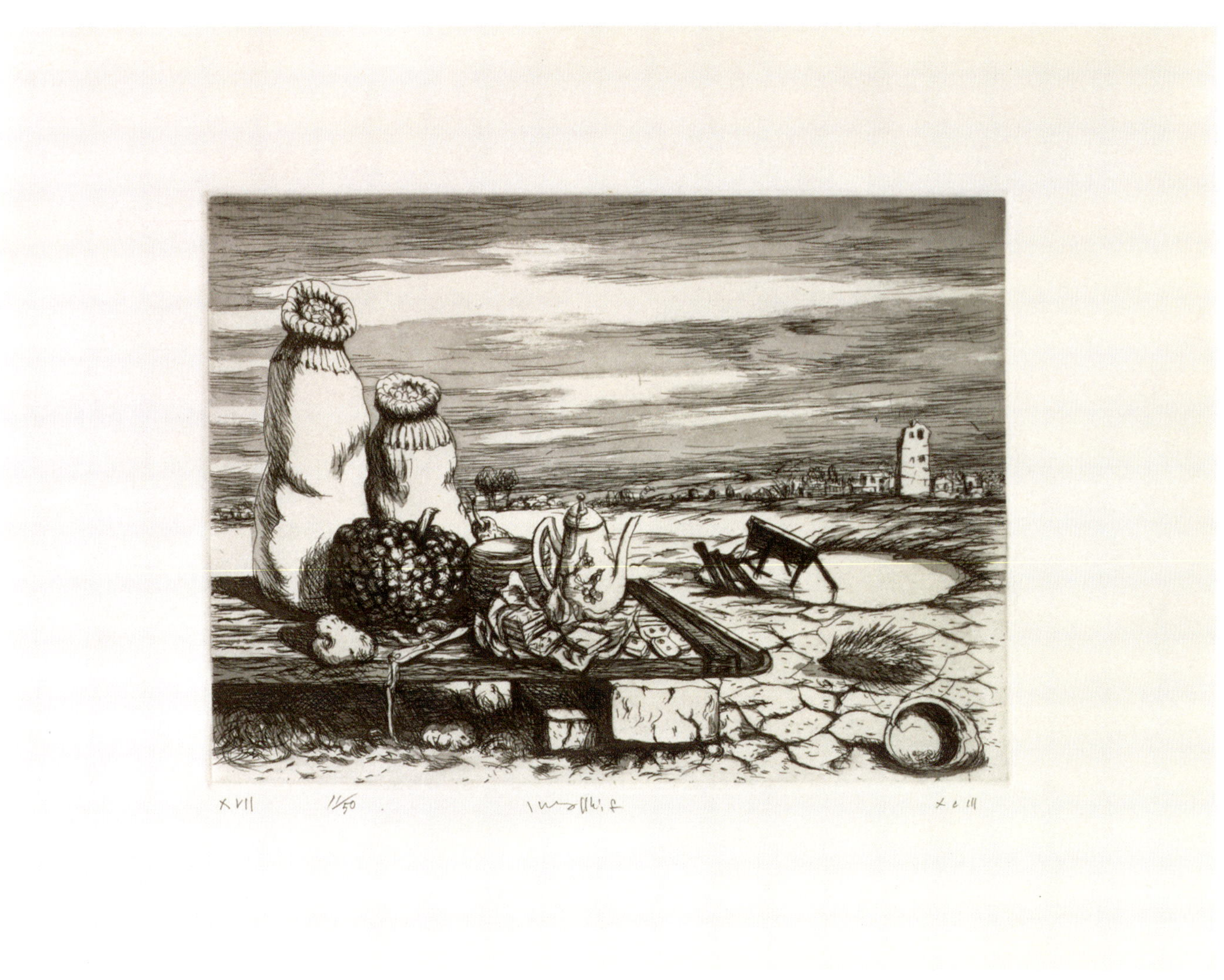

96
Table of Plundered Poverty (The poorest Chinese peasants are robbed so that we may live)

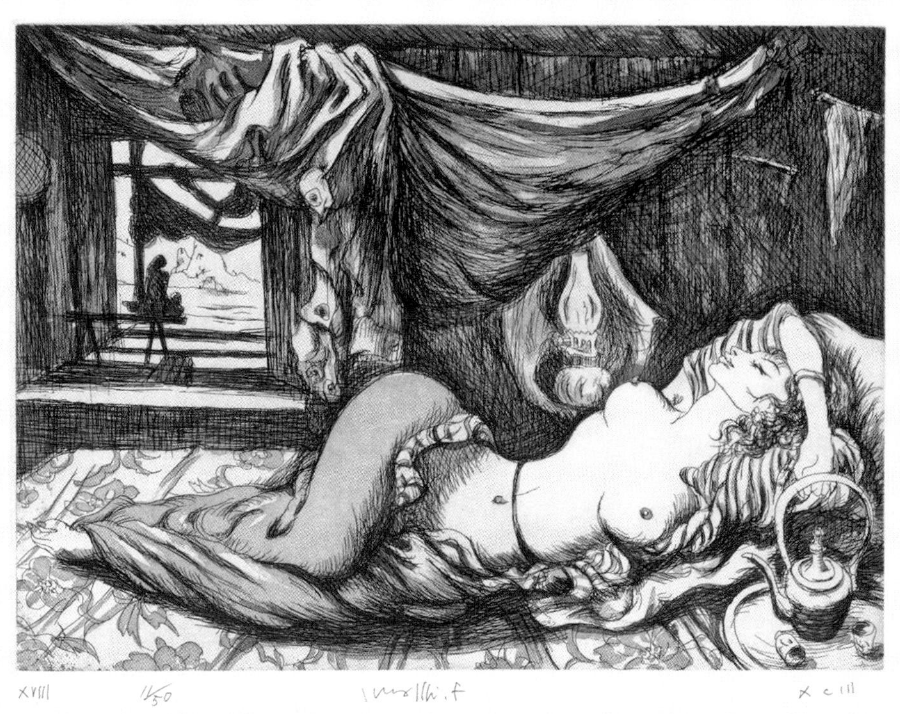

97
Poor White Thread (Sad beauty: a prostitute in a military camp)

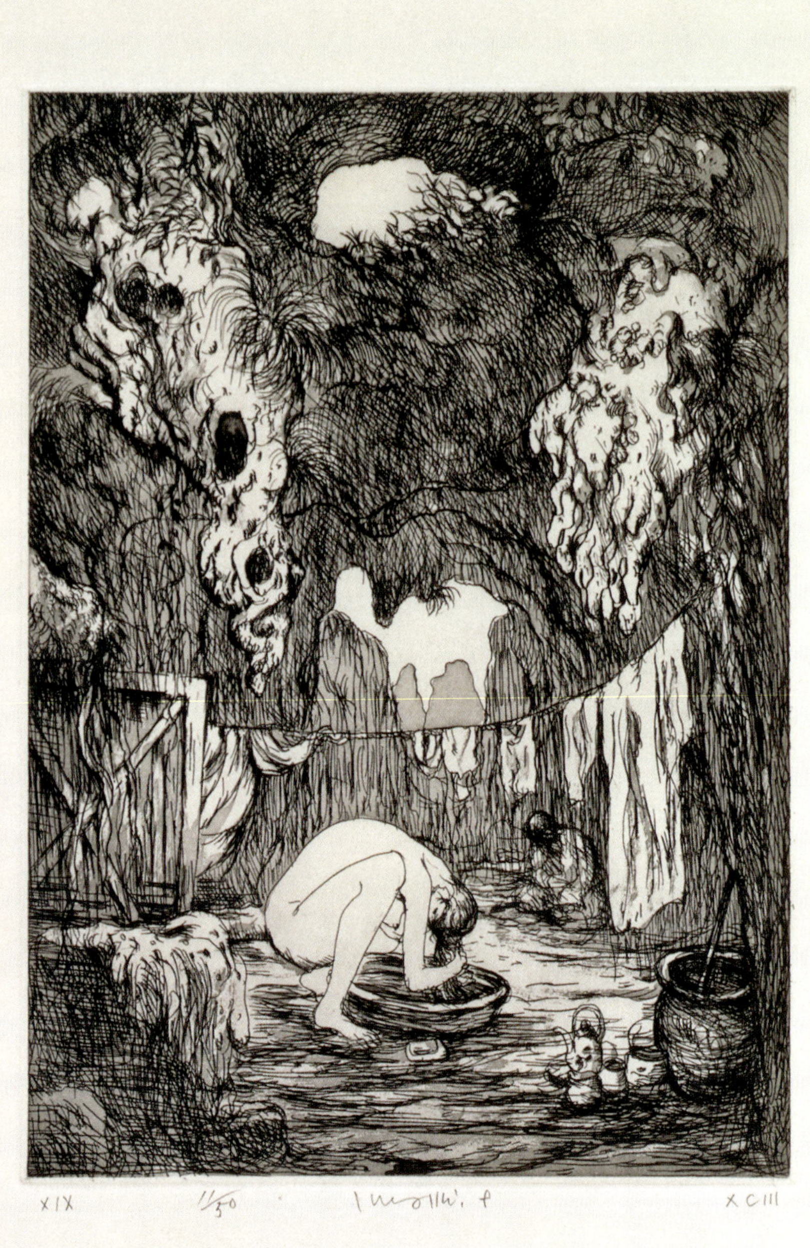

98
Grotto

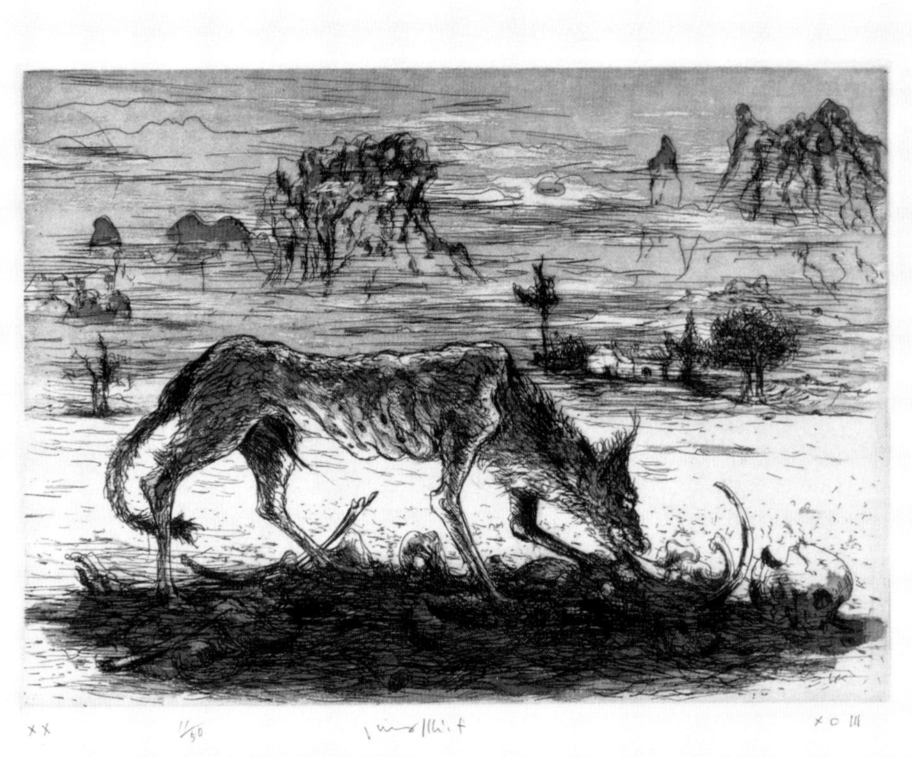

99
Blue Dusk

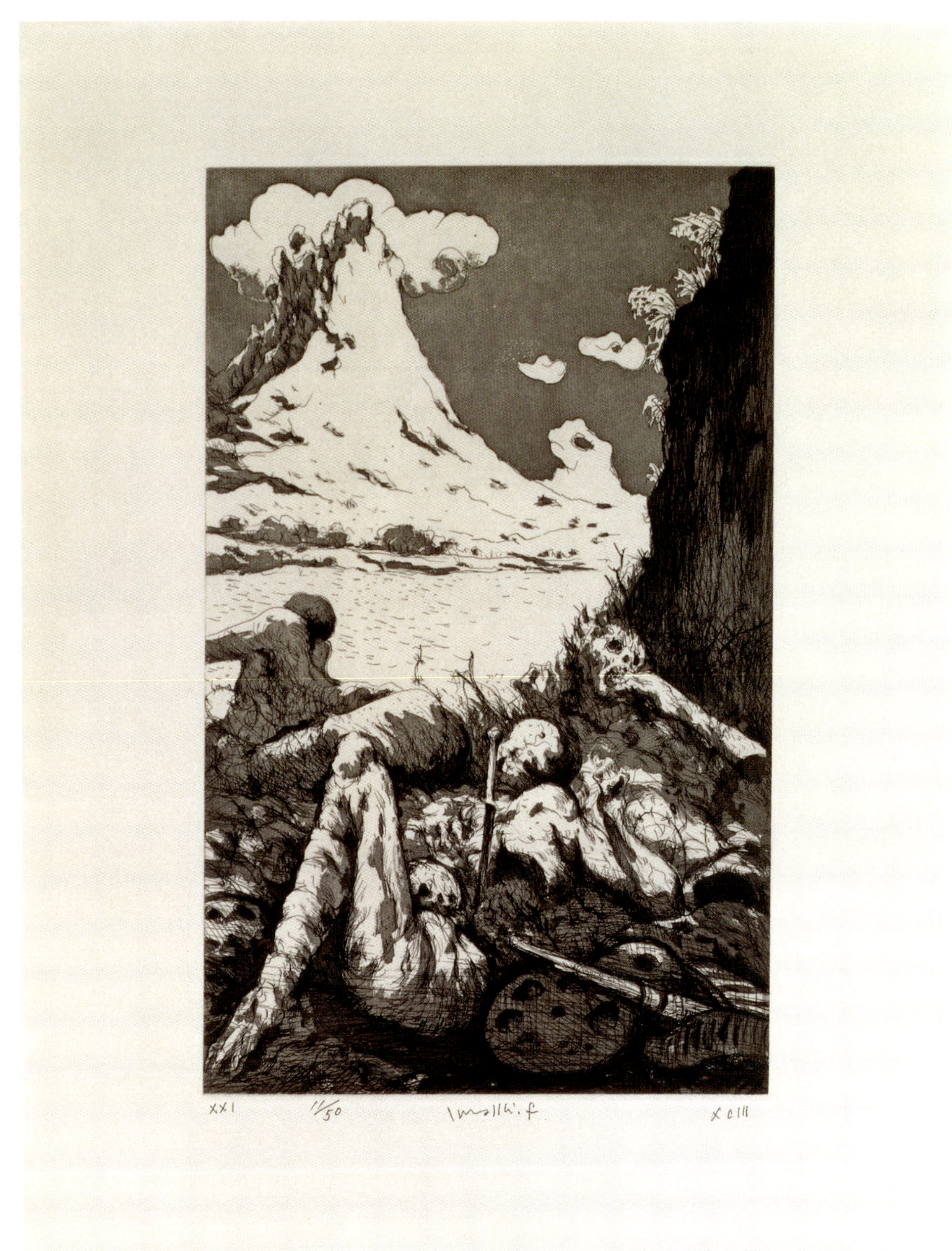

100
Corpse

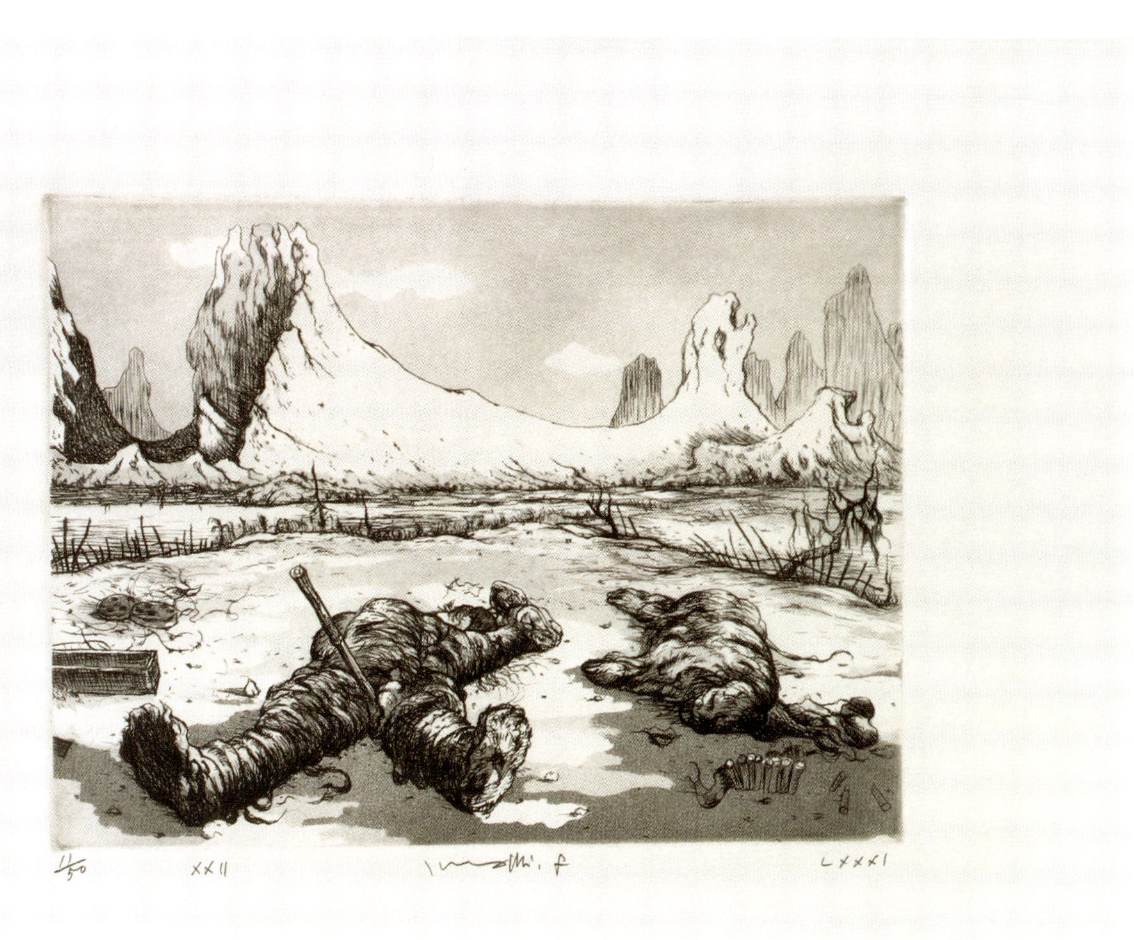

101
Field of Peach Blossoms

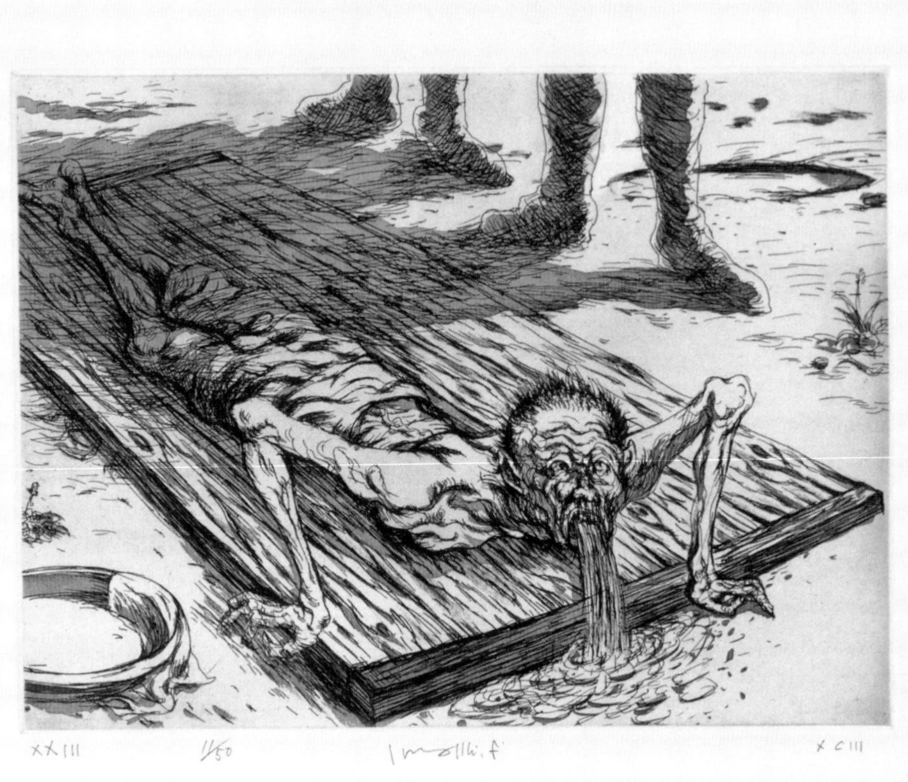

102
Cholera

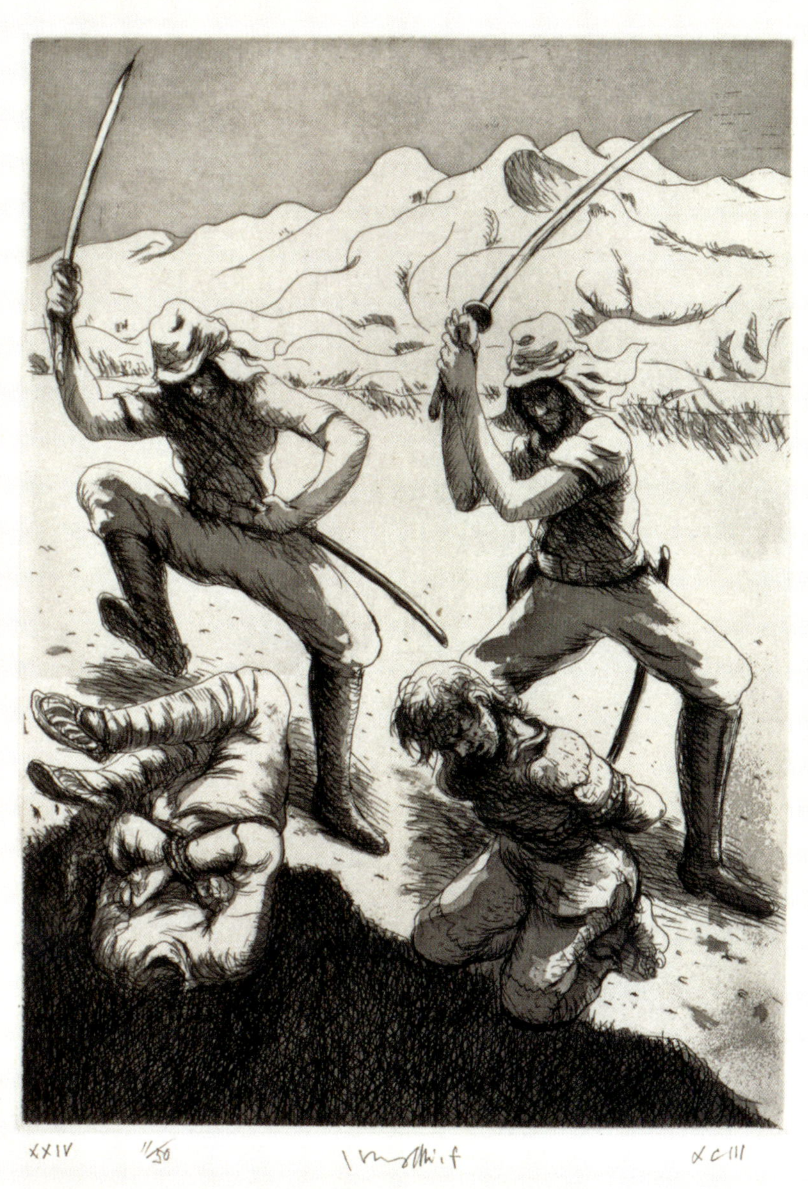

103
Beheading

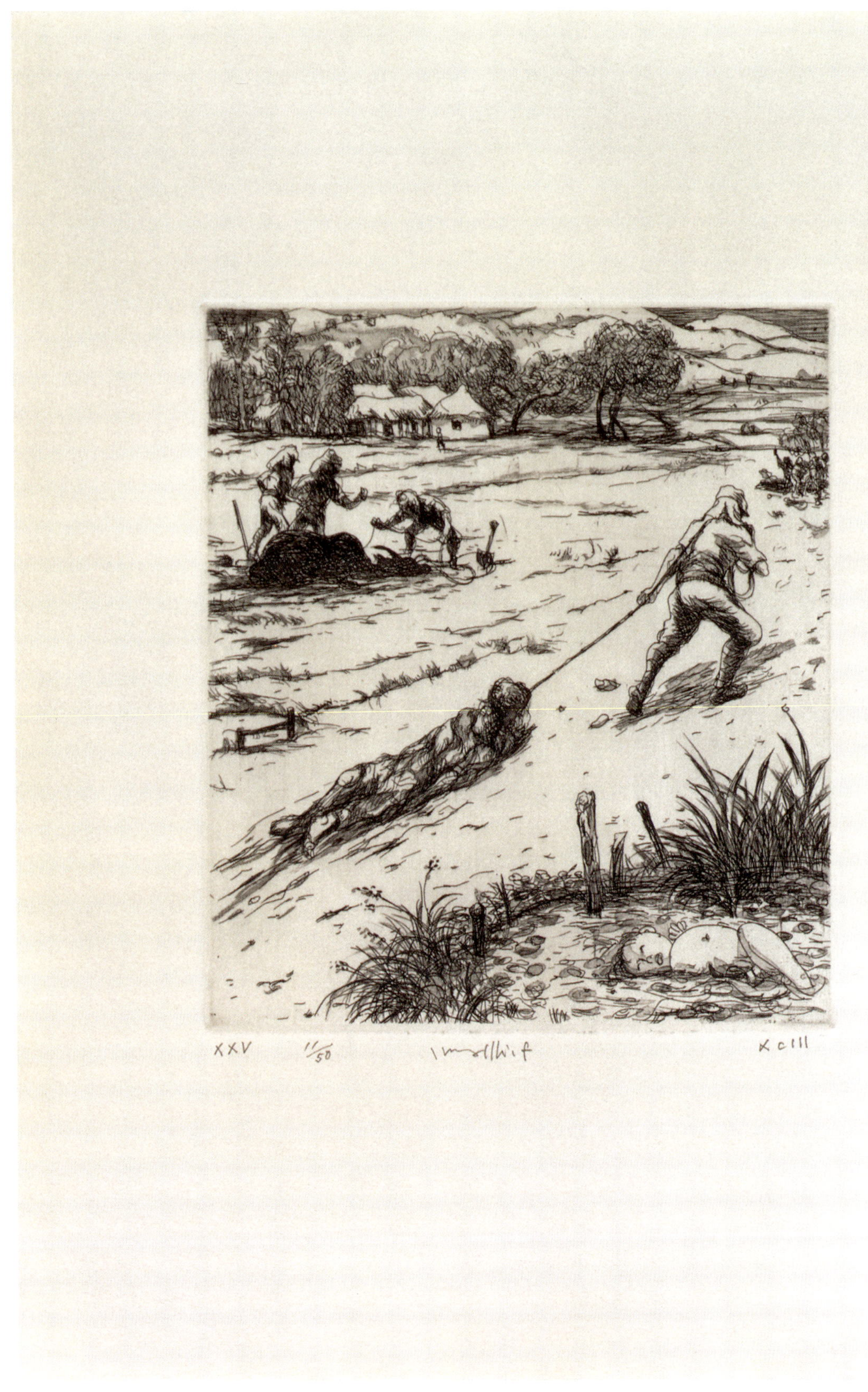

104
Cleansing Dead Bodies

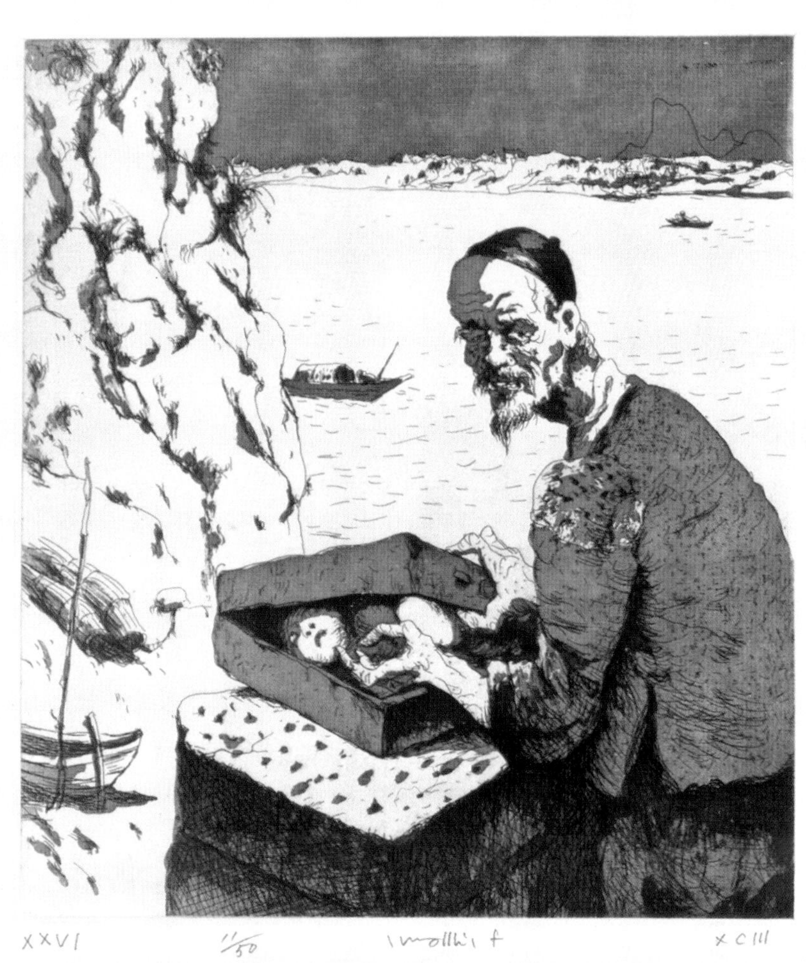

105
Failure?

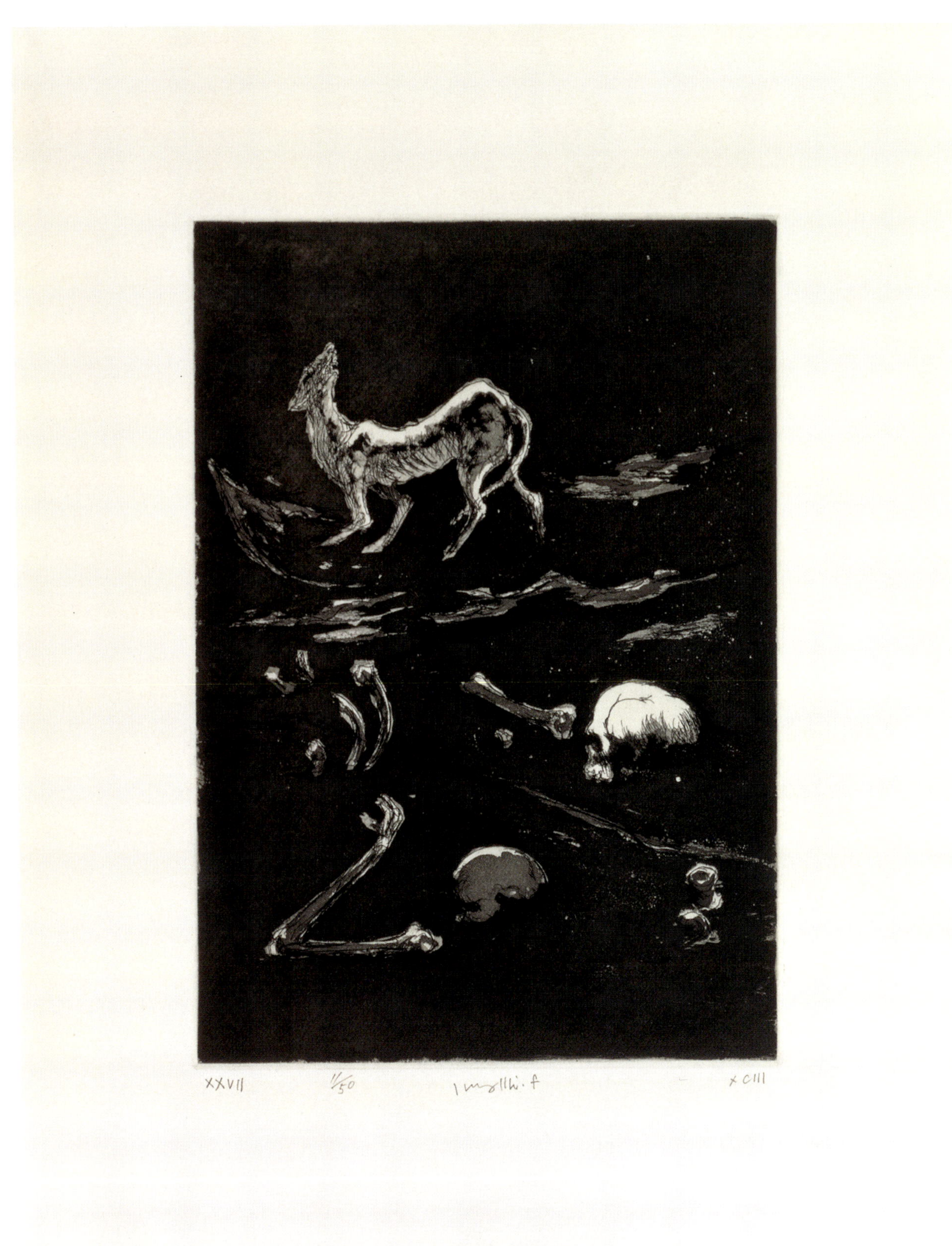

106
Darkness

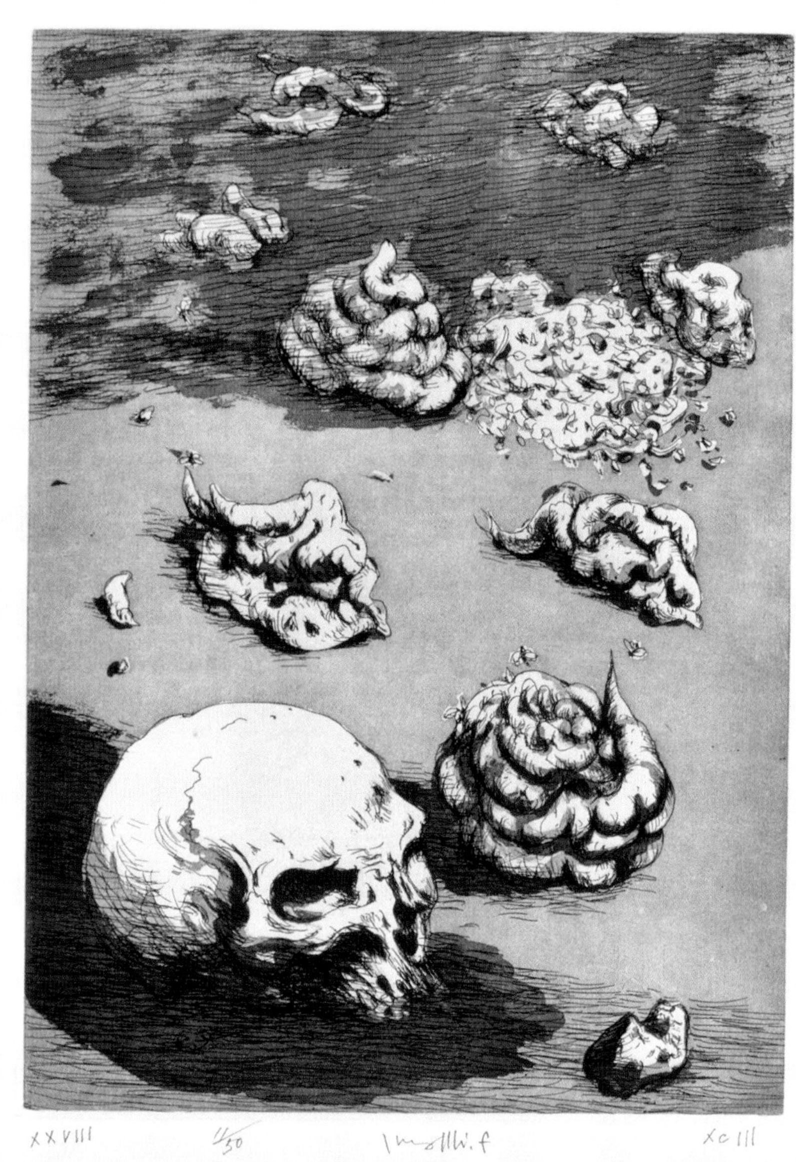

107
Excrement and Bones

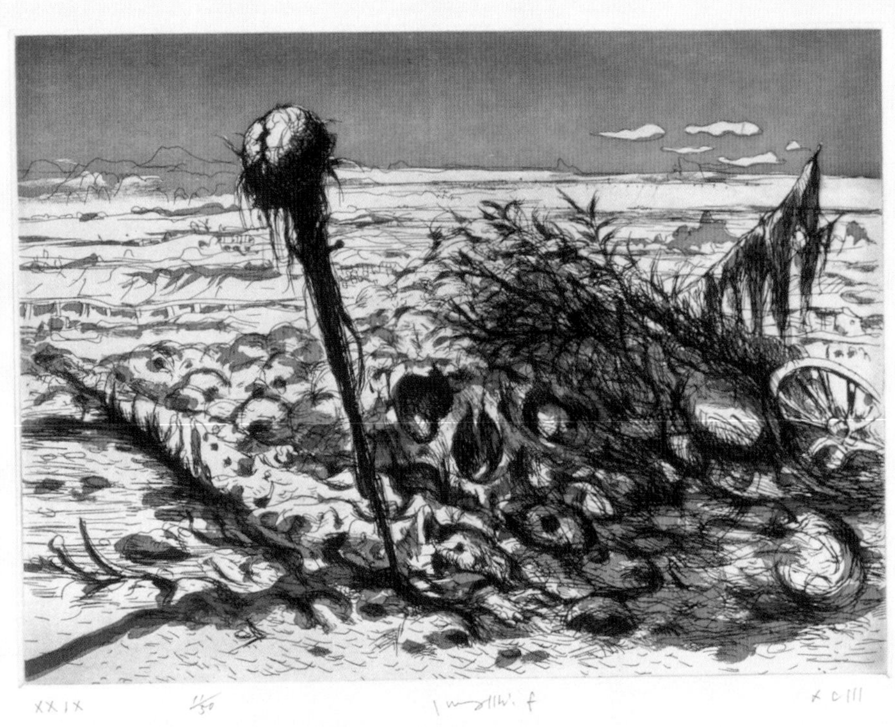

108
Fallen Soldier

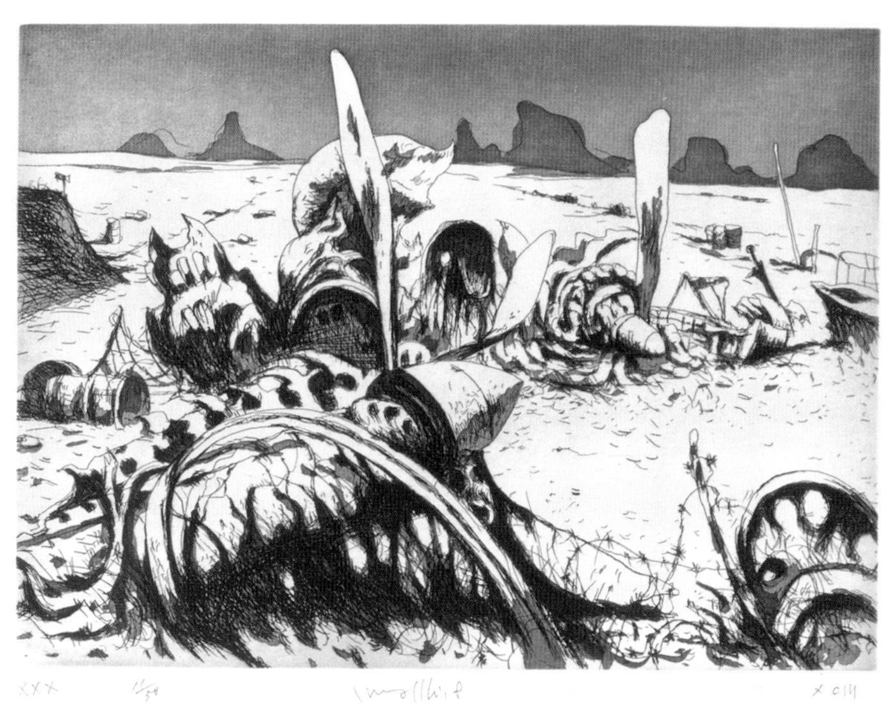

109
Shattered, Rotting Wing

THE ARTISTS

ABE NOBUYA

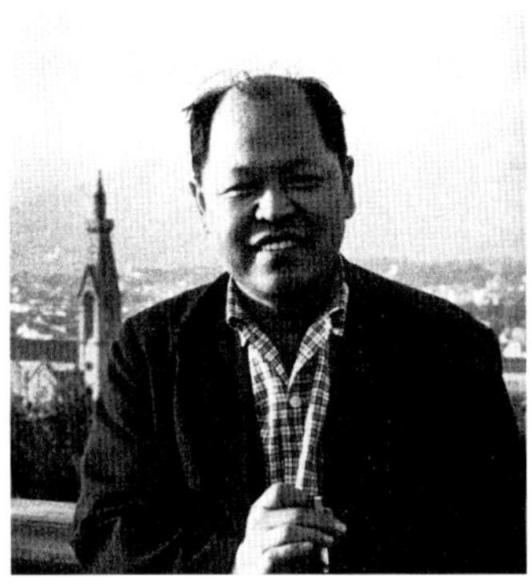

1913 Born in Goizumi, Niigata Prefecture.
Real Christian name: Yoshifumi.
1937 *Yosei-no-kyori* (Distance of the Nymphs), an illustrated collection of poems with surrealistic drawings and poems by Takiguchi Shuzo.
1938 Co-founder of the Bijutsubunka-kyôkai Society (Art and Culture Society).
1949 Active art critic.
1952 Withdraws from the Bijutsubunka-kyôkai Society.
1953 Seven-months stay in India.
Founder of the International Art Club.
1955 *Contemporary American Art* is published.
1957–58 Travels through Europe (Yugoslavia, Paris, Zurich, Vienna) and then the USA, after receiving an invitation from the American Foreign Ministry.
1959 A stay in Rome, Member of the Executive Committee of the LAPA.
1960 Member of the jury for the Guggenheim Art Prize.
Member of the committee for the Ljubljana *International Graphic Art Biennial.*
1969 Travels to Sarajevo upon receiving an invitation from the Yugoslav Republic.
1970 Travels to Europe (Bulgaria, Ireland).
1971 Dies after suddenly falling ill.

Solo Exhibitions

1951 Takamiya Gallery, Tokyo
1957 Yoseido Gallery, Tokyo
1960 Galleria Grataceo, Milan
1961 Galleria Alberto, Rome
1962 Galleria George Lester, Rome
1964 Galleria Naviglio, Milan
Galleria George Lester, Rome
Galleria Paganini Lester, Milan
1965 Galleria Cavaglino, Venice

Group Exhibitions

1932 *2nd Dokuritsubijutsu-kyôkai,* Tokyo
1940 *1st Bijutsubunka-kyôkai,* Tokyo
1950 *2nd Yomiuri Independant,* Tokyo
1951 *1st São Paulo Biennial,* São Paulo
1952 *39th Carnegie International Art Exhibition,* New York
Nihon Kokusai-bijutsu-ten (International Art Exhibition), Tokyo
1953 *Abstraction and Fantasy,* National Museum of Modern Art, Tokyo
1954 *1st Nihon Gendai-bijutsu-ten* (Exhibition of contemporary Japanese art), Tokyo
1961 *International Watercolor Exhibition,* Brooklyn Museum, New York
1963 *San Marino Biennial,* San Marino
1964 *43th Carnegie International Art Exhibition,* New York
1965 *Zero Avantgarde,* Milan
1967 *46th Carnegie International Art Exhibition,* New York

AI-MITSU

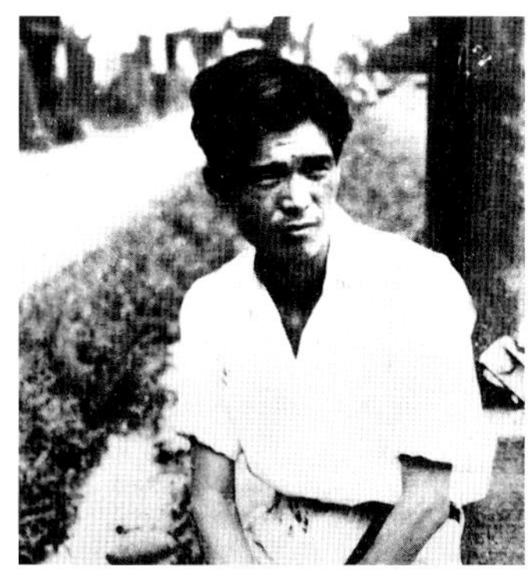

1907 Born in Mibu-chô, Yamagata district, Hiroshima Prefecture. Real name: Ishimura Nichirô.
1922 Starts works at the Ibuki Design company, Osaka.
1923 Studies at the Tensai School for Painting in Osaka, uses the name Aikawa Mitsurô.
1924 Moves to Tokyo. Visits the Taiheiyôgakai Institute.
1926 First Prize at the *13th Nika-ten,* assumes the name Ai-Mitsu.
1929 Founds the Kôgenkai Society together with Tsuruoka Masao and others.
1938 First prize for *Landscape (Landscape with Eyes)* at the *8th Dokuritsubijutsu-kyôkai* (Independent Artists Association).
1939 Co-founder of the Bijutsubunka-kyôkai (Art and Cultural Association).
1940 Founds Shinjingakai (New Painters Association) together with Matsumoto Shunsuke, Asô Saburô, Tsuruoka Masao and others.
1944 Becomes seriously ill in Wuchang at the end of the war.
1946 Dies of his illness in Shanghai.

Selected Solo Exhibitions

1938 Newspaper *Chûgoku,* Hiroshima
1943 Hotel Yamato, Dalian, China
1949 Hokusô Gallery, Tokyo
1954 Pedagogic Faculty at the University of Tokyo
1961 Gallery of the Bungeishunjû Publishing House, Tokyo (Organizer: Nantenshi Gallery)
1979 Odakyû Grand Gallery, Tokyo
1988 Nerimaku Art Museum, Tokyo
1994 Prefecture Museum of Modern Art, Tokushima Prefecture
1998 Odakyû Museum of Art, Tokyo

Selected Group Exhibitions

1923 *13th Nika-ten,* Tokyo
1932 *Nova,* Tokyo
1933 *Independent Art Association,* Tokyo
1940 *Art and Culture Association,* Tokyo
1943 *Shinjingakai* (New Painter Association) together with Maruki Iri, Sera Gallery, Hiroshima
1967 *Ai-Mitsu and Sekine Shôji,* Kanagawa Prefecture Museum of Modern Art, Kamakura
1971 *Raisan Yô, Minami Kunzô and Ai-Mitsu,* Prefecture Art Museum, Hiroshima Prefecture
1977 *Ai-Mitsu and Matsumoto Shunsuke, New Beginnings in Post-war Art,* Municipal Art Museum, Tokyo
1986 *Japon des Avantgardes 1910–1970,* Centre Georges Pompidou, Paris

EI-KYÛ

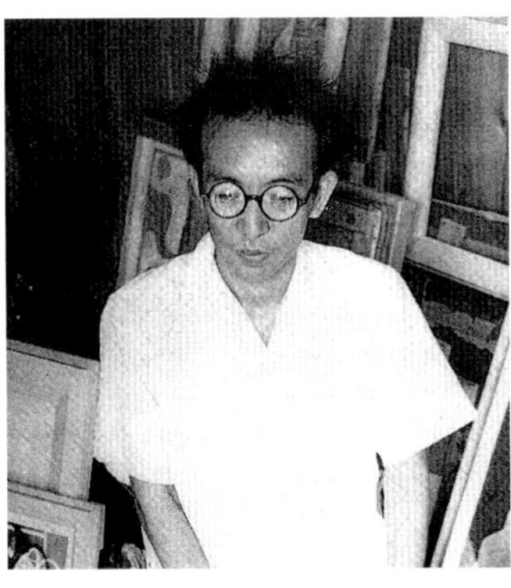

1911	Born in Miyazaki, Miyazaki Prefecture. Real name: Sugita Hideo.
1925	Studies Western painting at the Nihon Bijutsu Gakkô Art School.
1927	Following his return to Miyazaki, he then goes back to Tokyo. While moving back and forth between Miyazaki and Tokyo he is particularly active as an art critic. Contributions in magazines, e.g. in *Atelier* or *Mizue.*
1930	Becomes a member of the Oriental Photographic School.
1936	Member of the Shinjidaiyôga-ten (Western painting of the New Age) Group. He creates the *Reasons for Sleep* photogrammes.
1937	His relations to the Association of Free Artists are up and down.
1951	Founds the Demokurâto Bijutsuka-kyôkai (Association of Democratic Artists), first exhibition. He designs *Dreams of Photographic Images* and produces his first etchings.
1960	He dies in Tokyo.

Selected Solo Exhibitions

1936	*Photodesign,* Kinokuniya Gallery, Tokyo (1950 Matsuzakaya, Tokyo; 1952 Takemiya Gallery, Tokyo; 1955 Takashimaya, Tokyo)
1950	Clubhouse, Miyazaki Prefecture
1952	Miyazaki Prefecture Library (and 1955,1957,1968,1975)
1954	Bunbôdô Gallery, Tokyo
1957	Takemiya Gallery, Tokyo
1960	Kabutoya Gallery, Tokyo
1971	Miyazaki Prefecture Museum for Art, Miyazaki (and 1980)
1979	Odakyû Grand Gallery, Tokyo
1996	Miyazaki Prefecture Museum for Art, Miyazaki

Selected Group Exhibitions

1934	*1st Exhibition of the Miyazaki Art Association*
1937	*1st Exhibition of the Association of Free Artists*
1951	*1st Democratic Art Exhibition,* Municipal Art Museum, Osaka
1955	*7th Japanese Independent Exhibition,* Municipal Art Museum, Tokyo
1957	*1st International Graphic Art Biennial Tokyo,* National Museum of Modern Art, Tokyo
1960	*The Unfolding of Surrealist Painting,* National Museum of Modern Art, Tokyo
1982	*Photogramme Exhibition: Man Ray, Moholy-Nagy, Ei-Kyû, Yamaguchi Masanari,* Municipal Art Museum, Fukuoka
1985	*Ei-Kyû and the Democratic Painters,* Museum of Modern Art, Kobe *Ei-Kyû and his Environment,* Prefecture Museum of Modern Art, Saitama Prefecture
1986	*Japon des Avantgardes 1910–1970,* Centre Georges Pompidou, Paris
1992	*Abstract Painting in Japan 1910–1945,* Itabashiku Art Museum, Tokyo (and other museums)
1997	*Traces of Light in Modernism: Onchi Kôshirô, Shiihara Osamu, Ei-Kyû,* National Museum of Modern Art, Tokyo

FURUZAWA IWAMI

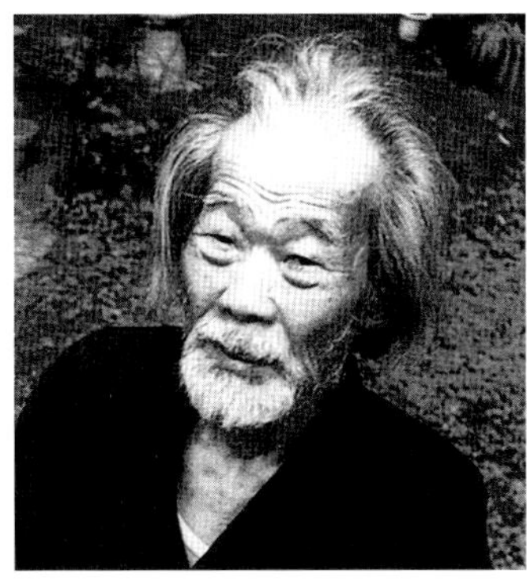

1912 Born in Saga Prefecture.

1928 Goes to Tokyo. Attends the Hongô Painting Institute. His painting style changes from Japanese to Western.

1938 Founds the Sôki Artists Association, which breaks up in the spring of 1939. Involved in founding the Bijutsubunka-kyôkai (Art and Culture Association).

1939 Receives an award in an illustration competition marking the 50th anniversary of the Asahi Newspaper.

1940 Sent to Peking as a special correspondent for drawing illustrations.

1943 He is drafted into the army.

1944 *Rank and File Soldiers and Officers of the Army in the Wuhan Region* is shown on Army Memorial Day. On the judges panel together with Okamoto Tarô and others.

1945 Prisoner of war in the Wuhang Region.

1946 Returns to Kagoshima.

1947 Moves to Maeno in the suburb of Itabashi (Tokyo). Joins the Japanese Avant-garde Artists Club.

1970 April, May: Travels to Europe (Greece, Italy).

1973 Goes to France. In Paris: Lithographies commissioned by Visions Nouvelles.

1975 Opens the Furuzawa Iwami art museum in Yamanashi.

1977 Works as a lithographer in Paris.

1979 He travels to Peking, Taiyuan and Xi'an (and other destinations) as the head of the 3rd Chinese goodwill delegation of Japanese and Chinese artists.

1981 He receives an invitation to visit the Soviet Union from the Soviet Ministry of Culture and Education. He travels to many places making sketches.

1986 Visits the Soviet Union after receiving an invitation from the Soviet Ministry of Culture and Education.

Selected Solo Exhibitions

1963 *Parisian Women and Streets,* Tsubaki-Kindai Gallery, Tokyo

1971 *Exhibition of Representative Works by Furuzawa Iwami: Strength and Aestheticism,* Tôkyô Cultural Centre, Tokyo and other locations

1975 *Furuzawa Iwami, 30 Post-war Years.* Memorial exhibition for the opening of the Central Bijutsukan Art Museum, Tokyo

1978 *Love and Illusion—Furuzawa Iwami,* Nichidô Salon, Tokyo

1982 *Furuzawa Iwami,* Itabashiku Art Museum, Tokyo

1984 *Female Nudes. Furuzawa Iwami,* Central Kaigakan Picture Gallery, Tokyo and other locations

1994 *The World of Eros and Mythos—Furuzawa Iwami,* Prefecture Art Museum, Saga Prefecture

1997 *In the Ikebukuro–Montparnasse series: Furuzawa Iwami* solo exhibition, Igarashi Gallery, Tokyo

Selected Group Exhibitions

1931 *6th Art Shundai Exhibition,* Art Museum of the Governmental District of Tokyo

1938 *8th Exhibition of the Association for Independent Art,* Art Museum of the Governmental District of Tokyo

1940 *1st Exhibition of the Association for Art and Culture,* Art Museum of the Governmental District of Tokyo

1949 *1st Japan Independent,* Art Museum of the Governmental District Tokyo

1951 *1st São Paulo Biennial,* São Paulo

1957 *1st Tokyo International Graphic Art Biennial,* Yomiuri-kaikan Hall

1960 *Surrealist Painting,* National Museum of Modern Art, Tokyo

1981 *The World of Modern Art. Works from the Ôhashi Kiichi Collection,* Prefecture Art Museum, Nara Prefecture
The Course of 35 Post-war Years to Osmosis, Central Bijutsukan Art Museum, Tokyo

1983 *100 Years of Nudes,* International Art Museum, Osaka

1995 *Itabashi '95, Furuzawa Iwami—Avant-garde of the Sixties,* Itabashiku Art Museum, Tokyo
Tokyo–Montparnasse and Surrealism, Itabashiku Art Museum, Tokyo

1996 *How Was The Female Expressed?*, Prefecture Art Museum, Okayama Prefecture

1999 *Attack/Damage,* Itabashiku Art Museum, Tokyo

HASEGAWA SABURÔ

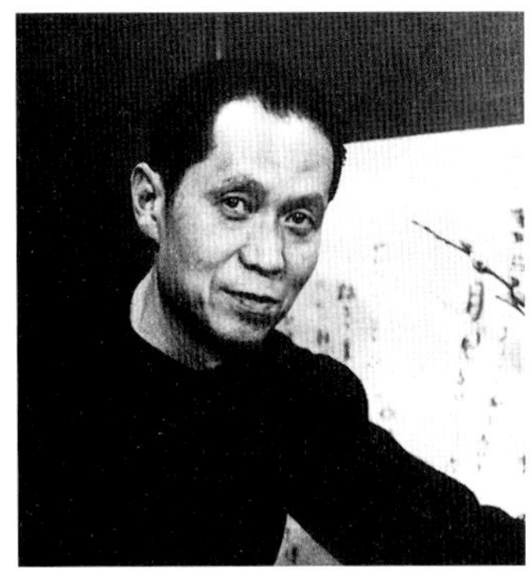

1906 Born in Chôfu, Yamaguchi Prefecture.
1929 Graduates from the Faculty of Literature at the Imperial University in Tokyo with a major in Aesthetics and Art. During this time, he took lessons at the Institute for Western Painting Shinanobashi in Osaka: He is taught by Koide Narashige. Study visits to the USA, England, France, Italy and Spain.
1932 Returns to Japan.
1934 Revives the Shinjidaiyôgaten (Exhibition of Western Painting, Yôga of the New Age).
1937 Founds the avant-garde artists group Jiyû Bijutsuka Kyôkai (Association of Independent Artists) together with Murai Masanari, Yamaguchi Kaoru, Yabashi Rokurô, Hamaguchi Yôzô and others; exhibits abstract pictures.
1950 Returns from evacuation to Fujisawa.
Friendship with Noguchi Isamu and others.
Overseas presentation of Japanese avant-garde art.
1951 Stops oil painting and turns his attention toward rubbing over inscriptions in stone and wood engravings as well as painting in Chinese ink.
1953 Moves to the USA. Following a brief return to Japan he then goes back to the USA where he lectures on Asian art and Zen at the Californian University for Art and Applied Art and at the American Institute for Asian Culture in San Francisco.
1957 He dies in San Francisco.

Selected Solo Exhibitions

1933 Kinokuniya Gallery, Tokyo
1934 Ginza Gallery, Tokyo
1935 Gakushi Club, Osaka
Koikawasuji Gallery, Kobe
1936 Kinokuniya Gallery, Tokyo
Bijutsu Shinronsha Gallery, Osaka
1953 New Gallery, New York
1954 Gallery New Contemporaries, New York
New Jersey College Art Gallery, New Jersey
1955 Rose Fried Gallery (with Al Copley and Michèle Seuphor)
1956 American Institute for Asian Culture, San Francisco
1957 Oakland Museum; Willard Gallery (exhibition of unpublished works)
1958 Unpublished works shown at the *2nd Exhibition of the Association of Independent Artists*
1959 Series: *Outstanding Artists. Hasegawa Saburô,* Shibuya Tôkyû, Tokyo
Rose Rabow Gallery, San Francisco (exhibition of unpublished works)
1964 Fujikawa Gallery, Osaka; Akiyama Gallery, Tokyo (exhibition of unpublished works)
1965 Imai Gallery, Kobe (small exhibition of unpublished works)
1974 Retrospective Hasegawa Saburô, Ôtani Memorial Museum, Nishimiya, Hyôgo Prefecture
1976 Rose Rabow Gallery, San Francisco (exhibition of unpublished works)
1977 *The 20th Anniversary of the Death of Hasegawa Saburô,* Hyôgo Prefecture Museum of Modern Art, Kobe
1982 *Hasegawa Saburô,* Satani Gallery, Tokyo
1985 *The Search for Reality of the Mind: Hasegawa Saburô,* Sanchiga Hall Gallery, Sanchiga
1986 *Hasegawa Saburô—A Pioneer of Modern Art,* The Contemporary Art Gallery, Tokyo

Selected Group Exhibitions

1924 *1st Exhibition of the Osaka Municipal Art Association,* Tennôji Kôen Kangyôkan, Osaka
5th Chûô, Takenodai Exhibition Hall in Ueno-Park, Tokyo
1932 *19th Nika-ten,* Municipal Art Museum, Tokyo
Elected to the *Salon d'automne*
1934 *1st Shinjidaiyôgaten,* Kinokuniya Gallery, Tokyo
1937 *1st Exhibition of the Association of Independent Artists,* Ueno-Park, Tokyo
1952 *Modern Japanese Art,* San Francisco; Saint Louis; Los Angeles; Seattle; Santa Barbara (Touring Exhibition)
1954 *18th American Exhibition of Abstract Art,* Riverside Museum of Art, New York
1958 *The Development of Abstract Painting,* National Museum of Modern Art, Tokyo
1965 *The Forerunners of Avant-garde Painting,* National Museum of Modern Art, Tokyo
1967 *Outstanding Contemporary Artists,* National Museum of Modern Art, Kyoto
1977 *Pioneers of Modern Art,* Tôkyô Central Art Museum, Tokyo
1986 *Ei-Kyû and his Environment,* Prefecture Museum for Modern Art, Saitama Prefecture; Miyazaki Prefecture Museum, Miyazaki; Prefecture Museum of Modern Art, Wakayama Prefecture
Japon des Avantgardes 1910–1970, Centre Georges Pompidou, Paris
1987 *The Progression of Western Painting at the End of the Shôwa Era,* Municipal Art Museum, Himeji
1992 *Abstract Painting in Japan 1910–1945,* Itabashiku Art Museum, Tokyo (and other museums)

IIDA YOSHIKUNI

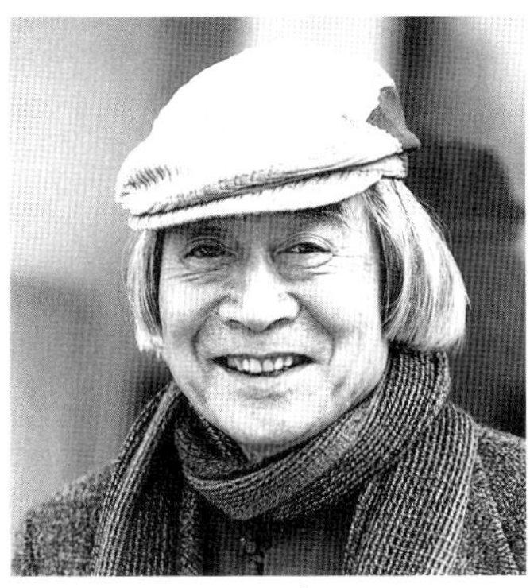

1923 Born in Ashikaga, Tochigi Prefecture.
1946–49 Studies aesthetics and art history at the Keio Gijuku Daigaku University.
1949–53 Studies oil painting with Umehara Ryûsaburô at the Tôkyô Geijutsu Daigaku University.
1953 Becomes a member of Mushanokôji Saneatsu's Atarashii mura (new village) Society.
1954 Commences the *Nocturnal Sight* cycle and joins the Hachinin-no-kai (Society of the Eight).
1956 Moves to Europe where he studies with Pericle Fazzini in Rome.
1957–63 Moves to Vienna where he initially turns his hand to copperplate engraving and oil painting. He is invited by Karl Prantl to participate in the European Sculptor's Symposium in St. Margareten.
1963–67 Moves to Berlin where he continues to work as a sculptor.
1967 Returns to Japan.
1978 Publishes his first collection of poems *Nancy's Armour.*
1987 *Iida Yoshikuni—Mirror Mobiles,* a collection of his works. He currently lives in Machida, Tokyo.

Selected Solo Exhibitions

1953 Maruzen Gallery, Tokyo
1960 Galerie Gurlitt, Munich
1961 Afro-Asiatisches Institut, Vienna
1963 Galleria Pagani, Milan
Galleria Il Canale, Venice
1967 Galerie Springer, Berlin
1972 Minami Gallery, Tokyo (together with the poet Nishiwaki Junzaburô)
1974 Denise René Gallery, New York
1979 Annely Juda Gallery, London
1987 *Sculptural Retrospective,* Prefecture Museum of Art, Mie Prefecture; Meguroku Art Museum, Tokyo; National Museum of Modern Art, Kyoto
1993 Tsuki no sabaku Memorial Museum; Meguroku Art Museum, Tokyo
1997–98 Sculptural and Painting Retrospective in Kanagawa Prefecture Museum of Modern Art, Kamakura

Selected Group Exhibitions

1953 *Japan Independent,* Tokyo
1954 *Society of the Eight*
1955 *Shinjukai Society,* Tokyo
1962 *Symposium of European Sculptors,* St. Margareten
1963 *Form Viva,* Yugoslavia
1964 *Symposium of European Sculptors,* Berlin
1967 Enters the City of Berlin's *Competition for a Monument* and wins first prize.
1968 Awarded a prize at the *Modern Japanese Art* exhibition in the Kanagawa Prefecture Museum of Modern Art, Kamakura
First prize at the *1st Exhibition of Modern Sculptures* in Sumarikyû Park, Kobe
Co-organizer of the *International Symposium on Iron and Steel,* Osaka
1985 *Reconstructions: Avant-garde Art in Japan 1945–1965,* The Museum of Modern Art, Oxford
1996 *Realism in Japan* (early oil-paintings), Municipal Art Museum, Nagoya

ISHIGAKI EITARÔ

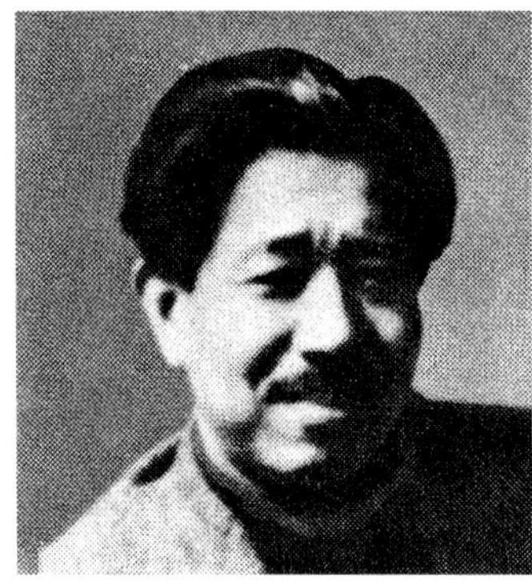

1893 Born in Taiji, Wakayama Prefecture.
1909 Moves to America with his father.
1910 Works on a casual basis.
1914 Studies at the California State University art school. Friendship with the socialist activist Katayama Sen.
1915 Becomes a pupil of John Sloane at the Art Students League in New York.
1918 Works as a typesetter for the Japanese weekly *New York Shinbô*. Becomes involved in Katayama Sen's Socialist Study Association.
1919 Co-editor of the worker's magazine *Kyôzon*.
1929 Co-founder of the John Read Club. Develops ties with the Mexican painters José C. Orozco and Rufino Tamayo.
1935 Paints mural for the Harlem courts of law, commissioned by the WPA (World Progress Administration).
1936 Co-founder of the American Artists' Congress. Member of the committee for various exhibitions.
1941 As a citizen of an enemy country, his liberties are restricted after the outbreak of war.
1951 He is arrested and then allowed to leave the country subject to fulfilling certain conditions. He returns to Japan where he lives in Mitaka near Tokyo.
1958 He dies in Tokyo.

Selected Solo Exhibitions

1936 A.C.A. Gallery, New York (and 1940)
1955 Chûôkôron Gallery, Tokyo
1958 Bungeishunjû Gallery, Tokyo
1988 Shoto Museum of Art
Shibuyaku Museum, Tokyo

Selected Group Exhibitions

1922 Gachôkai Civic Club, New York
1925 Society of Independent Artists, New York
1927 *Japanese Artists in America,* The Art Center, New York (organized by the weekly magazine *New York Shinbô*)
1933 *Proletaria,* Moscow
1936 *8th New York Art Exhibition,* Municipal Community, New York
1955 Tenten-kai Club, Matsuya, Tokyo (and 1956, 1957, 1958)
1982 *Japanese Painters Who Studied in the USA,* National Museum of Modern Art, Tokyo (and other museums)

ISHII SHIGEO

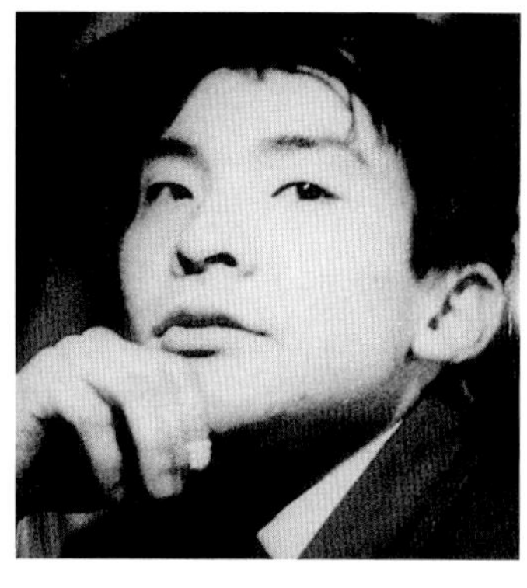

1933 Born in the Tokyo-Bunkyôku district.
1945 Student of Miwa Takashi (Asagaya Art Institute).
1950 Graduates from the Bunka Gakuin College with a major in art.
1955 Founds Seisakusha Kondankai (The Artists Discussion Group).
1956 The Soviet Ministry for Culture and Education purchases some of his works at the Peace and Goodwill Festival, Moscow.
1958 Studies Graphic Art with Sugano Yô.
1959 Member of the Association of Avant-garde Artists.
1960 Awarded a prize by the Japanese Graphic Art Association.
1962 His chronic asthma worsens resulting in his death.

Selected Solo Exhibitions

1954 Yôseidô Gallery, Tokyo (with Shimamura Kiyoshi)
1955 Yôseidô Gallery, Tokyo
1956 Muramatsu Gallery, Tokyo
1957 Muramatsu Gallery, Tokyo
1962 *30th Exhibition of the Japanese Graphic Art Association* (unpublished works)
15th Avant-garde Art Exhibition (unpublished works)
1966 Aoki Gallery, Tokyo (unpublished works)
1994 *Ishii Shigeo: Painter and Society. Unpublished Works on the 33rd Anniversary of his Death,* Tamaki Gallery, Tokyo

Selected Group Exhibitions

1950 *24th Exhibition of the Kokugakai Association,* Municipal Art Museum, Tokyo

1954 *6th Yomiuri Independent,* Municipal Art Museum, Tokyo

1955 *Exhibition by 43 People,* Ginza Matuzakaya, Tokyo
Peace and Goodwill Festival of the Young People and Students of the World, Moscow

1956 *5th Regional Exhibition of the Seisakusha Kondankai* (The Artists Discussion Group), Hankyû department store, Osaka
Group 30—Painting is not Expensive, Muramatsu Gallery, Tokyo

1958 *Images,* Shinjuku Fûgetsudô, Tokyo

1959 *7th Nippo,* Municipal Art Museum, Tokyo

1960 *Modern Japanese Graphic Art in the Soviet Union*
28th Exhibition of the Japanese Graphic Art Association
13th Avant-garde Art Exhibition (Recommencement), Municipal Art Museum, Tokyo

1979 *Painters who Died Young—An Overview of the Work of Young Japanese Modernists,* Municipal Art Museum, Chiba

1981 *Directions in Modern Art. The Fifties—Light and Dark,* Municipal Art Museum, Tokyo

1982 *Modern Japanese Art since 1945,* National Museum of Modern Art, Tokyo

1985 *Reconstructions: Avant-garde Art in Japan 1945–1965,* The Museum of Modern Art, Oxford

1986 *Japon des Avantgardes 1910–1970,* Centre Georges Pompidou, Paris

1990 *Tokyo, an Avant-garde Forest,* Itabashiku Art Museum, Tokyo

1991 *Painting in the Shôwa Era, Part 3: Post-war Art. Its Reanimation and Development,* Prefecture Art Museum, Miyagi Prefecture

KAMBARA TAI

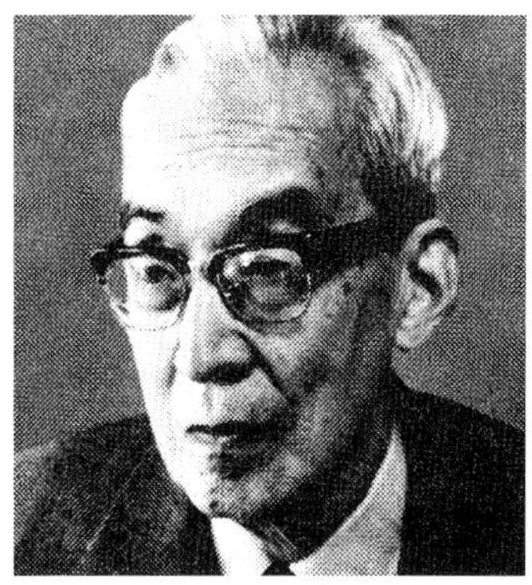

1898 Born in Sendai, Miyagi Prefecture. Soon moves to Tokyo.

1920 Publication of the *First Manifesto* by Kambara Tai.

1922 Founds Action, an avant-garde artists group.
Numerous publications (e.g. on futurism).
Correspondence with F. T. Marinetti.

1924–30 Involved in founding several groups and magazines.

1990 Donates material on the futurists and Picasso to the Ôhara Art Museum and names it "Kambara Tai Library."

1997 Dies in Yokohama.

Selected Solo Exhibitions

1920 Society of the Imperial Railway, Tokyo

1933 Sanseidô Gallery, Tokyo

1972 Nichidô Salon, Tokyo

1986 Nantenshi Gallery, Tokyo

1994 Nantenshi Gallery, Tokyo

Group Exhibitions

1917 *4th Nika-ten,* Tokyo

1923 *Action,* Mitsukoshi, Tokyo

1925 *Sanka Society,* Matsuzakaya, Tokyo

1926 *Zôkei Group,* Matsuya, Tokyo

1936 *Kayû* (Friends of Pictures), Itôya, Tokyo

1986 *Japon des Avantgardes 1910–1970,* Centre Georges Pompidou, Paris

1988 *The Twenties in Japan,* Municipal Art Museum, Tokyo (and other museums)

1989 *Action,* Yûrakuchô Asahi Gallery, Tokyo (and other museums)

1992 *Abstract Painting in Japan 1910–1945,* Itabashiku Art Museum, Tokyo (and other museums)

1993 *Japan and Europe 1543–1929,* Martin Gropius Building, Berlin

KATSURA YUKI

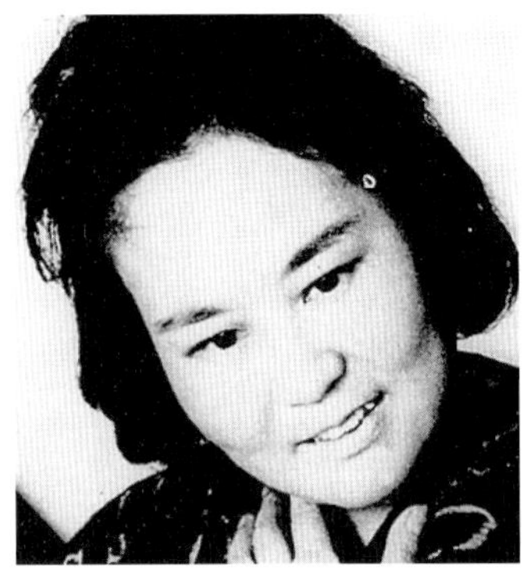

1913 Born in Hongôsendagi-machi district, Tokyo.
1933 Attends the Institute for Western Avant-garde Painting. Her teacher is Fujita Tsuguji.
1938 Founding member of the Kyûshitsukai (Society of the Ninth Space).
1946 Founds the Joryû Gaka-kyôkai (Association of Female Painters) together with Migishi Setsuku and others.
1947 Helps to found the Japanese Avant-garde Artists Club.
1949 Awarded a prize by the Association for Female Painters.
1950–56 Member of the Nika jury.
1961 Quits Nika.
1963 Wins the Culture Award of the Mainichi publishing house for *A Woman Goes to the Special Hamlet Gensi.*
1991 Dies in Tokyo.

Selected Solo Exhibitions

1935 *Katsura Yuki Collagen,* Kindai Gallery, Tokyo
1938 Nichidô Gallery, Tokyo
1943 Firma Aoki, Osaka
1944 *New Oil Paintings,* Mihodô, Tokyo
1956 Kabutoya Gallery, Tokyo
1961 Tôkyô Gallery, Tokyo
1980 Prefecture Art Museum, Yamaguchi Prefecture; Garandô Gallery, Nagoya
1985 *Katsura Yuki—Shapes of Red Silk,* Ina Gallery, Tokyo
1986 *Between Body and Image—Katsura Yuki,* The Contemporary Art Gallery, Tokyo
1989 Tôkyô Galerie, Tokyo
1991 Shimonoseki City Art Museum, Yamaguchi Prefecture
1998 *The World of Katsura Yuki—A Painter's Point of View in Pictures and Collages,* Prefecture Museum of Modern Art, Ibaraki Prefecture

Selected Group Exhibitions

1939 *26th Nika-ten,* Tokyo
1947 *32nd Nika-ten,* Tokyo
1950 *35th Nika-ten,* Tokyo
1952 *Retrospective. A View of Modern Japanese Painting,* National Museum of Modern Art, Tokyo
1953 *Abstraction and Surrealism—What do they mean?,* National Museum of Modern Art, Tokyo
1955 *International Watercolor Exhibition,* Brooklyn, New York
1957 *1st Tokyo International Graphic Art Biennial,* Tokyo
International Female Artists Exhibition, Musée d'Art moderne, Paris
1959 National exhibition with works from the *Premio Lissone* international art exhibition, Ginza Gallery, Tokyo
International Contemporary Painting, Arizona University-Art Gallery, USA
1960 *The Development of Surrealism,* National Museum of Modern Art, Tokyo
Abstract Japanese Art, Gres Gallery, Washington, D.C.
1961 *27th Corcoran Biennial,* Washington Corcoran Gallery, Washington, D.C.
Awarded a prize for outstanding contributions at the *6th International Art Exhibition of Japan*
1966 1st Prize at the *7th Japanese Exhibition of Modern Art*
1967 *Modern Japanese Water Colors and Drawings,* National Museum of Modern Art, Tokyo
1976 *The Pre-war Avant-garde,* Municipal Art Museum, Tokyo
1979 *Post-war Modern Art,* Kanagawa Prefecture Museum of Modern Art, Kamakura
1980 *Japanese-Western Painting. From before the War until after the War,* Prefecture Museum of Modern Art, Gunma Prefecture
Japanese-Western Painting. The Marks of 20 Post-war Years, Municipal Art Museum, Kyoto
1982 *Japanese-Western Painting. An Overview of 30 Post-war Years,* Prefecture Art Museum, Hiroshima Prefecture
1989 *Dolls from the Land of Art,* Prefecture Art Museum, Miyagi Prefecture
1990 *Surrealism in Japan 1925–1945,* Municipal Art Museum, Nagoya
1992 *Abstract Painting in Japan 1910–1945,* Itabashiku Art Museum, Tokyo (and other museums)
1995 *Modern Art Techniques (1): the Collage,* Nerimaku Art Museum, Tokyo
1996 *10 Years of Avant-garde Artists—Transformations and Continuity of the Self,* Itabashiku Art Museum, Tokyo
1997 *Swaying Women, Swaying Image—From the Birth of Feminism to the Present,* Prefecture Art Museum, Tochigi Prefecture
1998 *Japanese Realism in the Post-war Years 1945–1960,* Municipal Art Museum, Nagoya
Beauty and Local Customs—Japan's Part in Modern Art, Hokkaidô Prefecture Art Museum, Asahikawa

KITAWAKI NOBORU

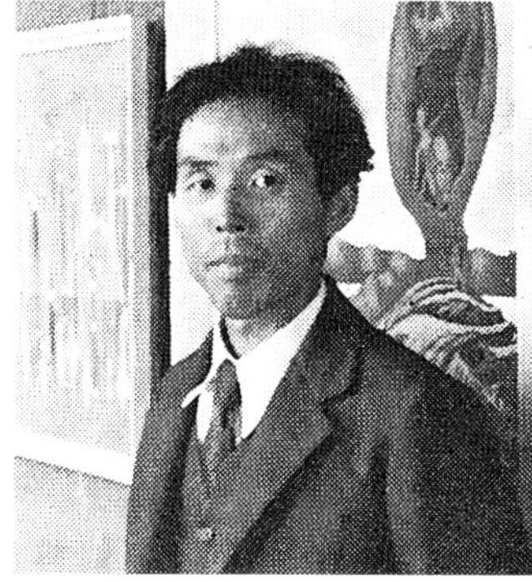

1901 Born in Nagoya, Aichi Prefecture.
1930 Commences studying at Tsuda Seifû's Painting School, Kyoto.
1932 First Prize at the *19th Nika-ten,* Tokyo.
Helps to found the Association for Western Painting, Kyoto.
1933 Founds the Dokuritsubijutsu Kyôto Kenkyûsho (Kyoto Institute for Independent Art).
1935–39 Participates in founding various art associations.
1946 Founds the Art and Culture Study Society.
1947 Participates in founding the Japanese Avant-garde Artists Club.
1951 He dies in Kyoto.

Selected Solo Exhibitions

1952 Exhibition of unpublished works at the *12th Exhibition of the Society for Art and Culture,* Municipal Art Museum, Tokyo
1953 Municipal Art Museum, Kyoto
1963 Aoki Gallery, Tokyo
1997 National Museum of Modern Art, Tokyo
National Museum of Modern Art, Kyoto
Aichi Prefecture Art Museum, Nagoya

Selected Group Exhibitions

1932 *19th Nika-ten,* Tokyo
1934 *4th Dokuritsubijutsu-kyôkai* (independent art association), Tokyo
1938 Sôki Art Association
1939 Asahi-kaikan Gallery, Kyoto (together with Komaki Gentarô)
1940 Art and Culture Association, Tokyo
1948 *Modern Art* (Organizer: Japanese Avant-garde Artists Club), Tokyo
1954 *Four Artists,* National Museum of Modern Art, Tokyo
1985 *Reconstructions: Avant-garde Art in Japan 1945–1965,* The Museum of Modern Art, Oxford
1986 *Japon des Avantgardes 1910–1970,* Centre Georges Pompidou, Paris
1990 *Surrealism in Japan 1925–1945,* Municipal Art Museum, Nagoya
1992 *Abstract Painting in Japan 1910–1945,* Itabashiku Art Museum, Tokyo (and other museums)

MAEDA JOSAKU

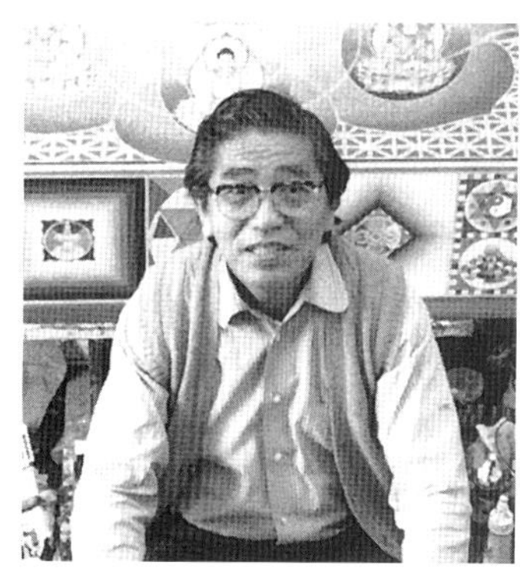

1926 Born in Shinkawa, Toyama Prefecture.
Real Christian name: Tsunesaku.
1949 Studies oil painting at the Musashino Art Academy, Tokyo.
1953 Becomes involved with the Seisakusha Kondankai Society (Society for Free Artist Discourse).
1955 The Night series is created, inspired by Hara Tamiki's atom bomb poems *Flowers in the Summer.*
1957 Grand Prize of *the Kokusai-seinen-bijutsuka-ten* (international exhibition for young artists), scholarship to study in Paris.
1958 Travels to France.
1962 Starts work on the series *Birth of Humanity.*
1963 Returns to Japan and is strongly influenced by the art of esoteric Buddhism (Mikkyo).
1965–66 Lives in France.
1970 Travels to India and Nepal.
1973 Travels to Iran and Iraq.
1977 Travels to India, Nepal, Sri Lanka, Indonesia and China.
1978 *Departing for Mandala* is published.
1979 11th Grand Japanese Art Prize: Nihon Geijutsu taish.
Professor at the Kyotoshi Geijutsudaigaku (Municipal Art Academy, Kyoto).
1988 Professor at the Musashino Art Academy.
1989 Series: *Pilgrimage in west Japan.*
1993 16th Grand Prize of the Togo Seiji Museum of the Yasuda-kasai insurance company.
1994 Rector of the Musashino Art Academy.
Lives in Tokyo.

Selected Solo Exhibitions

1955 Takemiya Gallery, Tokyo
1956 Takemiya Gallery, Tokyo
1957 Sato Gallery, Tokyo
1959 L'Envers Gallery, Tokyo
1960 Galleria Galatea , Torino
1965 Galerie Carl Flinker, Paris
1966 Galerie Europa, Berlin
1969 Tokyo Gallery, Tokyo
1970 Tokyo Gallery, Tokyo
1971 Central Art Museum, Tokyo
1976 Tokyo Gallery, Tokyo
Museum in the House of the People, Toyama Prefecture
1989 *Retrospective,* Prefecture Museum of Modern Art, Toyama
1990 *Maeda Josaku—Departing for Mandala,* Meguroku Art Museum, Tokyo; Ohara Art Museum, Kurashiki (Touring Exhibition)

MATSUMOTO SHUNSUKE

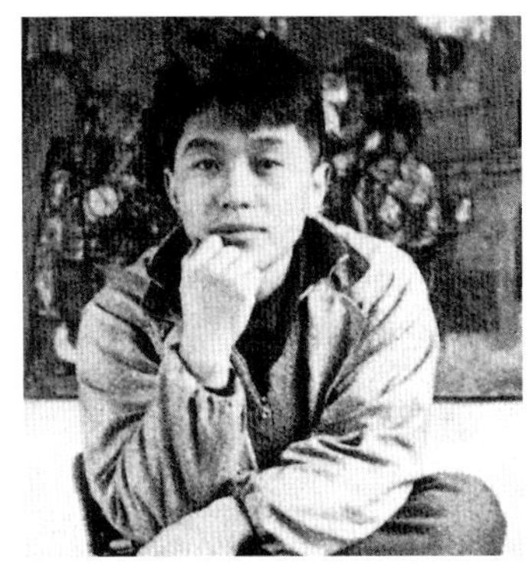

1912 Born in Tokyo.
1913 Moves to Hanamaki in Iwate Prefecture.
1925 Loses his hearing due to illness.
1929 Returns to Tokyo. Attends theTaiheiyôga Kenkyûsho Institute.
1931 Founds the Taiheiyô Kindaiyôga Kenkyûkai study society. Involved in publishing the group magazine *Sen* (Line).
1932 Founds the Akamamekai Society.
1933 Co-editor of *Seimei no geijutsu* magazine.
1936 Marriage.
First issue of *Zakkichô* magazine.
1940 Member of Kyûshitsukai (Society of the Ninth Space).
1941 Publishes the essay "Living Painters" in *Mizue* magazine.
1942 Founds the Shinjingakai (New Painters Association).
1944 Works for the film company Rikeneigasha.
1946 Publishes "Discussion with Japanese Artists" and "Recommendation for a Japanese Artists Union" in *Bijutsu* magazine.
1947 Member of the Association of Free Artists.
1948 He dies in Tokyo.

Selected Solo Exhibitions

1933 *Little Paintings,* Misaki, Tokyo
1940 Nichidô Gallery, Tokyo
1942 Nichidô Gallery, Tokyo
1968 Kanagawa Prefecture Museum of Modern Art, Kamakura
1986 National Museum of Modern Art, Tokyo
1998 *Retrospective,* Nerimaku Art Museum, Tokyo; Aichi Prefecture Art Museum, Nagoya; Prefecture Art Museum, Iwate Prefecture

Group Exhibitions

1949 *13th Jiyu Bijutsuka Kyôkai* (Free Artists Society), Tokyo
1955 *8th Japanese Independent Exhibition,* Tokyo
1957 *1st Exhibition of Young Asian Artists,* Tokyo
1958 *Japanese Artists in Paris,* Galerie Galeria, Paris
1959 *Moment of Vision,* Rome
Young International Artists Exhibition, Vienna
1st Young Artists Biennial in Paris, Paris
10th Premio Lissone Young International Artists Exhibition, Paris: Awarded a prize
1960 *Nouvelle Realité–1960,* Museé d'Art moderne de la ville de Paris, Paris
1965 *Contemporary Japanese Art by 15 Artists,* Kunsthaus, Zurich
1966 *The Eye of the Present—an East Asian Fantasy,* National Museum of Modern Art, Tokyo
1968 *1st Indian Triennial*
1971 *2nd Indian Triennial*
1980 *Asia's Contemporary Art,* Municipal Art Museum, Fukuoka
1985 *Japanese Contemporary Art by 83 Artists,* Indian National Museum of Modern Art, New Delhi

MURAI MASANARI

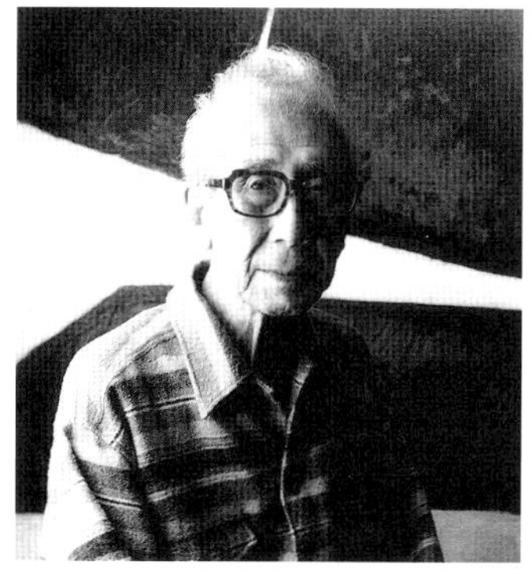

1905	Born in Ôgaki, Gifu Prefecture.
1925	Art degree at the Bunkagakuin University.
1927	First Prize at the *14th Nika-ten,* Tokyo.
1928	Graduation. Moves to Paris. Meets Fujita Tsuguharu, Ebihara Kinosuke and others
1932	Returns to Japan and settles down in Tokyo.
1934	Forms the Shinjidaiyôgaten (Western painting of the New Age) Group together with Hasegawa Saburô, Yabashi Rokurô, Yamaguchi Kaoru and others. Organization of the first exhibition.
1937	Founds the Association of Free Artists with the members of Shinjidaiyôgaten.
1938	Lecturer at the Bunkagakuin University.
1947	Founds the Japanese Avantgarde Artists Club together with Fukuzawa Ichirô, Okamoto Tarô and others.
1950	Leaves the Jiyû Bijutsuka Kyôkai. Founds the Kyôkai Association of Modern Art together with Yamaguchi Kaoru, Yabashi Rokurô and others.
1953	Founds the Abstract Art Club of Japan together with Onchi Kôshirô, Hasegawa Saburô, Yamaguchi Takeo, Yoshihara Jirô and others .
1954–75	Professorship for Western painting at the Musashino Art Academy.
1955	Awarded a prize at the *3rd International Japanese Art Exhibition.*
1962	First Prize at the *5th Exhibition of Japanese Contemporary Art.* Receives the Minister of Culture and Education Prize at the *3rd International Biennial for Graphic Art,* Tokyo.
1999	He dies.

Selected Solo Exhibitions

1934	Kinokuniya Gallery, Tokyo
1951	Takemiya Gallery, Tokyo
1956	Yôseidô Gallery, Tokyo
1963	Akiyama Gallery, Tokyo
1973	Kanagawa Prefecture Museum of Modern Art, Kamakura
1974	Art Library, Musashino Art Academy
1979	Prefecture Museum of Modern Art, Wakayama Prefecture
1984	Kamakura Gallery, Tokyo
1993	Setagayaku Museum, Tokyo Inokuma Genichirô Museum of Modern Art, Marugame

Selected Group Exhibitions

1933	Hokuto Society
1935	*Nova-ten,* Tokyo
1940	*Kyûshitsukai* (Society of the Ninth Space), Tokyo
1941	Kawatoku Gallery, Morioka (together with Funakoshi Yasutake)
1946	Nichidô Gallery, Tokyo (together with Funakoshi Yasutake and Asô Saburô)
1947	*1st and 2nd Shinjingakai* (New Painters Association) *Exhibition,* Tokyo
1958	Kanagawa Prefecture Museum of Modern Art, Kamakura (together with Shimazaki Keiji)
1977	*Ai-Mitsu and Matsumoto Shunsuke—Upheaval in Post-war Art,* Municipal Art Museum, Tokyo
1986	*Matsumoto Shunsuke and Friends of Zakkichô Magazine,* Kanagawa Prefecture Museum of Modern Art, Kamakura
1988	*Ikebukuro – Montparnasse,* Seibu department store, Tokyo
1990	*Matsumoto Shunsuke and his Friends,* Itami Municipal Museum, Hyôgo Prefecture

1995 Kanagawa Prefecture Museum of Modern Art, Kamakura; Ôhara Museum; Prefecture Art Museum, Gifu Prefecture; Prefecture Museum of Modern Art, Toyama; Prefecture Museum of Modern Art, Wakayama Prefecture (Touring Exhibition)

Selected Group Exhibitions

1930 *41st Salon des Indépendents,* Grand Palais, Paris
1937 *1st Jiyû Bijutsuka Kyôkai* (Association of Free Artists)
1951 *1st Modern Art, Mitsukoshi-Nihonbashi,* Tokyo
1st São Paulo Biennial, São Paulo (*7th Biennial* 1963, *9th Biennial,* 1967).
1953 *Carnegie International Art Exhibition,* Carnegie Museum of Art, Pittsburgh
Abstraction and Surrealism—What do they mean?, National Museum of Modern Art, Tokyo
1958 *Contemporary Japanese Art* (Exhibition shown in five Australian and four New Zealand cities)
1959 *Murai Masanari and Yamaguchi Kaoru,* Kanagawa Prefecture Museum of Modern Art, Kamakura
1981 *The Sixties—A Time for Change in Modern Art,* National Museum of Modern Art, Tokyo (and other museums)
1986 *Japon des Avantgardes 1910–1970,* Centre Georges Pompidou, Paris
1992 *Abstract Painting in Japan 1910–1945,* Itabashiku Art Museum, Tokyo (and other museums)

NISHIMURA ISAKU

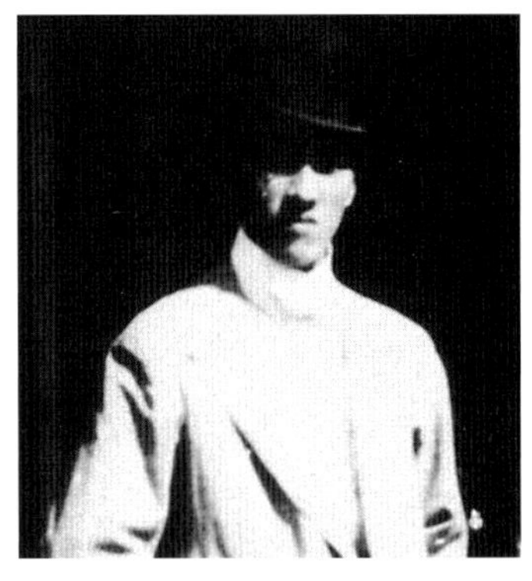

1886 Born in Shingu, Wakayama Prefecture.
Real name: Oishi.
1887 Adopted by the Nishimura family.
1904 Opposes the Russian-Japanese War, socialist and pacifist.
1912 Founds a kindergarten.
1913 Turns his attention to painting.
1918 Becomes increasingly interested in abstract painting and ceramics.
1921 Motivated by liberal ideologies, he founds the Bunka-gakuin school (Cultural Academy) private in Tokyo; founds the Nishimura Architects Office.
1938 Extension of the Bunka-gakuin school building with reinforced concrete based on his own design.
1943 Is suspected of treason and is arrested. The Bunka-gakuin school is closed and then reopened in 1946.
1951 Continues to pursue his interest in ceramics.
1950 Publishes his autobiography *I have something Good.*
1968 He dies.

Solo Exhibition

1914 Hibiya Art Museum, Tokyo (Oil and tempera paintings)

OKAMOTO TARÔ

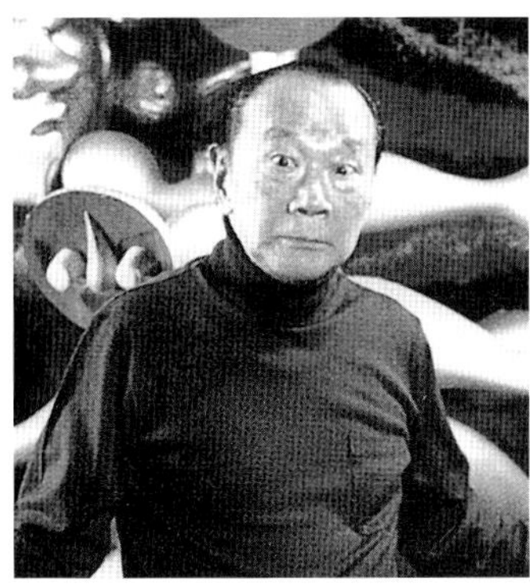

1911 Born in Kawasaki-Takatsu. His father is the caricaturist Okamoto Ippei, his mother the Waka poet and writer Okamoto Kanoko.
1929 Attends the Tôkyô Bijutsu Gakkô art school, breaks off his studies after half a year. Accompanies his parents to Paris.
1931 Studies at the University of Paris, where one of his subjects is philosophy.
1932 His encounter with Picasso's avant-garde art shocks him. He then pursues this course. Befriends internationally renowned avant-garde artists such as Brancusi and Kandinsky.
1939 Graduates from the University of Paris with a degree in ethnology.
1940 Returns to Japan following the German invasion of France.
1941 Awarded a prize at the *28th Nika-ten,* Tokyo.
1942 He is drafted and serves in the military campaign against China. Returns after a year. Prisoner of war in 1946.
1959 A wall mural in the former Tokyo town hall is awarded the Grand International Prize for Architecture and Painting.
1961 His book *Forgotten Japan* is awarded the Culture Prize of the Mainichi Publishing house.
1970 Completes *Taiyô no tô* (Tower of the Sun), *Haha no tô* (Tower of the Mother) and *Seishun no tô* (Tower of Youth) in the center of the Symbol Zone of the World Fair in Osaka.
1984 The French government makes him an *Officier de l'Ordre National du Mérite.*
1989 The French government makes him a *Grand Officier de l'Ordre des Arts et des Lettres.*
1993 He is made an honorary citizen of the City of Kawasaki.
1996 He dies.
1998 The atelier in his house in Aoyama (Tokyo) is opened to the public as the Okamoto Tarô Memorial Museum.
1999 Opening of the Okamoto Tarô Art Museum in Kawasaki, Kanagawa Prefecture.

Selected Solo Exhibitions

1941 Ginza Mitsukoshi, Tokyo
1953 Galerie Creuzevault, Paris
1954 International House, Washington, D.C.
1961 Tôkyô Gallery, Tokyo
1970 *Explosion Tarô,* Touring Exhibition in Europe
1976 *Okamoto Tarô: Challenge, Flame, Opening,* Nihonbashi Takashimaya, Tokyo; later in Paris
1979 *The World of Okamoto Tarô—The Present and the Myth,* Ôtani Memorial Museum of the City of Nishimiya, Hyôgo Prefecture
1980 *Challenge—Okamoto Tarô,* Odakyû Grand Gallery, Tokyo
1981 *Okamoto Tarô,* Prefecture Art Museum, Yamanashi Prefecture, Funabashi Seibu Art Museum and others (Touring Exhibition)
1986 *The World of Okamoto Tarô,* Nagoya Meitetsu, Aichi Prefecture and others (Touring Exhibition)
Okamoto Tarô, Yorozu Tetsugorô Memorial Museum, Tôwa, Iwate Prefecture
1991 *Kawasaki's Famous Personalities: Okamoto Tarô,* Citizens Museum of the City of Kawasaki, Kanagawa Prefecture
1995 Municipal Museum of Modern Art, Hiroshima

Selected Group Exhibitions

1932 *Salon of the Independent Jury*
1934 *Salon of the Independent Jury*
1938 *International Surrealism Exhibition,* Paris
1941 *28th Nika-ten,* Tokyo
1952 *Salon de Mai,* Paris
1953 *2nd São Paulo Biennial,* São Paulo
1954 *27th Venice Biennale,* Venice
1955 *3rd International Art Exhibition of Japan*
1957 *11th Milan Triennial,* Milan
1972 *Surrealism,* Haus der Kunst, Munich
1985 *Tokyo—Montparnasse and Surrealism,* Itabashiku Art Museum, Tokyo
Reconstructions: Avant-garde Art in Japan 1945–1965, The Museum of Modern Art, Oxford
1986 *Japon des Avantgardes 1910–1970,* Centre Georges Pompidou, Paris
1990 *Surrealism in Japan,* Aichi Prefecture Art Museum, Nagoya
1994 *Spirit of the Earth,* Watari-um-Art Museum, Tokyo
1995 *Traces of Post-war Culture,* Meguroku Art Museum, Tokyo (and other museums)
50th Day of Remembrance of the Dropping of the Atom Bomb: Since Hiroshima, Municipal Museum of Modern Art, Hiroshima
1998 *Beauty and Local Customs—Japan and Modern Art,* Hokkaidô Prefecture Art Museum, Asahikawa

ONCHI KÔSHIRÔ

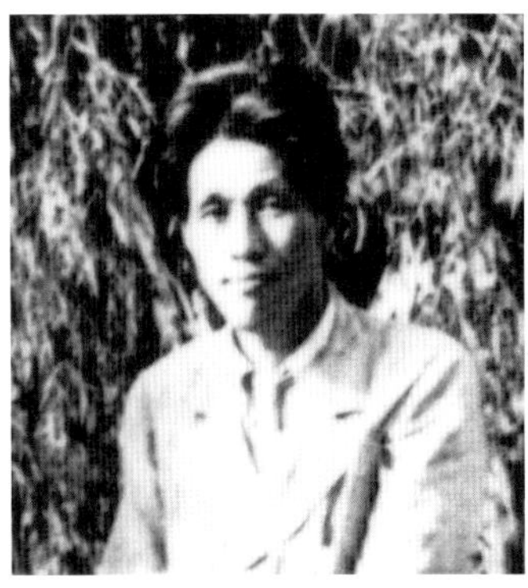

1891 Born in Tokyo.
1910 Visits the Pre-school for European Art at the Art Academy in Tokyo. Studies at the Institute of the Hakuba-kai Society for European Art.
1911 Starts sculpting.
1913 Cover design for Takehisa Yumeji's (1884–1934) *Dontaku* (Sunday).
1914 Founding of a literary group in conjunction with the *Tsukihae* (Reflection of the Moon) newspaper, together with Tanaka Kyoichi.
1915 He graduates from the Tokyo Art Academy.
1917 He designs the book *Tsukini hoeru* (Barking at the Moon) by Hagiwara Sakutar (1886–1942).
1918 Becomes involved with the Nihon Sosakuhanga-kyôkai Society (Society for Creative Prints).
1921 Publishes the art magazine *Naizai* (looking within).
1923 Involvement in the Encho-kai Society under the guidance of Yorozu Tetsugorô.
Founds the Dontaku-zuan-sha Society (Dontaku Prints Society) with Takehisa Yumeji.
1930 Lecturer at the institute of the above-mentioned society.
1931 Member of the Nihon Hanga-kyôkai (Society for Japanese Prints).
1934 Publishes *Umi no dowa* (Fairytales of the Sea), a collection of poems and wood engravings and *Hiko kanno* (Soaring Sensuality).
1935 Founds the magazine *Shoso* (Library) and remains with the editing team until the final issue in 1944.
1936 Member of the Kokuga-kai Society (Society for National Painting) in which he works for the prints department.
1939 Travels to China.
1942 Essays: *Kobo zakki* (From the Atelier).
1943 *Insects, Fishermen, Muscles,* an illustrated collection of poems.
1955 He dies.

Selected Solo Exhibitions

1946 Marunouchid-towa Gallery, Tokyo
1950 Nihonbashi Mitsukoshi, Tokyo
1952 Nihonbashi Mitsukoshi, Tokyo
1956 Unpublished works, Nihon Hanga-kyôkai Society, Tokyo
1958 Toyoko-hyakkaten, Tokyo
1964 San Francisco Museum of Modern Art, San Francisco
1976 *Onchi Kôshirô and Tsukihae,* National Museum of Modern Art, Tokyo
1982 Shibuyaku Shoto Art Museum, Tokyo
1994 *Onchi Kôshirô—Poets of Color and Shape,* Yokohama Art Museum, Yokohama; Miyagi Art Museum; Prefecture Museum of Modern Art, Wakayama Prefecture (Touring Exhibition)

Group Exhibitions

1914 *1st Minato-ya,* Tokyo
1919 *Nihon Sosakuhanga-kyôkai,* Mitsukoshi, Tokyo
1931 *Nihon Hanga-kyôkai,* Mitsukoshi, Tokyo
1934 *Japanese Wood Engravings,* Musée des Arts Décoratifs, Paris
1936 *Japanese Prints,* Municipal Museum, Geneva
Kokuga-kai, Tokyo
Shinkobijutsuka-kyôkai (Young Artist's Society), Tokyo
1947 *Union of Art Associations,* Municipal Art Museum, Tokyo
1951 *1st São Paulo Biennial,* São Paulo
1952 *International Wood Engraving Exhibition,* Lugano
1954 *18th Exhibition of American Abstract Art,* Riverside Art Museum, New York
Contemporary Art in Japan, Municipal Art Museum, Tokyo
1963 *Modern Japanese Art from 1914,* National Museum of Modern Art, Tokyo
1973 *Changes in Abstract Art in the Development of Post-war Art in Japan,* National Museum of Modern Art, Tokyo
1981 *Exhibition of Wood Engravings by Onchi Kôshirô, Tanaka Kyokichi and Hayami Toru,* Prefecture Museum of Modern Art, Wakayama Prefecture
1986 *Japon des Avantgardes 1910–1970,* Centre Georges Pompidou, Paris
1988 *Art in the 1920s,* Municipal Art Museum, Tokyo; Aichi Prefecture Art Museum, Nagoya; Prefecture Art Museum, Yamaguchi Prefecture; Hyôgo Prefecture Museum of Modern Art, Kobe (Touring Exhibition)
1991 *Onchi Kôshirô and his Contemporaries,* Okawa Art Museum, Okawa
1992 *Abstract Painting in Japan 1910–1945,* Itabashiku Art Museum, Tokyo (and other museums)

ONOSATO TOSHINOBU

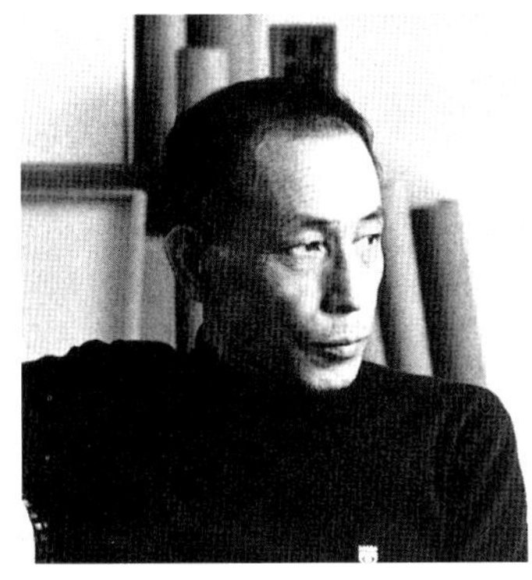

1912 Born in Iida, Nagano Prefecture.
1931 Starts studying engineering, from which he withdraws after one year deciding to become a painter.
Studies Western painting with Tsuda Seifû.
1935 Founds the Kokushokuyôga-ten group in conjunction with the Tsuda Seifû school.
1937 Involved in founding the Jiyû Bijutsuka Kyôkai (Association of Free Artists).
1942 Drafted into the army.
1945 In Manchuria at the end of the war. Imprisoned for three years in Siberia.
1948 Return to Japan (Kiryû, Gunma Prefecture).
1949 Member of the Association of Free Artists.
1955 Member of the Art Club.
1963 Awarded a prize at the *Seventh International Art Exhibition of Japan,* Municipal Art Museum, Tokyo.
1978 Publishes *Flight to Reality—An Anthology by Onosato Toshinobu.*
1986 He dies.
1988 *Paths to Abstraction—A Picture Anthology by Onosato Toshinobu* is published.

Selected Solo Exhibitions

1953 Takemiya Gallery, Tokyo
1961 *Toshinobu Onosato—Recent Paintings,* Gres Gallery, Washington, D.C.
1962 Minami Gallery, Tokyo (and 1966, 1969)
1971 Honma Museum, Sakata, Yamagata Prefecture
1972 *Onosato,* Galerie Kornfeld, Zurich
1980 Jiyûgaoka Gallery, Tokyo
1981 Ueda Gallery, Tokyo
1989 Nerimaku Art Museum, Tokyo
1993 Ôkawa Museum Kiryû, Gunma Prefecture

Selected Group Exhibitions

1935 *22nd Nika-ten*
1st Kokushokuyôga-ten Exhibition, Kindai Gallery, Tokyo
1937 *Jiyû Bijutsuka Kyôkai* (Association of Free Artists)
1953 *Abstraction and Surrealism—What do they mean?,* National Museum of Modern Art, Tokyo
1964 *32nd Venice Biennial,* Venice
1965 *The New Japanese Painting and Sculpture,* San Francisco Museum of Modern Art; MOMA, New York
1966 *33rd Venice Biennial,* Venice
1968 *Ornamental Tendencies in Contemporary Painting,* Haus am Waldsee, Berlin
1973 *Development of Post-war Japanese Art. Abstract and Non-Figurative,* National Museum of Modern Art, Tokyo
1974 *Traditional and Modern Japan,* Städtisches Kunstmuseum, Düsseldorf (and other museums)
1981 *The Fifties—Light and Dark,* Municipal Art Museum, Tokyo
The Sixties— A Time for Change in Modern Art, National Museum of Modern Art, Tokyo (and other museums)
1986 *Japon des Avantgardes 1910–1970,* Centre Georges Pompidou, Paris
1992 *Abstract Painting in Japan 1910–1945,* Itabashiku Art Museum, Tokyo (and other museums)

SAITÔ YOSHISHIGE

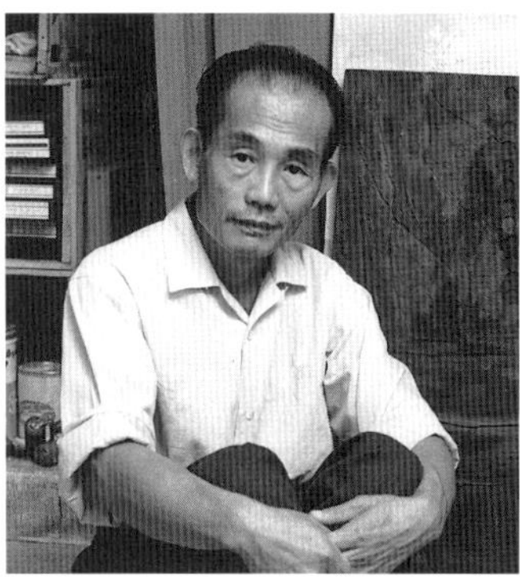

1904 Born in Tokyo.
1920 He is shocked by an exhibition showing works of the Russian futurist David Burluck.
1924 He becomes interested in literature. Connections with the Mavo Group of Murayama Tomoyoshi and with Sanka.
1932 Attends the Institute for Western Avant-garde Painting. The academic approach disappoints him.
1936 Meets Yoshihara Jirô.
1938 Co-founder of the Kyûshitsukai (Society of the Ninth Space) group, the first Japanese abstract-group.
1939 Co-founder of the Ky-shitsu-kai (Society for Art and Literature) society but is only involved in the first exhibition.
1945 Many works are lost following a bombing raid.
1954–60 Worsening of his health.
1957 *Devil,* his contribution to the 4th *Japanese Exhibition of International Art* receives the Critics Prize.
1959 Awarded the Prize of the National Museum of Modern Art at the 5th *Japanese Exhibition of International Art* and the Prize of the International Art Critics Association.
1960 Awarded the Grand Prize of the *Exhibition of Contemporary Japanese Art.*
First trip to Europe (Italy, France, Switzerland).
Awarded a prize at the *International Art Exhibition* in the Solomon R. Guggenheim Museum, New York.
1961 Awarded the Prize for International Painting at the 6th *São Paulo Biennial,* São Paolo.
1963 Teacher at the Tama Bijutsu Daigaku University, Tama Art Academy in Tokyo.
1973 He retires. Recreates several works from the thirties and the fifties which were burned or stolen in the war.
1982 Teacher at the Tokyo Art School.
1985 Asahi Prize.
He currently lives in Yokohama.

Selected Solo Exhibitions

1958 Tôkyô Gallery, Tokyo
1964 Galerie Friedrich Dahlem, Munich
1965 Galleria d'Arte de Naviglio, Milan
1976 Sakura Gallery, Nagoya
1977 Galerie in the Citizen's Hall, Kanagawa Prefecture
1978 *Retrospective,* National Museum of Modern Art, Tokyo
1984 Municipal Art Museum, Tokyo; Prefecture Art Museum, Tochigi; Hyôgo Prefecture Museum of Modern Art, Kobe; Prefecture Art Museum, Fukui; Ôhara Museum, Kurashiki (Touring Exhibition)
1985 Gallery Hyundai, Seoul
1988 Annely Juda Gallery, London
1992 Annely Juda Gallery, London
1993 Yokohama Art Museum, Yokohama; Prefecture Museum of Modern Art, Fukushima Prefecture
1996 Gallery T&S, Tôkyô Art College, Tokyo
1998 Nyûzen Power Station Museum, Takayama

Group Exhibitions

1936 *Nika-ten,* Tokyo
1938 Exhibition of the Zettaishôha Association
1939 *Kyûshitsukai* (Society of the Ninth Space), Tokyo
1940 *Bijutsubunka-kyôkai* (Art and Cultural Society), Tokyo
1957 Annual exhibition of the Kyô-no-shinjin (New People of the Modern Day) Group, Tokyo
1959 Awarded the National Museum of Modern Art Prize, Tokyo, at the 5th *Japanese Exhibition of International Art*
1959–61 5th /6th *São Paulo Biennial,* São Paulo
1960 Awarded the 4th Exhibition of Modern Japanese Art Prize
Awarded the National Museum of Modern Art Prize at the 7th *Japanese Exhibition of International Art*
1960–64 30th /31st *Venice Biennial,* Venice
1974 *Japan in Louisiana,* The Louisiana Museum of Modern Art, Denmark (Touring Exhibition)
1981 *Modern Japanese Art—Directions in Japanese Art in the Seventies,* Art Gallery of the Culture and Art Association, Seoul
1983 *Modern Japanese Art,* Museum für Geschichte und Kunst, Geneva
1986 *Reconstructions: Avant-garde Art in Japan 1945–1965,* The Museum of Modern Art, Oxford
1986 *Japon des Avantgardes 1910–1970,* Centre Georges Pompidou, Paris
1989 *Europalia—Japan 1989,* Brussels
1994 *Japanese Art after 1945: Scream against the Sky,* Yokohama Art Museum, Yokohama; Solomon R. Guggenheim Museum, New York (and other museums)
1998 *Modern Art in Japan and Korea,* Meguroku Art Museum, Tokyo

SHIRAGA KAZUO

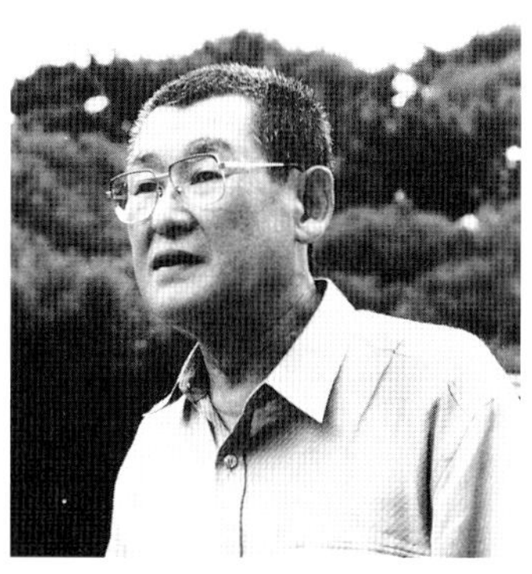

1924 Born in Amagasaki, Hyôgo Prefecture.
1948 Graduates from the Municipal Painting College in Kyoto with a major in Japanese painting (Nihonga).
1952 Participates in the Gendai Bijutsu Kondankai (Modern Art Discussion Group).
1953 Founds the Zero Group together with Kanayama Akira, Murakami Saburô and others.
From this time on he paints with his feet.
1955 Member of the Gutai Art Association.
1965 Awarded a prize at the 8th *International Art Exhibition of Japan* for outstanding achievements.
1987 Receives the Culture Award of the Hyôgo Prefecture.

Selected Solo Exhibitions

1962 Galerie Stadler, Paris
1964 Tôkyô Gallery, Tokyo
1974 Fujimi Gallery, Osaka; Shinano Gallery, Osaka; Kintetsu department store, Osaka
1976 Asahi Gallery, Kyoto
Shinano Gallery, Osaka
1977 Imabashi Gallery, Osaka
1978 Toarodo Gallery, Kobe
Miyako Gallery, Osaka
1979 Toarodo Gallery, Kobe
1980 Tôkyô Gallery; Tokyo
1982 Haku Gallery, Osaka
1984 Tôkyô Gallery, Tokyo
1985 Be-Art Gallery, Kyoto
Prefecture Art Museum, Hyôgo Prefecture
The Contemporary Art Gallery, Tokyo
1987 *Passé et présent au Japon,* La Vieille Charité, Marseille
1988 *Berlin—Tokyo,* Galerie Georg Nothelfer, Berlin (West)
1993 Art Center of the Pyrenees Area, Toulouse

Selected Group Exhibitions

1955 Participates in the *1st Gutai Art Exhibition*
1957 *Gendai Sekai Geijutsuten* (World Modern Art Exhibition), Bridgestone Art Museum, Tokyo; Daimaru, Osaka
1959 *Metamorphism,* Galerie Stadler, Paris
Awarded a prize at the *11th Premio Lissone Art Exhibition*
1961 *Abstract Painting of the World,* Munich
1963 *Directions in Modern Painting—The West and Japan,* National Museum of Modern Art, Kyoto
1965 *The New Japanese Painting and Sculpture,* San Francisco Museum of Modern Art; MOMA, New York
1969 *Abstraction and Space,* Galleria Cortina, Milan
1970 *Art Exhibition of the World Fair,* Section: *Contemporary Movements,* Art Museum of the World Fair, Osaka
1973 *Changes in Abstract Art during the Development of Japanese Post-war Art,* National Museum of Modern Art, Tokyo
1981 *The Sixties—A Time for Change in Modern Art,* National Museum of Modern Art, Tokyo; National Museum of Modern Art, Kyoto
1985 *A Tempest in Painting—The Fifties,* National Museum for International Art, Osaka
Reconstructions: Avant-garde Art in Japan 1945–1965, The Museum of Modern Art, Oxford
1986 *Gutai—Actions and Painting,* Spanish National Museum of Modern Art and Yugoslavian National Museum of Modern Art
1990 *Japanese Avant-garde—The Gutai Group in the Fifties,* National Museum of Modern Art, Rome
1991 *Gutai—Japanese Avant-garde 1954–1965,* Städtisches Museum Mathildenhöhe, Darmstadt

SUGAI KUMI

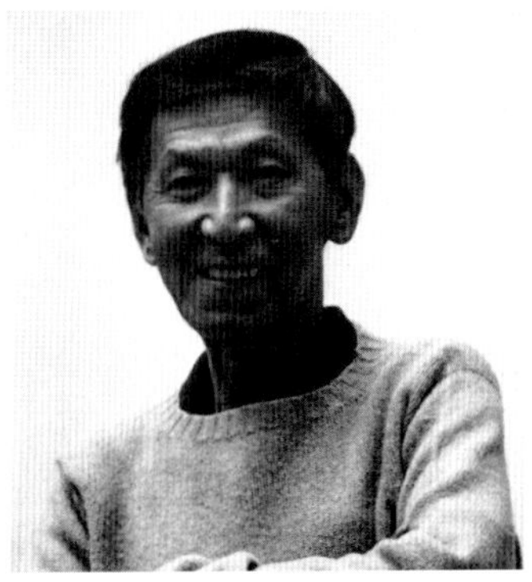

1918 Born in Hyôgo Prefecture.
1933 Studies at the Gotenyama Art School, Osaka.
1937 Employed by Hanshinkyûden Railway PLC as a poster designer in the advertising department.
1947 Studies "Nihonga" (Japanese painting).
1949 Quits Hanshinkyûden Railway PLC.
1952 Moves to France where he is taught by Goerg at the Académie Grande Chaumière. Becomes friends with Tabuchi Yasukazu, Nomiyama Gyûji and others.
1955 Starts lithographing.
1956 *Eternal Quest,* a collection of pictures and poems created together with Jean-Clarence Lambert.
1966 Receives the Annual Prize of the Family Minister Geijutsu Senshô.
1967 Seriously injured in a car accident.
1969 Returns temporarily to Japan.
Paints a mural in the lobby of the National Museum of Modern Art, Tokyo.
Returns to France. Lives in France and Japan.
1981 Works on poems and pictures together with Ôoka Makoto.
1995 Returns to Japan and dies in Kobe.

Selected Solo Exhibitions

1954 Galerie Craveu, Paris
1958 Galerie Creuzevault, Paris
1960 *Retrospective 1952–1960,* Municipal Art Museum Leverkusen, Germany
1962 Kootz Gallery, New York
1963 Galerie Creuzevault, Paris
1964 *Retrospective 1952–1963,* Die Insel, Hamburg
1969 National Museum of Modern Art, Kyoto
1977 Umeda Museum of Modern Art, Osaka
1983 Seibu Museum, Tokyo
1988 Galerie Brusberg, Berlin (in connection with the exhibitions *Contemporary Art Berlin—Tokyo. Galleries exchange their artists.*)
1991–92 Nantenshi Gallery SOKO, Tokyo; Ashiya Municipal Art Museum, Ôhara; Museum and Memorial Museum of Kojiki Torajirô (Touring Exhibition)
1997–98 *Sugai Kumi. Prints 1955–1995,* Takamatsu Municipal Art Museum; Hamamatsu Municipal Art Museum; Machida City International Graphic Art Museum; Tendô Municipal Art Museum; Kaga Art Gallery; Ashiya Municipal Art Museum, Ôhara

Selected Group Exhibitions

1941 Awarded a prize by the newspaper *Asahi Shinbun* at the *Exhibition for Aviation and Art*
1953 *Salon d'Octobre* (following a recommendation by Tajiri Shinkichi)
1955 Carnegie Museum of Art, Pittsburgh
1956 *Salon de la Nouvelle Réalité,* Paris
1957–89 *Salon de Mai,* Paris
1959 Awarded the Prize of the Museum of Modern Art of the City of Zagreb at the *3rd Ljubljana International Graphic Art Biennial,* Ljubljana
1960 *2nd International Graphic Art Biennial,* National Museum of Modern Art, Tokyo
1961 *4th Ljubljana International Graphic Art Biennial,* Ljubljana
Awarded the Prize of the *Tokyo International Art Exhibition*
1962 *31st Venice Biennial,* Venice
1965 *8th São Paulo Biennial,* São Paulo. Awarded the first prize for foreign artists
1966 Grand Prize of the *1st International Graphic Art Biennial,* Krakow
1968 *French Painting 1900–1967 in America,* Krakow
1972 *1st Norwegian International Graphic Art Biennial.* Honorary Prize.
1985 His works are shown at the exhibition *Localizing Contemporary Graphic Art,* Prefecture Art Museum, Fukushima Prefecture

TAKAMATSU JIRÔ

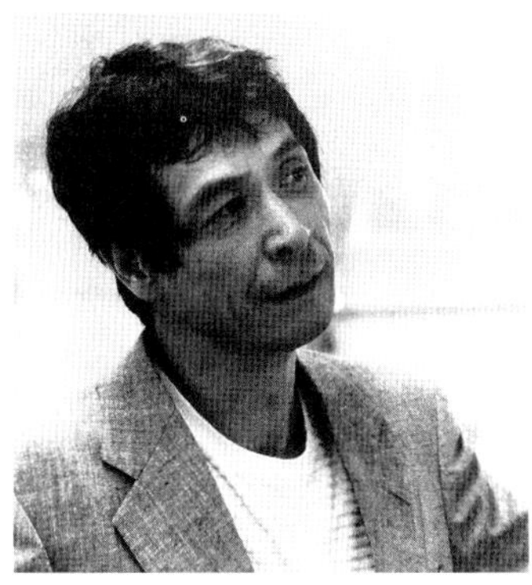

1936 Born in Tokyo.
1958 Finishes studying oil painting at the Geidai State Art Academy, Tokyo.
1963 Founds the Hi-Red-Center with Nakanishi Natsuyuki and Akasegawa Genpei.
1965 First Prize at the 9th *Shell-Prize Exhibition.*
1967 Awarded a prize by the Kanagawa Prefecture Museum of Modern Art at the 9th *International Japanese Art Exhibition* as well as other prizes.
1968 Receives the Minister of Culture and Education Prize for Young Artists at the *18th Geijutsusenshô.*
Lecturer at the Tama Academy (until 1973).
1969 Awarded a prize by the Ôhara Art Museum at the *9th Exhibition of Contemporary Japanese Art.*
1970 Construction of the *Sunday Square of Perspectives* at the World Fair in Osaka.
1972 Grand Prize at the *8th Tokyo International Graphic Art Biennial.*
1977 Paints the *Shadows* mural for the National Museum of International Art, Osaka.
1998 Dies in Tokyo.

Selected Solo Exhibtions

1966 Tôkyô Gallery, Tokyo (and 1969, 1971, 1976, 1978, 1979, 1982, 1987)
1967 Galleria d'Arte del Naviglio, Milan
1976 Kaneko Art Gallery, Tokyo (and 1978, 1980)
1986 The Contemporary Art Gallery, Tokyo
1989 Ikeda Akira Gallery, Nagoya and Tokyo (and 1990, 1992, 1993, 1994, 1995)
1996 Museum of Art, Niigata
1999 National Museum of International Art, Osaka

Selected Group Exhibitions

1958 *10th Yomiuri Independent,* Municipal Art Museum, Tokyo
1966 *A New Generation of Contemporary Art,* National Museum of Modern Art, Tokyo
Modern Art in Japan, San Marco, Venice
1968 *34th Venice Biennial,* Venice
1971 *International Art Exhibition,* Solomon R. Guggenheim Museum, New York
1973 *12th São Paulo Biennial,* São Paulo
1974 *Japan—Tradition and the Present,* Städtisches Kunstmuseum, Düsseldorf (and other museums)
1977 *Dokumenta VI,* Kassel
1980 *2nd Exhibition of Contemporary Artists: Takamatsu Jirô and Motonaga Sadamasa,* National Museum of International Art, Osaka
1981 *The Sixties— A Time for Change in Modern Art,* National Museum of Modern Art, Tokyo (and other museums)
1985 *Reconstructions: Avant-garde Art in Japan 1945–1965,* The Museum of Modern Art, Oxford
1986 *Japon des Avantgardes 1910–1970,* Centre Georges Pompidou, Paris
1994 *Avant-garde Art in Post-War Japan (Japanese Art after 1945: Scream against the Sky),* Yokohama Art Museum, Yokohama; Solomon R. Guggenheim Museum, New York and other museums (Touring Exhibition)

TANAKA ATSUKO

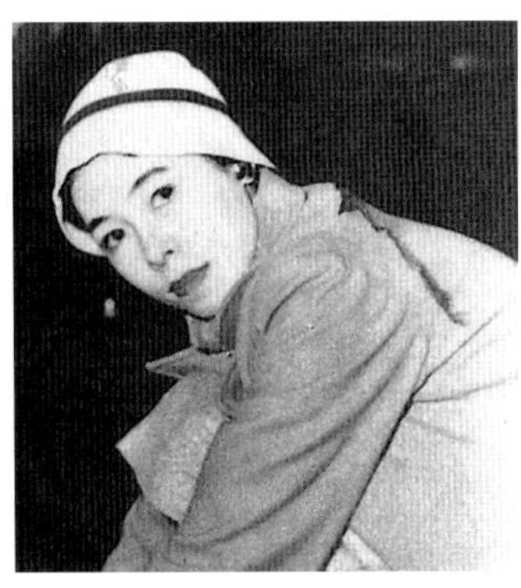

1932 Born in Osaka.
1955 Becomes a member of the Gutai Concrete Art Association (until 1965).
1964 Awarded a prize at the 6th *Exhibition of Contemporary Japanese Art.*
1965 The MOMA, New York, purchases one of her works.
She currently lives in Asuka, Nara Prefecture.

Selected Solo Exhibitions

1963 Minami Gallery, Tokyo
Gutai Pinacotheca, Osaka
1972 Minami Gallery, Tokyo
Fujibi Gallery, Osaka
1975 Kasahara Gallery, Osaka
1978 Asahi Gallery, Kyoto
Imabashi Gallery, Osaka
1983 Takagi Gallery, Nagoya
1985 The Contemporary Art Gallery Seibu, Tokyo
1987 Galerie Stadler, Paris
1990 Kita Museum of Art, Nara
1998 Ham Gallery, Nagoya

Selected Group Exhibitions

1958 *World Exhibition of New Painting: Informel and Gutai,* Takashima, Osaka
Gutai—New York, Martha Jackson Gallery, New York
1961 *International Exhibition of Contemporary Painting and Sculpture,* Carnegie Museum of Art, Pittsburgh
Experiments in Contemporary Art, National Museum of Modern Art, Tokyo
1964 *Guggenheim International Award 1964,* Solomon R. Guggenheim Museum, New York
1965 *The New Japanese Painting and Sculpture,* San Francisco Museum of Modern Art; MOMA, New York
1979 *Yoshihara Jirô, Gutai and What Followed,* Hyôgo Prefecture Museum of Modern Art, Kobe
1981 *The Sixties—A Time for Change in Modern Art,* National Museum of Modern Art, Tokyo (and other museums)
1983 *Dada in Japan: Japanese Avant-garde 1920–1970,* Städtisches Kunstmuseum, Düsseldorf
1985 *A Tempest in Painting: The Fifties—Informel,* Gutai-Art and Cobra, National Art Museum, Osaka
Pintura y acción Grupo Gutai, Museo Español de Arte Contempráneo, Madrid (and other museums)
1986 *Japon des Avantgardes 1910–1970,* Centre Georges Pompidou, Paris
1991 *Gutai—Japanese Avant-garde 1954–1965,* Städtisches Museum Mathildenhöhe, Darmstadt
1993 45th *Venice Biennial,* Venice
1994 *Japanese Art after 1945: Scream against the Sky,* Yokohama Museum of Art, Yokohama; Solomon R. Guggenheim Museum, New York (and other museums)

YAMAGUCHI TAKEO

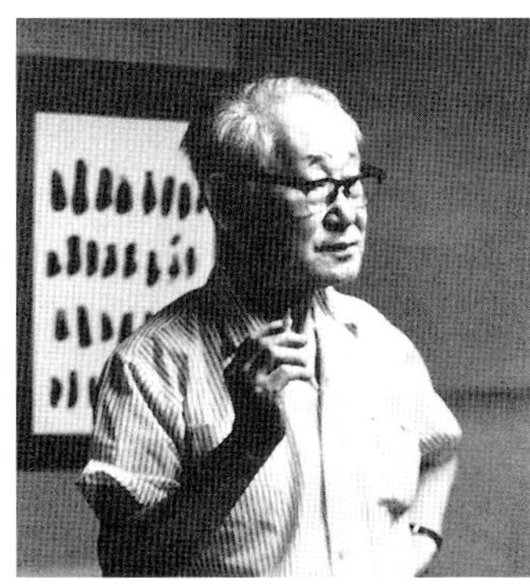

1902 Born in Korea.
1921 Moves to Tokyo, attends the Hongo Painting Institute. Taught by Okada Saburosuke.
1922 Studies European painting at the Art Academy in Tokyo.
1926 Walks between all 53 stops on the Tokaido (East Sea Road) from Tokyo to Kyoto.
1927 Travels to France with Ogisu Takanori, visits Ossip Zadkine.
1928 Sketch-trip with Saeki Yuzo, Ogisu Takanori, Yokote Sadami and Ohashi Ryosuke.
1931 Returns to Seoul.
1938 Co-founder of the Kyushitsu-kai Society (Society of the Ninth Space).
1946 Moves to Japan with his family.
1947 Involvement in the Society of Avant-garde Japanese Artists.
1953 Founds the Japanese Abstract Art Club.
1954 Teacher at the Musashino Art Academy. Awarded a prize at the *First Exhibition of Contemporary Japanese Art.*
1955 "From primitiveness to modern design," published in *Bijutsu-techo* (Art Notebook).
1958 *Nika-kaiin Doryoku-sh:* Awarded a prize.
1974 Goes into retirement.
1983 He dies.

Selected Solo Exhibitions

1939 Ginza Seijusha Gallery, Tokyo
1968 Musashino Art Academy, Tokyo
Minami Gallery, Tokyo
1970 Yamagata-ya, Kagoshima
1976 Ashiya Gallery, Ashiya
Merry Exhibition (Ceramic Pictures), Osaka
1978 Suzukawa Gallery
1979 Morioka Daiichi Gallery, Morioka
1980 Municipal Art Museum, Kitakyûshu

Group Exhibitions

1931 *Nika-ten,* Tokyo (regular participation until 1963)
1939 *Kyushitsu-kai*
1947 *Union of Art Associations Exhibition* (Bijutsudantai-rengo-ten); regular participation until 1951
1953 *Abstraction and Fantasy,* National Museum of Modern Art, Tokyo
1954 *18th Exhibition of American Abstract Art,* New York
1955 *3rd São Paulo Biennial,* São Paulo
Japanese and American Abstract Art, National Museum of Modern Art, Tokyo
1958 *Contemporary Japanese Painting* (Exhibition touring eleven European cities)
1965 *The New Japanese Painting and Sculpture,* San Francisco Museum of Modern Art; MOMA, New York
1970 *Aso Saburo, Osawa Shosuke, Yamaguchi Takeo,* Saison Gallery, Tokyo
1974 *Traditional and Modern Japan,* Städtisches Kunstmuseum, Düsseldorf
Japan in Louisiana, The Louisiana Museum of Modern Art, Denmark (Traveling Exhibition)
1980 *Yamaguchi Takeo and Horiuchi Masakazu,* National Museum of Modern Art, Tokyo
1986 *Arishima Ikuma, Togo Seiji, Yamaguchi Takeo,* Municipal Art Museum, Kagoshima

YOROZU TETSUGORÔ

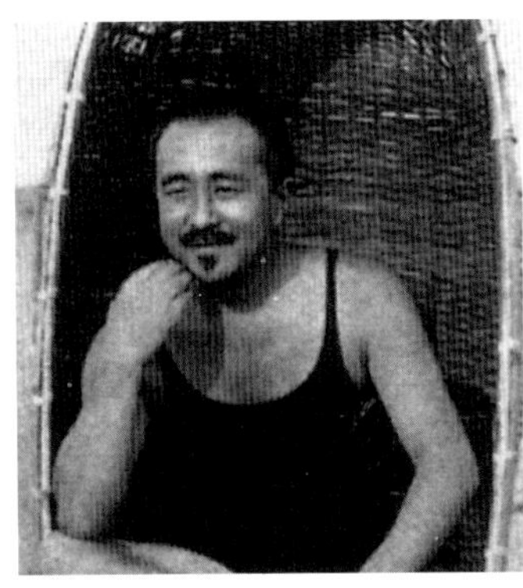

1885 Born in Tsuchizawa, Iwate prefecture.
1889 Teaches himself traditional Nihonga painting and develops a keen interest in seal-carving.
1901 Turns his attention to watercolors.
1903 Goes to Tokyo, where he studies at the Waseda Chugaku and continues painting with watercolors.
1905 Studies oil painting at the Second Institute for European Painting of the Hakuba-kai Artists Society.
1907 Studies European art at the Tokyo Art Academy.
1912 Graduation works: *The Naked Beauty* and *Self-Portrait.* Co-founder of the Fu-zan-kai Society (Fusain: Charcoal). Participates in exhibitions.
1913 Designs the sets for the Geijutsuza theater group and the poster for Maeterlinck's Monna Vanna.
1917 Shows *Leaning figure* at the *4th Nika-ten:* his understanding of cubism arouses interest.
1919 Falls ill with weak nerves and tuberculosis. Travels to Chigasaki, Kanagawa prefecture.
1922 Co-founder of the Shunyo-kai (Spring Sunshine) Society; he concentrates on painting of literati (Bunjinga).
1923 Founder of the Encho-kai (Round Bird) Society. Relationships to young avant-garde artists such as Onchi Kôshirô and Maeta Kanji.
1925 Publishes *About Tani Buncho* (a famous painter of literati, 1763–1840).
1927 Dies in Chigasaki.

Selected Solo Exhibitions

1923 *Yorozu Tetsugorô Nihonga,* Nojima Yasujiro, Tokyo
1924 *Tetsujin Hoga-kai,* Murata Gallery, Tokyo
Yorozu Tetsugorô, Morioka
1997 *Yorozu Tetsugorô,* National Museum of Modern Art, Tokyo

Group Exhibitions

1911 Exhibition of the members of the Absent Society, Tokyo
1912 *1st Zasso-kai* (Weeds), Tokyo
1913 *2nd Fyuzan-kai,* Tokyo
1917 *2nd Nihonbijutsuka-kyôkai* (Society of Japanese Artists), Tokyo
1918 *4th Nika-ten,* Tokyo
4th In-ten, Department for European Art, Tokyo
1918 *5th In-ten,* Department for European Art, Tokyo
5th Nihonsuisaiga (Japanese Watercolor), Tokyo
1919 *1st Nihon Sosakuhanga-kyôkai* (Society for Creative Prints), Tokyo
6th Nika-ten, Tokyo
1921 *8th Nihonsuisaiga,* Tokyo
1922 *4th Nihon Sosakuhanga-kyôkai,* Tokyo
9th Nihonsuisaiga, Tokyo
1923 *10th Nihonsuisaiga,* Tokyo
1st Shunyo-kai, Tokyo
1st Encho-kai, Tokyo
1924 *11th Nihonsuisaiga,* Tokyo
2nd Shunyo-kai, Tokyo
2nd Encho-kai, Tokyo
1925 *12th Nihonsuisaiga,* Tokyo
3rd Shunyo-kai, Tokyo
1926 *4th Shunyo-kai,* Tokyo
1927 *5th Shunyo-kai,* Tokyo

YOSHIHARA JIRÔ

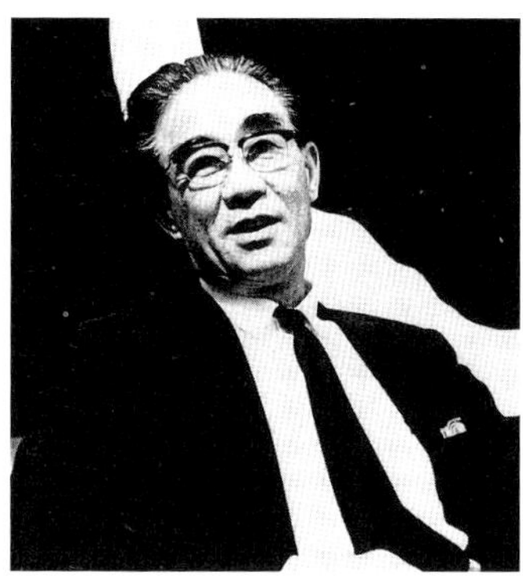

1905 Born in Osaka.
1928 Graduates from the Kansai-Gakuin University (Commercial Science).
1934 Guest member of the Nika Association.
1938 Involved in founding the Kyûshitsukai (Society of the Ninth Space).
1945 Member of the Nika Association.
1954 Founds the Gutai Artists Association.
1972 Dies in Ashiya, Hyôgo Prefecture.

Selected Solo Exhibitions

1928 Ôsaka Asahi Kaikan Hall, Osaka
1934 Ginza Kinokuniya Gallery, Tokyo
1967 Tôkyô Gallery, Tokyo
1970 Gutai Pinacotheca, Osaka
1973 *People who Create Tomorrow—Yoshihara Jirô,* Kanagawa Prefecture Museum of Modern Art, Kamakura; Municipal Art Museum, Kyoto
1975 Tôkyô Gallery, Tokyo
1984 *The Unknown Yoshihara Jirô,* Prefecture Museum of Modern Art, Hyôgo Prefecture
1985 Contemporary Art Gallery, Tokyo

Selected Group Exhibitions

1952 *International Exhibition of Modern Painting and Sculpture,* Carnegie Institute Pittsburgh, New York
1955 *Abstract Painting in Japan,* National Museum of Modern Art, Tokyo
1957 *The World's Modern Art,* Bridgestone-Art Museum, Tokyo; Daimaru, Osaka
1959 *Metamorphism,* Galerie Stadler, Paris
1961 *Continuité et Avantgarde au Japon,* Torino. Represented at the *12th Premio Lissone International Art Exhibition.*
1962 *Strutture è stile,* Municipal Museum of Modern Art, Torino
1963 *Directions in Modern Painting—The West and Japan,* National Museum of Modern Art, Kyoto
1964 *4th Guggenheim Prize Exhibition,* Solomon R. Guggenheim Museum, New York
Modern Japanese Art after the War, Kanagawa Prefecture Museum of Modern Art, Kamakura
1965 *The New Japanese Painting and Sculpture,* San Francisco Museum of Modern Art; MOMA, New York
1967 Grand Prize (National Category) at the *9th International Art Exhibition of Japan*
1970 Art Exhibition of the World Fair, Section: *Contemporary Movements,* Art Museum of the World Fair, Osaka
1971 *A Chronicle of Post-war Art,* Kanagawa Prefecture Museum of Modern Art, Kamakura
Gold Medal at the *2nd Triennial of India*
1979 *Yoshihara Jirô: Gutai and What Followed,* Prefecture Museum of Modern Art, Hyôgo Prefecture
1985 *Yoshihara Jirô and Gutai,* Ashiya Citizens Center, Hyôgo Prefecture
1992 *20 Years after His Death: Yoshihara Jirô,* Municipal Art Museum, Ashiya, Hyôgo Prefecture

The authors of the biographies are:
Fukuda Saori, Furuta Ryô, Matsumoto Tôru, Mizusawa Tsutomu, Nagato Saki, Sasaki Eriko, Suzuki Katsuo

This book is published in conjunction with the exhibition *Japanese Modern Art—Painting from 1910 to 1970*

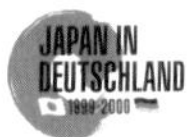

The exhibition is part of a program of events entitled "Japan in Germany 1999–2000." Patrons are His Royal Highness the Crown Prince of Japan and the President of the Federal Republic of Germany.

KULTUR-STIFTUNG

Deutsche Bank Gruppe

The catalogue was made possible thanks to funds provided by the Kultur-Stiftung of the Deutsche Bank.

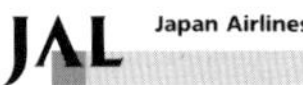

With the generous support of Japan Airlines, Frankfurt/Main.

Kunstsammlungen Chemnitz
Director Ingrid Mössinger
Theaterplatz 1
D–09111 Chemnitz
Tel. 0049/371 488 44 24
Fax 0049/371 488 44 99
September 12th to October 24th, 1999

Schirn Kunsthalle Frankfurt
Director Hellmut Seemann
Römerberg
D–60311 Frankfurt/Main
Tel. 0049/69/299 88 20
Fax 0049/69/299 88 240
January 18th to March 18th, 2000

Editorial direction by Sara Schindler, Mirjam Ghisleni-Stemmle, Lisa Briner
Translation from the German by Julian Cooper, Pauline Cumbers, John S. Southard
Layout and Typography by Giorgio Chiappa, Zurich, Switzerland
Typesetting and Lithography by Alpha Druckereiservice GmbH, Radolfzell, Germany
Printed by Spefa Druck AG, Zurich, Switzerland
Bound by Buchbinderei Burkhardt AG, Mönchaltorf, Switzerland

ISBN 3-908161-86-X